Business Data Analytics
Second Edition

Lucy Scott

ISBN: **979-8-3304-3929-4**

ISBN: **979-8-3304-3929-4**

CONTENTS

DISCLAIMER

The names 'Python', "Anaconda", "Pandas", "NumPy", "Matplotlib", "MATLAB", "Seaborn", "statsmodels", "sklearn", "ARIMA", "Excel", "Windows", "Google Sheet", "Zillow", "SAS", "SPSS", "STATA" and "JupyterLab" are registered trademarks and belong to their respective owners. The use of these names in this book is for reference and educational purposes only and is not intended to imply endorsement by the trademark owners. The author and publisher of this book do not claim any ownership or affiliation with these trademarked names. All rights belong to their respective owners.

NOTICE OF LIABILITY

The author and publisher have made every effort to ensure the accuracy of the information herein. However, the information contained in this book is sold without warranty, either express or implied. Neither the author nor the publisher will be held liable for any damages to be caused either directly or indirectly by the instructions contained in this book, or by the software or hardware products described herein

ACKNOWLEDGMENTS

We express our gratitude to Dr. Youlong Zhuang for the invaluable contributions to this edition, including the review process and authorship of Chapter 9 (Levels of Data Analytics). This chapter offers a comprehensive overview of business data analytics, delineating four distinct levels of analytics that are key for understanding and leveraging data effectively in business contexts.

Practice Files

http://bit.ly/3DladjM

Chapter 1: Introduction to Python

Chapter Learning Objectives:

1.1 Recall the basic syntax of the Python language.
1.2 Install the Anaconda IDE.
1.3 Utilize the NumPy library for performing simple statistical operations.
1.4 Showcase proficiency in using JupyterLab for data analysis.

1.1 What is Python?

This book is about data analytics. Data refers to raw facts that possess meaning and can be measured. Data analytics involves the study of analyzing data to extract information for business purposes. Many data analytics processes have been automated using a programming language called Python.

Python is a versatile programming language that can be utilized for constructing various applications, ranging from web applications to desktop applications. Python is renowned for its simplicity, readability, and flexibility. It is commonly employed in the fields of data science and machine learning. Programmers utilize Python syntax to instruct computers on how to construct models based on given data and to analyze data in order to generate meaningful outcomes.

Python's versatility extends beyond just web and desktop applications. It is also widely used in business data analytics due to its powerful libraries and frameworks such as Pandas, NumPy, and SciPy which are designed specifically for data analysis. These libraries provide high-performance, easy-to-use data structures and data analysis tools that make Python an excellent choice for manipulating, processing, and analyzing data.

In business, Python can be used to perform tasks such as predictive analysis, statistical analysis, and data visualization. For instance, Python's Scikit-learn library can be used to build predictive models, which are important in making informed business decisions. Python's Matplotlib and Seaborn libraries are excellent for creating static, animated, and interactive visualizations in Python.

Moreover, Python's simplicity and readability make it a great language for beginners. Its syntax is clear and intuitive, which makes it an excellent choice for individuals who are new to programming. This is particularly beneficial in a business setting where not everyone may have a background in computer science.

Before you can start coding in Python, you will need to set up a Python development environment on your computer. This involves downloading and installing Python, as well as setting up a code editor or Integrated Development Environment (IDE) such as PyCharm or Jupyter Notebook. These tools provide features like syntax highlighting and code completion that make writing Python code easier and more efficient.

Review Question 1.1
What is the definition of data in the context of data analytics?
a. Processed information used for decision-making
b. Raw facts with meaning and measurability
c. Statistical analysis of business operations
d. Information extracted from Python programming

Review Question 1.2
According to the author, which language is commonly used in data science and machine learning?
a. Java
b. Python
c. C++
d. Ruby

Review Question 1.3
What is Python known for?
a. Complexity and rigidity
b. Security and speed
c. Simplicity, readability, and flexibility
d. Advanced graphics and visualization

Review Question 1.4
What is the purpose of data analytics?
a. To automate programming processes
b. To analyze data for business insights
c. To develop web and desktop applications
d. To retrieve information for data science

Review Question 1.5
What is the recommended step before a beginner starts hands-on coding in Python?
a. Conducting a feasibility study
b. Learning data science principles
c. Installing an editor and setting up Python
d. Understanding programming syntax

1.2 Install Anaconda and Use Jupyter Lab

We will be using Anaconda on Windows throughout this book. Anaconda is an integrated development environment (IDE) that encompasses both an editor and Python. With Anaconda, you can type code directly into the editor and run it seamlessly without having to switch out of the editor.

To download Anaconda, you can search the web for 'Anaconda download.' The first link you find will likely be the "Individual Edition" download page. Click on the link provided, which will direct you to anaconda.com, where you should encounter a download page. Just click to download.

In your local computer, find the installer (executable file) you just downloaded. Double click on it to install.

After the installation, expand "Anaconda3" and select "Anaconda Navigator (Anaconda3)" in your start program menu of Windows to launch Anaconda Navigator:

The Navigator has many pre-installed applications:

On Anaconda Navigator, click on the "Launch" button of the "JupyterLab" tile to start JupyterLab. A new browser tab called JupyterLab will open.

JupyterLab allows you to organize your analyses in a spreadsheet-style format, with each analysis represented by a Notebook (ipynb file). Within each Notebook, you can write small blocks of code in cells that can be executed individually. Unlike a traditional spreadsheet, where only one formula is allowed per cell, a Notebook cell in JupyterLab can contain multiple instructions.

Moreover, JupyterLab's Notebook offers a unique feature that sets it apart from most programming editors, such as VS Code. In VS Code, you typically run the entire program at once. However, in a Notebook, you have the flexibility to run any section of the code as long as it is inside a cell. This allows for more granular control and testing of your code. Additionally, while it's often easier to understand the code when cells are run sequentially, JupyterLab does not enforce this. You have the freedom to run the cells in any order you choose, further enhancing the flexibility and interactivity of your coding environment.

To start a new Notebook, click on the "File", "New", and "Notebook".

On the popup, select the default option 'Python 3 (ipykernel).' A Jupyter kernel is a program responsible for executing the code within a notebook document. When you initiate a new kernel, any code written in a previous kernel will be lost.

A new Notebook tab with one cell is ready for you to type in the instructions.

Before you start coding, it's advisable to save your file with a meaningful name in the appropriate directory. To do this, first, choose the default directory for your file. You can find the Folder icon on the left panel; click on it to navigate through your directories. You have the option to create a new directory or use the existing default one. For the purposes of this book, we will assume that all files are saved in the default directory.

Next, click on "File", "Save Notebook As…" and name this file as "MyFirstNotebook.ipynb"

A file named MyFirstNotebook.ipynb will appear inside the default directory.

Let's start coding. Our task is to instruct Python to display the message "Welcome to Python for business data analytics!" on the Notebook. To accomplish this, enter the following command in the first cell of the Notebook:

```
print("Welcome to Python for business data analytics!")
```

Next, click on the "Run" icon (represented by a small play triangle) located directly above the first line of code. You should then see the message "Welcome to Python for business data analytics!" (without the quotation marks) appear right below the cell.

You might observe that the square bracket to the left of the cell transitions from [ ] to [*] and then to [1] in quick succession. This indicates that the cell is being executed and has finished running. Initially, it appears as a blank square bracket [ ], signifying that the cell is idle and has not been executed yet. As you run the cell, the bracket changes to an asterisk [*], indicating that the cell is currently in execution. Once the execution is complete, the bracket displays a number [1], denoting the order in which the cell was executed.

To save your Python code, locate the 'save' icon in the top left corner of the interface and click on it. A black dot appearing on the top right of a tab signifies that the file has not been saved yet. Once you click on the 'Save' icon, the dot will change into a cross (x) symbol, confirming that the file has been successfully saved.

Review Question 1.6
Anaconda is a(n) _________ both an editor and python.
a. advanced language that includes
b. IDE that includes
c. programmer who invented
d. Scientist who invented

Review Question 1.7
The _______ lets you organize your analyses in spreadsheet style with one Notebook (ipynb file) for each analysis.
a. Anaconda
b. Anaconda Navigator
c. JupyterLab
d. MS Excel

Review Question 1.8
Within each _______ of JupyterLab, you write small blocks of code in cells to execute, one cell at a time.
a. Anaconda
b. Anaconda Navigator
c. Notebook
d. MS Excel

Review Question 1.9
A Jupyter _______ is a program that executes the code you write in a notebook document. When you start a new _______, the code you write in a previous _______ is gone.
a. kernel, kernel, kernel
b. file, file, file
c. kernel, file, kernel
d. file, kernel, file

Review Question 1.10
In JupyterLab, a black _______ on the top right of a tab indicates the file is not saved yet. Click on the "Save" icon will turn the _______ into _______.
a. circle dot, circle dot, blank
b. cross, cross, circle dot
c. circle dot, circle dot, cross
d. blank, blank, circle dot

1.3 Variables and Operators in Python

In programming, we often use variables to store data. Think of a variable as a storage box that holds a value.

We assign a name to this box, and we can use this name later for calculations or to display the value it holds.

When naming variables in Python, there are a few rules to keep in mind:

- A variable name must start with a letter or an underscore (_).

- The rest of the variable name can consist of letters, numbers, or underscores.

- Python is case-sensitive, which means myVariable and myvariable would be considered two different variables.

However, it's important to note that spaces are not allowed in variable names in Python. If you try to create a variable name with a space, you'll get a syntax error. Instead, you can use underscores to separate words in a variable name, like my_variable.

Now, let's see this in action with an example.

Example 1.1

Write Python code to convert the temperature in Fahrenheit to Celsius. First, prompt the user for a degree in Fahrenheit, then convert it to Celsius, and finally, display the result in both measurements.

Solution:

Start Jupyter Notebook, and enter the following code in a cell:

```python
fahrenheit = float(input("Enter temperature in Fahrenheit: "))
celsius = (fahrenheit - 32) * (5/9)
celsius = round(celsius, 2)
print(f"{fahrenheit} degrees Fahrenheit is {celsius} degrees Celsius.")
```

Click on the "Run" button, the program will prompt for an input:

Enter a number, say "32.3" (without quotation marks).

Press the "Enter" key on keyboard to continue. The following will be displayed right below the cell:

```
Enter temperature in Fahrenheit:  32.3
32.3 degrees Fahrenheit is 0.17 degrees Celsius.
```

let's break down this Python code line by line:

Line 1: `fahrenheit = float(input("Enter temperature in Fahrenheit: "))`

This line of code does two things. First, it uses the input() function to prompt the user to enter a temperature in Fahrenheit. The entered value is a string. Then, it uses the float() function to convert this string to a floating-point number. The result is stored in the variable fahrenheit.

Line 2: `celsius = (fahrenheit - 32) * (5/9)`

This line of code converts the temperature from Fahrenheit to Celsius using the formula (Fahrenheit - 32) * 5/9. The result is stored in the variable celsius.

Line 3: `celsius = round(celsius, 2)`

This line of code rounds the value of celsius to two decimal places using the round() function.

Line 4: `print(f"{fahrenheit} degrees Fahrenheit is {celsius} degrees Celsius.")`

This line of code uses the print() function to display the result. It uses an f-string (formatted string literal), also known as string interpolation, which enables the inclusion of variables within a pair of curly braces {}. By placing an f directly before the string you are creating, you activate a special string mode that allows you to incorporate {} within the string, with the variable name positioned between the { and the }. When displaying a string literal to the user, string interpolation proves to be convenient. This formatting technique facilitates the embedding of Python expressions within string constants.

When declaring a variable in Python, you are not required to explicitly specify its data type. Nevertheless, Python does assign a data type to each variable. Some commonly used data types include `int` for integers, `float` for decimal numbers, `str` for string text, `bool` for True or False values, and `range` for a sequence of integers. To determine the data type of a variable, you can utilize the built-in type() function in Python. In the following example, the displayed output will be 'int' because the value 5 is an integer.

```
x = 5
type(x)
```

A number entered from the keyboard is of the str data type by default (where 'str' stands for string). To enable arithmetic operations on the entered value, the built-in float() function can be used to convert the str value into a float data type. The following line of code will display 'str' (even if you entered 5):

```
x = input('Enter a number:')
type(x)
```

In addition to providing instructions for computers to follow, as demonstrated in this section, there are instances where you may wish to include notes within your code for personal reference or to aid others in understanding your code. These notes are referred to as comments and are disregarded by Python. Adding the # symbol as the first character in a line designates that line as a comment. For example, if we rewrite the Example 1.1 code as follow, you may notice the benefits of using comments:

```
# Prompt the user for a degree in Fahrenheit
fahrenheit = float(input("Enter temperature in Fahrenheit: "))
```

```python
# Convert it to Celsius
celsius = (fahrenheit - 32) * (5/9)

# Round it with 2 decimal places
celsius = round(celsius, 2)

# Display the result in both measurements
print(f"{fahrenheit} degrees Fahrenheit is {celsius} degrees Celsius.")
```

Review Question 1.11
In coding, you often store data in a _______ and perform _______ on it.
a. variable, cleansing
b. variable, operations
c. data type, cleansing
d. data type, operations

Review Question 1.12
Which of the following is NOT a legal variable name in Python?
a. myName2
b. 2myName
c. _myName
d. _my_name

Review Question 1.13
Which of the following is NOT a legal variable name in Python?
a. x
b. x_2
c. x2
d. x 2

Review Question 1.14
Which of the following is NOT a legal variable name in Python?
a. x$2
b. x_2
c. x2
d. X2

Review Question 1.15
The 'student' and 'Student' are _______ variable names in Python indicating that variable names in python are case _______.
a. the same, insensitive
b. the same, sensitive
c. different, insensitive
d. different, sensitive

Review Question 1.16
When displaying a string literal to the user, it is convenient to use string _______, or _______. Such formatting lets you embed Python expressions inside string constants.

a. manipulation, s-string
b. interpolation, s-string
c. manipulation, f-string
d. interpolation, f-string

Review Question 1.17
The built-in float() function converts a _______ value to a _______ data type so that arithmetic operations
can apply to it.
a. int, bool
b. decimal, float
c. str, float
d. bool, int

Review Question 1.18
Which of the following is NOT a commonly used data type in Python?
a. int
b. double
c. bool
d. str

Review Question 1.19
At run time, a number entered in keyboard is a ________ data type in Python by default
a. int
b. double
c. bool
d. str

Review Question 1.20
You can check the data type of a variable by using the Python built-in _______ function
a. int()
b. type()
c. bool()
d. str()

Review Question 1.21
Add _______ symbol as the first character in a line makes the line as a comment and ignored by Python.
a. /
b. //
c. --
d. #

Exercise 1.1

Write Python code to convert distance in miles to kilometers. First, prompt the user for a distance in miles,
then convert it to kilometers, and finally, display the result in both measurements (One mile = 1.60934km).

1.4 Python Lists

A variable is capable of holding only one value at a time. However, in real-world scenarios, there are often multiple values that need to be stored at the same time. For instance, a business may have numerous customers, or an exam may generate multiple scores, each corresponding to a student. To accommodate multiple values simultaneously, you can utilize a **list**. Enter and run the following example in a cell:

```python
scores = [87, 60, 79, 95, 100]
```

You now have a variable called 'scores' representing a list that contains five test scores for a class. A list is a collection of values stored in sequential order, enclosed within square brackets and separated by commas. Unlike some other data types, a list is mutable, meaning you can modify, add, or delete values within it.

A list in Python allows for the inclusion of values of different data types. In fact, a list can even contain other lists. For instance, you can create a list consisting of five inner lists, with each inner list containing a student's name and their corresponding score. Here is an example:

```python
students = [["Scott", 87], ["Thomas", 60], ["Eric", 79], ["Mary", 95], ["Lisa", 100]]
```

To access a specific element within a list, you can utilize its index. Each element in a list possesses a unique index based on its position. The first element has an index of 0, the second element has an index of 1, the third element has an index of 2, and so on.

Another way to access an element of a list is counting backward. The last element has the index of -1. The second to the last element has the index of -2, and so on. If you give an index that is not in the list, you will get a "list index out of range" error.

In addition to accessing a specific element using a single index, you can also access a block of elements using a technique called **list slicing**. List slicing involves using two indices: one for the beginning of the block and the other for the end. However, it's important to note that the element at the ending index is not included in the slice. For example, let's consider the scenario of displaying the middle three scores from our 'scores' list (from the second position to the fourth position, inclusive), denoted by indices 1 to 3:

```python
middle3Scores = scores[1:4]
```

The resulting 'middle3Scores' list is a slice of the original 'scores' list. It starts at the index 1, corresponding to a score of 60, and ends at the index 4 (excluding the element itself), which is associated with a score of

100. Therefore, the last element included in the slice is 95, which corresponds to the index 3. Consequently, the variable 'middle3Scores' is a list containing three values. Type the variable name in the cell:

```
middle3Scores
```

You will see the following output:

```
[60, 79, 95]
```

When slicing a list, if you omit the starting index, the slice will start from the beginning of the list (index 0). Likewise, if you omit the ending index, the slice will extend to the end of the list, including the last element. For example, 'scores[:2]' would be [87, 60], and 'scores[3:]' would be [95, 100]. Lastly, 'scores[:]' represents the entire original list, including all elements.

Similarly, you can access a list of lists using two indices. For instance, let's consider the question: What is Thomas' test score in the 'students' list? Since Thomas is at index 1 in the 'students' list, and his score is stored at index 1 within his sublist, you can retrieve Thomas' score using the expression 'students[1][1]'. Similarly, to find Mary's score of 95, you would use 'students[3][1]'.

To modify one or more values within a list, you can assign new values to the corresponding indices. For example, if you wish to change the value of the first element in the 'scores' list from 87 to 78, you can accomplish this by executing the following assignment: `scores[0] = 78`

Furthermore, you have the ability to modify multiple elements simultaneously. For instance, if you want to replace the values of the first two elements in the 'scores' list with 55 and 66, respectively, you can use slicing notation with assignment: `scores[0:2] = [55, 66]`

It's worth noting that if the number of elements on the right side of the assignment exceeds the number of elements being replaced on the left side, the original elements will be removed, and the additional elements on the right will be inserted into the list. Enter the following in a new cell to see how it works:

```
scores = [87, 60, 79, 95, 100]
scores[0:2] = [55, 66, 100]
print(scores)
```

will display:

```
[55, 66, 100, 79, 95, 100]
```

To add additional elements to a list, you can utilize the "+" sign. For instance, let's say you want to include a new score of 99 to the existing 'scores' list. You can achieve this by creating a new list called 'newScores' that combines the original 'scores' list with the additional score: `newScores = scores + [99]`

Similarly, if you want to add two scores, such as 98 and 87, to the 'scores' list, you can use the same approach: `newScores = scores + [98, 87]`

Alternatively, the list object provides a method called 'append()' that allows you to add elements to the end of the list directly. For example, if you have a list called 'students' and you wish to add a new sublist representing the student "Lucy" with a score of 98, you can use the 'append' method:

```
students.append(["Lucy", 98])
```

To remove an element from a list, you can utilize the del() function by specifying the index of the element you want to remove. For instance, if you want to delete the second element from the 'scores' list, you can use the following code: `del(scores[1])`

However, it's important to note that when you remove an element from a list, the remaining elements' indices are readjusted to accommodate the change. This means that the indices of the elements following the one being removed will be shifted accordingly. Now, let's consider the following code snippet:

```
del(scores[0])
del(scores[1])
```

In this case, the intention seems to be to remove the first two elements from the 'scores' list. However, due to the shifting of indices after each deletion, the second line del(scores[1]) will not remove the desired second element, but rather the element that previously occupied the third position. This happens because the index of the remaining elements changes after the first deletion. To correctly remove the first two elements from the 'scores' list, you can simply reverse the order of deletion, starting from the higher index first, like this:

```
del(scores[1])
del(scores[0])
```

A Python list is considered a **reference variable**, meaning that the list variable itself holds a memory address rather than the values directly. Let's take an example: `x = ["a", "b", "c"]`

If you assign x to y like this: `y = x`

Then y will hold the memory address of x. If you print out the list y, Python will access the same memory address where the list values ("a", "b", "c") are stored, resulting in the same output. Any changes made to y will also affect x, and vice versa. For instance, if you modify the first element of y:

```
y[0] = "d"
```

Python will update the list values of both x and y to "d", "b", "c". This behavior occurs because there is only one list with two different names. Therefore, changes made to either list will reflect in the shared values. In short, if you print either x or y, you will get "d", "b", "c".

To avoid such a result and create a new list with the same values and its own address, you can use the list() function or the slicing syntax [:]. For example:

```
y = list(x)
```

Or

```
y = x[:]
```

By using either of these methods, if you update the y list by modifying an element, such as y[0] = "e", Python will only update the value in the y list and leave the value in the x list unaffected. This is because each list now has its own distinct set of values stored in different memory addresses.

If you want to perform a task on each element of a list, you can utilize a **for** loop. Let's consider the following example:

```
curved_scores=[]
for score in scores:
    curved_scores.append(score+10)
```

In this code, a new list called curved_scores is created, and for each element in the scores list, the corresponding element is increased by 10 and added to the curved_scores list. As a result, the curved_scores list will contain each element from the scores list incremented by 10.

An alternative and more concise way to achieve the same result is by using **list comprehension**:

```
curved_scores=[score+10 for score in scores]
```

The above code utilizes list comprehension syntax to iterate over each element in the scores list, perform the operation score + 10, and create a new list curved_scores with the modified values. List comprehension provides a more compact and expressive way to combine the loop and append operations into a single line.

Python also provides a built-in function called range() that generates a sequence of numbers within a specified range. When given a single argument, range() starts from 0 and goes up to, but does not include, the given number. It is commonly used in conjunction with a for loop. For example:

```
for number in range(3):
    print(number)
```

The above code will display the numbers 0, 1, and 2, as range(3) generates a sequence starting from 0 and ending before 3.

Additionally, the range() function can be supplied with two arguments, where the first argument specifies the starting point of the range, and the second argument is used as the exclusive upper limit. For example:

```
for number in range(10, 12):
    print(number)
```

In this case, the code will display the numbers 10 and 11, as the range starts from 10 and ends before 12.

You can determine the index or location of a specific item in a list by using the index() method of a list. Here's an example:

```
scores = [87, 60, 79, 95, 100]
index_of_79=scores.index(79)
```

In the given code, the index() method is called on the scores list with the argument 79. This method searches the list for the first value of 79 and returns its index, which in this case is 2 because 79 is the third element in the list (remembering that indices start from 0). Therefore, the variable index_of_79 will hold the value 2. Using the index() method allows you to quickly determine the position of a specific item within a list.

Review Question 1.22
A variable in Python can only hold one value at a time. A(n) _______, on the other hand, can hold many values at once.
a. multi-value variable
b. array
c. list
d. array or a list

Review Question 1.23
All values in a Python list _______.
a. must have the same data type
b. can only be string
c. can only be string or int
d. can be any data type

Review Question 1.24
Suppose you have the following list in a Python program:
```
scores = [87, 60, 79, 95, 100]
```
What is the value of scores[3]?
a. 60
b. 79
c. 95
d. list index out of range error.

Review Question 1.25
Suppose you have the following list in a Python program:
```
scores = [87, 60, 79, 95, 100]
```
What is the value of scores[0]?
a. 60
b. 87
c. 95
d. list index out of range error.

Review Question 1.26
Suppose you have the following list in a Python program:
```
scores = [87, 60, 79, 95, 100]
```
What is the value of scores[-2]?
a. 60
b. 87
c. 95
d. list index out of range error.

Review Question 1.27
In addition to access a specific element with one index, you can access a block of elements, called _______.
a. list slicing
b. block list
c. elements
d. general elements.

Review Question 1.28
Suppose you have the following list in a Python program:
```
scores = [87, 60, 79, 95, 100]
```
What is(are) the value(s) of scores[1:2]?
a. [87]
b. [60]
c. [60, 79]
d. list index out of range error.

Review Question 1.29
Suppose you have the following list in a Python program:
```
scores = [87, 60, 79, 95, 100]
```
What is(are) the value(s) of scores[:2]?
a. [87, 60]
b. [87, 60, 79]
c. [60, 79]
d. list index out of range error.

Review Question 1.30
Suppose you have the following list in a Python program:
```
scores = [87, 60, 79, 95, 100]
```
What is(are) the value(s) of scores[3:]?
a. [95, 100]
b. [79, 95, 100]
c. [60, 79]
d. list index out of range error.

Review Question 1.31
Suppose you have the following list in a Python program:
```
scores = [87, 60, 79, 95, 100]
```
What is(are) the value(s) of scores[:]?
a. []
b. [87]
c. [87, 60, 79, 95, 100]
d. list index out of range error.

Review Question 1.32
Suppose you have the following list in a Python program:
```
students = [["Scott", 87], ["Thomas", 60], ["Eric", 79], ["Mary", 95],
["Lisa", 100]]
```
What is(are) the value(s) of students[1][1]?
a. Scott
b. 87
c. Thomas
d. 60

Review Question 1.33
Suppose you have the following list in a Python program:
```
students = [["Scott", 87], ["Thomas", 60], ["Eric", 79], ["Mary", 95],
["Lisa", 100]]
```
What is(are) the value(s) of students[1][2]?
a. Scott
b. ["Scott", 87]
c. ["Thomas", 60]
d. list index out of range error.

Review Question 1.34
Suppose you have the following list in a Python program:

```
scores = [87, 60, 79, 95, 100]
newScores = scores + [10]
```
What are in the newScores?
a. [97, 60, 79, 95, 100]
b. [97, 70, 89, 105, 110]
c. [87, 60, 79, 95, 100, 10]
d. list index out of range error.

Review Question 1.35
Suppose you have the following list in a Python program:
```
scores = [87, 60, 79, 95, 100]
newScores = scores.append(10)
```
What is in the newScores?
a. [97, 60, 79, 95, 100]
b. [97, 70, 89, 105, 110]
c. [87, 60, 79, 95, 100, 10]
d. An error, the second line must be newScores = scores.append([10])

Review Question 1.36
Suppose you have the following list in a Python program:
```
scores = [87, 60, 79, 95, 100]
del(scores[1])
```
What is in the scores now?
a. [87, 79, 95, 100]
b. [60, 79, 95, 100]
c. [86, 59, 78, 94, 99]
d. An error, 1 is not a value in the scores list

Review Question 1.37
Python list is a(n) _______ variable, which means the list variable just holds a computer memory address, not the values themselves.
a. list
b. array
c. reference
d. memory

Review Question 1.38
What is the following code in Python called?
```
curved_scores=[score+10 for score in scores]
```
a. list
b. list comprehension
c. curved list
d. for loop list

Review Question 1.39
What is the result of executing the following code in Python (The end parameter indicates no new line)?
```
for number in range(3):
    print(number, end='')
```
a. 3
b. 123

c. 12
d. 012

Review Question 1.40
What is the result of executing the following code in Python (The end parameter indicates no new line)?

```python
for number in range(1, 3):
    print(number, end='')
```

a. 3
b. 123
c. 12
d. 012

Review Question 1.41
What is the result of executing the following code in Python?

```python
scores = [87, 60, 79, 95, 100]
scores.index(79)
```

a. 0
b. 1
c. 2
d. 0, 1, 2

Review Question 1.42
What is the result of executing the following code in Python?

```python
x = ["a", "b", "c"]
y = x
y[0] = "d"
print(x[0])
```

a. a
b. b
c. c
d. d

Review Question 1.43
What is the result of executing the following code in Python?

```python
x = ["a", "b", "c"]
y = list(x)
y[0] = "d"
print(x[0])
```

a. a
b. b
c. c
d. d

Review Question 1.44
What is the result of executing the following code in Python?

```python
scores = [87, 60, 79, 95, 100]
scores[0:2] = [55, 66]
print(scores)
```

a. [87, 60, 79, 95, 100]
b. [55, 66, 87, 60, 79, 95, 100]
c. [55, 66, 79, 95, 100]
d. [55, 60, 66, 79, 95, 100]

Review Question 1.45
What is the result of executing the following code in Python?

```
scores = [87, 60, 79, 95, 100]
scores[0:2] = [55, 66, 100]
print(scores)
```

a. [87, 60, 79, 95, 100]
b. [55, 66, 87, 60, 79, 95, 100]
c. [55, 66, 100, 79, 95, 100]
d. [55, 60, 66, 100, 79, 95, 100]

Exercise 1.2

Task 1: Declare a variable, hourly_wages, to store these five values: 45, 98, 23, 31, and 19.
Task 2: Declare a variable, employee_wages, to store the wages of these five employees: Scott (45), Thomas (98), Eric (23), Mary (31), and Lisa (19).
Task 3: Display the second value in hourly_wages using its index.
Task 4: Display the last value in hourly_wages using its index.
Task 5: Display the middle three values in hourly_wages using list slicing.
Task 6: Display Scott's wage using the employee_wages index.
Task 7: Add two values to hourly_wages using two different methods.
Task 8: Remove the first two values from hourly_wages.
Task 9: Create a copy of hourly_wages and name it hourly_wages1. If a change is made to either list, the other should also change. Write code to demonstrate this.
Task 10: Create another copy of hourly_wages and name it hourly_wages1. If a change is made to one list, the other should not be affected. Write code to demonstrate this.
Task 11: Use a for loop to add 5 to each value in hourly_wages.
Task 12: Use list comprehension to achieve the same result as Task 11.
Task 13: Display all numbers from 10 to 19 using the method introduced in the book.
Task 14: Display all numbers from 0 to 10 using the method introduced in the book.
Task 15: Find the index of the value 98 in hourly_wages.

1.5 Working with Strings

A string is a sequence of characters enclosed within quotes. Both single and double quotes are acceptable, but not a mix of the two. The data type for strings in Python is 'str'. Python does not have a separate character data type. Even single characters, such as 'a' or 'b', are stored as strings. Like lists, strings are internally stored as sequences but are immutable, meaning they cannot be modified. The best you can do is create a new string and assigned to the same variable. Single-line strings can be defined using either single or double quotes. To assign a multi-line string to a variable, you can use triple quotes (either single or double):

```python
x = 'Python is fun!'
y = "Python is really fun!"
z = '''Python string can
    take multiple lines.'''
print(x)
print(y)
print(z)
```

Various functions can be used with strings, and some of them are explained here. The 'len()' function can be used to calculate the length of a string. The following code will display 6 because the string has 6 characters:

```python
len('Python')
```

To extract individual characters from a string, you can use the indexing operator '[]'. The following code will return 'y' because the indexing starts at 0, and 'y' is the second character in the string::

```python
x='Python'
x[1]
```

Slicing refers to extracting a portion or subset of an object, such as a string. Similar to other iterable objects like lists, slicing in strings is done using the colon operator with optional start, stop, and step indices. To display the string from the 10th character to the end, which is 'fun!', you can use the following code:

```python
x='Python is fun!'
x[10:]
```

To display the first 10 characters, including the ending space 'Python is ', you can use the following code:

```python
x='Python is fun!'
x[:10]
```

To display the word 'is', you can use the following code:

```python
x='Python is fun!'
x[7:9]
```

To change the case of a string, you can use the 'upper()' or 'lower()' method. The following code will display 'PYTHON IS FUN!':

```python
x='Python is fun!'
x.upper()
```

To check whether a string starts or ends with a given character, you can use the 'startswith()' or 'endswith()' methods. The following line will display True because the '!' is at the end of the string:

```python
x='Python is fun!'
```

```
x.endswith('!')
```

To remove leading or trailing spaces from a string, you can use the 'strip()' method (to remove spaces at both ends), 'rstrip()' method (to remove spaces from the right end), or 'lstrip()' method (to remove spaces from the left end). The following line removes the leading space from ' Python ' and displays 'Python ':

```
x=' Python '.lstrip()
x
```

There are several methods to check the content of a string, such as 'isalpha()', 'isupper()', 'isdigit()', 'isalnum()', and more. These methods return 'True' only if all the characters in the string satisfy the given condition. The following lines will display 'True' for variable 'x' and 'False' for variable 'y':

```
x = '123'.isdigit()
y = 'ABc'.isupper()
print(x)
print(y)
```

The 'split()' method breaks down a string into a list of individual words and returns a list where each word is an element. If you pass only one word to this method, it will return a list containing just that word and won't split the string further. The following line of code turns a string into a list: ['Python', 'is', 'fun!']:

```
'Python is fun!'.split()
```

The 'join()' method does the opposite of the 'split()' method. It combines a list of strings into one string. On the left-hand side of the 'join()' method, you specify the delimiter in quotes that will be used to join the strings. On the right-hand side, you pass the list of individual strings. The following code turns a list into a string 'Python is fun!':

```
' '.join(['Python', 'is', 'fun!'])
```

Other methods are used for locating substrings. The 'in' keyword in Python is a good way to detect a substring, although 'index()' and 'find()' can also be used. The following code returns 'True':

```
x = "Python is fun!"
"fun" in x
```

You can also use 'index()' or 'find()':

```
x.index("fun")
x.find("fun")
```

Both of the above statements return 10, indicating the starting position of "fun". Note that the difference between 'find()' and 'index()' is that the 'index()' method raises an exception with the message 'ValueError: substring not found' if the string is not found, while 'find()' returns -1 if the string is not found.

Additionally, you can use the 'count()' method to return the number of occurrences of a particular substring. The following code will return 1:

```
x.count("fun")
```

The 'replace()' method substitutes occurrences of one pattern with another but does not change the original string:

```
x.replace("fun", "amazing")
```

Review Question 1.46
What is the data type for x with the following code in Python?
```
x = "88"
```
a. int
b. double
c. number
d. str

Review Question 1.47
What is the data type for x with the following code in Python?
```
x = 'a'
```
a. char
b. character
c. string
d. str

Review Question 1.48
Strings in Python are internally stored as sequences and are immutable. What does immutable mean?
a. will not be affected by virus
b. more secure
c. cannot be modified
d. invented during a pandemic

Review Question 1.49
What is the output of the following Python code?
```
len('Python')
```
a. Py
b. Pyth
c. 5

d. 6

Review Question 1.50
What is the output of the following Python code?
```
x='Python'
x[1]
```
a. P
b. p
c. Y
d. y

Review Question 1.51
What is the output of the following Python code?
```
x='Python is fun!'
x[10:]
```
a. blank space
b. Python is
c. is
d. fun!

Review Question 1.52
What is the output of the following Python code?
```
x='Python is fun!'
x[:9]
```
a. blank space
b. Python is
c. is
d. fun!

Review Question 1.53
What is the output of the following Python code?
```
x='Python is fun!'
x[7:9]
```
a. blank space
b. Python is
c. is
d. fun!

Review Question 1.54
What is the output of the following Python code?
```
x='Python is fun!'
x.endswith('!')
```
a. True
b. False
c. n!
d. fun!

Review Question 1.55
In Python, use the _______ method to remove spaces at both ends of a string.
a. remove()

b. removespaces()
c. strip()
d. space()

Review Question 1.56
What is the output of the following Python code?

```python
y = 'ABc'.isupper()
```

a. True
b. False
c. ABC
d. 'ABC'

Review Question 1.57
What is the output of the following Python code?

```python
x = "Python is fun!"
x.find("fun")
```

a. True
b. False
c. 3
d. 10

Review Question 1.58
What is the output of the following Python code?

```python
x = "Python is fun!"
x.count("fun")
```

a. True
b. False
c. 1
d. 3

1.6 Python Tuples

Similar to lists, tuples in Python can be used to store a collection of values. Tuples are written as a list of comma-separated items surrounded by parentheses. Unlike lists, tuples are immutable, meaning you cannot assign items to a tuple. Tuples have the count() and index() methods. The count() method returns the number of elements in the tuple, while the index() method returns the index of the first element with a specified value. Here is an example of tuple packing (parentheses are optional, and the elements don't have to be of the same data type): `t = ('12345', '12346', '12347').` Similar to a list, the following code will display '12346': `t[1]`

To convert a list to a tuple, you can use the following syntax: `t1 = tuple(['12345', '12346'])`
Additionally, tuples can be nested: `t2 = (('12345', 77, 89), '12346')`

However, you cannot assign values to a tuple. The following code will generate a TypeError: 'tuple' object does not support item assignment:

```
t = ('12345', '12346', '12347')
t[1] = '123'
```

If you have a tuple with a list in it, although the tuple itself is immutable, the list is mutable. You can assign values to items in the list:

```
t3 = (['a', 11, 22], 33)
t3[0][0]='b'
t3
```

Tuples are often used in **tuple unpacking**, where each item from a tuple is assigned to its corresponding variable in order.

```
x, y = t3
print(x)
print(y)
```

In this example, the value of x will be assigned the list ['b', 11, 22], and the value of y will be assigned the value 33 assuming you followed the example prior to this.

Even though you cannot append any elements to a tuple, you can create a new one from the existing one, like this:

```
original_tuple = (1, 2, 3)
new_elements = (4, 5)
expanded_tuple = original_tuple + new_elements
expanded_tuple  # Output: (1, 2, 3, 4, 5)
```

Similar to list comprehension, tuples also have **tuple comprehension**. The following code will generate a tuple (0, 1, 4, 9, 16): `tuple([x**2 for x in range(5)])`

In this code, the expression inside the square brackets generates a list containing the squares of numbers from 0 to 4. The tuple() function then converts that list into a tuple, resulting in the tuple (0, 1, 4, 9, 16).

Review Question 1.59
What is the "a" object of the following Python code?

```
a = ('12345', '12346', '12347')
```
a. array
b. list
c. tuple
d. string

Review Question 1.60
What is the result of the following Python code?
```
t = ('12345', '12346', '12347')
t[1] = '123'
```
a. an updated t tuple
b. the first element of the t tuple is now '123'
c. the second element of the t tuple is now '123'
d. TypeError

Review Question 1.61
What is the result of the following Python code?
```
t = (['12345', '12346'], '12347')
t[0][1] = '123'
```
a. an updated t tuple
b. the first element of the t tuple is '123'
c. the second element of the t tuple is '123'
d. TypeError

Review Question 1.62
Suppose t3 is a tuple. What is the following Python code called/do?
```
x, y = t3
```
a. tuple comprehension
b. x, y tuple
c. list comprehension
d. tuple unpacking

Review Question 1.63
What is the following Python code called/do?
```
tuple([x**2 for x in range(5)])
```
a. tuple comprehension
b. range of 5
c. list comprehension
d. tuple unpacking

1.7 Statements Flow Control

Sometimes, the instructions for computers to follow are not sequential. What you want the computer to do may depend on a condition. For example, if you ask the user to guess a number between 1 and 9, you can provide feedback to the user based on how close their guess is. In such cases, you can use an **if statement**. An if statement allows you to change the execution sequence of instructions based on certain conditions.

Example 1.2

Write a program that generates a random number between 1 and 9 and asks the user to guess. If the guess is correct, display the feedback "Your guess is correct." If the guess is within a range of +1 or -1 from the actual number, display the feedback "Your guess is close." Otherwise, display the feedback "Your guess is incorrect."

Solution:

```python
import random
list = [1, 2, 3, 4, 5, 6, 7, 8, 9]
target = random.choice(list)
guess = input("Enter a number between 1 and 9:")
guess = int(guess)
if guess == target:
    print("Your guess is correct.")
elif guess <= target+1 and guess >= target-1:
    print("Your guess is close.")
else:
    print("Your guess is incorrect.")
```

The random is a module in Python which contains classes and functions. We import the module in the first line so that we can use its function in the third line. The if, elif, and else statements are followed by a colon (:). The next line must be indented to indicate the block of code inside the if statement. Additionally, the "and" and "or" logical operators can be used to combine two or more conditions.

A **shorthand if statement** is also commonly used. The following code is equivalent to the previous code (note that the backward slash \ is a line continuation character):

```python
guess = input("Enter a number between 1 and 9:")
guess = int(guess)
print("Correct.") if guess == target else print("Close.") if\
guess<=target+1 and guess > target-1 else print("Incorrect")
```

In this code, the user is asked to enter a number between 1 and 9. The input is converted to an integer. Then, using the shorthand if statement, the program checks if the guess is equal to the target number. If it is, the message "Correct." is printed. If not, the program checks if the guess is within a range of +1 or -1 from the target number. If it is, the message "Close." is printed. If neither condition is met, the message "Incorrect." is printed.

In addition to using sequential and conditional statements to execute a block of code in Python, there are situations where you may want the computer to repeat a certain action. Take Example 1.2 as reference. In scenarios where you want the user to keep guessing a number until they get the correct one, you can utilize a **while loop**. A while loop is used when you want to execute specific instructions as long as a condition remains "True". Once the block of code executes, the execution returns to the beginning of the block and checks the condition again to determine if another round of loop is necessary.

Example 1.3

Same as Example 1.2. This time, Repeat the guessing process until the user guesses the correct number.

Solution:

```python
import random
list = [1, 2, 3, 4, 5, 6, 7, 8, 9]
target = random.choice(list)
correct = False
while(not correct):
    guess = input("Enter a number between 1 and 9:")
    guess = int(guess)
    if guess == target:
        print("Your guess is correct.")
        correct = True
    elif guess <= target+1 and guess >= target-1:
        print("Your guess is close.")
    else:
        print("Your guess is incorrect.")
```

You can also utilize the **for loop** for repetition. The for loop is used to execute a block of code a predetermined number of times. It is commonly used with iterable objects, such as lists, tuples, and strings. Furthermore, the for loop is frequently used in combination with the range function. The range function creates a range object, which represents a sequence of evenly spaced integers.

Example 1.4

Write Python code to calculate the sum of the first ten odd integers.

Solution:

```python
sum=0
for i in range(1,20,2):
  sum=sum+i
print(sum)
```

The range() function accepts three arguments: the start argument, the stop argument, and the step argument. None of these arguments are mandatory. To generate numbers from 0 to 19 (both 0 and 19 included), you can use any of the following: range(20), range(0, 20), or range(0, 20, 1). The default start argument is 0, and the default step argument is 1. The 'step' indicates the increment.

Review Question 1.64
How to write Python if statement?
a. use the if keyword followed by a condition in a single line, add a block of statements in new lines.
b. use the if keyword followed by a condition in a single line, add a block of statements in a pair of curly braces.
c. use the if keyword followed by a condition and a colon, add a block of statements in new lines.
d. use the if keyword followed by a condition and a colon, add a block of statements in new lines indented by four spaces.

Review Question 1.65
What is the output of the following code?
```python
x = 5
if x > 3:
    print("x is greater than 3")
elif x > 4:
    print("x is greater than 4")
else:
    print("x is not greater than 3 or 4")
```
a. `x is greater than 3`
b. `x is greater than 4`
c. `x is not greater than 3 or 4`
d. Nothing can be displayed because of an error.

Review Question 1.66
What is the output of the following code (The end parameter indicates a space in between the print)?
```python
for i in range(5):
    print(i, end= ' ')
```
a. `0 1 2 3 4`
b. `0 1 2 3 4 5`
c. `1 2 3 4 5`
d. I and 5

Exercise 1.2

Our online store sells only soda, milk, chips, eggs, and bread. Prompt the user to enter a grocery item they want to buy. If the item is on the list, display "You have good taste." If the item is not on the list, display "Sorry, we don't sell that."

1.8 Python Dictionary

Lists and tuples allow you to store multiple values and access them by their index in the sequence. However, there are situations when you want to access values using predefined keys that do not change. For example, if you want to store student scores and access them by their student ID, a list or tuple may not be ideal.

In such cases, dictionaries come in handy. A dictionary allows you to store variables and access them using keys. It is an unordered collection of key-value pairs, where both the key and value can be Python objects. Each key is associated with a value, making it easy to retrieve, insert, modify, or delete data. As such, keys must be unique. If you provide more than one value for the same key, the last value will be stored.

Dictionaries in Python are created using curly brackets. An element can be retrieved from a dictionary by using its key. For example:

```python
scores = {12345:87, 12346:60, 12347:79, 12348:95, 12349:100}
scores[12347]
```

The above code creates a dictionary called "scores" with five items, where each item consists of a key and a value. The value represents the actual data, while the key allows us to access that data. In this case, accessing the element with the key "12347" (`scores[12347]`) will return the value 79.

The key and value in a dictionary are separated by a colon, and each key-value pair is separated by a comma. Similar to lists, we use square brackets to indicate the key when accessing data in a dictionary. You can add additional key-value pairs to a dictionary. For example, let's say a student with an ID of 21345 has scored 83. You can add this to the "scores" dictionary using the following code:

```python
scores[21345] = 83
scores
```

If you access an element with a key that does not exist in the dictionary, you will encounter an error. For instance, accessing scores[22222] will result in an error. To avoid this, you can use the get method, which will return "None" instead of an error:

```python
print(scores.get(22222))
```

To check if a dictionary contains a specific key, you can use an if statement. For example:

```python
student_id = int(input("Enter a student ID:"))
if student_id in scores:
    print(f"Student {student_id} has a score.")
else:
    print("The ID does not exist.")
```

In this code, the user is prompted to enter a student ID. If the ID exists in the "scores" dictionary, it will print a message indicating that the student has a score. Otherwise, it will display a message stating that the ID does not exist.

To delete values from a dictionary, you can use either the del keyword or the pop() method, which simultaneously returns the value and deletes the key. For example:

```python
del scores[12349]
score_12346=scores.pop(12346)
```

When looping over a dictionary, you will iterate over the keys by default. For example:

```python
for x in scores:
    print(x)
```

If you want to loop over the values instead, you can use the values() method on dictionaries. For example:

```python
for x in scores.values():
    print(x)
```

If you want to loop over the dictionary and access both the keys and values, you can use the items() method. Since each iteration will give you two items (key and value), you need to provide two variables in the for loop declaration. For example:

```python
for student_id, score in scores.items():
    print(f"ID: {student_id} Score: {score}")
```

In this code, each loop iteration will assign the key to the student_id variable and the corresponding value to the score variable. The print statement will then display the ID and score for each student in the dictionary.

Example 1.5:

Write a Python code that prompts the user for a message and then encodes that message into Morse code, which uses dots and dashes.

Solution:

```python
# A dictionary mapping each alphanumeric character
letter_to_morse = {
    'a':'.-', 'b':'-...', 'c':'-.-.', 'd':'-..', 'e':'.',
    'f':'..-.', 'g':'--.', 'h':'....', 'i':'..', 'j':'.---',
    'k':'-.-', 'l':'.-..', 'm':'--', 'n':'-.', 'o':'---',
    'p':'.--.', 'q':'--.-', 'r':'.-.', 's':'...', 't':'-',
    'u':'..-', 'v':'...-', 'w':'.--', 'x':'-..-', 'y':'-.--',
    'z':'--..', '0':'-----', '1':'.----', '2':'..---',
    '3':'...--', '4':'....-', '5':'.....', '6':'-....',
    '7':'--...', '8':'---..', '9':'----.', ' ':'/'
}
message = input("Enter a message (no punctuation):").lower()
# `an empty list to hold each character of the message in Morse
morse = []
# loop through the message
for letter in message:
    morse_letter = letter_to_morse[letter]
    morse.append(morse_letter)
# Join together Morse code letters with spaces into a message
morse_message = " ".join(morse)
# Display both messages
print(f"Your message: {message}")
print(f"Morse encoded: {morse_message}")
```

Example 1.6

A store has only three products. Create a dictionary named unit_price with product names as keys and product prices as values. Next, suppose an order consists of one unit of product1 and four units of product3. Create a dictionary named order with product names as keys and the number of units in the order as values. Finally, calculate the total cost of the order using a for loop and display the total as output.

Solution:

```python
unit_price = {
    "product1": 1.20,
    "product2": 2.50,
    "product3": 1.90
}
order = {
    "product1": 1,
    "product3": 4,
}
order_total = 0
for product, count in order.items():
```

```python
    order_total += unit_price[product] * count
print(f"Your order total: ${order_total:.2f}")
```

Review Question 1.67
Lists let you store many values, and to access them by their location or index in the list. For the same element, the index may change over time when elements are removed or inserted. To have fixed indices, you can use ________.
a. fixed index list
b. dictionary
c. tuple
d. loop

Review Question 1.68
A dictionary lets you store variables and access them using a ________.
a. key
b. value
c. key: value pair
d. colon

Review Question 1.69
Given the following code in Python:
```python
scores = {12345:87, 12346:60, 12347:79, 12348:95, 12349:100}
scores[12347]
```
What will be the output?
a. 87
b. 60
c. 79
d. 95

Review Question 1.70
Given the following code in Python:
```python
scores = {12345:87, 12346:60, 12347:79, 12348:95, 12349:100}
```
How do you change the score for student 12345?
a. 87 = 100
b. scores[12345] = 100
c. scores[87] = 100
d. You cannot change the value of a dictionary.

Review Question 1.71
Given the following code in Python:
```python
scores = {12345:87, 12346:60, 12347:79, 12348:95, 12349:100}
scores[12344]
```
What is the output?
a. too small
b. 86
c. None
d. Error

Review Question 1.72
Given the following code in Python:
```
scores = {12345:87, 12346:60, 12347:79, 12348:95, 12349:100}
print(scores.get(12344))
```
What is the output?
a. too small
b. 86
c. None
d. Error

Review Question 1.73
How do you delete an element in Python dictionary?
a. use keyword del
b. dictionary method pop()
c. use keyword del or dictionary method pop()
d. use keyword del and immediately followed by dictionary method pop()

Review Question 1.74
Suppose scores is a Python dictionary. How do you loop through all keys in the scores?
a. `for x in scores:`
b. `for x in scores.keys:`
c. `for x in scores.values():`
d. `for x, y in scores.items():`

Review Question 1.75
Suppose scores is a Python dictionary. How do you loop through all values in the scores only?
a. `for x in scores:`
b. `for x in scores.keys:`
c. `for x in scores.values():`
d. `for x, y in scores.items():`

Review Question 1.76
Suppose scores is a Python dictionary. How do you loop through all keys and values in the scores?
a. `for x in scores:`
b. `for x in scores.values:`
c. `for x in scores.keys&values():`
d. `for x, y in scores.items():`

Exercise 1.3

Prompt the user for a message in Morse code and convert it to plain text. To test your program, run
Example 1.5, which provides a message in Morse code. Then, convert the Morse code message to plain text.
Compare the converted text with your original message. Are they the same? (hint: Use the following code to
switch the keys and values in a dictionary: new_dict = {value: key for key, value in original_dict.items()})

1.9 Python Functions

Functions provide a way of encapsulating code into reusable and user-friendly components. For instance, the built-in print() function handles all the details of printing text, so all you need to do is provide the text as input, and it takes care of the rest. A function can be thought of as a "black box" where the user doesn't need to worry about how it works internally. It takes an input, processes it, and produces an output.

By creating your own functions, you can package your own logic, avoid repetition, and make your code more readable. A function in Python is defined using the *def* keyword, followed by the function name and one or more optional parameters. Parameters are variables that exist only within the function. Variables defined within a function have local scope, which means they cannot be accessed outside the function.

Example 1.7:

Write a Python function to generate weekly pay stubs for employees. Each employee has a name, hours worked, and pay rate. If an employee worked 40 hours or less, the regular pay amount is calculated by multiplying the hours worked by the pay rate. If an employee worked more than 40 hours, the first 40 hours are paid at the regular rate, and any additional hours are paid at a rate of 1.5 times the regular rate.

Solution:

```python
def weekly_pay_stub(name, hours, rate):
    regualar_pay = 0.0
    overtime_pay = 0.0
    if hours <= 40:
        regular_pay = hours * rate
    else:
        regular_pay = 40 * rate
        overtime_pay = (hours-40) * rate * 1.5
    return f"Name: {name} Regular pay: {regular_pay:.2f} Overtime pay:\
{overtime_pay:.2f} Total pay: {regular_pay+overtime_pay:.2f}"
```

When you execute the cell, you won't see any output. This is because a function needs to be called in order to be executed. To use, or call, the function, just type the function name, providing the argument values for the parameters. For example, if Lucy Scott worked 50 hours at a pay rate of $40 per hour, the employee should be paid $2,200.00. Make sure to provide the values in the specific order as expected by the function:

```python
weekly_pay_stub('Lucy Scott', 50, 40)
```

Alternatively, you can send the arguments using the key-value syntax:

```python
weekly_pay_stub(hours=50, name='Lucy Scott', rate=40)
```

This way, the order of the arguments doesn't matter as long as you specify the correct parameter names and values.

Example 1.8

Prompt the user to enter a sentence. Then, categorize the words in the sentence based on their first letter. For example, if the sentence is "Python program is fun," there would be two words starting with the letter 'p' ('p': ['python', 'programs']), one word starting with the letter 'i' ('i': ['is']), and one word starting with the letter 'f' ('f': ['fun']). Case sensitivity should be ignored in this categorization.

To accomplish this, define a function that breaks down a sentence into a list of words. Then, extract the first letter of each word and count how many words start with each letter. Specifically:

1. Prompt the user to enter a sentence.

2. Convert the sentence to all lower case so that we can ignore the case from now on.

3. Pass the sentence to a function that splits it into a list of words.

4. Iterate through the words and extract the first letter of each word.

5. If the the letter does not exit, create a new category. Otherwise, append the word to an existing letter.

6. Display the results.

Solution:

```python
def sentence_to_words(sentence):
    return [word for word in sentence.split()]
sentence = input("Enter a sentence:").lower()
words = sentence_to_words(sentence)
category_by_first_letter = {}
for word in words:
    first_letter = word[0]
    if first_letter not in category_by_first_letter:
        category_by_first_letter[first_letter] = [word]
    else:
        category_by_first_letter[first_letter].append(word)
category_by_first_letter
```

Sometimes, you may find it useful to use anonymous or *lambda* functions for their compact way of defining functions without binding them to a name. Consider the following code:

```python
(lambda x, y: x+y) (3, 2)
```

This code will display 5. Note the syntax of a lambda expression. It starts with the lambda keyword, followed by the parameters (in this case, 'x' and 'y'). After the colon, there is an expression that is evaluated and returned. At this point, the benefit of using a lambda may not be apparent. However, as you progress through future chapters, you will come to appreciate the conciseness and usefulness of lambda functions.

Review Question 1.77
Functions provide a way of wrapping statement code into _______ and easy-to-use components.
a. reusable
b. concise
c. executable
d. one-line

Review Question 1.78
Which of the following is NOT required in a regular Python function definition?
a. def keyword
b. name of the function
c. a pair of parentheses
d. parameter(s)

Review Question 1.79
Which of the following is NOT required in a regular Python function definition?
a. def keyword
b. name of the function
c. a colon
d. argument(s)

Review Question 1.80
What do you call an anonymous function in Python?
a. nameless
b. beta
c. lambda
d. alpha

Review Question 1.81
What do you call the x and y in the following Python code?
```
(lambda x, y: x+y) (3, 2)
```
a. lambda
b. parameters
c. global variables
d. return values

1.10 NumPy

Lists are useful when you have a group of data points, but they can be inconvenient for performing

calculations. Let's consider an example where we have two lists of test scores for five students:

```
score1 = [56, 74, 97, 88, 95]
score2 = [69, 78, 95, 83, 59]
```

If we want to calculate the total scores for each student, we have to use loops. It would be great if we could simply do something like this:

```
total_score = score1 + score2
```

However, as you know, this would result in a list of 10 scores. To perform such calculations efficiently on lists and handle similar operations, Travis Oliphant created an open-source Python library called NumPy. NumPy, short for "Numerical Python," is a foundational package for numerical computing in Python. It is a library or module that contains reusable code, eliminating the need to reinvent the wheel.

To use the NumPy library, simply add the following line:

```
import numpy as np
```

In this case, the "as np" is optional. It creates an alias for NumPy as "np." This alias is commonly used among data scientists and allows you to use "np" instead of typing out "numpy" every time you need to access its functionalities.

NumPy is designed for efficiency when working with large datasets. It stores data internally in a contiguous block of memory, resulting in lower memory usage compared to built-in Python sequences. Additionally, NumPy provides faster computation without the need for Python's for loops, thanks to its optimized C language-based algorithms.

One of the key features of NumPy is its N-dimensional array object, known as **ndarray**. This array is a fast and flexible container specifically designed for handling large datasets in Python.

The simplest way to create a NumPy ndarray is by using the array function provided by the NumPy library. This function accepts various sequence-like objects, including other arrays, and returns a new NumPy array:

```
import numpy as np
score1 = [56, 74, 97, 88, 95]
score2 = [69, 78, 95, 83, 59]
score1np = np.array(score1)
score2np = np.array(score2)
print(score1np)
print(score2np)
```

In the code above, we first import the NumPy library using the line "import numpy as np". Then, we create NumPy arrays score1np and score2np by passing the corresponding lists score1 and score2 to the np.array()

function. Finally, we print the arrays to verify the results.

You can also create multidimensional arrays by nesting lists. For example:

```
scoresnp=np.array([score1, score2])
scoresnp
```

In this case, scoresnp becomes a two-dimensional NumPy array. We can confirm this by examining the ndim and shape attributes of the array:

```
print(scoresnp.ndim)
print(scoresnp.shape)
print(type(scoresnp))
```

Output:

```
2
(2, 5)
<class 'numpy.ndarray'>
```

This output indicates that scoresnp is a two-dimensional array with a shape of (2, 5). The ndim attribute tells us the number of dimensions of the array, and the type function confirms that scoresnp belongs to the ndarray class provided by NumPy.

Arithmetic operations with NumPy arrays are known as **vectorization**. When performing arithmetic operations between equal-sized arrays, the operation is applied element-wise. Let's compare the outputs of addition operations on Python lists and NumPy arrays using the following examples:

First, let's add two Python lists score1 and score2:

```
score1 + score2
```

In this case, the + operator concatenates the two lists, resulting in a new list that combines the elements of score1 and score2. The elements are not added element-wise.

Now, let's perform the same addition operation using NumPy arrays score1np and score2np:

```
score1np + score2np
```

Here, the + operator performs element-wise addition on the NumPy arrays. Each corresponding pair of elements from score1np and score2np is added together, resulting in a new NumPy array with the element-wise sum.

Moving on to arithmetic operations with scalars, let's add a scalar value of 10 to each element in a Python list score1:

```
score1 + 10
```

In this case, the addition operation is not supported between a list and a scalar, resulting in an error.

Now, let's perform the same operation using a NumPy array score1np:

```
score1np + 10
```

In this case, the scalar value of 10 is added to each element in the score1np array. The operation is applied element-wise, resulting in a new NumPy array where each element is increased by 10.

Similarly, let's compare two NumPy arrays score1np and score2np to check if each corresponding element in score1np is greater than the corresponding element in score2np:

```
score1_greater_than_score2 = score1np > score2np
score1_greater_than_score2
```

The result of this comparison will be a NumPy array of Boolean values. Each element in the resulting array represents the outcome of the comparison between the corresponding elements of score1np and score2np. If the element in score1np is greater than the corresponding element in score2np, the value will be True; otherwise, it will be False.

Indexing and slicing in NumPy arrays are similar to Python lists:

```
# display the element with index of 2
print(score1np[2])
# display the elements with index of 2 and 3
print(score1np[2:4])
# assign the third element a new value of 66
score1np[2] = 66
# display the whole array
print(score1np)
```

When working with a two-dimensional NumPy array scoresnp, you need to provide two indices:

```
# display the scoresnp array
print(scoresnp)
# second row, fifth element
print(scoresnp[1, 4])
# first row, second element
print(scoresnp[0][1])
# middle three elements of the second row
```

```
print(scoresnp[1, 1:4])
```

It's important to note that when you assign a slice of a NumPy array to a new array, any changes made to the new array will be reflected in the original array, as they share the same memory location (reference type):

```
# get the last two elements from score1np to a new array
last_scores = score1np[-2:]
# modify the first element of the new array
last_scores[0] = 100
# the second-to-last element of the original array is modified
score1np # output: array([ 56,  74,  97, 100,  95])
```

NumPy arrays also allow Boolean indexing, which enables you to select elements based on a Boolean condition:

```
import numpy as np
# Create a NumPy array
a = np.array([1, 3, 6])
# Use Boolean indexing to select elements that are greater than 5
b = a[a > 5]
print(b).
```

The output is: [6].

In this example, the condition a > 5 returns a Boolean array, which is then used to index into the original array a, resulting in a new array **b** that contains only the elements from **a** that are greater than 5.

You can also set values using Boolean arrays by assigning values to the locations where the Boolean array's values are True::

```
# Boolean array of scores above mean in scoresnp
print(scoresnp > scoresnp.mean())
# display scores above mean
print(f"Scores above mean: {scoresnp[scoresnp > scoresnp.mean()]}")
# Boolean array of scores above 60 percentile in scoresnp
sixty_pct = scoresnp > np.percentile(scoresnp, 60)
# display scores above 60 percentile
print(f"Scores abve 60 percentile: {scoresnp[sixty_pct]}")
```

This code demonstrates using Boolean arrays to filter elements in scoresnp based on specific conditions.

This section just provides a brief review of NumPy. For more information, visit: https://numpy.org/.

Review Question 1.82

Suppose you have two Python lists of five student test scores, each list represents an exam:

```
score1 = [1, 2, 3, 4, 5]
score2 = [2, 3, 4, 5, 6]
```

What is in the total_score after executing the following statement?

```
total_score = score1 + score2
```

a. [3, 5, 7, 9, 11]
b. [1, 2, 3, 4, 5, 6]
c. [1, 2, 3, 4, 5, 2, 3, 4, 5, 6]
d. An error. You cannot "plus" anything other than scalar numbers.

Review Question 1.83

Suppose you have two NumPy arrays of five student test scores, each array represents an exam:

```
score1 = np.array([1, 2, 3, 4, 5])
score2 = np.array([2, 3, 4, 5, 6])
```

What is in the total_score after executing the following statement?

```
total_score = score1 + score2
```

a. [3, 5, 7, 9, 11]
b. [1, 2, 3, 4, 5, 6]
c. [1, 2, 3, 4, 5, 2, 3, 4, 5, 6]
d. An error. You cannot "plus" anything other than scalar numbers.

Review Question 1.84

Suppose you have a Python list of five student quiz scores:

```
score = [1, 2, 3, 4, 5]
```

What is in the new_score after executing the following statement?

```
new_score = score + 1
```

a. [2, 2, 3, 4, 5]
b. [2, 3, 4, 5, 6]
c. [1, 2, 3, 4, 5, 1]
d. An error. You cannot "plus" a number to a list.

Review Question 1.85

Suppose you have a NumPy array of five student quiz scores:

```
score = np.array([1, 2, 3, 4, 5])
```

What is in the new_score after executing the following statement?

```
new_score = score + 1
```

a. [2, 2, 3, 4, 5]
b. [2, 3, 4, 5, 6]
c. [1, 2, 3, 4, 5, 1]
d. An error. You cannot "plus" a number to a list.

Review Question 1.86

Suppose you have a Python list of five student quiz scores:

```
score = [1, 2, 3, 4, 5]
```

How do you make a NumPy array with the data from the Python list score, assuming numpy is imported by following the convention?

a. score.numpy()
b. score.np.array()
c. numpy(score)
d. np.array(score)

Review Question 1.87
If a slice of a NumPy array is assigned to a new array, any change made to the new array will ______.
a. be reflected in the original array, but not in the new array
b. be reflected in both original array and the new array
c. not be reflected in the original array, just the new array
d. not be reflected in either original array nor the new array

Review Question 1.88
NumPy arrays allow you to use ________, which allows you to select elements from an array based on a Boolean condition.
a. Boolean indexing
b. Boolean condition
c. binary indexing
d. binary condition

Review Question 1.89
What is the output of the following code execution?
```
a = np.array([1, 3, 5, 7, 9])
b = a[a > 5]
print(b).
```
a. [7, 9]
b. [no, no, no, yes, yes]
c. [False, False, False, True, True]
d. [1, 3, 5]

1.11 Basic Skills for Working with JupyterLab:

In JupyterLab, you can use the Markdown language to document your code in a cell. To switch a cell to Markdown, select "Markdown" from the drop-down menu in the toolbar. Any text entered in the cell will be treated as documentation. To organize your document, you can use hash symbols (#) to create headings of different levels. One hash symbol represents the most important heading, and you can use up to six hash symbols for subsection headings. These headings correspond to HTML heading tags from <h1> to <h6>.

To edit the text in a Markdown cell, double-click on the cell and modify the text. After making your changes, you can run the cell to see the updated formatting. Markdown cells support various formatting options such as boldface, italics, numbered lists, bulleted lists, and more. For example, you can make text bold by enclosing it with two asterisks (** **). Let's practice with the following lines in a Markdown cell:

```
# Chapter 1: Introduction to Python
## 1.11 Basic Skills for working with JupyterLab
You can **bold one or more words** like this and *italicize one or more words* as well.
```

When working in a code cell, JupyterLab offers two useful features that can enhance your productivity. The first feature is **Tab completion**, which can be activated by pressing the Tab key after typing an object name followed by a dot. Upon pressing Tab, JupyterLab displays a drop-down list containing all the attributes and methods associated with that object. You can scroll through the list to find the desired attribute or method, or you can refine the entries by typing the first few letters of the specific attribute or method.

The second feature is the **tooltip**, which can be activated by pressing Shift+Tab after typing an attribute or method name. The tooltip provides a convenient way to access the documentation for each attribute or method. By scrolling through the tooltip, you can quickly view relevant information about the attribute or method, helping you understand its functionality and usage.

JupyterLab provides certain commands known as **Magic Commands**, which are specific to JupyterLab and not part of the Python language itself. One such example is the %time command, which measures the execution time of a single Python statement. This command can be useful when you're working on optimizing the performance of your code and need to assess the time it takes to run a particular statement.

Additionally, the %%time command is used at the beginning of a cell that contains multiple statements. When applied, it measures the execution time for the entire cell, allowing you to analyze the overall performance of a code block comprising multiple statements.

Example 1.9

Comparing Performance of NumPy Arrays and Python Lists

Solution:

To compare the execution time of operating on a NumPy array versus a Python list, follow these steps:

Create the two objects, a NumPy array and a Python list, by entering the following code in the first cell:

```python
import numpy as np
np_array = np.arange(1000000)
py_list = list(range(1000000))
```

In a new cell, measure the time required for operating on the NumPy array using the %time command:.

```python
%time for _ in range(20): new_np_array = np_array * 3
```

In another new cell, measure the time required for operating on the Python list:

```python
%time for _ in range(20): new_py_list = [x * 3 for x in py_list]
```

You can further practice using the %%time command in a new cell with the following code:

```
%%time
for _ in range(20):
    new_np_array = np_array * 3
for _ in range(20):
    new_py_list = [x * 2 for x in py_list]
```

Similarly, the %who command can be used to obtain a table of active variables, including their data types and other relevant information. This information is particularly useful during debugging, as certain methods can only be applied to specific data types. Simply type %who to execute this command. Another handy Magic Command is %magic, which provides documentation for all available Magic commands. Generally, commands starting with % apply to a single statement, while those starting with %% apply to all statements within a cell.

1.12 Chapter Summary

In this chapter, you have gained familiarity with the basic syntax of the Python language. The topics covered include variables, operators, flow control, functions, lists, tuples, dictionaries, and an introduction to the NumPy library, which is essential for data science. Additionally, you have installed the JupyterLab integrated development environment (IDE), which offers a spreadsheet-like environment where you can write and execute code to obtain immediate results. One of the key distinctions between Python and other programming languages like Java or C# is the absence of semicolons to terminate statements. In Python, indentation is crucial, and it is achieved using four spaces instead of a pair of curly braces. Another significant difference is that programmers do not need to specify the data type for variables in Python; the language automatically determines the type based on the assigned value.

1.13 Solutions to the Review Questions

1.1 B; 1.2 B; 1.3 C; 1.4 B; 1.5 C; 1.6 B; 1.7 C; 1.8 C; 1.9 A; 1.10 C; 1.11 B; 1.12 B; 1.13 D; 1.14 A; 1.15 D; 1.16 D; 1.17 C; 1.18 B; 1.19 D; 1.20 B; 1.21 D; 1.22 C; 1.23 D; 1.24 C; 1.25 B; 1.26 C; 1.27 A; 1.28 B; 1.29 A; 1.30 A; 1.31 C; 1.32 D; 1.33 D; 1.34 C; 1.35 C; 1.36 A; 1.37 C; 1.38 B; 1.39 D; 1.40 C; 1.41 C; 1.42 D; 1.43 A; 1.44 C; 1.45 C; 1.46 D; 1.47 D; 1.48 C; 1.49 D; 1.50 D; 1.51 D; 1.52 B; 1.53 C; 1.54 A; 1.55 C; 1.56 B; 1.57 D; 1.58 C; 1.59 C; 1.60 D; 1.61 A; 1.62 D; 1.63 A; 1.64 D; 1.65 A; 1.66 A; 1.67 B; 1.68 A; 1.69 C; 1.70 B; 1.71 D; 1.72 C; 1.73 C; 1.74 A; 1.75 C; 1.76 D; 1.77 A; 1.78 D; 1.79 D; 1.80 C; 1.81 B; 1.82 C; 1.83 A; 1.84 D; 1.85 B; 1.86 D; 1.87 B; 1.88 A; 1.89 A;

Chapter 2: Pandas Basics

Chapter Learning Objectives:

2.1 Demonstrate a basic understanding of Pandas.
2.2 Compare and contrast Series and DataFrame in Pandas.
2.3 Illustrate indexing techniques in Pandas.
2.4 Select and filter data using Pandas DataFrame.
2.5 Perform statistical computations using Pandas.

2.1 Introduction to Pandas

Imagine you're working with a spreadsheet full of data, where each row and column has specific meaning and context. Now, think about how you could manipulate, analyze, and visualize that data with ease, all within Python. That's where Pandas comes in—your go-to library for transforming raw data into actionable insights.

Introduced in 2010, Pandas is an open-source library that has quickly become a cornerstone for data manipulation in Python. While NumPy, which you explored in Chapter 1, excels at handling homogeneous data (like arrays of numbers), Pandas is designed to handle more complex, tabular data—the kind you might find in spreadsheets or SQL tables. With Pandas, you can seamlessly work with datasets that include mixed data types, such as numbers, text, and dates.

At the heart of Pandas are two key structures: the Series and the DataFrame. Understanding these is essential for anyone who wants to master data manipulation in Python.

Series: Think of a Series as a single column in a spreadsheet—a one-dimensional array with labels (known as an index) that make data retrieval and operations straightforward. It's perfect for when you're working with a simple list of data points. Each element in a Series is associated with a label, which allows for fast and flexible data access.

DataFrame: A DataFrame is like a full spreadsheet or a SQL table. It's two-dimensional, with rows and columns, and each column can contain different data types. Just like a Series, a DataFrame has an index that labels the rows, making it easy to select and manipulate specific parts of your data. Additionally, each column in a DataFrame is also labeled, allowing you to access and work with data intuitively. This structure makes DataFrames incredibly versatile for handling real-world data, where you might have columns of dates, text, and numbers all mixed together.

When you load data into a Pandas DataFrame or Series, you're setting the stage for powerful data manipulation. Whether you're cleaning messy data, transforming it into different formats, or plotting trends, Pandas provides the tools you need—all with intuitive, built-in methods and attributes.

Review Question 2.1
Similar to the NumPy package you learned in Chapter 1, Pandas is an open source _______ that was introduced in 2010.
a. animal
b. virtual animal
c. module
d. mobile app

Review Question 2.2
The pandas adopts many coding idioms from NumPy with one major difference: pandas is designed for working with _______.
a. animal or living data
b. larger data set
c. tabular data
d. homogeneously typed data

Review Question 2.3
Pandas is built around two objects: _______.
a. Series and array
b. DataFrame and array
c. Series and DataFrame
d. array and list

Review Question 2.4
The Series and DataFrame objects are the underlying _______ in Pandas.
a. foundations
b. building blocks
c. functions
d. data structures

Review Question 2.5
A _______ in Pandas is a one-dimensional sequence, such as a column of a table.
a. Series
b. DataFrame

c. Pandas
d. field

Review Question 2.6
A _______ in Pandas is a two-dimensional sequence, such as a table or a spreadsheet with rows and columns.
a. Series
b. DataFrame
c. Pandas
d. field

Review Question 2.7
Each value stored in a Series or a DataFrame has _______ attached to it, which speeds up retrieval and access to data.
a. a number
b. a name
c. a label or an index
d. a primary key

2.2 Series Basics

In the Pandas library, a Series is a one-dimensional labeled array similar to a column in a spreadsheet. Each element has an index, which can be an integer or a string, allowing easy access to values. By default, the index is a range starting from 0, but it can be customized when creating the Series.

To create a Series in Pandas, you can use the Series function and provide a Python list, dictionary, or a NumPy array as the input. Here's an example:

```python
import numpy as np
import pandas as pd

# Create a Series from a list
s1 = pd.Series([1, 12, 5, np.nan, 8])
print(s1)

# Create a Series from a dictionary
s2 = pd.Series({'a': 1, 'b': 12, 'c': 5, 'd': np.nan, 'e': 18, 'f': 8})
print(s2)

# Create a Series from an array
s3 = pd.Series(np.array([1, 12, 5, np.nan, 16, 8]))
print(s3)
```

In the example, the special value np.nan represents "Not a Number" and is commonly used to denote missing or null values in numerical data. The output displays the index on the left column and the corresponding values on the right column. If you don't specify an index explicitly, Pandas will create a default index consisting of integers from 0 to N-1, where N is the length of the data. An index is an object with its own data type and a set of values. The default data type for an index object is RangeIndex.

You can obtain the index object and the values of a Series by accessing the index and values attributes of the Series, respectively. Here's an example:

```
print(s1.index)
print(s1.values)
```

Output:

```
RangeIndex(start=0, stop=5, step=1)
[ 1. 12.  5. nan  8.]
```

The index attribute displays the type of index, which in this case is a RangeIndex. The RangeIndex is specified within the parentheses and indicates that the index starts at 0, increases by 1, and stops at 5 (exclusive). The values attribute returns a NumPy array containing the actual values stored in the Series.

Often, it is desirable to create a Series with custom index labels to identify each data point. To add custom index labels, you can pass the index parameter to the Series constructor when creating a new Series object.

```
score = [56, 74, 97, 88, 95]
student_id = ['12345', '12346', '12347', '12348', '12349']
score_series=pd.Series(score, index=student_id)
print(score_series)
```

Output:

```
12345    56
12346    74
12347    97
12348    88
12349    95
dtype: int64
```

If you print the index attribute of the score_series, you will see that it is not a RangeIndex:

```
print(score_series.index)
print(score_series.values)
```

Output:

```
Index(['12345', '12346', '12347', '12348', '12349'], dtype='object')
[56 74 97 88 95]
```

You can use the index to access individual values in two ways: by using the index label or by using the corresponding integer position. You can also use a list of indices to select multiple values. By using double square brackets, you are specifying a list of indices or labels to access specific elements in the Series object. If you use double square brackets to retrieve a single element, you will get a single element series (not recommended). Additionally, you can still use integer-based indexing. Most features of Pandas Series are similar to NumPy. For example, filtering with a Boolean array, performing scalar addition, applying mathematical functions, will preserve the index-value relationship.

```python
print("With custom index, you can access an element in two ways:")
print(score_series['12346'])
print(score_series[1])
print("----------")
print(score_series[['12346', '12348']])
print(score_series[[1, 3]])
print("----------")
print(score_series[score_series >= score_series.mean()])
print("----------")
print(score_series + 10)
```

Output:

```
With custom index, you can access an element in two ways:
74
74
----------
12346    74
12348    88
dtype: int64
12346    74
12348    88
dtype: int64
----------
12347    97
12348    88
12349    95
dtype: int64
----------
12345     66
12346     84
12347    107
12348     98
12349    105
dtype: int64
```

Some people find it helpful to think of a Series as a fixed-length and ordered dictionary because it represents a mapping of index values to data values. In many contexts, you can use a Series similar to how you would use a dictionary. For example, the following code will display "True" if the index value '12349' is present in the score_series:

```python
print('12349' in score_series)
```

Additionally, both the Series object itself and its index can have a name attribute, which integrates with other functionalities in pandas. You can assign a name to the score_series and a name to its index using the following code:

```
score_series.name = 'exam1'
score_series.index.name = 'studentID'
score_series
```

A Series's index can be modified in-place by assignment. The following code replaces the student IDs with names for the indexes, removing the custom index name:

```
score_series.index=['Lucy', 'Lucky', 'Rich', 'Adam', 'Matt']
score_series
```

Output:

```
Lucy      56
Lucky     74
Rich      97
Adam      88
Matt      95
Name: exam1, dtype: int64
```

In this output, you can see that the Series now has index labels represented by names instead of the original student IDs.

In addition to indexes, a Series object in Pandas has various attributes and methods that you can use. To determine the number of elements in a series, you can utilize the size or shape attribute of the series. Alternatively, you can use the len() function in Python:

```
print(score_series.size)
print(score_series.shape)
print(len(score_series))
```

In the output, you might observe that the shape attribute output appears as (5,). It seems like a number is missing after the comma. This occurs because the shape attribute is shared with DataFrame, which has a second dimension. You will learn about DataFrames in the next section.

You can apply aggregate methods to a Series, such as mean(), sum(), and median(). This process is known as data aggregation. You can directly call these methods using the dot operator:

```
print(score_series.mean())
print(score_series.median())
print(score_series.count())
print(score_series.sum())
```

If you need to apply multiple aggregate functions, there is a better way to do it. You can pass them as a list to the agg() method of the Series:

```
score_series.agg(['mean', 'median', 'count', 'sum'])
```

The value_counts() method of a Series returns the number of occurrences of each unique value in the Series. It is commonly used with categorical variables to obtain insight into the distinct values they contain. The result is a frequency table.

```
Score2_series = pd.Series([88, 74, 97, 88, 97, 88, 88])
Score2_series.value_counts()
```

In a separate cell, you can enter the following code for a categorical variable:

```
Score3_series = pd.Series(['B', 'C', 'B', 'A', 'B', 'B'])
Score3_series.value_counts()
```

You can apply multiple methods to a series and chain them together. This technique, known as **method chaining**, can be applied to both Series and DataFrame objects. For example, you can apply the sort_index() and head(2) methods to display only the counts for values 'A' and 'B' in score3_series:

```
Score3_series.value_counts().sort_index().head(2)
```

Review Question 2.8
In the Pandas library, a Series is a one-dimensional _______.
a. array
b. labeled array
c. Pandas
d. labeled Pandas

Review Question 2.9
In the Pandas library, a Series is similar to a column in a spreadsheet or a list, but with a label for each element. The label is also called _______.
a. index
b. Series
c. Pandas
d. DataFrame

Review Question 2.10
You can access the value of each element of a Pandas Series by its _______.
a. index
b. Series
c. Pandas
d. DataFrame

Review Question 2.11
Which of the following statements about a Series' index is correct?

a. By default, there is no index, and you cannot specify your own index labels when creating a Series.
b. By default, the index is a range of integers starting from 0, and you cannot specify your own index labels when creating a Series.
c. By default, there is no index, but you can specify your own index labels when creating a Series.
d. By default, the index is a range of integers starting from 0, but you can also specify your own index labels when creating a Series.

Review Question 2.12
From which of the following, you CANNOT create a Series by calling the Series function of Pandas?
a. Python set
b. Python list
c. Python dictionary
d. NumPy array

Review Question 2.13
The numpy.nan is a special floating-point value that represents _______.
a. Python None
b. 0
c. 0.0
d. Not a Number

Review Question 2.14
The default type for an index object of a Pandas series is _______.
a. int
b. Index
c. Range
d. RangeIndex

Review Question 2.15
How do you get the index object of a Pandas Series s?
a. s.index
b. s.getIndex()
c. s.values
d. s.getValue()

Review Question 2.16
How do you get the values of a Pandas Series s?
a. s.index
b. s.getIndex()
c. s.values
d. s.getValue()

Review Question 2.17
Suppose you have a Pandas Series s. How do you access the second element of s?
a. s(1)
b. s[1]
c. s(2)
d. s[2]

Review Question 2.18

Suppose you have a Pandas Series s. How do you access the first and third elements of s?
a. s(1, 3)
b. s[1, 3]
c. s[0, 2]
d. s[[0, 2]]

Review Question 2.19
Suppose you have a Pandas Series s. How do you retrieve all elements more than the average of s?
a. s[s>s.mean()]
b. s[[s>s.mean()]]
c. s>s.mean()
d. [s>s.mean()]

Review Question 2.20
Suppose you want to know if k is a key of a Pandas Series s. What is the correct code?
a. k in s
b. k in s.key
c. k in s.key()
d. k in s.value

Review Question 2.21
Both the Pandas Series object and its index have a(n) _______ attribute.
a. index
b. label
c. object
d. name

Review Question 2.22
Suppose you have a Pandas Series s. How do you find out the number of elements in s?
a. s.len
b. s.len()
c. s.size
d. s.size()

Review Question 2.23
Suppose you have a Pandas Series s. How do you find out the number of elements in s?
a. s.len
b. s.len()
c. s.shape
d. s.shape()

Review Question 2.24
Suppose you have a Pandas Series s. How do you find out the number of elements in s?
a. s.len
b. s.len()
c. len(s)
d. len.s

Review Question 2.25
Suppose you have a numerical Pandas Series s. How do you calculate the total of the s?

a. s.total

b. s.total()

c. s.sum

d. s.sum()

Review Question 2.26

Suppose you have a Pandas Series s. How do you find the total and the average of the s?

a. s.sum().mean()

b. s.mean().sum()

c. s.(mean, sum)

d. s.agg(['mean', 'sum'])

Review Question 2.27

Suppose you have a Pandas Series s. How do you get a frequency table out of the s?

a. s.frequency()

b. s.counts()

c. s.value_counts()

d. s.frequency_table()

Review Question 2.28

Suppose you have a Pandas Series s. How do you get the top 2 frequencies out of the s?

a. s.value_counts().sort_index().head(2)

b. s.counts(2)

c. s.value_counts(2)

d. s.frequency_table(2)

Review Question 2.29

Given a series scoreseries50 of 50 integer scores for a class, the expression:

Scoreseries50 == 100

will return:

a. TypeError

b. Single boolean value

c. Boolean Series

d. Series filled with 100s.

Exercise 2.1

Launch JupyterLab and start a new notebook file called "Exercise2-1".

Task 1: Create a Pandas Series called "employee" with the following dataset of hours worked for 10 employees: 31, 20, 19, 22, 30, 42, 29, 30, 35, 32. Display the series and identify the index for the "employee" series.

Task 2: Replace the default RangeIndex with the following corresponding employee IDs: 02345, 12345, 22345, 32345, 42345, 52345, 62345, 72345, 82345, 92345. Display the series and verify that the index has been changed by calling the properties of the series.

Task 3: Display the hours worked for employee ID 12345 in two different ways.

Task 4: Display the hours worked for all employees who worked more than the average hours.

Task 5: Add one hour to the hours worked data for all employees using Pandas' scalar addition.

Task 6: Modify the index of employee IDs to employee names. Create nine names and use your own name as the first employee.

Task 7: Write code to confirm that your name is indeed in the series by displaying "True".

Task 8: Display the hours worked for all employees who work 30 or more hours.
Task 9: Calculate and display the mean, median, count, and sum of the hours worked using aggregate functions.
Task 10: Create a frequency table for the hours worked, displaying the count of occurrences for each hour.

2.3 DataFrame Basics

A DataFrame is a two-dimensional labeled data structure that consists of columns, similar to Pandas Series. It can be visualized as a collection of Series objects, where each Series represents a column in the DataFrame. The DataFrame has both a row index and a column index, forming the axes of the DataFrame.

In comparison to a Series, which has values and index labels attached to those values, a DataFrame extends this concept by including three components: the column object, index object, and a NumPy array object that holds the values. The index and columns together form the axes of the DataFrame with 0 for row index and 1 for column index.

A DataFrame can be created from various sources, including a dictionary. The code snippet provided below demonstrates creating a DataFrame from a Python dictionary.:

```python
import pandas as pd
data = {'studentID':['12345', '12346', '12347', '12348', '12349'],
        'exam1':[56, 74, 97, 88, 95],
        'exam2':[98, 88, 85, 78, 92]}
score_df=pd.DataFrame(data)
score_df
```

Output:

	studentID	exam1	exam2
0	12345	56	98
1	12346	74	88
2	12347	97	85
3	12348	88	78
4	12349	95	92

In the example, the dictionary named data contains three key-value pairs. Each key represents a column name, and the corresponding value is a list of values for that column. The pd.DataFrame() function from the Pandas library is used to create a DataFrame object, passing the data dictionary as the input. The resulting DataFrame object, named score_df, is displayed in tabular format. The column names ('studentID', 'exam1', 'exam2') are displayed as the header of each column. The leftmost column shows the row index or label, which starts from 0 by default and increases for each subsequent row.

To retrieve specific rows or columns from a DataFrame object, you can utilize different methods. Here are the steps for each scenario:

1. Retrieving Rows:

To retrieve one or more rows based on a condition, you can use the query() method of the DataFrame. For example, to retrieve the row where the 'studentID' is equal to "12346", you can use:

```
score_df.query('studentID == "12346"')
```

If you want to retrieve rows with multiple student IDs, you can use the in operator:

```
score_df.query('studentID in ["12346", "12349"]')
```

2. Retrieving Columns:

To retrieve one or more columns from a DataFrame object, you can pass the column names as a list to the DataFrame object. For example, to retrieve the 'exam1' and 'exam2' columns::

```
score_df[['exam1', 'exam2']]
```

3. Retrieving Specific Rows and Columns:

If you want to retrieve specific rows and specific columns, you can combine the above methods. First, filter the rows using the query() method, and then select the desired columns using their labels. For example, to retrieve the 'exam1' and 'exam2' columns for the rows with 'studentID' values "12346" and "12349":

```
score_df.query('studentID in ["12346", "12349"]')[['exam1', 'exam2']]
```

You can add one or more columns to a DataFrame by passing a list to the DataFrame. For example, the following code adds two columns labeled "exam3" and "exam4" with all 0s for the values:

```
score_df[['exam3', 'exam4']] = 0
```

When assigning lists or arrays to a column, the length of the values must match the length of the DataFrame. If you assign a Series, its labels will be aligned to the DataFrame's index, inserting missing values for any index values not present. For example, you can assign a Series named final with values [77, 85, 67, 99, 94] and index [3, 2, 4, 1, 0] to the 'final' column of the DataFrame::

```
final = pd.Series([77, 85, 67, 99, 94], index= [3, 2, 4, 1, 0])
score_df['final'] = final
score_df
```

Output:

	studentID	exam1	exam2	exam3	exam4	final
0	12345	56	98	0	0	94
1	12346	74	88	0	0	99
2	12347	97	85	0	0	85
3	12348	88	78	0	0	77
4	12349	95	92	0	0	67

To replace values in a DataFrame, you can use the replace() method. The replacements can be specified in a dictionary format, where the key:value pairs represent the old and new values. For example, to replace the value 0 with 50 and replace 56 with 66 anywhere in the DataFrame, you can use:

```
score_df.replace({0:50, 56:66})
```

Output:

	studentID	exam1	exam2	exam3	exam4	Final
0	12345	66	98	50	50	94
1	12346	74	88	50	50	99
2	12347	97	85	50	50	85
3	12348	88	78	50	50	77
4	12349	95	92	50	50	67

The replace() method allows you to selectively replace values in the DataFrame based on your specified mapping.

Review Question 2.30
A _______ is a two-dimensional labeled data structure that contains an ordered, named collection of columns.
a. Pandas
b. Series
c. DataFrame
d. Pandas Table

Review Question 2.31
A DataFrame can be thought of as a collection of _______ all sharing the same index.
a. Pandas
b. Series
c. Rows
d. Columns

Review Question 2.32
The Series object contains _______ components. The DataFrame object contains _____ components.
a. one, two
b. two, three
c. three, four
d. two, one

Review Question 2.33
The index and columns of a DataFrame are collectively called the ______.
a. rows and columns
b. rows and fields
c. records and columns
d. axes

Review Question 2.34
The index of a DataFrame forms the axis ______ and the columns of a DataFrame form the axis ______.
a. 0, 1
b. 1, 2
c. 1, 0
d. 2, 1

Review Question 2.35
A DataFrame can be created from a variety of sources such as a dictionary or a NumPy array by calling the ______ function of the pandas.
a. Pandas()
b. DataFrame()
c. Series()
d. CreateFrame()

Review Question 2.36
To retrieve one or more rows, you can use the ______ method of a DataFrame object.
a. select()
b. retrieve()
c. where()
d. query()

Review Question 2.37
To retrieve one or more columns, you can pass the column names ______ to the DataFrame object.
a. as a list
b. as strings
c. as a dictionary
d. as a tuple

Review Question 2.38
To retrieve data for certain row(s) and certain column(s), you will first filter the rows by the ______ method, then select column(s) on the result by ______:
a. rows, columns
b. rows, column label(s)
c. query, columns
d. query, columns label(s)

Review Question 2.39
Suppose df is a DataFrame object that does not have column1 and column2. What will the following code do?

```
df[['column1', 'column2']] = 0
```

a. replace values in column1 and colum2 with 0s.
b. add two new columns to the df.

c. add two new columns called column1 and column2 to the df.
d. add two new columns called column1 and column2 to the df with all 0s for the new columns.

Review Question 2.40
Suppose df is a DataFrame object. What will the following code do?

```
df.replace({0:50, 56:66})
```

a. replace values in column1 and colum2 with 0s.
b. replace values in column1 with values from 0 to 49 inclusive and similarly replace values in column2.
c. replace values in column1 with values 0 and 50, replace values in column2 with 56 and 66.
d. replace the value 0 with the value of 50 and replace the value 56 with the value of 66 anywhere in the DataFrame.

2.4 DataFrame's Index Objects

In Pandas, an index labels DataFrame rows, acting as a unique identifier similar to spreadsheet row numbers. It's key to efficient data organization, retrieval, and access in Pandas. Setting a suitable index enhances performance with large datasets and simplifies data operations.

By default, when creating a DataFrame, Pandas assigns a range of integer labels to each row, starting from 0 and incrementing by 1. However, you have the flexibility to specify a different index for the DataFrame during its creation or change the index of an existing DataFrame using the `set_index()` method. While the index of a DataFrame identifies each row, the column labels are used to identify and access the data in each column of the DataFrame.

When a Pandas DataFrame or Series is created, it is assigned a default index of the type RangeIndex, as mentioned earlier. The RangeIndex starts with a label value of 0, corresponding to the first item in the DataFrame or Series, and follows an arithmetic progression with a spacing of one integer.

However, you can customize the index by using the index parameter or attribute. In the next example, a DataFrame named grade_df is created from a dictionary. Since no custom index is specified, the default RangeIndex is used.

To access the index object of a DataFrame, you can use the index attribute. This allows you to view and work with the index labels. Additionally, you can access the actual values of the index object using the values attribute of the index object. Similarly, the columns attribute provides access to the column labels of the DataFrame:

```python
import pandas as pd
grade = {'exam1':[56, 74, 97, 88, 95],
         'exam2':[98, 88, 85, 78, 92]}
grade_df=pd.DataFrame(grade)
# Display the DataFrame
print("The DataFrame")
print(grade_df)
# Display the index object
print("The index object")
print(grade_df.index)
# Display the values in the index object
print("The values in the index object")
print(grade_df.index.values)
# Display the columns object
print("The columns object")
print(grade_df.columns)
# Display the values in the columns object
print("The values in the columns object")
print(grade_df.columns.values)
```

Output:

```
The DataFrame
   exam1  exam2
0     56     98
1     74     88
2     97     85
3     88     78
4     95     92
The index object
RangeIndex(start=0, stop=5, step=1)
The values in the index object
[0 1 2 3 4]
The columns object
Index(['exam1', 'exam2'], dtype='object')
The values in the columns object
['exam1' 'exam2']
```

In the above code, the output displays the DataFrame, the index object (RangeIndex), the values in the index object (an array of labels), the columns object (an Index object), and the values in the columns object (an array of column labels).

The index parameter in Pandas DataFrame() function can be used to specify custom values for the index labels when defining a DataFrame. In the following example, a DataFrame named student_df is created with student IDs as the index labels.

By passing the index parameter with the studentID list, the DataFrame is created with the specified index labels. Each student ID corresponds to a row in the DataFrame, while the 'exam1' and 'exam2' columns contain the respective exam scores:

```python
import pandas as pd
studentID = ['12345', '12346', '12347', '12348', '12349']
data1 = {'exam1':[56, 74, 97, 88, 95],
         'exam2':[98, 88, 85, 78, 92]}
student_df=pd.DataFrame(data1, index = studentID)
student_df
```

Output:

	exam1	exam2
12345	56	98
12346	74	88
12347	97	85
12348	88	78
12349	95	92

When accessing the student_df.index attribute, the output displays the Index object, which contains the student IDs as the row labels.

```python
student_df.index
```

Output:

```
Index(['12345', '12346', '12347', '12348', '12349'], dtype='object')
```

You can also see what the column object is. The columns attribute gives you information about the columns (their names and data type):

```python
print(student_df.columns)
print(type(student_df.columns))
```

Output:

```
Index(['exam1', 'exam2'], dtype='object')
<class 'pandas.core.indexes.base.Index'>
```

In Pandas, both the index and column objects are types of index objects. The index object defaults to a type called RangeIndex when no custom index is specified. On the other hand, the column object is of type Index. The values in the index object serve as the row labels, while the values in the column object act as the column labels. You can use numeric indexing to access specific elements in the index object. For instance, student_df.index[2] will return the third element in the Index, which corresponds to the student ID '12347'.

```python
student_df.index[2]
```

Output:

```
'12347'
```

It's important to note that Index objects are immutable, meaning they cannot be modified. This design ensures safety and consistency. Attempting to modify an Index object will result in a TypeError because mutable operations are not supported:

```
student_df.index[2] = '21347'
```

Output:

```
TypeError: Index does not support mutable operations
```

You can rename the columns of a DataFrame in Pandas using the rename() method. This method takes a dictionary as an argument, where the keys represent the current column names and the values represent the new column names. The following example renames the columns 'exam1' to 'quiz1' and 'exam2' to 'quiz2':

```
student_df.rename(columns={'exam1':'quiz1', 'exam2':'quiz2'})
```

Output:

	quiz1	quiz2
12345	56	98
12346	74	88
12347	97	85
12348	88	78
12349	95	92

When you execute the student_df.rename() method, it returns a new DataFrame with the renamed columns, but it doesn't modify the original DataFrame. You can take a look with the following code:

```
student_df
```

To make the changes stay in the DataFrame, you can add the inplace=True parameter to the rename() method:

```
student_df.rename(columns={'exam1':'quiz1', 'exam2':'quiz2'},
inplace=True)
```

If you want to rename columns by accessing the columns attribute directly, you can assign a new list of column names to it. The following example renames the columns back to 'exam1' and 'exam2':

```
student_df.columns=['exam1', 'exam2']
```

It's important to note that a Pandas Index can contain duplicate labels. If you have duplicate labels in your DataFrame, selections based on those labels will select all occurrences of that label.

Additionally, you can add additional rows using the concat() method. In the given example, a new dataframe named new_student is created and added to the student_df DataFrame:

```
new_student = pd.DataFrame({'exam1':66, 'exam2': 77}, index=['12345'])
```

```python
student_df = pd.concat([student_df, new_student])
```

To retrieve rows based on duplicate labels, you can use the query method. In the provided code, student_df.query('index=="12345"') selects all rows with the index label '12345':

```python
student_df.query('index=="12345"')
```

Output:

	exam1	exam2
12345	56	98
12345	66	77

To reset the index of a Pandas DataFrame and create a new object with the values rearranged to align with the new index, you can use the reset_index() method. By default, this method will reset the index to a range of integers from 0 to the number of rows minus one. The old index is stored in a column named "index":

```python
student_df.index.name = 'student_id'
student_df.reset_index()
```

Output:

	student_id	exam1	exam2
0	12345	56	98
1	12346	74	88
2	12347	97	85
3	12348	88	78
4	12349	95	92
5	12345	66	77

In the above code, the line student_df.index.name = 'student_id' sets the name of the index to 'student_id'. Then, when you call student_df.reset_index(), it creates a new DataFrame where the index is reset and a new default integer index is assigned.

To set the index of a Pandas DataFrame using an existing column, use the set_index() method and specify the column to use as the index, creating a new object with values rearranged to match the new index.

```python
student1_df = student_df.reset_index()
student1_df.set_index(['student_id'])
```
Output:

student_id	exam1	exam2
12345	56	98
12346	74	88
12347	97	85
12348	88	78
12349	95	92
12345	66	77

In the example given, score_df.set_index(['studentID']) sets the 'studentID' column as the index of the DataFrame. It returns a new DataFrame object with the index set as 'studentID'.

Review Question 2.41
In Pandas, a(n) _______ is a way to label rows in a DataFrame.
a. row
b. row number
c. sequence
d. index

Review Question 2.42
What is the default index when creating a DataFrame without setting an index?
a. No index
b. np.nan
c. None
d. Integers range from 0 to the number of rows -1.

Review Question 2.43
You can specify a custom index for a DataFrame when you create it by using the _______.
a. index() method
b. index attribute
c. index parameter
d. add_index() method

Review Question 2.44
If you want to set the index of a Pandas DataFrame using an existing column, you can use the _______.
a. index() method
b. index attribute
c. set_index() method
d. set_index attribute

Review Question 2.45
The _______ will reset the index to a range of integers from 0 to the number of rows minus one.
a. reset_index() method
b. reset_index attribute
c. set_index() method
d. set_index attribute

Review Question 2.46
The reset_index() method will reset the index to a range of integers from 0 to the number of rows minus one. The default field name for the old index is _______:
a. index
b. reset_index
c. set_index
d. np.nan

Review Question 2.47

You can access the index object of a DataFrame using the _______.
a. index attribute
b. index() method
c. access_index attribute
d. access_index() method

Review Question 2.48
You can access the values of the index object using the _______.
a. index method
b. values() method
c. index attribute of the index object
d. values attribute of the index object

Review Question 2.49
What is the index object name for a DataFrame object with default index?
a. Index
b. RangeIndex
c. RowIndex
d. ColumnIndex

Review Question 2.50
What is the column object name for a DataFrame object with default column index (column headers exist)?
a. Index
b. RangeIndex
c. RowIndex
d. ColumnIndex

Review Question 2.51
Index objects are _______ and cannot be modified.?
a. fixed
b. fixed-position
c. immutable
d. non-immutable

Review Question 2.52
Suppose df is a DataFrame object with student ID as its index. What is the output of the following code?
```
df.index[2] = '21347'
```
a. The first student ID will be changed to 21347.
b. The second student ID will be changed to 21347.
c. The third student ID will change to 21347.
d. An error because the index is immutable.

Review Question 2.53
Write code to rename column headings of a DataFrame df from exam1 to quiz1 and exam2 to quiz2:
a. df.rename(columns={'quiz1', 'quiz2'})
b. df.rename(columns=['quiz1', 'quiz2'])
c. df.rename(columns={'exam1':'quiz1', 'exam2':'quiz2'})
d. df.rename(columns=['exam1', 'exam2']:['quiz1', 'quiz2'])

Review Question 2.54

To rename the column headings of a DataFrame df with the elements in the headings list, you can use the following code:
a. df.rename(headings)
b. df.rename(columns=headings)
c. df.columns = headings
d. df.columns.labels = headings

Review Question 2.55
Pandas DataFrame keeps its column labels in an object of the following type:
a. pandas.core.indexes.base.Index
b. pandas.core.indexes.base.Labels
c. pandas.core.indexes.base.ColumnNames
d. pnadas.core.indexes.base.Columns

2.5 Selection on DataFrame

There are multiple ways to select single or multiple columns from a Pandas DataFrame. You can use the square bracket [] operator to select a single column or a list of columns based on their labels. Additionally, you can use the dot (.) operator to select a single column by its label. For single column selection, you can use either the [] operator or the dot (.) operator. However, for selecting multiple columns, only the [] operator is applicable. It's important to note that the dot operator may be less intuitive and readable, especially when the column label contains spaces or special characters. In such cases, it is recommended to use the [] operator instead. Here's an example based on the score_df DataFrame created earlier:

```
# Select a single column
print(score_df['exam1'])
# Another way to select a single column.
print(score_df[['exam1']])
# Another way to select a single column
print(score_df.exam1)
# Select multiple columns
print(score_df[['exam1', 'exam2']])
```

This code snippet demonstrates the different ways to select columns. The first three print statements show different ways to select a single column, while the fourth statement selects multiple columns.

Filtering enables you to extract a subset of a DataFrame based on specific criteria. This is particularly useful when you need to select specific rows that satisfy certain conditions. Pandas provides several methods for filtering DataFrames. Earlier in this chapter, you learned about one method called query(), which allows you to specify a boolean condition using a string.

Another method is Boolean indexing, where you create a Boolean mask that specifies the rows you want to retain. Here's an example using the score_df DataFrame created earlier:

```python
# Select rows where exam1 is less than 80.
mask = score_df['exam1'] < 80
# Use the mask to filter the DataFrame
filtered_df = score_df[mask]
print(filtered_df)
```

In this example, we create a mask by evaluating the condition score_df['exam1'] < 80. The resulting mask is a Boolean Series with True or False values indicating whether each corresponding row satisfies the condition. We then use this mask to filter the DataFrame and assign the filtered result to filtered_df. Finally, we print filtered_df, which contains only the rows where the 'exam1' score is less than 80.

The rest of this section will cover how to properly select data in Pandas using the **loc** and **iloc** attributes. The loc allows you to select data by labels, while iloc allows you to select data by position. Understanding and utilizing these attributes will help you perform data selection tasks consistently, obtaining the expected results without encountering errors or warnings.

In Pandas, labels refer to the row and column names of a DataFrame. The loc stands for "location" and enables you to select data based on labels. This means you can select data using the row and column names of a DataFrame. For example, to select the value of the second student's "exam2" using loc, you would write `score_df.loc[1, "exam2"]`. The loc indexer works by selecting data using index labels, similar to how data is accessed in dictionaries in Python, using keys associated with values.

Positions, on the other hand, refer to the numerical index of each label, starting from 0. The iloc attribute allows you to select data using these positions. iloc stands for "integer location" and enables you to select data based on positions. This means you can select data using the numerical index of each row and column, rather than the row and column labels. Positions start at 0, so to select the value in the 4th row and 3rd column using iloc, you would write df.iloc[3, 2]. For example, to select the value of the second student's "exam2" using iloc, you would write `score_df.iloc[1, 2]` (indexes start at 0, and the student ID is in column 0). The iloc indexer is similar to how individual elements are accessed in lists and arrays.

Here are some examples demonstrating the usage of both attributes:

```python
# Display the score_df again for convenience
print(score_df)
# Select the first row and second column using loc
```

```python
print("First row second column")
print(score_df.loc[0, "exam1"])
# Select the first row and second column using iloc
print(score_df.iloc[0, 1])
# Select all rows and the first two columns using loc
print("All rows and the first two columns")
print(score_df.loc[:, ["studentID", "exam1"]])
# Select all rows and the first two columns using iloc
print(score_df.iloc[:, 0:2])

# Select the second and third rows and all columns using loc
print("Second and third rows and all columns")
print(score_df.loc[1:2, :])
# Select the second and third rows and all columns using iloc
print(score_df.iloc[1:3, :])
```

It's important to note that the indexers loc and iloc are used with square brackets, not round brackets as with functions or methods. The index values before the comma in the indexer refer to the row indices, while the index values after the comma refer to the column indices. If only the row indices are mentioned, and no column indices are specified, all columns are selected by default. Although we can skip the column indices, we cannot skip the row indices. For example:

```python
student_df.loc['12346'] #work
student_df.loc['exam1'] #not work
```

Boolean indexing allows you to select rows and columns of a DataFrame based on a boolean condition.

Here are some examples of using loc and iloc to select rows and columns using boolean indexing:

```python
# Select rows where the value in the "exam1" is greater than 80
# using loc
print(score_df.loc[score_df["exam1"] > 80, :])

# Select rows where the value in the "exam1" is greater than 80
# using iloc
print(score_df.iloc[score_df.iloc[:, 1].values > 80, :])

# Select columns where the heading starts with "exam"
print(score_df.loc[:, score_df.columns.str.startswith("exam")])

# Select columns where the heading starts with "exam"
print(score_df.iloc[:, score_df.columns.str.startswith("exam")])
```

In these examples, the boolean condition is placed inside the square brackets when using loc or iloc. The condition is evaluated for each element in the DataFrame, and the rows or columns where the condition is True are selected.

For selecting index values, it is recommended to use the "loc" operator over the indexing "[]" operator. This is because using the "[]" operator for indexing can handle integers differently based on the index's data type. Additionally, slicing with labels treats the endpoint differently.

The indexing operator can be employed to select a consecutive set of rows:

```
student_df[:3]
```

However, it cannot be used to select a series of nonconsecutive rows, as it will raise an error. The following statement would not work:

```
student_df[[3, 5]] # not work
```

Another limitation of the indexing operator is that it cannot select rows and columns simultaneously. The following statement would also not work:

```
student_df[:, 2] # not work
```

When adding two Pandas objects, the index labels of each object are compared. If the labels match, the corresponding values in each object are added or combined. If the labels do not match, the resulting object will have a null value (np.NaN) at that index.

```
# Create two Pandas objects
df1 = pd.DataFrame({'A': [1, 2, 3], 'B': [4, 5, 6], 'C': [7, 8, 9]})
df2 = pd.DataFrame({'A': [10, 20, 30], 'B': [40, 50, 60], 'C': [70, 80,
90]})
# Uncomment the following line to see NaN when labels do not match.
#df2 = pd.DataFrame({'A': [10, 20, 30], 'B': [40, 50, 60]})
# Add the two objects
result = df1 + df2

# Print the resulting object
print(result)
```

Review Question 2.56
What are the different ways to select a single column from a Pandas DataFrame?
a. Square bracket [] operator
b. Dot (.) operator
c. Both square bracket[] and dot(.) operator
d. Neither square bracket[] nor dot(.) operator

Review Question 2.57
What are the different ways to select multiple columns from a Pandas DataFrame?

a. Square bracket [] operator
b. Dot (.) operator
c. Both square bracket[] and dot(.) operator
d. Neither square bracket[] nor dot(.) operator

Review Question 2.58
Which operator is recommended when the column label contains spaces or special characters?
a. Square bracket [] operator
b. Dot (.) operator
c. Both square bracket[] and dot(.) operator
d. Neither square bracket[] nor dot(.) operator

Review Question 2.59
What is the purpose of filtering a DataFrame?
a. To modify the structure of the DataFrame
b. To extract a subset of the DataFrame based on specific criteria
c. To sort the DataFrame in ascending order
d. To merge multiple DataFrames together

Review Question 2.60
Which method in Pandas allows you to specify a boolean condition using a string for filtering a DataFrame?
a. .filter()
b. .extract()
c. .query()
d. .select()

Review Question 2.61
What is Boolean indexing in the context of filtering DataFrames?
a. A method for creating a new DataFrame with the filtered rows for Boolean columns
b. A technique for sorting the DataFrame based on specific criteria
c. A way to select specific rows using a Boolean mask
d. A method for renaming column labels in the DataFrame

Review Question 2.62
In the provided code example, what does the variable 'mask' represent?

```
mask = score_df['exam1'] < 80
```

a. The filtered DataFrame
b. The original DataFrame
c. The boolean condition for filtering
d. The selected columns from the DataFrame

Review Question 2.63
How is the resulting mask represented after evaluating the condition in Boolean indexing?
a. A numeric value representing the number of rows that satisfy the condition
b. A boolean series with True or False values for each row
c. A string value indicating the condition's outcome
d. An integer value representing the total number of rows in the DataFrame

Review Question 2.64
What does the filtered_df DataFrame contain in the provided code example?

```
mask = score_df['exam1'] < 80
filtered_df = score_df[mask]
```
a. The rows where the 'exam1' score is greater than or equal to 80
b. The rows where the 'exam1' score is less than 80
c. The rows where the 'exam1' score is equal to 80
d. The rows where the 'exam1' score is not available (NaN)

Review Question 2.65
What is the purpose of using the loc attribute in Pandas?
a. To select data based on labels
b. To select data based on positions
c. To modify the structure of the DataFrame
d. To sort the DataFrame in descending order

Review Question 2.66
What does the iloc attribute in Pandas allow you to do?
a. Modify the DataFrame's column names
b. Select data based on labels
c. Select data based on positions
d. Sort the DataFrame in ascending order

Review Question 2.67
What is the key difference between loc and iloc in Pandas?
a. loc uses labels, while iloc uses positions for data selection
b. loc uses positions, while iloc uses labels for data selection
c. loc works with integers, while iloc works with floating-point numbers
d. loc works with positions, while iloc works with labels for data selection

Review Question 2.68
For a DataFrame object score_df with each row represents a student and columns labeled by exam
numbers. How would you select the value of the second student's "exam2" using loc?
a. score_df.loc[1, "exam2"]
b. score_df.loc[0, "exam2"]
c. score_df.loc["exam2", 1]
d. score_df.loc["exam2", 0]

Review Question 2.69
What does iloc stand for in Pandas?
a. Index Location
b. Integer Location
c. Information Locator
d. Indexed Location

Review Question 2.70
The score_df is a DataFrame with the studentID and exam1 as the first two column names. How would you
select all rows and the first two columns of a DataFrame using loc or iloc?
a. score_df.loc[:, ["studentID", "exam1"]]
b. score_df.loc[0:2, :]
c. score_df.iloc[:, 0:1]
d. score_df.iloc[1:3, :]

Review Question 2.71
What does it mean if only the row indices are mentioned in the loc indexer?
a. All columns are selected by default
b. All rows are selected by default
c. An error will occur because it's an incomplete syntax
d. The DataFrame will be sorted in ascending order

Review Question 2.72
What happens if the row indices are skipped in the loc indexer (comma is skipped also)?
a. An error will occur because row indices are required
b. The resulting DataFrame will be empty
c. All columns are selected by default
d. All rows are selected by default

Review Question 2.73
For score_df DataFrame, how would you select the second and third rows and all columns using loc or iloc?
a. score_df.loc[1:2, :]
b. score_df.loc[:, 1:3]
c. score_df.iloc[1:2, :]
d. score_df.iloc[:, 1:3]

Review Question 2.74
Which indexing attribute is used with square brackets, not round brackets?
a. .at
b. .get
c. .loc
d. .ix

Review Question 2.75
What do the index values before the comma represent in the loc and iloc indexers?
a. Row indices
b. Column indices
c. Boolean conditions
d. String labels

Review Question 2.76
Which operator is recommended for selecting index values in Pandas?
a. loc
b. iloc
c. []
d. :

Review Question 2.77
Which operator exclusively uses labels for indexing in Pandas?
a. loc
b. iloc
c. []
d. :

Review Question 2.78
What is a limitation of the indexing operator [] in Pandas?
a. It cannot handle non-integer indices
b. It cannot select a consecutive set of rows
c. It cannot select rows and columns simultaneously
d. It cannot perform arithmetic operations on DataFrames

Review Question 2.79
What happens when adding two Pandas objects with mismatched index labels?
a. An error is raised
b. The resulting object will have a null value (np.NaN) at the mismatched index
c. The resulting object will have duplicate labels
d. The resulting object will be sorted in ascending order

Exercise 2.2

Pandas Series and DataDrame have loc and iloc operators for label-based (loc) and integer-based (iloc) indexing. In a new cell, enter the following lines to set up a DataFrame object student_df:

```python
import pandas as pd
studentID = ['12345', '12346', '12347', '12348', '12349']
data1 = {'exam1':[56, 74, 97, 88, 95],
         'exam2':[98, 88, 85, 78, 92],
         'exam3':[95, 91, 56, 79, 88]}
student_df=pd.DataFrame(data1, index = studentID)
student_df
```

1. Use the loc operator to retrieve three students' exam 2 and exam 3 grades. The three students are the second (12346), the fifth (12349) and the first (12345). The output should be in this sequence.
2. Use the iloc operator to retrieve the same three students' same grades.
3. Use the loc operator to slice students from 12346 to 12348 inclusive and exam2 and larger number exams.
4. Use the iloc operator to slice students from 12346 to 12348 inclusive and exam2 and larger number exams.

2.6 Methods of the DataFrame

The DataFrame class has many methods, and one of them is the drop() method. It enables the removal of rows or columns from a DataFrame object. The drop() method accepts two main parameters: labels and axis. The labels parameter represents a list of row or column labels to be removed. The axis parameter, which is optional, specifies the axis along which the labels will be removed. By default, its value is 0, indicating the removal of rows. If axis is set to 1, it removes columns instead.

When using the drop() method, a new object is returned with the specified values deleted. For example, calling drop() with a sequence of labels will drop the corresponding rows from the DataFrame::

```
student_df.drop(['12348'])
```

To remove columns instead of rows, you can set the axis parameter to 1. For example, the following code will drop the 'exam2' column::

```
student_df.drop(['exam2'], axis=1)
```

Some methods, including drop(), can modify the size or shape of a Series or DataFrame. They can either return a new object or modify the existing one in-place. To modify the object in-place, you can use the inplace parameter or assign the result to the original variable:

```
student_df.drop(['12348'], inplace=True)
```

Be careful with the inplace, as it destroys the old one.

By default, if any of the specified labels do not exist in the DataFrame, the drop() method raises an error. However, you can control this behavior using the errors parameter. When errors='ignore', the drop method ignores any labels that do not exist, eliminating the possibility of an error. When errors='raise' (the default), a KeyError is raised if any of the labels do not exist, and no rows or columns are dropped.

Here's an example of using the drop() method to remove rows based on index labels while ignoring labels that do not exist:

```
# Create a sample DataFrame
df = pd.DataFrame({'A': [1, 2, 3], 'B': [4, 5, 6], 'C': [7, 8, 9]})
# Remove rows with index label 1 and 2, ignore labels that do not exist
df = df.drop([1, 2, 3], errors='ignore')
print(df)
```

In the above code, the second and third rows are dropped. If you remove the errors parameter, no rows will be dropped, and an error will be displayed because row index 3 does not exist.

The drop() method can also be used to remove rows or columns based on a condition. You can utilize the index or columns attributes of the DataFrame object along with a Boolean indexing expression. Here's an example that removes rows where the value in column A is greater than 2:

```
# Create a sample DataFrame
df = pd.DataFrame({'A': [1, 2, 3], 'B': [4, 5, 6], 'C': [7, 8, 9]})
# Remove rows where column A is greater than 2
df = df.drop(df[df['A'] > 2].index)
print(df)
```

In this case, only the first two rows will be displayed since the third row has a value in column A greater than 2.

Sorting datasets is essential in data analysis. In Pandas, use sort_index() for lexicographic sorting by row or column index. By default, the sort_index() method sorts the data in ascending order. However, you can also sort it in descending order by setting the ascending parameter to False. Here's an example of sorting the DataFrame student_df lexicographically by column index in descending order:

```
student_df.sort_index(axis=1, ascending=False)
```

Output:

student_id	exam2	exam1
12345	98	56
12346	88	74
12347	85	97
12349	92	95
12345	77	66

To sort a DataFrame based on one or more columns as the sort keys, you can use the sort_values() method. Simply pass the column names to the "by" parameter (optional) of sort_values. Here's an example of sorting the DataFrame student_df by the 'exam1' column:

```
student_df.sort_values(['exam1'])
```

If you want to sort by multiple columns, you can provide a list of column names. The DataFrame will be sorted based on the columns' order in the list, with the first column being the primary sort key, the second column being the secondary sort key, and so on.

There are many other methods available. For instance, idxmax() will return the index label corresponding to the first occurrence of the maximum value.

Review Question 2.80
Given that score_df is a DataFrame with 5 students and each student has 2 exam scores. Which of the following will return the full row with the highest exam1 value?
a. score_df.loc[score_df['exam1'].idxmax(), :]
b. score_df.iloc[score_df['exam1'].idxmax(), 'exam1']
c. score_df.loc[score_df['exam1'].max(), 'exam1']
d. score_df.iloc[score_df['exam1'].max(), :]

Review Question 2.81
Suppose we create a DataFrame like this:

```
df = pd.DataFrame([[11, 12], [21, 22]])
```
What will be the output with df[1, 1] ?
a. 11
b. 12
c. 22
d. KeyError

Review Question 2.82
Suppose we create a DataFrame like this:
```
df = pd.DataFrame([[11, 12], [21, 22]])
```
What will be the output with df[1][1]?
a. 11
b. 12
c. 22
d. KeyError

Review Question 2.83
By default, which axis is selected for removal when using the drop() method?
a. 0
b. 1
c. Both rows and columns are removed simultaneously.
d. It depends on the size of the DataFrame.

Review Question 2.84
How can you remove columns instead of rows using the drop() method?
a. Set the inplace parameter to True.
b. Specify the axis parameter as 1.
c. Use the errors parameter with the value 'columns'.
d. It is not possible to remove columns with the drop() method.

Review Question 2.85
What does the inplace parameter (True) do when using the drop() method?
a. It modifies the original DataFrame in-place without returning a new object.
b. It raises an error if any labels do not exist in the DataFrame.
c. It controls the sorting order of the labels.
d. It specifies whether rows or columns are dropped.

Review Question 2.86
What happens if a label specified in the drop() method does not exist in the DataFrame?
a. An error is raised by default.
b. The label is ignored without raising an error by default.
c. The entire DataFrame is dropped.
d. The label is automatically created in the DataFrame.

Review Question 2.87
What happens if a label specified in the drop() method does not exist in the DataFrame?
a. An error is raised if the label specified cannot be derived from the existing ones by default.
b. The label is ignored without raising an error when errors='ignore'.
c. The entire DataFrame is dropped.
d. The label is automatically created in the DataFrame.

Review Question 2.88
Which method in Pandas is used to achieve lexicographic sorting based on row or column index?
a. sort_values()
b. sort_index()
c. sort()
d. order_by()

Review Question 2.89
By default, how does the sort_index() method sort the data?
a. In descending order
b. In ascending order
c. Randomly
d. Alphabetically

Review Question 2.90
How can you sort the data in descending order using the sort_index() method?
a. By setting the sort_order parameter to 'desc'
b. By passing False to the ascending parameter
c. By using the reverse() method after sorting
d. By calling the sort_descending() function

Review Question 2.91
Which method is used to sort a DataFrame based on one or more columns as the sort keys?
a. sort()
b. order_by()
c. sort_values()
d. sort_index()

Review Question 2.92
How do you specify the columns to be used as sort keys when using the sort_values() method?
a. Using the sort_keys parameter
b. Passing a list of column names to the by parameter
c. Calling the sort_columns() function
d. Specifying the sort_by attribute

Review Question 2.93
In a DataFrame, how does the sort_values() method prioritize the columns when sorting by multiple columns?
a. It sorts the columns in alphabetical order.
b. It sorts the columns randomly.
c. It uses the columns' order in the list, with the first column being the primary sort key.
d. It sorts the columns based on their data types.

2.7 Function Application and Mapping

You can use the apply() method of a DataFrame to apply a function to each element of the DataFrame.

Let's consider a DataFrame that contains the exam scores of five students. We also have a function called grade_curve that increases a given number by 10. You can apply this function to the DataFrame to increase all scores by 10.

To set up the DataFrame, you can enter the following code in a cell::

```
studentID = ['12345', '12346', '12347', '12348', '12349']
data1 = {'exam1':[56, 74, 97, 88, 95],
         'exam2':[98, 88, 85, 78, 92],
         'exam3':[95, 91, 56, 79, 88]}
student_df=pd.DataFrame(data1, index = studentID)
student_df
```

Next, you need to define the grade_curve function and apply it to the DataFrame:

```
# Define a function to create a score by 10
def grade_curve(score):
    return score+10
# Apply the function to the DataFrame
student_df.apply(grade_curve)
```

This will apply the grade_curve() function to each element of the DataFrame, resulting in all scores being increased by 10.

The apply() method allows you to apply a function to a DataFrame, with an optional axis argument to specify the axis along which the function should be applied. By default, axis=0, which applies the function vertically across the rows of the DataFrame. Setting axis=1 applies the function horizontally across the columns.

Example 2.1

Define a function called dispersion_range that calculates the statistical range (maximum minus minimum) of a Series. We can apply this function to each column of the DataFrame student_df using the apply() method:

Solution:

```
def dispersion_range(x):
    return x.max() - x.min()
student_df.apply(dispersion_range)
```

In this case, the dispersion_range() function is invoked once on each column of the DataFrame, and the result is a Series with the columns of student_df as its index.

Example 2.2

Apply the same dispersion_range() function to each row (across the columns) of the DataFrame. We can achieve this by passing axis=1 to the apply() method:

Solution:

```
student_df.apply(dispersion_range, axis=1)
```

Here, the function is invoked once per row, and the result is a Series with the rows of student_df as its index.

You can also use the apply() method on a specific column or row of the DataFrame. For instance, if you want to increase the exam2 scores by 10, you can apply the grade_curve function to that specific column:

```
student_df['exam2'].apply(grade_curve)
```

Additionally, you can use the applymap() method to apply an element-wise Python function to each element of the DataFrame. For example, if you want to format each floating-point value in student_df with two decimal places, you can define the function two_decimal_places() and apply it using applymap():

```
def two_decimal_places(x):
    return '%.2f'%x
student_df.applymap(two_decimal_places)
```

The apply() and applymap() methods in Pandas are both used to apply a function to a DataFrame, but they work in different ways. The apply() is used to apply a function along an axis of the DataFrame (either rows or columns). It returns a Series or DataFrame, depending on the function. The applymap() is used to apply a function to each element of the DataFrame. It always returns a DataFrame.

Review Question 2.94
What does the apply() method of DataFrame do?
a. Applies a function to each column of the DataFrame
b. Sorts the DataFrame based on a specific criterion
c. Drops a label that doesn't exist in the DataFrame
d. Sets the value of a specific element in the DataFrame

Review Question 2.95
By default, along which axis is the apply() method applied?
a. axis=0 (rows)

b. axis=1 (columns)
c. axis=None
d. axis=2

Review Question 2.96
What does the applymap() method do?
a. Applies a function to each element of the DataFrame
b. Applies a function to each column of the DataFrame
c. Applies a function to each row of the DataFrame
d. Applies a function to a specific column of the DataFrame

Review Question 2.97
When should you use the applymap() method instead of the apply() method?
a. When applying a function to each element of the DataFrame
b. When applying a function to a specific column or row of the DataFrame
c. When applying a function to the DataFrame along an axis
d. When applying a function that converts a Series into a scalar value

Exercise 2.3

Use the following code to create a DataFrame:

```python
import pandas as pd
# Create a sample DataFrame
df = pd.DataFrame({'A': [1, 2, 3], 'B': [4, 5, 6], 'C': [7, 8, 9]})
# Display the DataFrame
df
```

Next, define a function that will multiply a given number by 2. Finally, apply the function to the above DataFrame.

2.8 Descriptive Statistics

Pandas objects offer a wide range of mathematical and statistical methods that are used to summarize and manipulate data in Series or DataFrame structures. These methods can generate single values, such as sums or means, or produce a series of values from the rows or columns of the DataFrame. While these methods share similarities with those found in NumPy arrays, they are specifically designed to handle missing data more effectively. To illustrate this, let's consider a small DataFrame::

```python
exam4 = pd.Series({'12345':88, '12346':89, '12347':87, '12348':88})
student_df['exam4'] = exam4
student_df
```

By calling the DataFrame's mean method, we obtain a Series containing the means of each column:

```python
student_df.mean()
```

If we pass axis='columns' or axis=1, we can compute means across the columns for each student:

```python
student_df['grade'] = student_df.mean(axis='columns')
student_df
```

The describe() method allows us to generate multiple summary statistics in a single call:

```python
student_df.describe()
```

Output:

	exam1	exam2	exam3	exam4	grade
Count	5.000000	5.000000	5.000000	4.000000	5.000000
Mean	82.000000	88.200000	81.800000	88.000000	85.183333
Std	17.102631	7.496666	15.578832	0.816497	3.943789
Min	56.000000	78.000000	56.000000	87.000000	81.250000
25%	74.000000	85.000000	79.000000	87.750000	83.250000
50%	88.000000	88.000000	88.000000	88.000000	84.250000
75%	95.000000	92.000000	91.000000	88.250000	85.500000
Max	97.000000	98.000000	95.000000	89.000000	91.666667

In cases where non-numeric data is present, describe() provides alternative summary statistics. For instance, if we introduce a letter grade column:

```python
letter_grade = pd.Series({'12345':'B', '12346':'B',
                          '12347':'B', '12348':'B',
                          '12349':'A'})
student_df['letter_grade'] = letter_grade
student_df.letter_grade.describe()
```

Output:

```
count           5
unique          2
top             B
freq            4
Name: letter_grade, dtype: object
```

Certain summary statistics, such as correlation and covariance, involve computations between pairs of arguments. The cov() and corr() methods of a Series compute the covariance or correlation between two Series, respectively:

```python
exam1 = student_df.exam1
exam2 = student_df.exam2
print(f'Covariance of Exam1 and Exam 2: {exam1.cov(exam2)}')
print(f'Correlation of Exam1 and Exam 2: {exam1.corr(exam2):.2f}')
```

By utilizing the cov and corr methods of a DataFrame, we can obtain a full covariance or correlation matrix:

```python
student_df.drop(['letter_grade'], axis=1).cov()
```

Output:

	exam1	exam2	exam3	exam4	grade
exam1	292.500000	-78.250000	-185.000000	-7.666667	8.854167
exam2	-78.250000	56.200000	65.550000	1.000000	11.933333
exam3	-185.000000	65.550000	242.700000	11.666667	34.420833
exam4	-7.666667	1.000000	11.666667	0.666667	1.416667
Grade	8.854167	11.933333	34.420833	1.416667	15.553472

Similarly, enter the following code into a new cell to see a matrix of correlations:

```
student_df.drop(['letter_grade'], axis=1).corr()
```

Output:

	exam1	exam2	exam3	exam4	Grade
exam1	1.000000	-0.610314	-0.694343	-0.525243	0.131272
exam2	-0.610314	1.000000	0.561267	0.147531	0.403627
exam3	-0.694343	0.561267	1.000000	0.814725	0.560238
exam4	-0.525243	0.147531	0.814725	1.000000	0.966315
Grade	0.131272	0.403627	0.560238	0.966315	1.000000

The last useful tool for summary statistics we would like to introduce is the unique() method, which provides an array of distinct values present in a Series. This method helps quickly identify the range of different values, essential for understanding the distribution and variability within the dataset. By summarizing the unique entries, it aids in the initial exploratory data analysis, offering insights into the diversity of data points. For instance, when applied to student_df.exam4, it returns all the unique scores from the exam4 column:

```
student_df.exam4.unique()
```

Output:

```
array([88., 89., 87., nan])
```

Review Question 2.98
What does the describe() method in Pandas provide?
a. Counts, means, and standard deviations
b. Unique values and frequencies
c. Correlation and covariance matrices
d. Counts, unique values, frequency, correlation and covariance

Review Question 2.99
What does the describe() method provide for non-numeric data?
a. Counts, unique values, and frequencies
b. Correlation and covariance matrices
c. Summary statistics such as mean and standard deviation
d. Counts and summary statistics such as mean

Review Question 2.100
What does the unique() method in Pandas return?
a. Counts of unique values
b. Frequencies of unique values
c. A matrix of unique values
d. An array of unique values

2.9 Chapter Summary

In this chapter, you learned the basic concepts of Pandas: Series and DataFrame. Pandas is a powerful and flexible open-source library for data analysis and manipulation in Python. It provides a comprehensive set of tools for working with structured data, such as tables. One key feature of pandas is its index, which provides a labeling mechanism for accessing data within a table. The index allows you to filter, sort, and select specific data based on row or column labels. Pandas offers various methods for performing data analysis, which we will cover in the rest of this book. These methods enable you to clean, prepare, filter, aggregate, and transform data to gain insights and draw meaningful conclusions.

2.10 Solutions to the Review Questions

2.1 C; 2.2 C; 2.3 C; 2.4 D; 2.5 A; 2.6 B; 2.7 C; 2.8 B; 2.9 A; 2.10 A; 2.11 D; 2.12 A; 2.13 D; 2.14 D; 2.15 A; 2.16 C; 2.17 B; 2.18 D; 2.19 A; 2.20 A; 2.21 D; 2.22 C; 2.23 C; 2.24 C; 2.25 D; 2.26 D; 2.27 C; 2.28 A; 2.29 C; 2.30 C; 2.31 B; 2.32 B; 2.33 D; 2.34 A; 2.35 B; 2.36 D; 2.37 A; 2.38 D; 2.39 D; 2.40 D; 2.41 D; 2.42 D; 2.43 C; 2.44 C; 2.45 A; 2.46 A; 2.47 A; 2.48 D; 2.49 B; 2.50 A; 2.51 C; 2.52 D; 2.53 C; 2.54 C; 2.55 A; 2.56 C; 2.57 A; 2.58 A; 2.59 B; 2.60 C; 2.61 C; 2.62 C; 2.63 B; 2.64 B; 2.65 A 2.66 C; 2.67 A; 2.68 A; 2.69 B; 2.70 A; 2.71 A; 2.72 A; 2.73 A; 2.74 C; 2.75 A; 2.76 A; 2.77 A; 2.78 C; 2.79 B; 2.80 A; 2.81 D; 2.82 C; 2.83 A; 2.84 B; 2.85 A; 2.86 A; 2.87 B; 2.88 B; 2.89 B; 2.90 B; 2.91 C; 2.92 B; 2.93 C; 2.94 A; 2.95 A; 2.96 A; 2.97 A; 2.98 A; 2.99 A; 2.100 D;

Chapter 3: Data Loading

Chapter Learning Objectives

3.1 Understand the process of loading text files into Pandas DataFrames.
3.2 Remember the steps to load binary files into Pandas DataFrames.
3.3 Apply the skills to load relational databases into Pandas DataFrames.
3.4 Analyze the benefits of saving Pandas DataFrames for future use.
3.5 Evaluate different approaches to manipulating Pandas DataFrames' column data types.

3.1 Read *csv* Files

To analyze data in JupyterLab, the first step is to load the data. The Pandas library offers a variety of

functions to do this, with the specific function depending on the file type. In this section, we'll focus on how

to load CSV files. We'll also learn the optional parameters of the read_csv() function, which can be

particularly useful when dealing with messy data. While we won't cover all the parameters, you can access a

full list by pressing Shift+Tab within the function in JupyterLab.

Start by opening a text editor like Notepad. Create "chapter3e1.csv" in your working directory and input

data below, ensuring no spaces after commas.

```
studentID,exam1,exam2
12345,78,89
12346,67,77
12347,89,99
```

Next, start a new JupyterLab file in the same folder and enter the following code in a new cell:

```
import pandas as pd
grade_book = pd.read_csv("chapter3e1.csv")
grade_book
```

Output:

	studentID	exam1	exam2
0	12345	78	89
1	12346	67	77
2	12347	89	99

Sometimes a file may not have a header row, and in such cases, you have the option to either let pandas assign default column names or specify the names yourself. To try this out, open the file "chapter3e1.csv" with Notepad and delete the first row. Save the file as "chapter3e2.csv".

```
12345,78,89
12346,67,77
12347,89,99
```

Next, enter the following lines in a new cell in JupyterLab Notebook tab:

```
grade_book1 = pd.read_csv("chapter3e2.csv", header=None)
grade_book1
```

Output:

	0	1	2
0	12345	78	89
1	12346	67	77
2	12347	89	99

For meaningful column names, provide them as a list and use the names parameter in the read_csv() function. To achieve this, use the following code in a new cell:

```
column_names = ["studentID", "exam1", "exam2"]
grade_book2 = pd.read_csv("chapter3e2.csv", names=column_names)
grade_book2
```

Output:

	studentID	exam1	exam2
0	12345	78	89
1	12346	67	77
2	12347	89	99

You can use the index_col parameter to set a column as an index in the returned DataFrame. For example, if you want the 'studentID' column to be the index, you can use the index_col parameter to specify either the column's index (0) or its name ('studentID'):

```
column_names = ["studentID", "exam1", "exam2"]
grade_book3 = pd.read_csv("chapter3e2.csv", names=column_names,
index_col=0)
grade_book3
```

or

```
column_names = ["studentID", "exam1", "exam2"]
grade_book4 = pd.read_csv("chapter3e2.csv", names=column_names,
index_col="studentID")
```

grade_book4

Output:

	exam1	exam2
studentID		
12345	78	89
12346	67	77
12347	89	99

If you don't like the column header provided in the CSV file, you can use custom column headers by specifying the header and names parameters of the read_csv() function:

```
column_names = ["studentID", "quiz1", "quiz2"]
grade_book5 = pd.read_csv("chapter3e1.csv", header=0,
names=column_names)
grade_book5
```

Output:

	studentID	quiz1	quiz2
0	12345	78	89
1	12346	67	77
2	12347	89	99

Sometimes, a CSV file may contain more than one line of header columns. In such cases, you may want to skip those lines and keep only the header line. You can use the skiprows parameter to achieve this. To see how it works, update the CSV file by adding a line of text on the top and save the file with a new name, "chapter3e1a.csv". Enter the following code in a cell to read the file with the first line skipped:

```
grade_book = pd.read_csv("chapter3e1a.csv", skiprows=1)
grade_book
```

Occasionally, you may have a data file that does not use a comma as a separator. Pandas can still read it as long as you specify the separator symbol. To see how it works, update "chapter3e1.csv" by replacing all commas with spaces and save the file as "chapter3e1b.csv". Enter the following code in a new cell:

```
grade_book = pd.read_csv("chapter3e1b.csv", sep=' ')
grade_book
```

Files often contain missing values, and these values may not be represented with a blank. Different symbols, such as "na" or "n/a," can be used to indicate missing values. You can use the na_values parameter to inform pandas about these missing values. To see how it works, update "chapter3e1.csv" by removing two values and replacing them with different symbols, as shown below. Save the file as "chapter3e1c.csv".

```
studentID,exam1,exam2
12345,78,89
12346,na,77
12347,89,n/a
```

Enter the following code in a cell will allow Pandas to correctly handle the null values:

```
grade = pd.read_csv("chapter3e1c.csv", na_values=['na', 'n/a'])
grade
```

Review Question 3.1
A csv file is a ________ text file.
a. common-separated
b. comma-separated
c. common-specific value
d. comma-specific value

Review Question 3.2
Suppose you have a csv file called a.csv in the working directory of the JupyterLab. Which of the following is a correct way to load a csv file into a DataFrame?
a. pandas.read_csv("a.csv")
b. df = pandas.read_csv("a.csv")
c. DataFrame.read_csv("a.csv")
d. df = DataFrame.read_csv("a.csv")

Review Question 3.3
When a csv file does not have a column header, you must add the ________ parameter to avoid the first line of data being used as the column header.
a. header
b. names
c. column
d. column_names

Review Question 3.4
When reading a csv file that does not have a column header, if you like a meaningful header, you can specify column names in a list. And add the ________ parameter of the read_csv() function.
a. header
b. names
c. column
d. column_names

Review Question 3.5
When reading a csv file, you can set a column as the index by using the ________ parameter of the read_csv() function.
a. header
b. names
c. index

d. index_col

Review Question 3.6
You can use a custom column header instead of the one that comes with the csv file by using the _______
parameter(s) of the read_csv() function.
a. renames
b. names
c. header and names
d. ignore_original

Review Question 3.7
What is the default behavior when reading a CSV file with no header row with 'header=None'?
a. The first row is used as the header row.
b. The first column is used as the header row.
c. Pandas assigns default column names.
d. Pandas raises an error.

Review Question 3.8
How can you skip a certain number of rows when reading a CSV file?
a. Use the 'skip_rows' parameter and set it to the number of rows to skip.
b. Use the 'skiprows' parameter and set it to the number of rows to skip.
c. Use the 'omit_rows' parameter and set it to the number of rows to skip.
d. Use the 'remove_rows' parameter and set it to the number of rows to skip.

Review Question 3.9
How can you specify the separator character when reading a CSV file?
a. Use the 'separator' parameter and set it to the separator character.
b. Use the 'sep' parameter and set it to the separator character.
c. Use the 'delimiter' parameter and set it to the separator character.
d. Use the 'divider' parameter and set it to the separator character.

Review Question 3.10
How can you handle missing values when reading a CSV file?
a. Use the 'missing_values' parameter and set it to a list of values to consider as missing.
b. Use the 'na_values' parameter and set it to a list of values to consider as missing.
c. Use the 'null_values' parameter and set it to a list of values to consider as missing.
d. Use the 'skipna' parameter and set it to True to skip missing values.

3.2 Read csv Files in Pieces

To optimize the processing of large files, it is often more efficient to read smaller chunks of the file or only

read a limited number of rows instead of the entire file. This can significantly speed up the process,

especially when working with large datasets. To read a small number of rows from a CSV file, you can use

the nrows parameter of the read_csv() function in the Pandas library. For example:

```python
column_names = ["studentID", "exam1", "exam2"]
grade_book6 = pd.read_csv("chapter3e2.csv", names=column_names, nrows=2)
```

```
grade_book6
```

Output:

	studentID	exam1	exam2
0	12345	78	89
1	12346	67	77

The default value for nrows is None, which means that the entire file will be read. If you specify a value that is greater than the number of rows in the file, all rows will be read as well.

While the nrows parameter only returns the specified number of rows, the chunksize parameter returns an iterator object that allows you to iterate over and process each chunk of data separately. For example:

```
column_names = ["studentID", "exam1", "exam2"]
chunker =pd.read_csv("chapter3e2.csv", names=column_names, chunksize=2)
counter = 1
for piece in chunker:
    if counter == 2:
        second_chunk = piece
    counter = counter + 1
second_chunk
```

Output:

	StudentID	exam1	exam2
2	12347	89	99

A common value for chunksize is between 500 and 2000 rows, but you can adjust it based on the size and complexity of your dataset.

Finally, to write a DataFrame to a CSV file, you can use the **to_csv()** method. Let's start by reading a CSV file into a DataFrame using the read_csv() function. After that, we can make any necessary modifications or add additional columns. Here's an example:

```
grade_book7 = pd.read_csv("chapter3e1.csv")
exam3 = [73, 83, 93]
grade_book7['exam3'] = exam3
grade_book7
```

Output:

	studentID	exam1	exam2	exam3
0	12345	78	89	73
1	12346	67	77	83
2	12347	89	99	93

To write the DataFrame to a CSV file, call the `to_csv()` method on the DataFrame and specify a file name. For example:

```
grade_book7.to_csv("chapter3e3.csv")
```

By default, the resulting file will be saved in the CSV format. However, you can specify a different delimiter using the sep parameter. For example, you can use sep='\t' to indicate that the data is separated by tabs. After executing the code, a new file with the specified name should appear in the left panel of JupyterLab.

Review Question 3.11
What is the purpose of the nrows parameter in the read_csv() function of the Pandas library?
a. To specify the number of rows to skip at the beginning of the file
b. To specify the number of rows to read from the file
c. To specify the delimiter used in the file
d. To specify the encoding of the file

Review Question 3.12
When using the nrows parameter, which of the following is NOT a valid value that can be passed?
a. A positive integer
b. A negative intege
c. 1000
d. The string "None"

Review Question 3.13
If you specify a value for nrows that is greater than the number of rows in a csv file, what will be the result?
a. All rows will be read.
b. It will raise an error.
c. Only one row will be displayed.
d. You will see a blank output.

Review Question 3.14
If you want to only read a small number of rows (avoiding reading the entire file) of a CSV file, you can use the _______ parameter.
a. head
b. header
c. rows
d. nrows

Review Question 3.15
To read a large file in pieces, you can specify the _______ parameter for the number of rows (usually 500 to 2000) at a time:
a. rowatime
b. numrows
c. chunksize

d. size

Review Question 3.16
Which of the following is the statement that writes a DataFrame called df to a CSV file called df.csv?
a. pd.write_csv("df.csv")
b. pd.to_csv("df.csv")
c. df.write_csv("df.csv")
d. df.to_csv("df.csv")

3.3 Read JSON file

JSON (short for JavaScript Object Notation) is a widely-used data interchange format for transmitting data over the internet between servers, web applications, or different systems. It is a lightweight and flexible data-serialization format that offers human-readability and versatility. One of the key advantages of JSON is its ability to represent diverse data structures, including lists, dictionaries, and nested objects. This flexibility makes JSON suitable for handling complex data scenarios. Here is an example of a JSON file. Type the following content into a notebook file called chapter3e4.json:

```
{
"exam1":{"12345":78, "12346":67, "12347":89},
"exam2":{"12345":89, "12346":77, "12347":99},
"exam3":{"12345":73, "12346":83, "12347":93}
}
```

To read this JSON file from the default location in JupyterLab, use the following code in a new cell::

```
grade_book8 = pd.read_json("chapter3e4.json")
grade_book8
```
Output:

	exam1	exam2	exam3
12345	78	89	73
12346	67	77	83
12347	89	99	93

JSON is a widely-used data interchange format commonly utilized in web APIs (Application Programming Interfaces). Web APIs serve as interfaces for web applications, enabling communication between various systems over the internet. They consist of defined methods for exchanging data, typically utilizing the HTTP protocol to facilitate communication between clients and servers. Web APIs can enable software systems to interact with each other or facilitate communication between different components within a system. They are often used to provide access to web-based services or expose data and functionality of servers or software applications to other systems.

To access such APIs, you can utilize the read_json() function in Python, providing the API's URL as a parameter. This function is part of the Pandas library. It allows you to retrieve JSON data from a URL and parse it into a Pandas DataFrame. Here is an example:

```python
url = "https://open.er-api.com/v6/latest/USD"
df = pd.read_json(url)
df
```

In the example above, we've kept things simple. However, in many real-world scenarios, we use additional tools to make our work easier. One such tool is the requests library, which we use to send and receive data over the internet. Another tool is the json_normalize function from the Pandas library. This function helps us organize JSON data that we receive from an API into a format that's easier to work with.

If a JSON file has only one level of nesting, it can be treated as tabular data and imported into a Pandas DataFrame using the read_json() method. However, most JSON files have multiple levels of nesting, making them unsuitable for direct conversion into a tabular structure. In such cases, the data needs to be downloaded to disk and read into a Python dictionary before it can be used to construct a Pandas DataFrame.

JSON shares many similarities with Python code with a few exceptions. For instance, JSON uses the value null to represent null values, whereas Python uses None. JSON also has some specific rules, such as disallowing trailing commas in lists. The basic data types in JSON include objects (similar to Python dictionaries), arrays (similar to Python lists), strings, numbers, booleans, and null values. All keys in a JSON object must be strings. There are several Python libraries available for reading and writing JSON data, with one of them being the built-in json library from the Python standard library. To convert a JSON string to a Python object, you can use the json.loads() function. To see how JSON string can be converted to a Python dictionary, create a json file called chapter3e5.json with the following content:

```json
{
  "id":"12345",
  "phones":["333-3456", "444-4567"],
  "courses":[{"title":"CS101", "grade":"A"},
      {"title":"CS102", "grade":"B"},
      {"title":"CS201", "grade":"A"}]
}
```

Then, enter the following lines in a new cell of JupyterLab:

```python
import json
import pandas as pd
grade_book9_dic = json.load(open("chapter3e5.json"))
grade_book9_dic
```

Output:

```
{'id': '12345',
 'phones': ['333-3456', '444-4567'],
 'courses': [{'title': 'CS101', 'grade': 'A'},
  {'title': 'CS102', 'grade': 'B'},
  {'title': 'CS201', 'grade': 'A'}]}
```

There are multiple approaches to convert a JSON object or a list of JSON objects into a Pandas DataFrame.

One convenient way to convert JSON data to a Pandas DataFrame is by passing a list of dictionaries to the

pd.DataFrame() constructor. Each dictionary represents a JSON object, with the keys representing the data

fields. You can then select a subset of the data fields to include in the DataFrame. Here's an example

illustrating how you can convert a list of JSON objects to a Pandas DataFrame:

```python
# Assume that json_data is a list of JSON objects
json_data = [
    {'name': 'John', 'age': 30, 'city': 'New York'},
    {'name': 'Jane', 'age': 25, 'city': 'Chicago'},
    {'name': 'Bob', 'age': 35, 'city': 'Los Angeles'}
]
# Convert the JSON data to a Pandas DataFrame
df = pd.DataFrame(json_data)
# Select a subset of the data fields
df = df[['name', 'age']]
print(df)
```

Output:

```
    name  age
0   John   30
1   Jane   25
2    Bob   35
```

In this example, json_data represents a list of JSON objects, each expressed as a dictionary. The

pd.DataFrame() constructor converts the list of dictionaries into a Pandas DataFrame, and the df[['name',

'age']] expression selects a subset of the data fields (name and age) to include in the DataFrame. The

resulting DataFrame will consist of two columns (name and age) and three rows, with each row

corresponding to a JSON object in the list.

Review Question 3.17
What is JSON short for?
a. JavaScript Object Notation
b. Java Object Notation
c. Justified Object Notation
d. JavaScript Oriented Notation

Review Question 3.18
JSON is a popular data interchange format that is used for _______ by HTTP request between a server and a web application or between different applications.
a. formatting websites
b. sending data over the internet
c. styling websites
d. storing data in a structured manner

Review Question 3.19
JSON is a _______, flexible, and lightweight _______ format that is often used for transmitting data between different systems.
a. small-size, relational data
b. small-size, data-serialization
c. human-readable, data-serialization
d. human-readable, relational data

Review Question 3.20
One of the main advantages of JSON is that it can represent _______ .
a. a three-dimensional data format
b. a more structured data format
c. a super-fast data structures
d. diverse data structures

Review Question 3.21
Acording to the book, JSON is well-suited for representing _______ data.
a. highly structured
b. complex
c. human-readable
d. machine-readable

Review Question 3.22
Which of the following is the correct way to retrieve data from a JSON file 'a.json' into a Pandas DataFrame?
a. df = pandas.retrieve("a.json")
b. df = pandas.retrieve_json("a.json")
c. df = pandas.read("a.json")
d. df = pandas.read_json("a.json")"

Review Question 3.23
JSON is a popular data interchange format that is often used in web _______.
a. APIs
b. databases
c. servers

d. websites

Review Question 3.24
Web _______ are often used to provide access to a web-based service or to expose data and functionality of a server or a software application to other systems.
a. APIs
b. databases
c. servers
d. websites

Review Question 3.25
Which Python library is required if you use the read_json() method to access a web API by URL and read its data into a Pandas DataFrame?
a. JSONs
b. Web APIs
c. requests
d. urls

Review Question 3.26
_______ JSON file can be considered as tabular data and can be imported into a Pandas DataFrame using the read_json() method.
a. Any
b. Only one level of nesting
c. Only one or two levels of nesting
d. Up to three levels of nesting

Review Question 3.27
The basic data types in JSON are objects (which are similar to Python dictionaries), arrays (which are similar to Python lists), strings, numbers, booleans, and null values. All keys in objects must be _______.
a. numbers
b. strings
c. objects
d. arrays

Review Question 3.28
JSON is a data interchange format that is similar to Python code in many ways, with a few exceptions. One of these exceptions is the use of the _______ value, which is represented as _______ in JSON and as _______ in Python..
a. null, null, null
b. null, null, None
c. null, None, null
d. None, null, null

Review Question 3.29
JSON is a data interchange format that is similar to Python code in many ways, with a few exceptions. JSON has some nuances, such as _______.
a. not allowing trailing commas at the end of lists
b. allowing not closed curly brace
c. not allowing strings in the keys
d. allowing numbers in the keys

Review Question 3.30
To convert a JSON string to a Python object, you use the _______ function.
a. json_list()
b. json_dic()
c. json.loads()
d. read_json()

Review Question 3.31
One convenient way to convert JSON data to a Pandas DataFrame is to pass a list of dictionaries to the _______.
a. pandas.DataFrame() constructor
b. pandas.JSON() constructor
c. DataFrame.JSON() method
d. DataFrame.convert() method

3.4 Read HTML Table from the Web

The pandas.read_html() function provides a convenient way to convert an HTML table from a webpage into a pandas DataFrame. This feature is useful for extracting data quickly without the need for manual HTML scraping. However, it is important to be aware that the data retrieved may require cleaning and formatting before it can be effectively analyzed. In this section, we will explore how to utilize the pandas.read_html() function to read and clean multiple HTML tables from Wikipedia, enabling further numerical analysis. By default, the function searches for and attempts to parse all tabular data enclosed within <table> tags, returning a list of pandas DataFrame objects. Here's an example:

```
medal_table =
pd.read_html('https://en.wikipedia.org/wiki/2022_Winter_Olympics_medal_table')
print(f'There are {len(medal_table)} tables on the page.')
```

Output:

```
There are 9 tables on the page.
```

To examine all nine tables, you can iterate over the list of DataFrame objects:

```
for i in range(8):
    print(medal_table[i])
```

The output is omitted for brevity. You can see that the table containing medals by country is the fourth table, you can assign it to a separate DataFrame for further analysis::

```
medal_2022 = medal_table[3]
medal_2022.head()
```

The read_html() function also offers optional parameters to customize its behavior. For instance, you can use the attrs parameter to specify HTML attributes that identify the desired tables to extract. The following code demonstrates how to retrieve table(s) with the wikitable class attribute::

```python
medal_table =
pd.read_html('https://en.wikipedia.org/wiki/2022_Winter_Olympics_medal_
table', attrs={'class': 'wikitable'})
print(f'There are {len(medal_table)} tables on the page.')
print(medal_table[0])
```

Output:

```
There are 1 tables on the page.
```

Additionally, you can pass an HTML document as a string to read_html(). In this case, you'll need to utilize the io module from the Python standard library to create a file-like object from the string::

```python
import io
html = '''
<table>
  <tr>
    <th>Column 1</th>
    <th>Column 2</th>
  </tr>
  <tr>
    <td>Value 1</td>
    <td>Value 2</td>
  </tr>
</table>
'''
# Create a file-like object from the HTML string
html_file = io.StringIO(html)
# Read the table from the file-like object
table = pd.read_html(html_file)[0]
# Print the table
print(table)
```

Output:

```
   Column 1 Column 2
0   Value 1  Value 2
```

In this example, an HTML table is passed as a string. The io.StringIO() function is used to create a file-like object, which is then read by read_html() to obtain the table as a DataFrame. Finally, the table is printed.

Review Question 3.32
The _______ function can be used to easily convert an HTML table on a website into a Pandas DataFrame.
a. pandas.convert_html_table()
b. pandas.convert_html()
c. pandas.read_html()
d. pandas.read_table()

Review Question 3.33
By default, the *pandas.read_html()* function searches for and tries to parse all tabular data contained within _______ tags, and returns a list of pandas DataFrame objects.
a. <table>
b. <data>
c. <list>
d. any

Review Question 3.34
Suppose the *pandas.read_html()* function returns a list of Pandas DataFrame objects from a webpage and assigns the list to df. How do you find out how many tables are on the webpage?
a. df.len
b. len(df)
c. count(df)
d. df.count

Review Question 3.35
The read_html() function has several optional parameters that you can be used to customize its behavior. For example, you can use the _______ parameter to specify the HTML attributes that identify the tables that you want to extract.
a. attr
b. attrs
c. attribute
d. attributes

Review Question 3.36
You can also pass an HTML document as a string to the read_html() function. In this case, you need to use the _______ module from the Python standard library to create a file-like object from the string.
a. html
b. document
c. io
d. input/output

3.5 Input and Output Pickle Files

Like other object-oriented programming, serialization is a process in which we convert a data structure or object state into a format that can be stored and reconstructed later in the same or another computer environment. When the resulting series of bits is reread according to the serialization format, it can be used to create a semantically identical clone of the original object.

Pickle is a Python module that implements binary protocols for serializing and de-serializing a Python object structure. In other words, it's a way to convert a python object into a byte stream. The idea is that this byte stream contains all the information necessary to reconstruct the object in another python script.

The `to_pickle()` method of Pandas objects is a handy tool that allows you to write the data to disk in pickle format. While you can save a DataFrame in a CSV or Excel file, these formats do not preserve all the attributes, data types, and methods of the DataFrame.

If you want to save and restore a DataFrame without losing any information, you should use pickle files. This is common when working with a dataset that requires significant cleaning and preparation. For example, you may want to save a DataFrame as a pickle file after you have cleaned and prepared it. Later, if you need to start your analysis again from this point, you can restore the DataFrame from the pickle file. This saves you the time of re-running the cells that clean and prepare the data.

Let's see how it works. Enter the following in a new cell to import an existing example:

```
grade_book = pd.read_csv("chapter3e1.csv")
grade_book
```

Enter the following code and execute it to save the DataFrame object to a pickle file:

```
grade_book.to_pickle('grade_book.pkl')
```

On the left panel of your JupyterLab, you should see a file named "grade_book.pkl". To retrieve the pickle file at a later time, issue the following code:

```
pd.read_pickle('grade_book.pkl')
```

An example where a Pandas DataFrame is better saved as a Pickle rather than a CSV is when the DataFrame contains complex data types such as Python objects, datetime objects with time zones, or multi-indexes that cannot be easily or efficiently represented in a CSV format.

Imagine you have a DataFrame that includes a column of lists and a column of dictionaries, in addition to standard numerical and textual data. For instance:

```
# Sample DataFrame with complex data types
data = {
    'ID': [1, 2, 3],
```

```
    'Name': ['Alice', 'Bob', 'Charlie'],
    'Scores': [[85, 90, 78], [88, 94, 81], [90, 92, 85]],
    'Preferences': [{'color': 'blue', 'food': 'pizza'}, {'color':
'green', 'food': 'sushi'}, {'color': 'red', 'food': 'pasta'}]
}
df = pd.DataFrame(data)
```

If you save this DataFrame to a CSV file, the lists and dictionaries will be converted to strings, losing their original data structures:

```
df.to_csv('data.csv', index=False)
```

The resulting CSV file will have the `Scores` and `Preferences` columns as plain text strings, which would require additional parsing and may lead to errors when attempting to restore the data to its original structure.

To preserve the complex data types and structure of the DataFrame, saving it as a Pickle file is more appropriate:

```
df.to_pickle('data.pkl')
```

When you load the DataFrame back from the Pickle file, all data types, including lists and dictionaries, are preserved exactly as they were:

```
df_loaded = pd.read_pickle('data.pkl')
df_loaded
```

The `df_loaded` DataFrame will be identical to the original `df`, with the `Scores` and `Preferences` columns retaining their original structures. This makes Pickle the better choice when working with DataFrames that contain complex or non-standard data types that cannot be easily or reliably represented in a flat file format like CSV.

Pickle is a handy tool for storing data that needs to persist or be shared between Python programs. However, it's crucial to be aware of potential security risks when using pickle for serialization.

Firstly, pickle is a Python-specific format. This means that objects serialized with pickle might not be readable by other programming languages. If you're using pickle to store data that needs to be shared with other systems or programs, those systems or programs might not be able to interpret the data.

Secondly, pickle is susceptible to security vulnerabilities. An attacker could create a malicious pickle file that, when deserialized, could run arbitrary code on the target system. Therefore, if you're using pickle to store sensitive data, it's important to exercise caution when deserializing pickle files, particularly if the source of the pickle file is untrusted.

Lastly, the pickle file format is recommended only for short-term storage. The problem with this format is that it's hard to guarantee its stability over time. An object pickled today might not be unpicklable with a future version of a library.

Review Question 3.37
What is serialization in the context of object-oriented programming?
a. The process of converting a data structure or object state into a format that can be stored and reconstructed later.
b. The process of converting a Python object into a character stream.
c. The process of writing data to disk in pickle format.
d. The process of saving a DataFrame in a CSV or Excel file.

Review Question 3.38
What does the Python module 'pickle' do?
a. It implements binary protocols for serializing and de-serializing a Python object structure.
b. It allows you to write data to disk in pickle format.
c. It saves a DataFrame in a CSV or Excel file.
d. It cleans and prepares a dataset.

Review Question 3.39
What is the purpose of the to_pickle() method in pandas?
a. It converts a Python object into a character stream.
b. It allows you to write data to disk in pickle format.
c. It saves a DataFrame in a CSV or Excel file.
d. It cleans and prepares a dataset.

Review Question 3.40
Why might you want to use pickle files when working with a DataFrame?
a. To convert a Python object into a character stream.
b. To save and restore a DataFrame without losing any information.
c. To implement binary protocols for serializing and de-serializing a Python object structure.
d. To write data to disk in CSV or Excel format.

Review Question 3.41
When might you want to save a DataFrame as a pickle file?
a. Before you have cleaned and prepared the data.
b. After you have cleaned and prepared the data.
c. When you want to convert a Python object into a character stream.
d. When you want to implement binary protocols for serializing and de-serializing a Python object structure.

Review Question 3.42
What is the benefit of restoring a DataFrame from a pickle file?
a. It allows you to convert a Python object into a character stream.

b. It saves you the time of re-running the cells that clean and prepare the data.

c. It allows you to implement binary protocols for serializing and de-serializing a Python object structure.

d. It allows you to write data to disk in CSV or Excel format.

Review Question 3.43

What is pickle used for in Python?

a. Serializing and deserializing Python objects.

b. Compiling Python code.

c. Debugging Python code.

d. Avoiding errors in Python code.

Review Question 3.44

How do you save a DataFrame df to a pickle file called a.pkl?

a. df.save("a.pkl")

b. df.to_pickle("a.pkl")

c. df.save_to_pickle("a.pkl")

d. df.save_pickle("a.pkl")

Review Question 3.45

How do you retrieve a pickle file called a.pkl to a DataFrame df?

a. pandas.retrieve_pickle("a.pkl")

b. pandas.read_pickle("a.pkl")

c. df.read_pickle("a.pkl")

d. df = pandas.read_pickle("a.pkl")

Review Question 3.46

Can objects serialized with pickle be easily read by other programming languages?

a. Yes

b. No

c. It depends on the programming language

d. It depends on the version of Python used to serialize the object

Review Question 3.47

Which of the following is NOT a risk of using pickle for serialization in Python?

a. Security vulnerabilities

b. Compatibility issues

c. Efficiency

d. vulnerability and compatibility

Review Question 3.48

The best format for saving a DataFrame on disk for near future use, provided that it will be only used by Python scripts, is what?

a. CSV

b. Pickle

c. XML

d. Plain text

3.6 Work with Spreadsheet Files

Another popular tabular data is spreadsheet. You can read an Excel file using pandas. You can either use the ExcelFile class or the pandas.read_excel() function. This section will demonstrate the use of read_excel().

Before proceeding, open the file named "Chapter3e1.csv" in Excel and add a new sheet by clicking the "+" sign on the bottom left. Keep the default sheet name as "sheet1". Enter the following data in the new sheet (sheet1):

studentID	exam1	exam2
12345	88	97
54321	76	83
12347	95	92

Then, save it as an Excel Workbook with a .xlsx file extension using the same file name. In a new cell of your JupyterLab, enter the following code:

```
grade_book10 = pd.read_excel("chapter3e1.xlsx")
grade_book10
```

You may notice that pandas opens the first sheet by default. If you want to open a specific sheet by its name, you can use the sheet_name parameter when reading the file with pandas. For example:

```
grade_book11 = pd.read_excel("chapter3e1.xlsx", sheet_name="Sheet1")
grade_book11
```

To write a pandas DataFrame back to an Excel file, you can use the to_excel() method:

```
grade_book11.to_excel("savedback.xlsx")
```

The saved Excel file will include the index column, which may not be of interest to the reader. To exclude the index column, you can use the optional parameter 'index' and set it to False.

You can also specify which column(s) to save. The **to_excel()** method allows you to select specific columns to include in the Excel file by passing a list of column names to the 'columns' parameter. Here is an example of how to use the to_excel() method to save only the specified columns to an Excel file:

```
# Create a DataFrame
df = pd.DataFrame({'Name': ['Alice', 'Bob', 'Charlie'],
                   'Score': [90, 80, 70],
                   'Grade': ['A', 'B', 'C']})
# Save the selected columns to an Excel file
```

```
df.to_excel('select.xlsx', index=False, columns=['Name', 'Score'])
```

This code will save only the 'Name' and 'Score' columns of the DataFrame to an Excel file named 'select.xlsx', without including the row indices. The 'index=False' parameter is used to exclude the indices from being saved to the Excel file.

In addition to working with Excel files, pandas can also handle many other binary formats, such as SAS, SPSS, and STATA.

Review Question 3.49
To read tabular data from an Excel file using Pandas, you can use the ________ class or the ________ function.
a. Pandas, pandas.read_excel()
b. DataFrame, pandas.read_excel()
c. ExcelFile, df.read_excel()
d. ExcelFile, pnadas.read_excel()

Review Question 3.50
When using the pandas.read_excel(), Pandas open the ________ by default.
a. first sheet
b. sheet0
c. sheet1
d. default_sheet

Review Question 3.51
If you want pandas to open a specific sheet with the sheet name, you can use the ________ parameter when reading in the file using pandas.
a. sheet
b. name
c. sheet_name
d. read_sheet

Review Question 3.52
How to save a DataFrame df to an excel file as "a.xlsx"?
a. df.to_excel("a.xlsx")
b. df.save_excel("a.xlsx")
c. pandas.to_excel("a.xlsx")
d. df=pandas.save_excel("a.xlsx")

Review Question 3.53
The saved excel file by using to_excel() method will have the ________ column which is often of no interest to the reader.
a. name
b. file record
c. decoding
d. index

Review Question 3.54
The saved excel file by using to_excel() method will have the index column which is often of no interest to the reader. To remove that, use optional _______ parameter and set it to _______.
a. index, False
b. index, None
c. index_column, False
d. index_column, None

Review Question 3.55
Suppose you want to save only certain columns with the to_excel() method to an Excel file. How do you specify that to the to_excel() method?
a. by passing a list of column names to the columns parameter.
b. by passing the column names to the headings parameter.
c. by adding the column names to the column_names parameter.
d. by adding the column names to the column_headings parameter.

3.7 Read Web APIs

To access public APIs that provide data feeds in JSON or other formats using Python, you can use the requests package. This package allows you to make HTTP requests to API endpoints and process the responses. An API endpoint is a specific URL where you can send requests and receive responses. With the requests library, you can access the data or functionality provided by the API. Here are the steps for accessing a web API using Python:

First, identify the API endpoint you want to access. Some popular APIs include the Twitter/X API, which allows you to access data such as tweets and user information; the Google Maps API, which provides access to data from Google Maps, including directions and geocoding information; and the Reddit API, which allows you to access data from the Reddit platform, including comments and posts.

Second, check if the API requires authentication. Some APIs may require you to provide an API key to access their data, while others may require authentication using OAuth. OAuth is an open standard for authorization that enables users to securely authorize access to their resources without sharing their credentials. It is commonly used to allow users to log in to a third-party application using their social media credentials, such as their Facebook or Twitter/X login.

Third, install any required libraries. Depending on the API you are accessing and the Python libraries you already have installed, you may need to install additional libraries to make API calls. For example, the requests library is commonly used for making HTTP requests in Python, and the json library is used for parsing JSON data. JupyterLab already has these libraries installed, so you can simply import them before using them.

Fourth, make an API call. Once you have the necessary libraries installed, you can use Python's requests library to make an HTTP request to the API's endpoint. The endpoint is the URL that specifies the location of the API resource you want to access. The API will return a response, which may include data or an error message.

Fifth, process the response. If the API call is successful, you will receive a response containing the requested data. You can use Python's json library to parse the response and access the data. If the API call is not successful, you may need to handle any error messages that are returned.

Here is an example of how to find the last 30 GitHub issues for Pandas on GitHub using the requests library. We make a GET HTTP request to the GitHub API endpoint and use the Response object's json() method to parse the JSON data into a native Python object:

```python
import requests
url = 'https://api.github.com/repos/pandas-dev/pandas/issues'
response = requests.get(url)
data = response.json()
data
```

Each element in the 'data' dictionary represents the data found on a GitHub issue page (except for the comments). We can pass the 'data' directly to a DataFrame and extract the fields of interest:

```python
issues = pd.DataFrame(data, columns=['title', 'labels', 'state'])
issues
```

The output is omitted for brevity.

Review Question 3.56
One way to access public APIs for websites that provide data feeds through JSON or other formats in Python is to use the _______ package
a. htmls
b. https
c. requests
d. requestAPIs

Review Question 3.57
The requests library allows you to make HTTP requests to API _______ and process the response you receive.
a. endpoints
b. clients
c. browsers
d. OS

Review Question 3.58
Which of the following is NOT a step for accessing a web API using Python?
a. Make an API call.
b. Install and import the required libraries.
c. Process the response.
d. Post API data on spreadsheets.

Review Question 3.59
Which of the following is NOT a step for accessing a web API using Python?
a. Validate data received from the API.
b. Install and import the required libraries.
c. Process the response.
d. Check if the API requires authentication.

Review Question 3.60
Which of the following is NOT a step for accessing a web API using Python?
a. Identify the API endpoint you want to access.
b. Install and import the required libraries.
c. Send the response back to the API server.
d. Check if the API requires authentication.

Review Question 3.61
Which of the following is NOT a step for accessing a web API using Python?
a. Identify the API endpoint you want to access.
b. Visit the website of your local/school libraries.
c. Process the response.
d. Check if the API requires authentication.

3.8 Read Relational Databases: SQLITE

Relational databases, along with their associated query language SQL (Structured Query Language), are widely utilized in business settings for efficient data storage and management. SQL Server, PostgreSQL, and MySQL are among the popular choices for implementing relational database systems. These databases offer robust features, performance optimization, data integrity, and scalability to meet the diverse needs of organizations. In this section, we will explore the fundamentals of working with relational databases and utilizing SQL for effective data manipulation and retrieval. Although SQLite may not be the most widely used database management system. SQLite has been chosen for its beginner-friendly nature, and most database management systems adhere to the SQL standard, making them similar to work with.

To interact with and manage a database, you require a database management system(DBMS). JupyterLab comes equipped with SQLite preinstalled, along with the necessary SQLite driver, sqlite3. We will create a database, define a table, and populate it with data, all from within JupyterLab.

The following code snippet demonstrates the creation of a database named "StudentDB" along with a table called "Student". The "Student" table consists of three columns: "studentID", "exam1", and "exam2". The "studentID" column is designated as the primary key, ensuring unique identification of each record within the table. Each row in the "Student" table represents an individual student:

```
import sqlite3
query = """
CREATE TABLE Student
(
    studentID CHAR(5) PRIMARY KEY,
    exam1 INTEGER,
    exam2 INTEGER
);"""
conn = sqlite3.connect('StudentDB.sqlite')
conn.execute(query)
conn.commit()
```

The above program employs the sqlite3 library, which enables Python programs to interact with SQLITE databases. By sending an SQL statement to the SQLITE DBMS, the Python program executes the desired operations. In the provided code, the SQL statement is responsible for creating the table.

The initial step involves establishing a connection between the Python program and the SQLITE database using the connect() function from the sqlite3 module. Subsequently, the execute() method of the connection object instructs the SQLITE DBMS to execute the specified query. Finally, the commit() method of the connection ensures that the executed changes are permanently saved..

After creating the database and table in your local computer, you can proceed to insert data into the table using the following code snippet in JupyterLab:

```
rowslist =  [('12345', 78, 89),
             ('12346', 67, 77),
             ('12347', 89, 99)]
insert_query = """INSERT INTO Student
    (studentID, exam1, exam2)
     VALUES(?, ?, ?);"""
```

```
conn.executemany(insert_query, rowslist)
conn.commit()
```

In this code, a list named rowslist is defined, containing the data rows to be inserted into the "Student" table. Each row consists of a student ID, an exam1 score, and an exam2 score. The insert_query variable holds the SQL statement responsible for inserting data into the table. The placeholders '?' in the query correspond to the values that will be provided later. By using the executemany() method of the connection object, the program executes the insert query multiple times, once for each row in the rowslist list. Lastly, the commit() method of the connection ensures that the changes are permanently saved to the database.

With data now present in our database table, we can move on to retrieving data from the database. The syntax for retrieving data from a table is as follows:

```
SELECT Column1, Column2, etc. FROM tableName;
```

By replacing the column names with an asterisk (*), you can select all columns in the table. In this SQL statement, "SELECT" and "FROM" are keywords that respectively indicate the selection of columns and the table to query. Executing an SQL SELECT statement returns a **cursor** object, which can be used to fetch the data. The fetchall() method of a cursor object retrieves all rows from the result set and stores them in a list of tuples. Here is an example code snippet that demonstrates retrieving all records from the "Student" table:

```
select_query = "SELECT * FROM Student;"
cursor = conn.execute(select_query)
rows = cursor.fetchall()
rows
```

In this code, a cursor object is created by executing the "SELECT" statement using the execute() method of the connection object. The fetchall() method is then used to fetch all rows from the result set and store them in the rows variable. This variable holds a list of tuples, with each tuple representing a row of data from the table. The cursor object allows you to iterate over the rows of the result set and process the returned data as needed.

For beginners who may encounter difficulties in table creation and need to start fresh, a convenient approach is to drop the entire table. The following code snippet illustrates this process:

```
drop_table_query = "DROP TABLE IF EXISTS Student;"
conn.execute(drop_table_query)
```

In this code, the SQL statement "DROP TABLE IF EXISTS Student;" is executed using the execute()

method of the connection object. This statement instructs the database to drop the "Student" table if it exists. By using the "IF EXISTS" clause, the code avoids any errors that could occur if the table does not exist.

After completing the execution of your queries, it is important to close both the cursor and the connection. Use the following code to accomplish this:

```
cursor.close()
conn.close()
```

By calling the close() method on the cursor and connection objects, you ensure that any resources associated with them are properly released.

The next time you want to work with the "StudentDB" database, you will need to establish a new connection by using the following code:

```
conn = sqlite3.connect('StudentDB.sqlite')
```

In summary, to enable Python to interact with an SQLite database, you need to establish a connection between the two. Once the connection is established, you can execute SQL statements on it and perform multiple queries using the same connection. Remember to close the connection when you have finished working with it.

Review Question 3.62
What is SQLITE?
a. A simplified version of SQL.
b. A portion of SQL for beginners.
c. A database management system.
d. A programming language.

Review Question 3.63
Which of the following is NOT a database management system?
a. SQL
b. SQLITE.
c. SQL Server.
d. MySQL.

Review Question 3.64
What is sqlite3 in Python?
a. The third generation of SQLITE.
b. The third generation of Python SQL.
c. The required driver for Python to work with SQLITE.

d. The required cable for Python clients to connect to a machine.

Review Question 3.65
Suppose you have a sqlite3 connection object called conn and an SQL statement stored in a string variable query. How do you run the SQL statement?
a. query.run(conn)
b. conn.run(query)
c. query.execute(conn)
d. conn.execute(query)

Review Question 3.66
In sqlite3, the execution of an SQL SELECT statement returns a _______ object.
a. select
b. sql_select
c. cursor
d. list of tuples

Review Question 3.67
In sqlite3, the fetchall() method of a cursor object returns a _______.
a. select object
b. sql_select object
c. cursor object
d. list of tuples

Review Question 3.68
In order for a Python program to interact with SQLITE databases, you must run _______ statement first.
a. a SQL
b. commit a SQL
c. a cursor
d. connection

Review Question 3.69
How do you run a SQL statement in SQLLITE from a Python program?
a. call the execute() method of the SQLLITE object
b. call the run() method of the SQLLITE object
c. call the execut() method of the connection object
d. call the run() method of the connection object

Review Question 3.70
What object is created when you execute a SELECT statement in SQLLITE from a Python program?
a. connection
b. selection
c. cursor
d. execution

Review Question 3.71
By calling the _______ method on the cursor and connection objects, you ensure that any resources associated with them are properly released.
a. connect()
b. close()

c. finish()
d. commit()

Exercise 3.1

Begin by creating a SQLite database named EmployeeDB. Within this database, you'll need to include a table named Employee. This table should be structured with five fields: EmployeeID, FirstName, LastName, HourlyRate, and HoursWorked. Once the table structure is in place, proceed to insert data for three fictitious employees. After the data insertion, display all the employee records. The format for each record should be as follows: "FirstName LastName works for HoursWorked hours at a rate of $HourlyRate per hour, earning a total of $TotalPay." An example of this format would be: "Lucy Scott works for 5 hours at a rate of $56 per hour, earning a total of $280.00." Remember to replace FirstName, LastName, HoursWorked, HourlyRate, and TotalPay with the actual values from each employee record. The TotalPay is calculated as HourlyRate multiplied by HoursWorked.

3.9 SQLAlchemy for Object-Relational Mapping

The sqlite3 library in Python provides a lightweight interface to the SQLite database engine. It allows you to execute SQL statements and perform various operations on the database, such as creating tables and inserting rows. This knowledge serves you well in your database interactions. However, if you need a more robust and flexible tool for working with databases, especially when utilizing an object-relational mapping (ORM), SQLAlchemy is a better option.

An ORM is a tool that enables you to interact with a database using an object-oriented approach. Here's how it operates: you define "classes" in your code that correspond to tables in the database. These classes possess "attributes" that map to columns in the table, and you can utilize "methods" to perform operations on the data stored in the table. The ORM handles the intricacies of translating your object-oriented code into the appropriate SQL commands for the database, and vice versa.

For instance, imagine you have a database table named "users" with columns such as "id," "username," and "email." By employing an ORM, you could define a "User" class with attributes like "id," "username," and "email," along with methods such as "save" and "delete" to create, update, and delete rows in the "users" table.

ORMs can be highly advantageous as they allow you to work with the database using a familiar object-oriented syntax, eliminating the need to write raw SQL queries. This can enhance the readability and maintainability of your code, while also facilitating easier switching between different databases.

When comparing sqlite3 to SQLAlchemy, it becomes evident that SQLAlchemy is a more extensive Python library that offers a higher-level interface to various database engines, including SQLITE. Apart from providing an API for executing SQL statements, it also incorporates a powerful Object-Relational Mapping (ORM) that facilitates the mapping of Python objects to database tables and vice versa. Let's explore some key distinctions between sqlite3 and SQLAlchemy:

Feature	Sqlite3	SQLAlchemy
API style	It provides a procedural API that allows for interaction with the database through function calls and statements.	It offers both a procedural API and an object-oriented API, providing more flexibility in how you interact with the database.
ORM support	It does not have built-in support for an ORM.	It includes a robust ORM that enables you to seamlessly map Python objects to corresponding database tables and vice versa.
Database Management Systems support	It is specifically designed for SQLITE and primarily focuses on interactions with this particular database engine.	It supports a wide range of database engines, including SQLITE, MySQL, PostgreSQL, and others. This versatility allows you to work with different database systems using a consistent API.
Complexity	It is a relatively straightforward library that is easy to learn and use, making it suitable for simpler database interactions.	It is a more comprehensive library that offers advanced features and functionality. While it provides powerful tools such as the ORM, utilizing these features may introduce additional complexity, especially for those new to SQLAlchemy.

SQLAlchemy simplifies the process of interacting with databases and abstracts away many of the intricacies and differences between various SQL database systems. This abstraction enables developers to write database-agnostic code, which can be seamlessly used across different database engines. The Pandas library, known for its powerful data manipulation capabilities, includes a convenient function called read_sql(). This function leverages SQLAlchemy to establish a connection to a database and retrieve data from it effortlessly. By using read_sql(), you can retrieve data from a table in a database without manually writing SQL queries.

In the following example, we demonstrate how to utilize SQLAlchemy to connect to a SQLite database and retrieve data from a previously created table (must install sqlachemy: `pip install sqlalchemy`):

```python
import sqlalchemy as sqla
db = sqla.create_engine('sqlite:///StudentDB.sqlite')
data = pd.read_sql('select * from Student', db)
data
```

In the above code snippet, we first create a SQLAlchemy engine by providing the connection URL to the

SQLite database file, 'StudentDB.sqlite'. Then, using the read_sql() function from pandas, we execute an SQL query to select all columns and rows from the "Student" table. The retrieved data is stored in the 'data' variable and subsequently displayed.

We conclude this section with an example showcasing the usage of SQLAlchemy to connect to a SQLite database and perform various operations::

```python
from sqlalchemy import create_engine, Column, Integer, String
from sqlalchemy.ext.declarative import declarative_base
from sqlalchemy.orm import sessionmaker

# Create a connection to the database
engine = create_engine('sqlite:///mydatabase.db')

# Declare a base for the models
Base = declarative_base()

# Define a model class
class Student(Base):
    __tablename__ = 'students'
    studentID = Column(String, primary_key=True)
    exam1 = Column(Integer)
    exam2 = Column(Integer)

# Create the tables in the database
Base.metadata.create_all(engine)

# Create a session to execute queries
Session = sessionmaker(bind=engine)
session = Session()


# Create two student objects
student1 = Student(studentID="12345", exam1=78, exam2=89)
student2 = Student(studentID="12346", exam1=67, exam2=77)
# Add the object to the session
session.add(student1)
session.add(student2)
# Save the changes to the database
session.commit()

# Select all students from the 'students' table
students = session.query(Student).all()

# Print the IDs of all students
```

```
for student in students:
    print(student.studentID)

# Close the session
session.close()
```

In this example, we start by creating a connection to the SQLite database using the create_engine() function from SQLAlchemy. Then, we define a model class Student that represents a table in the database. The class uses SQLAlchemy's declarative syntax, where we define the table name and columns as class attributes.

After defining the model class, we use Base.metadata.create_all(engine) to create the corresponding table in the database.

Next, we create a session using sessionmaker(bind=engine) to handle the execution of queries. We add two student objects to the session using session.add() and save the changes to the database using session.commit().

To retrieve data from the database, we execute a query using session.query(Student).all(), which returns a list of all student objects. We iterate over the list and print the student IDs.

Finally, we close the session using session.close() to free up resources.

Similar to inserting a new row into a table, updating a row can be accomplished using a session in SQLAlchemy. The process involves retrieving the object from the session, modifying its attributes, and then committing the changes to the database. Here is an example:

```
# Get the student with id=12345
student = session.query(Student).filter(Student.studentID=='12345').one()
# Update the student's exam1 score
student.exam1 = 100
# Save the changes to the database
session.commit()
```

To delete a row from a table using SQLAlchemy, you need to locate the specific row, remove the corresponding object from the session using the session.delete() method, and then save the changes to the database using session.commit(). Here is an example:

```
# Get the student with id=12345
student = session.query(Student).filter(Student.studentID=='12345').one()
```

```
# Delete the student
session.delete(student)

# Save the changes to the database
session.commit()
```

Review Question 3.72
Compared to sqlite3, the _______ is a better choice if you need a more powerful and flexible tool for working with databases in Python.
a. sqlite4
b. sqlite5
c. SQLAlchemy
d. powerSQL

Review Question 3.73
In addition to providing an API for executing SQL statements, SQLAlchemy also includes a powerful _______ that allows you to map Python objects to database tables and vice versa.
a. database engine
b. ORM
c. object-oriented programming
d. stored procedure

Review Question 3.74
How to use SQLAlchemy to create a connection to a SQLITE database?
a. connect()
b. create_connection()
c. create_engine()
d. create_sqlalchemy()

Review Question 3.75
The pandas library includes a _______ function that allows you to easily read data from a SQLAlchemy connection.
a. read_sqlalchemy()
b. read_sql()
c. read_from_connection()
d. read_by_pandas()

Exercise 3.2

Use SQLAlchemy to create a SQLite database named 'BookDB'. This database should include a table named 'Book'. The 'Book' table should have four fields: 'ISBN', 'Title', 'Author', and 'TotalCopy'.
Insert data for three fictitious books into the 'Book' table. Then, display all the ISBNs of the books.
Next, update the 'TotalCopy' field of one of the books using its ISBN. Finally, delete a book from the table using its ISBN.

3.10 Data Types in Pandas

Pandas is a powerful Python library designed to handle large and complex datasets efficiently. It introduces several key data types that facilitate data manipulation and analysis. Let's explore some of the main data types in Pandas:

Series: A Series is a one-dimensional array-like object that resembles a column in a spreadsheet. It can store data of any type, such as numbers, strings, or dates. You can create a Series by utilizing the pandas.Series() function and passing a list of values.

DataFrame: A DataFrame is a two-dimensional table of data with labeled rows and columns. It resembles a spreadsheet or a SQL table. DataFrames are versatile and widely used in data analysis. You can construct a DataFrame by employing the pandas.DataFrame() function, passing various data structures like NumPy arrays, Python dictionaries, or lists of lists.

Index: An Index is an immutable array that labels the rows and columns of a DataFrame. It serves as an identifier for each row and column. Although an Index can hold any data type, it typically consists of strings or integers.

DatetimeIndex: A DatetimeIndex is a specialized type of Index used for labeling time series data. It handles timestamps, dates, and times efficiently and offers various operations specific to time-based data analysis.

Apart from these fundamental data types, Pandas also supports other data types, including:

object: Suitable for storing mixed data types, such as a combination of numbers and strings.
int64: Used for storing integer values.
float64: Used for storing floating-point numbers with decimal places.
datetime64: Specifically designed for storing date and time information.
category: Optimized for variables with a limited number of distinct values, like nominal variables.

To determine the data types of the columns in a Pandas DataFrame, you can utilize the dtypes attribute of the DataFrame object. Let's consider an example where we create a CSV file named "chapter3e6.csv" with the following data:

```
Cohort,GPA,FavoriteColor,BodyTemperature,ShoeSize,DateofBirth
Freshman,3.4,Blue,97.3,8,5/12/1992
Junior,3.9,Green,Not measured,7,11/4/2001
Junior,2.7,White,99.3,11,5/22/2000
```

We can then read the CSV file into a DataFrame and use the dtypes attribute to examine the data types of the columns:

```
student_data = pd.read_csv("chapter3e6.csv")
student_data
```

Output:

	Cohort	GPA	FavoriteColor	BodyTemperature	ShoeSize	DateofBirth
0	Freshman	3.4	Blue	97.3	8	5/12/1992
1	Junior	3.9	Green	Not measured	7	11/4/2001
2	Junior	2.7	White	99.3	11	5/22/2000

To obtain the data types, we use the following code:

```
student_data.dtypes
```

Output:

```
Cohort                object
GPA                   float64
FavoriteColor         object
BodyTemperature       object
ShoeSize              int64
DateofBirth           object
dtype: object
```

From the output, we can observe the data types assigned to each column. For example, the "Cohort" and "FavoriteColor" columns are of type object (string), the "GPA" column is of type float64 (floating-point number), the "ShoeSize" column is of type int64 (integer), and the "BodyTemperature" and "DateofBirth" columns are also represented as object (string) due to their mixed data type values.

To convert the data type of a column in a Pandas DataFrame, you can use the **astype()** method. This method allows you to specify the desired data type for the column, and it will convert the values in the column accordingly. Let's consider an example where we convert the data type of the "Cohort" column from 'object' to 'category', and the "DateofBirth" column from 'object' to 'datetime64':

```
student_data['Cohort'] = student_data['Cohort'].astype('category')
student_data['DateofBirth'] =
student_data['DateofBirth'].astype('datetime64[ns]')
student_data.dtypes
```

Output:

```
Cohort                category
GPA                   float64
FavoriteColor         object
BodyTemperature       object
ShoeSize              int64
DateofBirth           datetime64[ns]
dtype: object
```

From the output, we can see that the "Cohort" column has been successfully converted to the 'category' data type, and the "DateofBirth" column has been converted to the 'datetime64' data type. By converting the data types appropriately, you can ensure that the data in your DataFrame is represented in the most suitable format for analysis and manipulation.

You can also use the astype() method to convert multiple columns at once. For example, to convert the "Cohort" and "FavoriteColor" columns to the category data type, you can use the following code:

```
student_data[['Cohort', 'FavoriteColor']] = student_data[['Cohort',
'FavoriteColor']].astype('category')
```

It's important to note that if you try to convert a column to a data type that is incompatible with the values in the column, you will encounter a ValueError. For instance, if you attempt to convert a column with values like 'a', 'b', and 'c' to the int64 data type, a ValueError will be raised because these values cannot be converted to integers.

Alternatively, you can use the **pd.to_numeric()** function to convert a column to a numeric data type (either int64 or float64). This function attempts to convert all values in the column to a numeric data type and returns a new Series with the converted values. If it encounters a value that cannot be converted, it assigns NaN (Not a Number) to that value.

Similarly, the **pd.to_datetime()** function can be used to convert a column to the datetime data type. It attempts to convert the values in the column to datetime objects and returns a new Series with the converted values.

Variables can be categorized into two types: categorical and continuous. Categorical variables are represented by data types such as 'object' or 'category' in Pandas, and they necessitate distinct analysis and graphing methodologies. On the other hand, continuous variables are represented by data types like 'int64' and 'float64', and they require different techniques for analysis and visualization.

Using the category data type instead of the object data type can significantly reduce memory usage, especially for large datasets. The category data type stores data more efficiently. For instance, if a column in your dataset contains a large number of unique values, using the object data type to store that column will consume more memory compared to using the category data type. Therefore, employing the appropriate data type can help optimize memory usage and enhance the performance of data analysis tasks.

Review Question 3.76
What is the "object" data type in Pandas used for?
a. Storing only numbers

b. Storing only strings
c. Storing mixed data types, such as numbers and strings
d. Storing only boolean values

Review Question 3.77
Which of the following is true about the "category" data type in Pandas?
a. It is for storing variables that can take on a large number of values.
b. It is for storing variables that can take on a small number of values.
c. It is for storing variables that contain only unique values.
d. It is for storing variables that contain missing values.

Review Question 3.78
To obtain information about the data types of the columns in a Pandas DataFrame, you can use the _______ attribute of the DataFrame object.
a. datatype
b. data_type
c. dt
d. dtypes

Review Question 3.79
In Pandas, you can convert the data type of a column in a DataFrame using the _______ method.
a. convert()
b. convert_type()
c. type()
d. astype()

Review Question 3.80
If you try to convert a column in a DataFrame with the values 'a', 'b', 'c' to the int64 data type by using the astype() method, you will get _______.
a. corresponding ASCII values
b. NaN values
c. empty spaces
d. a ValueError

Review Question 3.81
If you try to convert a column in a DataFrame with the values 'a', 'b', 'c' to the int64 data type by the pandas.to_numeric() function, you will get _______.
a. corresponding ASCII values
b. NaN values
c. empty spaces
d. a ValueError

Review Question 3.82
If you have a column in your dataset with unique values that contains many rows, using the _______ data type to store that column will take up more memory than using the _______ data type.
a. string, category
b. category, string
c. object, category
d. category, object

Review Question 3.83
After reading the data from a csv file into a Pandas DataFrame, you observed that the column "body temperature" in the DataFrame is identified as the 'Object' data type. What is the most likely explanation for this observation?
a. There are some text (e.g. 'Not measured') in this column
b. There are some empty entries in this column
c. DataFrame columns read from files are always of type 'Object'
d. You just need to apply astype() method.

3.11 Representing Dates and Times in Pandas

Pandas offers the **Timestamp()** function as a convenient way to define dates, times, or a combination of both. Unlike Python's approach, which requires separate objects for representing dates, times, or both, the Timestamp() function in Pandas serves as a unified solution. It is equivalent to the datetime.date, datetime.time, and datetime.datetime functions in Python.

The Pandas Timestamp() function is highly versatile and accommodates input in various formats. The examples below demonstrate different formats that yield the same Timestamp object:

```
print(pd.Timestamp(year=2024, month=12, day=25))
print(pd.Timestamp('25/12/2024'))
print(pd.Timestamp('12/25/2024'))
print(pd.Timestamp('25 December 2024'))
print(pd.Timestamp('December 25 2024'))
pd.Timestamp('25-12-2024')
```

Output (duplication removed):

```
2024-12-25 00:00:00
```

The pandas.Timestamp() function proves valuable for representing dates, times, or a combination of both. However, if the need arises to represent a duration of time, the pandas.Timedelta() function comes into play. This function generates an object designed to store a duration of time and is analogous to Python's datetime.timedelta function.

Similar to the Timestamp() function, the Timedelta() function in Pandas also provides flexibility in accepting input parameters. The examples below all generate the same output:

```
pd.Timedelta('3 days 7 minutes')
pd.Timedelta(days=3,minutes=7)
```

We can use the 'unit' parameter with the Timedelta() function to specify the desired unit of time. In the following example, the value of 'unit' is set to 'm' to represent minutes, and 4327 minutes are added to the base time of 00:00:00:

```
pd.Timedelta(4327, unit='m')
```

This creates a Timedelta object representing a duration of 4327 minutes. Other units that can be utilized with the 'unit' parameter include 's' for seconds, 'h' for hours, 'd' for days, and 'w' for weeks.

In Pandas, the Timedelta() function proves to be a valuable tool for performing arithmetic operations with time series data, including calculations of the time between events or the number of days, hours, minutes, and so on, between two dates. For instance, let's consider two dates as shown below. We can calculate the duration between these dates using the Timedelta() function as follows:

```
start_date = pd.Timestamp('2024-01-01')
end_date = pd.Timestamp('2024-01-03')
duration = end_date - start_date
print(duration)
```

This snippet would output "2 days 00:00:00," indicating that the duration between the two dates is two days.

The Timedelta() function in Pandas allows us to perform arithmetic operations with durations, such as addition or subtraction. For instance, we can add a duration of two days to the start date as shown:

```
new_date = start_date + pd.Timedelta(days=2)
print(new_date)
```

This code snippet would output "2024-01-03 00:00:00," which is the same as the end date.

Pandas provides the pd.to_datetime() function, which enables the conversion of date representations in the form of strings into Timestamp objects. These Timestamp objects can be utilized for various date operations, including comparison, duration addition/subtraction, and component extraction (e.g., day, month, year). The pd.to_datetime() function can handle dates that are not in the typical "day-month-year" or "month-day-year" formats.

Let's consider an example where we have a date represented as the string "11:20 AM, April 2nd 2023." We can use the pd.to_datetime function and specify the format parameter to correctly parse the individual components (hour, minute, day, month, year) of this date. The format parameter utilizes formatting codes such as %H for hour, %M for minute, %d for day, %m for month, and %Y for year.

```
a=pd.to_datetime('11:20,02/04/2023', format='%H:%M,%d/%m/%Y')
a
```
Output:

```
Timestamp('2023-04-02 11:20:00')
```

Now that the date has been converted into a Timestamp object, we can perform operations on it. For example, we can add four days to this date:

```
a+pd.Timedelta(4,unit='d')
```
Output:

```
Timestamp('2023-04-06 11:20:00')
```

After using the pd.to_datetime() function to convert a date string into a Pandas Timestamp object, we can access the individual components (e.g., year, month, day) of the date by using the corresponding attributes of the Timestamp object. For instance, we can extract the month, year, and day components as follows:

```
#extracting the month
print(f"Month: {a.month}")
#extracting the year
print(f"Year: {a.year}")
#extracting the day
print(f"Day: {a.day}")
```

Output:

```
Month: 4
Year: 2023
Day: 2
```

We can also utilize the minute and hour attributes to extract the minutes and hour from the date.

Review Question 3.84
Pandas provides a single function called _______ for defining dates, times, or a combination of both.
a. datetime
b. date
c. time
d. Timestamp

Review Question 3.85
How can the individual components of a date be accessed after converting it to a Pandas Timestamp object?
a. By using the extract_date_components function
b. By using the corresponding attributes of the Timestamp object
c. By calling the strftime method

d. By using the date function

Review Question 3.86
How can a time duration be added to or subtracted from a given date when working with Pandas Timestamp objects?
a. By using the add_duration function
b. By using the timedelta function
c. By using the duration function
d. By using the add method

Review Question 3.87
What is the purpose of the format parameter in the pd.to_datetime function?
a. To specify the format of the input date string
b. To specify the format of the output Timestamp object
c. To extract the individual components of the input date string
d. To compare two dates

Review Question 3.88
We can use the _______ parameter with the Timedelta function to specify the unit of time we want to use.
a. unit
b. format
c. time
d. use

3.12 Chapter Summary

This chapter covered reading and manipulating various data files using Pandas, highlighting tools for handling text files, binary files, and databases. We discussed the significance of data types and their impact on analysis performance, including converting DataFrame columns for effective manipulation. Pandas' handling of dates and times was explored, showcasing Timestamp for time representation and Timedelta for working with durations. Mastering these techniques enhances your proficiency in complex analysis tasks.

3.13 Solutions to the Review Questions

3.1 B; 3.2 B; 3.3 A; 3.4 B; 3.5 D; 3.6 C; 3.7 C; 3.8 B; 3.9 B; 3.10 B; 3.11 B; 3.12 B; 3.13 A; 3.14 D; 3.15 C; 3.16 D; 3.17 A; 3.18 B; 3.19 C; 3.20 D; 3.21 B; 3.22 D; 3.23 A; 3.24 A; 3.25 C; 3.26 B; 3.27 B; 3.28 B; 3.29 A; 3.30 C; 3.31 A; 3.32 C; 3.33 A; 3.34 B; 3.35 B; 3.36 C; 3.37 A; 3.38 A; 3.39 B; 3.40 B; 3.41 B; 3.42 B; 3.43 A; 3.44 B; 3.45 D; 3.46 B; 3.47 C; 3.48 B; 3.49 D; 3.50 A; 3.51 C; 3.52 A; 3.53 D; 3.54 A; 3.55 A; 3.56 C; 3.57 A; 3.58 D; 3.59 A; 3.60 C; 3.61 B; 3.62 C; 3.63 A; 3.64 C; 3.65 D; 3.66 C; 3.67 D; 3.68 D; 3.69 C; 3.70 C; 3.71 B; 3.72 C; 3.73 B; 3.74 C; 3.75 B; 3.76 C; 3.77 B; 3.78 D; 3.79 D; 3.80 D; 3.81 B; 3.82 C; 3.83 A; 3.84 D; 3.85 B; 3.86 B; 3.87 A; 3.88 A;

Chapter 4: Data Cleaning

Chapter Learning Objectives

4.1 Handle missing data effectively.
4.2 Detect and eliminate duplicate data.
4.3 Manipulate strings within data.
4.4 Perform data transformations to enhance analysis.
4.5 Identify and address outliers in the dataset.
4.6 Discretize continuous data for categorical analysis.

4.1 Introduction

Data cleansing, also known as data cleaning or data scrubbing, is the process of preparing a dataset in a pandas DataFrame by identifying and rectifying any issues present in the data. These issues can include errors, missing values, duplicates, and formatting inconsistencies. By leveraging the powerful capabilities of Pandas and the Python programming language, data cleansing can be performed efficiently and flexibly.

When working with datasets, it is common to encounter several issues that require cleansing. Some of these issues include:

1. *Missing values*: This is one of the most common issues. Data may be absent either because it was not collected or not provided by the data source. The missing data needs to be handled appropriately, either by filling it with a meaningful value (imputation) or by removing the data point entirely.
2. *Inconsistent column names*: Different individuals or sources may refer to the same entity using varying names or conventions.
3. *Inconsistent data*: This refers to data that is inconsistent in format, units, or representation. For example, dates might be represented differently in different parts of the dataset, or measurements might be recorded in different units.
4. *Complex data within columns*: A single column may contain multiple variables or complex data structures.
5. *Outliers*: Outliers are data points that are significantly different from other observations. They might be due to variability in the data or may indicate experimental errors. Outliers can significantly skew the results and need to be handled carefully.
6. *Data duplication*: Digital data can be inadvertently duplicated, for instance, if a user accidentally submits the same data multiple times. Duplicate data can lead to biased analysis and incorrect results. Therefore, it's important to identify and remove duplicates.
7. *Misaligned data structure*: The data may be structured incorrectly, such as being arranged horizontally instead of vertically or vice versa.
8. *Categorical data requiring numeric representation*: Variables may be categorical in nature, but they might need to

be converted to a numeric format for analysis and visualization purposes.

9. *Incorrect data type recognition*: The data type of a variable may not be accurately identified, leading to potential analysis errors.

10. *Incorrect formatting*: The data may contain extraneous spaces, commas, special symbols, or other formatting irregularities that require cleaning.

In this chapter, we will explore various techniques to address these data issues and perform data cleansing. You will learn how to handle missing and duplicate data. By acquiring these skills, you will be equipped to ensure the cleanliness and reliability of your datasets, enabling accurate analysis and interpretation of the underlying information.

Review Question 4.1

The process of cleaning up a dataset that has been loaded into a pandas dataframe is called data _______.

a. abstracting
b. cleansing
c. getting ready
d. identifying

Review Question 4.2

Which of the following is NOT a common task involved in data cleansing?

a. Identifying and correcting errors.
b. Identifying and correcting missing values.
c. Identifying and correcting duplicates or formatting issues.
d. Identifying and correcting rarely used data.

Review Question 4.3

Which of the following is a common issue that can arise in datasets?

a. Missing values.
b. Comprehensible column names.
c. Consistent organization.
d. Simple data in columns.

Review Question 4.4

Which of the following is a common issue that can arise in datasets?

a. Simple data in columns.
b. Single observational units.
c. Data duplication.
d. Aligned data structure.

Review Question 4.5

What is an example of a formatting issue that might need to be addressed through data cleansing?

a. A column containing multiple variables
b. Data structured around the wrong axis
c. Data containing spaces, commas, or special symbols
d. Categorical data that needs to be numeric

Review Question 4.6
What is data cleansing?
a. The process of organizing and formatting data for analysis and visualization.
b. The process of identifying and correcting errors or inconsistencies in a dataset.
c. The process of using methods like pivot, stack, and melt to manipulate data.
d. The process of converting data from wide to long format.

4.2 Handling Missing Data

Dealing with missing data is a crucial aspect of data analysis as it can significantly impact the validity and reliability of analytical results. Missing values have the potential to introduce biases, distort relationships between variables, and diminish the statistical power of tests employed in the analysis.

To illustrate this point, consider a scenario where a dataset contains missing values, and the objective is to build a predictive model. The presence of missing values can introduce bias into the model, potentially skewing the results. For instance, if certain groups are more likely to have missing values, the model might underrepresent these groups, leading to biased predictions. Consequently, drawing conclusions based on such a biased model may lead to erroneous interpretations and decisions.

Similarly, in statistical testing, the inclusion of missing values can impact the power of the test. Power refers to the ability of a statistical test to detect differences or relationships between variables. Improper handling of missing values can diminish the test's power, potentially resulting in false negatives (failure to detect actual differences) or false positives (erroneous detection of differences).

Given these considerations, it becomes imperative to handle missing data appropriately, taking into account the nature of the data and the specific analysis being conducted. Several strategies can be employed to address missing data, such as imputing missing values by replacing them with estimated values, excluding rows or columns with missing data, or employing advanced techniques like multiple imputation to consider the uncertainty introduced by the missing values.

Pandas employs the special numeric value NaN (Not a Number) as the default representation for missing data in numeric arrays. This sentinel value serves to indicate the absence or nullity of a value within such arrays. In non-numeric arrays, Pandas utilizes either the built-in Python value None or NaN from the Pandas library.

To gain hands-on experience with missing data handling in pandas, you can begin by executing the provided code snippet, which generates a sample dataset::

```python
import numpy as np
import pandas as pd
data = {'studentID':['12345', '12346', '12347', '12348', '12349'],
        'exam1':[56, 74, np.nan, 88, 95],
        'exam2':[98, 88, 85, None, 92],
        'exam3':[95, 91, 56, 79, 88]}
score_df=pd.DataFrame(data)
score_df
```

Output:

	studentID	exam1	exam2	exam3
0	12345	56.0	98.0	95
1	12346	74.0	88.0	91
2	12347	NaN	85.0	56
3	12348	88.0	NaN	79
4	12349	95.0	92.0	88

To identify the locations of missing data, the *isna()* method can be employed. This method returns a DataFrame of the same shape as the original DataFrame, where each position contains a Boolean value indicating whether the corresponding element is missing (True) or not (False). Executing the following:

```python
score_df.isna()
```

Output:

	studentID	exam1	exam2	exam3
0	False	False	False	False
1	False	False	False	False
2	False	True	False	False
3	False	False	True	False
4	False	False	False	False

The returned DataFrame is often called 'Boolean DataFrame', or 'mask DataFrame'. Using this Boolean mask, you can index the DataFrame to select only the rows or columns that contain missing values. Additionally, you can count the number of missing values in each column or across all columns. For example, the following operations can be performed:

```python
mask=score_df.isna()
# Select rows with missing values
missing_row=score_df[mask.any(axis=1)]
# Select columns with missing values
missing_column=score_df.loc[:, mask.any()]
# Count the number of missing values in each column
column_missing_count=score_df.isna().sum()
```

```python
# Count the number of missing values in all columns
all_missing_count=score_df.isna().sum().sum()
# Display
print(missing_row)
print(missing_column)
print(column_missing_count)
print(all_missing_count)
```

The mask.any(axis=1) expression allows you to select rows that contain at least one missing value, while mask.any() selects columns with missing values. The .sum() method is used to calculate the number of missing values within each column, and .sum().sum() provides the total count of missing values across the entire DataFrame.

When working with the axis=1 parameter, the specified function or operation is applied to each row of the DataFrame. The resulting values are then returned as a new DataFrame, which maintains the same number of rows but may have a different number of columns.

In statistical analysis, missing data (NA values) can arise from various factors like uncollected data or inherent collection issues. Handling missing data is crucial for data cleansing, as it can reveal collection problems or introduce biases. Examining missing data helps decide whether to impute values or remove rows with missing data.

There are two primary options for addressing missing data: dropping the values or replacing them with a suitable measure, such as the mean, median, or mode. These methods will be discussed in the subsequent sections.

Various approaches exist for filling in missing data, and the choice of method depends on the specific characteristics of the dataset and the underlying reasons for the missing values. Some commonly employed methods for handling missing data include:

1. *Mean/Median/Mode imputation*: When dealing with numerical missing values, one can substitute them with the mean, median, or mode of the non-missing values within the respective column.
2. *Predictive imputation*: Utilizing a machine learning model, missing values can be predicted based on the remaining values within the dataset.
3. *Interpolation*: If the missing values follow a time-based pattern and there are available data points both preceding and succeeding the missing values, interpolation can be employed to estimate the missing values by considering the surrounding data.
4. *Extrapolation*: In cases where the missing values exhibit a time-based trend, but there are only data points either before or after the missing values, extrapolation can be utilized to estimate the missing values by considering the data's overall trend.

5. *Dropping rows or columns*: If the missing values are too numerous or pervasive to be accurately imputed, one may opt to eliminate the rows or columns containing missing values altogether.

It is essential to carefully evaluate which method is most suitable for a given dataset, as employing an inappropriate approach can lead to biased or misleading results.

Review Question 4.7
Why is it important to handle missing data in data analysis?
a. To ensure that the data is complete and accurate.
b. To reduce the risk of biases and distortions in the results.
c. To ensure that nothing is left uncounted.
d. To reduce the probability of incorrect data input.

Review Question 4.8
In data analysis, which of the following is NOT an issue for missing values?
a. Lower total statistics.
b. Introduce biases
c. Distort relationships between variables
d. Reduce the power of statistical tests

Review Question 4.9
Depending on the _______ of the missing values, the mean may be higher or lower than it would be if the missing values were present.
a. number
b. frequency
c. distribution
d. number and distribution

Review Question 4.10
The ability of a statistical test to detect a difference or relationship between variables is called _______.
a. ability
b. power
c. force
d. hypotheses tests

Review Question 4.11
It is important to handle missing data in a way that is appropriate for the data and the analysis being performed, in order to ensure that the results are _______.
a. as expected
b. accurate
c. reliable
d. accurate and reliable

Review Question 4.12
Pandas handles missing data with the numeric value _______ by default.
a. None
b. NaN

c. Null

d. empty space

Review Question 4.13

In non-numeric arrays, Pandas uses the _______ by default.

a. None

b. NaN

c. Null

d. None or NaN

Review Question 4.14

The isna() method in pandas is used to detect and return a _______ mask indicating whether each value in a DataFrame is missing.

a. integer

b. floating-point

c. Boolean

d. str

Review Question 4.15

Suppose you have a DataFrame df and a mask that was assigned the df.isna(). How do you select rows with missing values?

a. rows=df[mask]

b. rows=df[mask.any()]

c. rows=df[mask.any(axis=0)]

d. rows=df[mask.any(axis=1)]

Review Question 4.16

Suppose you have a DataFrame df and a mask that was assigned the df.isna(). How do you select columns with missing values?

a. columns=df[mask]

b. columns=df.loc[:, mask.any()]

c. columns=df[mask.any(axis=0)]

d. columns=df.loc[mask.any(axis=1)]

Review Question 4.17

Suppose you have a DataFrame df and a mask that was assigned the df.isna(). How do you count the number of missing values in each column?

a. counts=df[mask].sum()

b. counts=df[mask].sum(axis=0)

c. counts=df[mask].sum(axis=1)]

d. counts=mask.sum()

Review Question 4.18

Suppose you have a DataFrame df and a mask that was assigned the df.isna(). How do you count the number of missing values in the whole DataFrame?

a. count=df.sum()

b. rows=df[mask].sum(axis=0)

c. rows=df[mask].sum(axis=1)]

d. rows=mask.sum().sum()

Exercise 4.1

The code snippet below generates a DataFrame that represents the sales records of five employees for the year 2024, broken down by quarters.

```python
import numpy as np
import pandas as pd
data = {
    'employeeID': ['12345', '12346', '12347', '12348', '12349'],
    'Q1 2024': [56, 74, np.nan, 88, 95],
    'Q2 2024': [98, 88, 85, None, 92],
    'Q3 2024': [95, 91, 56, 79, 88],
    'Q4 2024': [81, 65, np.nan, 55, 91]
}
sale_df = pd.DataFrame(data)
sale_df
```

Complete the following tasks:
Task 1: Generate a Boolean DataFrame of the same size as sale_df. Each cell should indicate whether the corresponding value in sale_df is null.
Task 2: Use the Boolean DataFrame to select rows in sale_df that contain missing values. Store these rows in a variable.
Task 3: Similarly, use the Boolean DataFrame to select columns in sale_df that contain missing values. Store these columns in a variable.
Task 4: Count the number of missing values in each column of sale_df and store the counts in a variable.
Task 5: Count the total number of missing values in sale_df and store this count in a variable.
Task 6: Display the values stored in the variables from Tasks 2 to 5.

4.3 Filtering Out Missing Data

In Pandas, there are multiple ways to filter out missing data in a DataFrame. One approach is to use the pandas.isna() function along with Boolean indexing to identify and remove rows or columns that contain missing values as you learned in the last section. Another method is to utilize the DataFrame.dropna() method, which, by default, drops any rows that have any missing values. For example, if we apply the dropna() method to the score_df DataFrame:

```python
score_df.dropna()
```

Output:

	studentID	exam1	exam2	exam3
0	12345	56.0	98.0	95
1	12346	74.0	88.0	91
4	12349	95.0	92.0	88

This resulting DataFrame contains only the rows that do not have any missing values.

The dropna() method in pandas provides flexibility for dropping rows or columns based on various conditions using optional parameters. These parameters allow you to specify criteria such as dropping rows or columns with all missing values or only those with a certain number of missing values. When using the dropna() method, you can use the how parameter to determine how missing values should be treated. The default value is how='any', meaning that any row or column containing at least one missing value will be dropped. To illustrate this, let's consider the score_df DataFrame with a new row of all missing values:

```
score_df.loc[len(score_df.index)] = None
score_df
```
Output:

	studentID	exam1	exam2	exam3
0	12345	56.0	98.0	95.0
1	12346	74.0	88.0	91.0
2	12347	NaN	85.0	56.0
3	12348	88.0	NaN	79.0
4	12349	95.0	92.0	88.0
5	NaN	NaN	NaN	NaN

To drop rows that are completely missing, you can use the following code:

```
score_df_cleaned = score_df.dropna(how='all')
score_df_cleaned
```
Output:

	studentID	exam1	exam2	exam3
0	12345	56.0	98.0	95.0
1	12346	74.0	88.0	91.0
2	12347	NaN	85.0	56.0
3	12348	88.0	NaN	79.0
4	12349	95.0	92.0	88.0

This creates a new DataFrame score_df_cleaned with the rows that are completely missing removed. Note that if you want to modify the original DataFrame in place, you can set the inplace parameter to True.

Similarly, you can drop columns with all missing values. First, add a column with all missing values:

```
score_df_cleaned.loc[:,'exam4'] = None
score_df_cleaned
```

Output:

	studentID	exam1	exam2	exam3	exam4
0	12345	56.0	98.0	95.0	None
1	12346	74.0	88.0	91.0	None
2	12347	NaN	85.0	56.0	None
3	12348	88.0	NaN	79.0	None
4	12349	95.0	92.0	88.0	None

In a new cell, add the following lines:

```
score_df_cleaned_column = score_df_cleaned.dropna(how='all', axis=1)
score_df_cleaned_column
```

Output:

	studentID	exam1	exam2	exam3
0	12345	56.0	98.0	95.0
1	12346	74.0	88.0	91.0
2	12347	NaN	85.0	56.0
3	12348	88.0	NaN	79.0
4	12349	95.0	92.0	88.0

The how parameter of the dropna() method has two possible values:

Parameter value	Explanation	Example
any (default)	Drops rows or columns that contain any missing values.	df.dropna(how='any') df.dropna(how='any', axis=1)
All	Drops rows or columns that are completely missing, i.e., all values in the row are missing.	df.dropna(how='all') df.dropna(how='all', axis=1)

To demonstrate the **thresh** parameter, let's replace student 12347's exam3 score with None:

```
score_df_cleaned_column.iloc[2, 3] = None
score_df_cleaned_column
```

Output:

	studentID	exam1	exam2	exam3
0	12345	56.0	98.0	95.0
1	12346	74.0	88.0	91.0
2	12347	NaN	85.0	NaN
3	12348	88.0	NaN	79.0
4	12349	95.0	92.0	88.0

Next, to keep rows with at least three non-missing values, you can use the thresh parameter:

```
score_df_cleaned_column_at_least_3 =
score_df_cleaned_column.dropna(thresh=3)
score_df_cleaned_column_at_least_3
```

Output:

	studentID	exam1	exam2	exam3
0	12345	56.0	98.0	95.0
1	12346	74.0	88.0	91.0
3	12348	88.0	NaN	79.0
4	12349	95.0	92.0	88.0

The dropna() method of a DataFrame includes a subset parameter that enables you to specify the columns to consider when searching for missing values. For instance, if your intention is to drop rows where values in the 'exam1' column are missing, you can set subset=['exam1']. Here's an example:

```python
# Drop any row that misses the exam1
score_df.dropna(subset=['exam1'])
```

Review Question 4.19
The DataFrame.dropna() method, by default, will drop _______.
a. any missing values
b. any rows that contain any missing values
c. no data
d. no data unless you use some of its parameters

Review Question 4.20
The DataFrame.dropna() method has a _______ parameter that allows you to specify a list of columns to check for missing values.
a. specify
b. list
c. subset
d. columns

Review Question 4.21
The DataFrame.dropna() method has a _______ parameter that allows you to specify a minimum number of non-missing values required in a row or column before it is retained.
a. min
b. max
c. thresh
d. non-missing

Review Question 4.22
The DataFrame.dropna() method has a _______ parameter that allows you to specify how missing values should be treated.
a. how
b. specify
c. treat
d. treated

Review Question 4.23
What is the default value for the how parameter of the DataFrame.dropna() method?
a. None
b. all
c. default
d. any

Review Question 4.24
Suppose you have a DataFrame df. What will the following code do?
```python
df.dropna(how='any')
```
a. Delete any rows with any missing values.
b. Delete any columns with any missing values.
c. Delete any rows or any columns with any missing values.
d. Delete rows or columns any way you desire.

Review Question 4.25
Suppose you have a DataFrame df. What will the following code do?
`df.dropna(how='any', axis=0)`
a. Delete any rows with any missing values.
b. Delete any columns with any missing values.
c. Delete any rows or any columns with any missing values.
d. Delete rows or columns any way you desire.

Review Question 4.26
Suppose you have a DataFrame df. What will the following code do?
`df.dropna(axis=0)`
a. Delete any rows with any missing values.
b. Delete any columns with any missing values.
c. Delete any rows or any columns with any missing values.
d. Delete rows or columns any way you desire.

Review Question 4.27
Suppose you have a DataFrame df. What will the following code do?
`df.dropna(how='any', axis=1)`
a. Delete any rows with any missing values.
b. Delete any columns with any missing values.
c. Delete any rows or any columns with any missing values.
d. Delete rows or columns any way you desire.

Review Question 4.28
Suppose you have a DataFrame df. What will the following code do?
`df.dropna(how='all', axis=1)`
a. Delete any rows with completely missing values.
b. Delete any columns with completely missing values.
c. Delete any rows or any columns with any missing values.
d. Delete any rows or any columns with completely missing values.

Review Question 4.29
Suppose you have a DataFrame df. What will the following code do? `df.dropna(how='all', axis=0)`
a. Delete any rows with completely missing values.
b. Delete any columns with completely missing values.
c. Delete any rows or any columns with any missing values.
d. Delete any rows or any columns with completely missing values.

Review Question 4.30
Suppose you have a DataFrame df. What will the following code do?
`df.dropna(how='all')`
a. Delete any rows with completely missing values.
b. Delete any columns with completely missing values.
c. Delete any rows or any columns with any missing values.
d. Delete any rows or any columns with completely missing values.

Review Question 4.31
The _______ parameter in the dropna() method of a pandas.DataFrame specifies the minimum number of

non-NA/null values required to keep a row (or column).
a. how
b. min
c. minnull
d. thresh

Exercise 4.2

In this exercise, you will be working with the **sale_df** DataFrame that you created in Exercise 4.1. Please note that the dataset may contain more than five employees. Your tasks are as follows:
Task 1: Remove all rows from the DataFrame that contain any missing data.
Task 2: Add a new record for an employee. This record should contain null values for all fields.
Task 3: Use the how parameter to remove all records that contain null values for all fields.
Task 4: Add a new column to the DataFrame named 'Q5 2024'. This column should contain null values for all records.
Task 5: Use the how parameter to remove all columns that contain null values for all records.
Task 6: Retain only those rows in the DataFrame that have at least four non-missing values.
Task 7: Remove all records of employees who do not have a value for 'Q2 2024'.

4.4 Imputation

Imputation is the process of replacing missing values with estimates. In Pandas, the fillna() method can be

used to substitute missing values with measures of central tendencies such as the mean, median, or mode.

Alternatively, you can use the fillna() method to fill missing values with a fixed or constant value, such as 0.

The fillna() method also allows you to use the forward fill technique to fill missing values with the value just

before it or the backward fill technique to fill missing values with the value just after it. Here is an example

code snippet to demonstrate how to fill missing values using different techniques:

```
data = {'studentID':['12345', '12346', '12347', '12348', '12349'],
        'exam1':[56, 74, np.nan, 88, 95],
        'exam2':[98, 88, 85, None, 92],
        'exam3':[95, 91, 56, 79, 88]}
score_df=pd.DataFrame(data)
score_df
```
Output:

	studentID	exam1	exam2	exam3
0	12345	56.0	98.0	95
1	12346	74.0	88.0	91
2	12347	NaN	85.0	56
3	12348	88.0	NaN	79
4	12349	95.0	92.0	88

```
# Forward fill technique
score_df_filled = score_df.fillna(method='ffill')
score_df_filled
```

Output:

	studentID	exam1	exam2	exam3
0	12345	56.0	98.0	95
1	12346	74.0	88.0	91
2	12347	74.0	85.0	56
3	12348	88.0	85.0	79
4	12349	95.0	92.0	88

```
# Backward fill technique
score_df_filled = score_df.fillna(method='bfill')
score_df_filled
```

	studentID	exam1	exam2	exam3
0	12345	56.0	98.0	95
1	12346	74.0	88.0	91
2	12347	88.0	85.0	56
3	12348	88.0	92.0	79
4	12349	95.0	92.0	88

```
# Fill with mean values
score_df_filled = score_df.fillna(score_df.mean())
score_df_filled
```

	studentID	exam1	exam2	exam3
0	12345	56.00	98.00	95
1	12346	74.00	88.00	91
2	12347	78.25	85.00	56
3	12348	88.00	90.75	79
4	12349	95.00	92.00	88

```
# Fill with constant values
score_df_filled = score_df.fillna(0)
score_df_filled
```

	studentID	exam1	exam2	exam3
0	12345	56.0	98.0	95
1	12346	74.0	88.0	91
2	12347	0.0	85.0	56
3	12348	88.0	0.0	79
4	12349	95.0	92.0	88

```
# Fill with different values for each column
score_df_filled = score_df.fillna({'exam1': 70, 'exam2': 0})
score_df_filled
```

	studentID	exam1	exam2	exam3
0	12345	56.0	98.0	95
1	12346	74.0	88.0	91
2	12347	70.0	85.0	56
3	12348	88.0	0.0	79
4	12349	95.0	92.0	88

Note that the fillna() method does not modify the original DataFrame without the inplace=True parameter. As we can see in the forward fill example, the exam1 field for student 12347 is filled with the corresponding value from student 12346 (the record that precedes it). The same applies to the exam2 field for student 12348. Similarly, the backward fill technique replaces missing values with the next valid observation from the row that follows. In the mean imputation example, it is worth noting that the average value for exam1 is 78.25, while the average value for exam2 is 90.75.

Review Question 4.32
In data science, _______ is the process of replacing missing values with estimates for a dataset.
a. imputation
b. replacing
c. substitution
d. estimation

Review Question 4.33
In Pandas, the _______ method can be used to substitute missing values with measures of central tendencies such as the mean, median, or mode.
a. central()
b. tendency()
c. central_tendency()
d. fillna()

Review Question 4.34
Suppose df is a DataFrame. What will the following code do?
```
df.fillna(method= 'ffill')
```
a. Fill a missing value with the value from the previous row of the same column.
b. Fill a missing value with the value from the previous column of the same row.
c. Fill a missing value with the value that is most close to it.
d. An error because two fs in the method parameter value should be just one f.

Review Question 4.35
Suppose df is a DataFrame. What will the following code do?
```
df.fillna(method= 'bfill')
```
a. Fill a missing value with the value from the next row of the same column.
b. Fill a missing value with the value from the next column of the same row.
c. Fill a missing value with the value that is most close to it.
d. An error because bf should be just f in the method parameter value.

Review Question 4.36
Suppose df is a DataFrame with some missing values. How do you fill a missing value with the mean of its column?
a. df.fillna(df.column.mean)
b. df.fillna(df.column.mean())

c. df.fillna(df.mean)
d. df.fillna(df.mean())

Review Question 4.37
Suppose df is a DataFrame with some missing values. How do you fill all missing values with 70?
a. df.fillna(70)
b. df.fillna(value=70)
c. df.fillna(missing=70)
d. df.fillna(missing_value=70)

Review Question 4.38
Suppose df is a DataFrame with some missing values. How do you fill all missing values in column1 with 70 and missing values in column2 with 80?
a. df.fillna(70, 80)
b. df.fillna(value=[70, 80])
c. df.fillna({'column1':70, 'column2':80})
d. You cannot fill in two values for the same DataFrame.

Exercise 4.3
In this exercise, you'll be working with the sale_df DataFrame, which you created in Exercise 4.1. Keep in mind that the dataset may include data for more than five employees. Display the result of each task without altering the original DataFrame. Here are your tasks:
Task 1: Replace any missing values with the value that precedes it in the same field.
Task 2: Replace any missing values with the value that follows it in the same field.
Task 3: Replace any missing values with the mean value of the respective column.
Task 4: Replace any missing values with a constant value of 30.
Task 5: For the quarters of 2024, replace any missing values as follows: 'Q1 2024' with 10, 'Q2 2024' with 20, 'Q3 2024' with 30, and 'Q4 2024' with 40.

4.5 Interpolation

Interpolation is a method used to estimate the value of a point that lies between two known points on a line or curve. The most commonly used interpolation method is linear interpolation, which involves calculating the value of the unknown point using the equation of a straight line. Linear interpolation requires two known points (x_0, y_0) and (x_1, y_1), and it estimates the value of the unknown point (x, y) using the following equation:

$$y - y_0 = \frac{y_1 - y_0}{x_1 - x_0} (x - x_0)$$

This equation determines the slope of the line between the two known points and uses it to estimate the value of the unknown point. Interpolation is particularly useful when dealing with datasets that contain missing values, as it allows for the estimation of those missing values.

The pandas library provides the interpolate() method, which is a useful tool for interpolating missing values in a DataFrame. To demonstrate its usage, consider the following line of code in a new cell:

```
score_df.interpolate(method = 'linear')
```

Output:

	StudentID	exam1	exam2	exam3
0	12345	56.0	98.0	95
1	12346	74.0	88.0	91
2	12347	81.0	85.0	56
3	12348	88.0	88.5	79
4	12349	95.0	92.0	88

Now, let's manually compute the exam1 value for student 12347 using linear interpolation. By default, the adjacent points above (0, 74) and below (2, 88) are considered, assuming equal distances between the points: Using the formula (x = 1):

$$y - y_0 = \frac{y_1 - y_0}{x_1 - x_0} (x - x_0); \quad y - 74 = \frac{88 - 74}{2 - 0} (1 - 0)$$

y = 14/2 + 74 = 7 + 74 = 81.

The interpolate() method in pandas supports various interpolation methods, including:

1. linear: Uses linear interpolation to fill missing values.
2. nearest: Fills missing values with the value of the nearest non-missing data point.
3. zero: Fills missing values with zeros.

Additionally, you can specify options such as the axis along which interpolation should be performed and the limit on the number of consecutive missing values to fill.

Review Question 4.39
The _______ is a method of estimating the value of a point that falls between two known points on a line or curve.
a. estimation
b. value estimation
c. line estimation
d. interpolation

Review Question 4.40
The _______ is a method of estimating the value of a point that falls between two known points on a straight line.
a. estimation
b. linear interpolation
c. line estimation

d. interpolation

Review Question 4.41
The most common interpolation method is ________, which uses the equation of a straight line to calculate the value of the unknown point.
a. estimation
b. linear interpolation
c. line estimation
d. interpolation

Review Question 4.42
The ________ method is a function in the pandas library that can be used to interpolate missing values in a DataFrame.
a. estimate()
b. linear()
c. interpolate()
d. interpolate_missing()

Review Question 4.43
There are several interpolation methods that you can use with the interpolate() method. Which of the following is NOT such a method in Pandas?
a. linear
b. nearest
c. zero
d. ffill

Exercise 4.4
In this exercise, you'll be working with the sale_df DataFrame, which you created in Exercise 4.1. Fill any missing values with interpolation (try both linear and nearest methods in two separate statements.).

4.6 Handle Data Duplication

Redundancy in data refers to the occurrence of the same information being repeated in multiple records within a dataset. This redundancy can lead to inefficiencies and inaccuracies in data analysis and storage.

Let's consider the following DataFrame as an example:

```python
import pandas as pd
data = {'studentID':['12345', '12346', '12347', '12348', '12349',
'12345'],
        'exam1':[56, 74, 96, 88, 95, 56],
        'exam2':[88, 88, 85, 94, 92, 88],
        'exam3':[95, 91, 56, 79, 88, 95]}
duplicated_df=pd.DataFrame(data)
duplicated_df
```

Output:

	studentID	exam1	exam2	exam3
0	12345	56	88	95
1	12346	74	88	91
2	12347	96	85	56
3	12348	88	94	79
4	12349	95	92	88
5	12345	56	88	95

In this DataFrame, the student with ID "12345" appears twice with the same exam scores.

To identify duplicate rows in a DataFrame, Pandas provides the duplicated() method. When applied to a DataFrame, this method returns a Boolean value for each row, indicating whether the row is a duplicate of a previously seen row. Using the above DataFrame as an example, we can detect duplicates as follows:

```
duplicated_df.duplicated()
```

Output:

```
0       False
1       False
2       False
3       False
4       False
5        True
dtype: bool
```

In the output, the value "True" indicates that the corresponding rows are duplicates of previously seen rows. For instance, row 5 is a duplicate of row 0 since it has identical values across all columns.

By using the sum() method in conjunction with duplicated(), we can determine the total number of duplicated rows in the DataFrame:

```
duplicated_df.duplicated().sum()
```
Output:

1

To eliminate duplicates, we can utilize the drop_duplicates() method:

```
duplicated_df.drop_duplicates()
```

Output:

	studentID	exam1	exam2	exam3
0	12345	56	88	95
1	12346	74	88	91
2	12347	96	85	56
3	12348	88	94	79
4	12349	95	92	88

Note: drop_duplicates() does not modify the original DataFrame unless the inplace parameter is specified.

By default, drop_duplicates() retains the first occurrence of a duplicate row. However, if we want to keep the last occurrence instead, we can use the keep='last' parameter:

```
duplicated_df.drop_duplicates(keep="last")
```

Output:

	studentID	exam1	exam2	exam3
1	12346	74	88	91
2	12347	96	85	56
3	12348	88	94	79
4	12349	95	92	88
5	12345	56	88	95

By default, drop_duplicates() considers all columns when detecting duplicates. However, you can specify a subset of columns using the subset parameter. For example, the following code removes two rows based on the exam2 column, as there are three occurrences of the value 88, and only the first occurrence is kept:

```
duplicated_df.drop_duplicates(subset=['exam2'])
```

Output:

	studentID	exam1	exam2	exam3
0	12345	56	88	95
2	12347	96	85	56
3	12348	88	94	79
4	12349	95	92	88

Review Question 4.44
Which of the following statements is true about a DataFrame that contains redundancy?
a. The DataFrame contains multiple records with different data.
b. The DataFrame contains multiple records with the same data.
c. The DataFrame contains a single record with different data.
d. The DataFrame contains a single record with the same data.

Review Question 4.45
Suppose df is a DataFrame. What is the result of the following code execution?
df.duplicated()
a. It returns a Boolean value for each row indicating whether the row is a duplicate of a previous row.
b. It returns a Boolean value for each column indicating whether the column is a duplicate of a previous column.
c. It returns all duplicated values of the df.

d. It returns a Boolean DataFrame for each cell indicating whether the cell is a duplicate of a previous one.

Review Question 4.46
Suppose df is a DataFrame. How do you find out total number of duplicated rows in it?
a. df.duplicated
b. df.duplicated()
c. df.duplicated().sum
d. df.duplicated().sum()

Review Question 4.47
Suppose df is a DataFrame. What is the result of the following code execution?
df.drop_duplicates()
a. Remove all duplicated cells.
b. Remove all duplicated rows.
c. Remove all duplicated rows except the first one.
d. Remove all duplicated rows except one.

Review Question 4.48
Suppose df is a DataFrame. How to remove all duplicate rows except the last row?
a. df.drop_duplicates(last)
b. df.drop_duplicates(drop_first)
c. df.drop_duplicates(keep_last)
d. df.drop_duplicates(keep="last")

Review Question 4.49
Suppose df is a DataFrame and based_columns is a list of columns. How to remove duplicates based on based_columns?
a. df.drop_duplicates(drop=based_columns)
b. df.drop_duplicates(subset=based_columns)
c. df.drop_duplicates(base=based_columns)
d. df.drop_duplicates(base_column=based_columns)

Exercise 4.5

The code snippet below generates a DataFrame that represents the sales records of five employees for the year 2024, broken down by quarters.

```python
import numpy as np
import pandas as pd
data = {
    'employeeID': ['12345', '12346', '12347', '12348', '12345'],
    'Q1 2024': [56, 56, np.nan, 88, 56],
    'Q2 2024': [98, 88, 85, None, 98],
    'Q3 2024': [95, 91, 56, 79, 95],
    'Q4 2024': [81, 65, np.nan, 55, 81]
}
sale_df = pd.DataFrame(data)
sale_df
```

Complete the following tasks:

Task 1: Generate a Boolean value for each row, indicating whether the row is a duplicate of a previously seen row.

Task 2: Calculate the total number of duplicated rows in the sale_df DataFrame.

Task 3: Eliminate duplicates and keep only the first occurrence.

Task 4: Eliminate duplicates and keep only the last occurrence.

Task 5: Eliminate duplicates based on employeeID and "Q1 2024" columns.

4.7 Transform Data

Data transformation involves converting data from one format or structure to another. This process prepares data for further analysis and visualization. It is particularly useful for cleaning and preprocessing data. For example, if you're working with a dataset of customer reviews for a product, the raw data might contain typos, missing ratings, or inconsistent date formats. Data transformation can help clean this data by correcting typos using spell check algorithms, imputing missing ratings with the average rating, and standardizing date formats to a common format like 'YYYY-MM-DD'.

Data transformation is also useful for enhancing interpretability. Let's say you have a large dataset of tweets about a particular event. The raw data might be hard to interpret due to the use of slang, abbreviations, and the sheer volume of tweets. Data transformation can help you select relevant tweets, aggregate them by themes using text analysis techniques, and summarize the sentiment of tweets, making the data more meaningful and easier to understand.

Data transformation prepares the data for advanced analysis techniques. Different analytical methods and tools require specific data formats or structures. For instance, some techniques may necessitate tabular data, while others may require specific data types (e.g., numerical or categorical). Data transformation assists in reshaping and converting the data into the required format or structure.

Data transformation improves the performance of analytical models. Certain models perform better when applied to transformed data rather than raw data. For example, a linear regression model may deliver superior results with data that follows a normal distribution, as opposed to skewed raw data. Data transformation aids in optimizing the performance of analytical models by converting the data into a more suitable format or structure.

Pandas provides the map() method, which can be used with a dictionary to transform the values in a Series or DataFrame. To utilize the map() method with a dictionary, pass the dictionary as an argument to the map() method. The dictionary should establish the mapping between the old values and the corresponding new values. Here's an example demonstrating the use of the map() method in a Series:

```python
# Create a series with some values
s = pd.Series([1, 2, 3, 4])
# Define a dictionary with the the old values and the new values
mapping = {1: 'one', 2: 'two', 3: 'three', 4: 'four'}
# Use the map() method with the dictionary to transform the values
s_transformed = s.map(mapping)
print(s_transformed)
```

The output of this code will be a new Series with the transformed values:

```
0       one
1       two
2     three
3      four
dtype: object
```

The map() method can also be used with a dictionary to transform the values in a DataFrame. To achieve this, specify the name of the column you want to transform and pass the dictionary as the argument:

```python
# Create a dataframe with some values
df = pd.DataFrame({'col1': [1, 2, 3, 4], 'col2': [5, 6, 7, 8]})
# Define a dictionary with the old values and the new values
mapping = {1: 'one', 2: 'two', 3: 'three', 4: 'four'}
# Use the map() method with the dictionary to transform the values
df['col1'] = df['col1'].map(mapping)
print(df)
```

The output of this code will be a new DataFrame with the transformed values in the 'col1' column:

```
    col1  col2
0    one     5
1    two     6
2  three     7
3   four     8
```

In addition to a dictionary, the map() method can also work on a function: For instance, let's consider the DataFrame provided earlier. We can use the map() method to apply a function to each element in the 'col2' column like this:

```python
def plus10(x):
    return x +10
df.col2.map(plus10)
```

The map() method returns a new Series with the transformed data:

```
0       15
1       16
2       17
3       18
Name: col2, dtype: int64
```

While the map() method is useful for applying simple transformations to a Series or DataFrame, it may not be suitable for more complex operations or transformations that involve multiple steps. In such cases, it is better to use other methods like apply() or applymap().

Example 4.1

Use map() method for abbreviations.

```
data = {'studentID':['12345', '12346', '12347', '12348'],
        'class':['Freshman', 'Sophomore', 'Freshman', 'Senior']}
score_df=pd.DataFrame(data)
score_df
```

Output:

	studentID	class
0	12345	Freshman
1	12346	Sophomore
2	12347	Freshman
3	12348	Senior

Next, enter the following:

```
class_abbr = {'Freshman':'F', 'Sophomore':'SO'}
score_df['class_abbr'] = score_df['class'].map(class_abbr)
score_df
```

Output:

	studentID	class	class_abbr
0	12345	Freshman	F
1	12346	Sophomore	SO
2	12347	Freshman	F
3	12348	Senior	NaN

Review Question 4.50
Data _______ is the process of converting data from one format or structure into another format or structure.
a. formation
b. transformation
c. structure
d. processing

Review Question 4.51
Why do we need data transformation in data analytics?
a. It helps to secure data from attackers.

b. It helps to clean and preprocess the data.
c. It helps data scientists who speak different languages.
d. It helps decision makers make better decisions.

Review Question 4.52
Why do we need data transformation in data analytics?
a. It helps to secure data from attackers.
b. It helps to retrieve data easier.
c. It helps to make the data more meaningful and understandable.
d. It helps decision makers make better decisions.

Review Question 4.53
Why do we need data transformation in data analytics?
a. It helps to secure data from attackers.
b. It helps to retrieve data easier.
c. It helps to take less room for storage.
d. It helps to prepare the data for further analysis.

Review Question 4.54
Why do we need data transformation in data analytics?
a. It helps to improve the performance of analytical models.
b. It helps to retrieve data easier.
c. It helps to take less room for storage.
d. It helps to both store and retrieve data faster.

Review Question 4.55
Given the following code:

```
df = pd.DataFrame({'col1': [1, 2, 3, 4], 'col2': [5, 6, 7, 8]})
mapping = {1: 'one', 2: 'two', 3: 'three', 4: 'four'}
```

How do you replace numbers in col1 to corresponding words?
a. df.mapping(map)
b. df.map(mapping)
c. df['col1'].mapping(map)
d. df['col1'].map(mapping)

Review Question 4.56
The _______ method is a function in the Python Pandas library that applies a function to every element in a series or dataframe.
a. function()
b. application()
c. map()
d. every()

4.8 Replace Values

To enhance the usefulness of data for analysis, it's often necessary to remove or replace certain values. The `replace()` method in Pandas is a powerful and flexible tool for this purpose. Unlike the `map()` method, which is more limited, `replace()` allows for the substitution of single values, lists, or dictionaries of values. This makes it particularly valuable in business data analytics, where maintaining data quality is crucial for accurate analysis and decision-making.

To use the replace() method, the values to be replaced must be specified as the first argument. This can be a single value or a list of values. For instance, to replace all occurrences of the value "White" with "Red" in a column, the following code can be used:

```python
student_data = pd.read_csv("chapter3e6.csv")
student_data
```

In a new cell, enter the following:

```python
student_data['FavoriteColor'].replace("White", "Red")
```

Alternatively, a dictionary of values can be specified for replacement. In this case, the keys of the dictionary represent the values to be replaced, and the values represent the replacements. To replace multiple values at once, the following code can be used:

```python
student_data['FavoriteColor'].replace({"Green": "G", "Blue":"B"})
```

The inplace argument can be set to True to make the replacement permanent:

```python
student_data['FavoriteColor'].replace("White", "Red", inplace=True)
student_data
```

Additionally, the replace() method offers several optional arguments that allow for further customization of replacements. For example, the regex argument can be used to specify a regular expression pattern to match against, and the method argument can be used to define how mismatches should be handled.

It is important to differentiate between the replace() method and the str.replace() method in the Pandas library. While both methods allow for value replacement, they operate differently and are best suited for different types of replacements.

The replace() method is a versatile tool that can replace values in a DataFrame with a specified value, list of values, or dictionary of values. It can be applied to any data type and is particularly useful for replacing multiple values at once.

On the other hand, the str.replace() method is specifically designed for replacing string values and is a method of the str attribute of a DataFrame. It operates by applying a regular expression pattern to the values in a column and replacing any matches with a specified value. Here's an example of using the str.replace() method to replace all occurrences of the string "Red" with "R" in a column:

```
student_data['FavoriteColor'].str.replace("Red", "R")
```

One key difference is that the replace() method can only replace exact values, whereas the str.replace() method can replace a character or utilize regular expressions to match and replace more complex patterns.

Review Question 4.57
How to replace all "red" with "green" in a DataFrame df column called "color"?
a. df['color'].replace("red", "green")
b. replace(df, "red", "green")
c. df.replace("red", "green")
d. df.replace("color", "red", "green")

Review Question 4.58
You can specify a _______ of values to the replace() method of a DataFrame. In this case, the _______ represent the values to be replaced, and the _______ represent the replacements.
a. list, elements of the list, indexes of the list
b. list, indexes of the list, elements of the list
c. dictionary, keys of the dictionary, values of the dictionary
d. dictionary, values of the dictionary, keys of the dictionary

Review Question 4.59
Which of the following statements is correct about the `replace()` method in Pandas?
a. The `replace()` method can only replace one value at a time in a single column.
b. The `replace()` method can be used to replace values in a single column or Series, but not across multiple columns.
c. The `replace()` method can replace values in multiple columns or Series at once.
d. The `replace()` method can only replace values if they are specified as a list or dictionary.

Review Question 4.60
What is a key difference between the replace method and the str.replace method in Pandas?
a. The replace method can only be used on string columns, while the str.replace method can be used on any data type.
b. The replace method can only replace exact values, while the str.replace method can use regular expressions to match and replace more complex patterns.
c. The replace method can only work on a single column at a time, while the str.replace method can work on multiple columns at once.
d. The replace method can be used to replace values in a single column or series, while the str.replace method can only be used to replace values across multiple columns.

4.9 Modify Axis

In data analysis and manipulation, transforming the axis labels of a dataframe is often necessary. A dataframe is a two-dimensional tabular data structure with rows and columns. The axis labels refer to the row and column labels of a dataframe. The row labels are also known as the index, while the column labels are simply called the columns. Transforming the axis labels can be done in various ways to meet the requirements of data analysis.

One approach to transform the axis labels of a dataframe is by utilizing the rename() method. This method enables renaming the columns or index of a dataframe. For instance, let's consider a dataframe df with columns 'col_1' and 'col_2', and we want to rename these columns to 'column_1' and 'column_2', respectively. The following code demonstrates this:

```python
df = df.rename(columns={'col_1': 'column_1', 'col_2': 'column_2'})
```

Similarly, the rename() method can be employed to rename the index labels of a dataframe. Suppose we have a dataframe df with index 'ind_1' and 'ind_2', and we wish to rename these index labels to 'index_1' and 'index_2', respectively. The code snippet below accomplishes this:

```python
df = df.rename(index={'ind_1': 'index_1', 'ind_2': 'index_2'})
```

Example 4.2

The following code will create a DataFrame df with five students and three exams:

```python
data = {'studentID':['lucy', 'lisa', 'scott', 'adam', 'bob'],
        'exam 1':[56, 74, 96, 88, 95],
        'exam 2':[88, 88, 85, 94, 92],
        'exam 3':[95, 91, 56, 79, 88]}
df=pd.DataFrame(data)
df.set_index('studentID', inplace=True)
df
```

Output:

studentID	exam 1	exam 2	exam 3
lucy	56	88	95
lisa	74	88	91
scott	96	85	56
adam	88	94	79
bob	95	92	88

In a new cell, the following code changes the index to title case and the columns to all capitals:

```
df=df.rename(index=str.title, columns=str.upper)
df
```

Output:

	EXAM 1	EXAM 2	EXAM 3
studentID			
Lucy	56	88	95
Lisa	74	88	91
Scott	96	85	56
Adam	88	94	79
Bob	95	92	88

In another cell, the following code removes spaces in the column headers:

```
df.columns = df.columns.str.replace(' ', '')
df
```

Output:

	EXAM1	EXAM2	EXAM3
studentID			
Lucy	56	88	95
Lisa	74	88	91
Scott	96	85	56
Adam	88	94	79
Bob	95	92	88

Review Question 4.61
Which of the following best describes the axis labels in a dataframe?
a. The values in the first column of the dataframe.
b. The values in the first row of the dataframe.
c. The row and column labels of the dataframe.
d. The values within the dataframe's cells.

Review Question 4.62
The index of a dataframe can be set to a specific column or set of columns using the _______ function, and the columns or index can be renamed using the _______ function.
a. set_index(), set_column()
b. set_index(), rename()
c. index(), set_column()
d. index(), rename()

Review Question 4.63
Suppose we have a dataframe df with columns 'col_1' and 'col_2', and we want to rename these columns to 'column_1' and 'column_2', respectively. How to accomplish that?
a. df.set_column(columns=['column_1', 'column_2'])
b. df.set_columns(colulmns=['column_1', 'column_2'])
c. df.rename(columns=['column_1', 'column_2'])
d. df.rename(columns={'col_1': 'column_1', 'col_2': 'column_2'})

Review Question 4.64
Suppose we have a dataframe df with an index 'ind_1' and 'ind_2', and we want to rename these index labels to 'index_1' and 'index_2', respectively. How to accomplish that?
a. df.set_index(indexes=['index_1', 'index_2'])
b. df.set_index(indexes={'ind_1': 'index_1', 'ind_2': 'index_2'})
c. df.rename(index=['index_1', 'index_2'])
d. df.rename(index={'ind_1': 'index_1', 'ind_2': 'index_2'})

4.10 Discretization

Understanding the nature of data is crucial in business data analytics. *Continuous data* can have any value within a specified range, in contrast to *discrete data* that can only take specific, separate values. Continuous data is commonly found in fields like physics, engineering, and economics, and it can represent various measurements such as time, distance, temperature, and more. As continuous data in its raw form can be complex and challenging to interpret, handling it is essential for simplifying analysis, improving visualization, enabling statistical techniques, optimizing storage and processing, and aiding decision-making. One approach to handling continuous data is through a process called discretization.

One common method of discretization is by discretizing data into "bins." This involves dividing the data into intervals or ranges, and assigning each data point to the corresponding bin based on its value. For instance, if we have a dataset of continuous temperature measurements, we might create bins for temperatures below zero, between zero and 32 degrees Fahrenheit, between 32 and 50 degrees, and so on.

There are several reasons why discretizing continuous data can be beneficial. Firstly, it makes the data easier to visualize and comprehend. When data is continuous, it can be challenging to discern patterns or trends merely by looking at a list of numbers. By organizing the data into bins, we can create histograms or other visualizations that provide a clearer representation of the data distribution.

Another advantage of discretizing continuous data is that it simplifies statistical analysis. Many statistical techniques, such as chi-squared tests, are designed to work more effectively with discrete data rather than continuous data. By discretizing the data, we can leverage these techniques to draw meaningful conclusions.

However, there are some limitations to consider when discretizing continuous data. One limitation is that it may result in the loss of detail and precision present in the original data. By assigning data to bins, we are essentially rounding off values to the nearest bin, which can introduce some inaccuracies. Additionally, the choice of bin size or intervals can significantly impact the analysis results. Using wide bins might cause important data patterns to be overlooked, while using narrow bins can lead to an overwhelming number of bins, making the analysis unwieldy.

Suppose you have data about a group of college students in a study, and you want to group them into discrete buckets based on the number of credit hours completed. First, let's set up the data::

```
data = {'studentID':['12345', '12346', '12347', '12348'],
        'hours_completed':[12, 30, 56, 90]}
credit_df=pd.DataFrame(data)
credit_df
```
Output:

	studentID	hours_completed
0	12345	12
1	12346	30
2	12347	56
3	12348	90

Next, we will define bins for our data. In this example, we'll create four bins based on the hours completed: 0 to 29.9, 30 to 59.9, 60 to 89.9, and 90 and above. We can use the *cut()* function from the pandas library to accomplish this. In the string representation of an interval, a parenthesis indicates an open side, while a square bracket indicates a closed side (inclusive). You can change which side is closed by specifying right=False. Additionally, you can override the default bin labels based on intervals by passing a list or array to the labels option.

```
bins = [0, 30, 60, 90, 120]
class_level=['Freshman', 'Sophomore', 'Junior', 'Senior']
credit_df['class_level'] = pd.cut(credit_df.hours_completed,
            bins, right=False, labels=class_level)
credit_df
```
Output:

	studentID	hours_completed	class_level
0	12345	12	Freshman
1	12346	30	Sophomore
2	12347	56	Sophomore
3	12348	90	Senior

By using the cut method, we assign each student to a class level based on the hours completed. Finally, the output shows the updated DataFrame with the additional class_level column.

If you use the cut() method and pass it an integer representing the number of bins, instead of specific bin edges, it will automatically create bins of equal length based on the minimum and maximum values in the data. For example, let's consider a case where uniformly distributed data is divided into three equal parts, representing the heights of fifteen 10-year-olds:

```python
import pandas as pd
height=[62, 52, 63, 58, 62, 53, 62, 50, 61, 54, 63, 52, 50, 55, 55]
pd.cut(height, 3, precision=1)
```

Output:

```
[(58.7, 63.0], (50.0, 54.3], (58.7, 63.0], (54.3, 58.7], (58.7, 63.0], ..., (58.7, 63.0], (50
.0, 54.3], (50.0, 54.3], (54.3, 58.7], (54.3, 58.7]]
Length: 15
Categories (3, interval[float64, right]): [(50.0, 54.3] < (54.3, 58.7] < (58.7, 63.0]]
```

The output displays the three bins. The first line shows a list of bins corresponding to the height of each student. For instance, the first student with a height of 62 inches falls into the bin (58.7, 63.0]. By default, the bin includes the right border value but not the left. The `precision=1` option limits the decimal place to one digit.

Another related function, `qcut()`, bins the data based on sample quantiles. Unlike `cut`, which may result in bins with varying numbers of data points depending on the data distribution, `qcut` creates roughly equally-sized bins:

```python
category = pd.qcut(height, 3, precision=1)
pd.value_counts(category)
```

Output:

```
(49.9, 53.7]    5
(53.7, 61.3]    5
(61.3, 63.0]    5
dtype: int64
```

In this example, the data is divided into three bins with roughly the same number of data points. Similarly, you can pass your custom quantiles (numbers between 0 and 1, inclusive) to qcut():

```python
pd.qcut(height, [0, 0.1, 0.5, 0.9, 1.]).value_counts()
```

Output:

```
(49.999, 50.8]    2
(50.8, 55.0]      6
(55.0, 62.6]      5
(62.6, 63.0]      2
dtype: int64
```

In the above example, the first bin contains the bottom 10% of the data, the second bin contains the next lowest 10% to 50%, and so on.

Review Question 4.65

_______ data refers to data that can take on any value within a given range.
a. Range
b. Any_range
c. Discrete
d. Continuous

Review Question 4.66

_______ data, which can only take on specific, separate values.
a. Range
b. Any_range
c. Discrete
d. Continuous

Review Question 4.67

One way that continuous data is often analyzed is by _______ it or separating it into "bins".
a. discretizing
b. continuing
c. modeling
d. regressing

Review Question 4.68

There are several reasons why it might be useful to discretize continuous data. One reason is that ______.
a. discretization makes data more realistic
b. continuous data is more realistic
c. it can make the data more secure from any attacks
d. it can make the data easier to visualize and understand

Review Question 4.69

There are several reasons why it might be useful to discretize continuous data. One reason is that ______.
a. discretization makes data more realistic
b. continuous data is more realistic
c. it can make the data more secure from any attacks
d. it can make it easier to perform statistical analysis

Review Question 4.70

Which function of pandas can be used to bin a continuous data set?
a. bin()
b. bins()
c. cut()
d. cuts()

Review Question 4.71

Which function of pandas can be used to bin continuous data based on sample quantiles?
a. bin()
b. qbin()
c. cut()
d. qcut()

Exercise 4.6

Suppose you have a dataset df with a column age representing the ages of a group of customer. Your task is to categorize these ages into different age groups:
Teenagers: under 20 years.
Young Adults: 20 or over, but less than 30 years.
Adults: 30 or over, but less than 50 years.
Middle-aged Adults: 50 or over, but less than 65 years.
Seniors: 65 years or above.
First, create the following dataframe:

```python
df = pd.DataFrame({
    'Name': ['Alice', 'Bob', 'Charlie', 'David', 'Eve'],
    'Age': [23, 50, 30, 19, 62]
})
```

Your task is to add a new column 'AgeGroup' in df and display the df.

4.11 Detect and Filter Outliers

Outliers are data points that deviate significantly from the range of the majority of data in a dataset. These points can arise due to errors or mistakes in data collection, or they may represent rare phenomena or events compared to the rest of the data. For instance, in a dataset of mortality rates, the year 2020 could be an outlier due to the COVID-19 pandemic, which caused a substantial increase in deaths compared to other years. Outliers can have a significant impact on data analysis results, making it crucial to identify and assess them during the data cleaning process. Depending on the situation, outliers may need to be fixed or removed to ensure more accurate results.

Let's see an example. The following code generates a random dataset of 500 normal distributed scores. Each row represents a student ID ranging from 1000 to 1499. There are three columns, each representing an exam. We set the seed to 42 so that you can compare your output with ours:

```python
np.random.seed(42)
rnd_score = pd.DataFrame(np.random.normal(80, 10,
size=1500).reshape((500, 3)),
                         index=range(1000, 1500, 1),
                         columns=['exam1', 'exam2', 'exam3'])
rnd_score.round(0).head()
```

Output:

	exam1	exam2	exam3
1000	85.0	79.0	86.0
1001	95.0	78.0	78.0
1002	96.0	88.0	75.0
1003	85.0	75.0	75.0
1004	82.0	61.0	63.0

Once we have our DataFrame, we can use the describe() method to generate a summary of the data, including minimum, maximum, and quartile values. This summary provides insights into the data's range, distribution, and allow you to manually check the potential outliers:

```
rnd_score.describe()
```

Output:

	exam1	exam2	exam3
count	500.000000	500.000000	500.000000
mean	81.145819	79.721108	80.604559
std	9.380479	9.989575	10.282711
min	51.037446	47.587327	51.514574
25%	74.470328	72.685705	74.058608
50%	81.273988	79.627282	80.691825
75%	86.666424	86.613263	87.087177
max	105.797093	110.788808	118.527315

We can use the boxplot() method of the DataFrame to visualize the data distribution and identify outliers. The boxplot displays a box that represents the interquartile range (IQR), which is the range between the 25th and 75th percentiles of the data. A line inside the box indicates the median value. Data points that fall outside the whiskers of the boxplot are considered potential outliers.

```
rnd_score.boxplot()
```

Output:

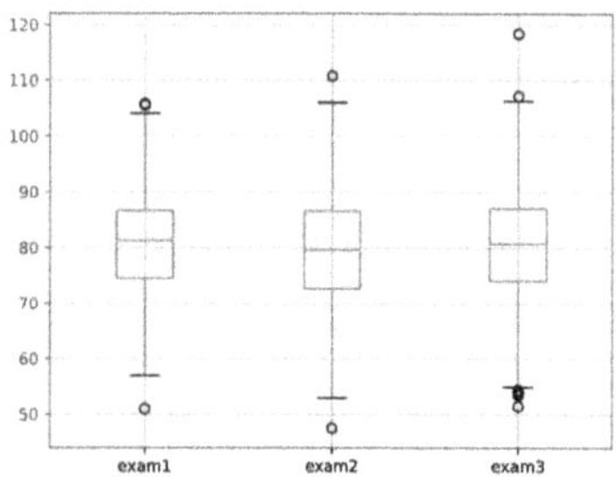

By default, the DataFrame.boxplot() method in pandas considers a data point to be an outlier if it is below $Q1 - 1.5 \times IQR$ or above $Q3 + 1.5 \times IQR$, where Q1 and Q3 denote the first and third quartiles, respectively, and IQR represents the interquartile range (Q3 - Q1). In other words, any data point more than 1.5 times the interquartile range below the first quartile or above the third quartile is deemed an outlier and plotted separately from the main boxplot.

You can modify this behavior by specifying the sym parameter, which determines the symbol used to plot the outliers. For example, setting sym='*' will use asterisks instead of circles for potential outliers.

Additionally, you can customize the whiskers—the lines extending from the box to the minimum and maximum data points—by using the whisker parameter. By default, the whiskers extend from the edges of the box to the minimum and maximum data points that are not considered outliers.

Another approach to identify outliers involves considering data points that deviate more than 3 standard deviations from the mean. To implement this, calculate the mean and standard deviation of the data and define a threshold beyond which any data point is considered an outlier. For instance, the following code identifies outliers in a Pandas DataFrame based on this criterion:

```
mean = rnd_score['exam1'].mean()
std = rnd_score['exam1'].std()
threshold = 3 * std
outliers = rnd_score[(rnd_score['exam1'] < mean - threshold) |
                     (rnd_score['exam1'] > mean + threshold)]
outliers
```

Finally, we can employ the zscore function to calculate the z-score for each data point, which represents the number of standard deviations each point deviates from the mean. Potential outliers are those data points with a z-score greater than 3 or less than -3. The following code displays all students whose exam1 score is an outlier:

```
from scipy.stats import zscore
z = rnd_score.apply(zscore)
outliers=rnd_score[z['exam1'].abs()>3]
outliers
```

Once potential outliers are identified, it is necessary to decide how to handle them. Depending on the circumstances, options include fixing errors, removing outliers, or retaining them as part of the dataset. Carefully considering the impact of outliers on analysis results is crucial in selecting the appropriate course of action.

Review Question 4.72
The _______ are data points that lie significantly outside the range of the majority of data in a dataset.
a. Outliers
b. Outsides
c. Out_of_ranges
d. Extreme points

Review Question 4.73
Which of the following statements best describes the causes of unusual data points in a dataset?
Statement1: Errors or mistakes in data collection

Statement2: Genuine phenomena or events that are rare compared to the rest of the data
a. Statement1 only.
b. Statement2 only.
c. Both Statements 1 and 2.
d. Neither Statement1 nor Statement2

Review Question 4.74
Outliers can significantly impact the results of data analysis, so it is important to identify and assess them as part of the data _______ process.
a. collecting.
b. cleaning
c. interpreting
d. presenting

Review Question 4.75
Once we have our DataFrame, we can use the _______ method to generate a summary of the data, including the minimum, maximum, and quartile values.
a. summary()
b. statistics()
c. basic_statistics()
d. describe()

Review Question 4.76
By default, the DataFrame.boxplot() method in pandas will consider a data point to be an outlier if it is less than _______ or greater than _______.
a. Q1, Q3
b. 0, 100
c. Q1 - 1.5×IQR, Q3 + 1.5×IQR
d. - 1.5×IQR, + 1.5×IQR

Review Question 4.77
What will be displayed with the following code?
```
mean = rnd_score['exam1'].mean()
std = rnd_score['exam1'].std()
threshold = 3 * std
x = rnd_score[(rnd_score['exam1'] < mean - threshold) |
                    (rnd_score['exam1'] > mean + threshold)]
x
```
a. All unknown values.
b. Outliers.
c. Outliers based on exam1 scores.
d. Threshold.

Review Question 4.78
What will be displayed with the following code?
```
from scipy.stats import zscore
z = rnd_score.apply(zscore)
x=rnd_score[z['exam1'].abs()>3]
x
```
a. All unknown values.

b. Outliers.
c. Outliers based on exam1 scores.
d. Threshold.

Review Question 4.79
Which of the following is NOT a technique described in the book for identifying outliers?
a. Use describe() method.
b. Use boxplot() method.
c. Use outliers() method.
d. Based on 3 standard deviations from the mean.

Review Question 4.80
Which of the following is NOT a technique described in the book for identifying outliers?
a. Use describe() method.
b. Use boxplot() method.
c. Use is_extreme() method.
d. Based on z-score greater than 3 or less than -3.

Exercise 4.7

You will be working with a dataset that is generated using the numpy.random.normal function. This dataset contains three columns and 500 data points. The data in each column is normally distributed with different means and standard deviations.

```python
np.random.seed(42)
rnd_sale = pd.DataFrame({
    'product1': np.random.normal(80, 10, 500),
    'product2': np.random.normal(80, 30, 500),
    'product3': np.random.normal(90, 5, 500)
}, index=range(1000, 1500))
rnd_sale.round(0).head()
```

Task 1: Generate summary statistics for the dataset. This includes count, mean, standard deviation, minimum value, 25th percentile (Q1), median (50th percentile), 75th percentile (Q3), and maximum value.
Task2: Create a plot for the dataset. This will give you a visual representation of the data distribution and potential outliers.
Task 3: Detect and filter out outliers that fall below Q1 - 1.5IQR or above Q3 + 1.5IQR. Create a new DataFrame without these outliers.
Task 4: Detect and filter out outliers that fall more than three standard deviations from the mean. Create a new DataFrame without these outliers.
Task 5: Filter out elements with a Z-score greater than 3 or less than -3. Create a new DataFrame without these outliers.

4.12 Chapter Summary

In this chapter, you have been introduced to various functions and methods in Pandas that are invaluable

for data cleaning. Cleaning data is a critical step for virtually all datasets since erroneous or incomplete data can result in inaccurate analyses and unfavorable business choices. Data cleaning encompasses several tasks, including identifying and managing missing data, performing imputation and interpolation, detecting and addressing duplicates, transforming data, replacing values, modifying axis labels, discretizing continuous data, and detecting and filtering outliers. By mastering these techniques, you can ensure the integrity and reliability of your data, paving the way for meaningful and robust analyses.

4.13 Solutions to the Review Questions

4.1 B; 4.2 D; 4.3 A; 4.4 C; 4.5 C; 4.6 B; 4.7 B; 4.8 A; 4.9 D; 4.10 B; 4.11 D; 4.12 B; 4.13 D; 4.14 C; 4.15 D; 4.16 B; 4.17 D; 4.18 D; 4.19 B. 4.20 C; 4.21 C; 4.22 A; 4.23 D; 4.24 A; 4.25 A; 4.26 A; 4.27 B; 4.28 B; 4.29 A; 4.30 A; 4.31 D; 4.32 A; 4.33 D; 4.34 A; 4.35 A; 4.36 D; 4.37 A; 4.38 C; 4.39 D; 4.40 B; 4.41 B; 4.42 C; 4.43 D; 4.44 B; 4.45 A; 4.46 D; 4.47 C; 4.48 D; 4.49 B; 4.50 B; 4.51 B; 4.52 C; 4.53 D; 4.54 A; 4.55 D; 4.56 C; 4.57 A; 4.58 C; 4.59 C; 4.60 B; 4.61 C; 4.62 B; 4.63 D; 4.64 D; 4.65 D; 4.66 C; 4.67 A; 4.68 D; 4.69 D; 4.70 C; 4.71 D; 4.72 A; 4.73 C; 4.74 B; 4.75 D; 4.76 C; 4.77 C; 4.78 C; 4.79 C; 4.80 C;

Chapter 5: Data Preparation

Chapter Learning Objectives

5.1 Combine DataFrames with merge, join, concat, and append methods
5.2 Reshape DataFrames with unstack and stack methods
5.3 Reshape DataFrames with pivot and melt methods
5.4 Prepare DataFrames with long or wide data

5.1 Hierarchical Indexing

In this chapter, we will learn the tools and techniques offered by Pandas for combining, joining, and reorganizing data. This is particularly useful when dealing with data that is spread across multiple files, databases, or has inconvenient formats for analysis.

Hierarchical indexing, also known as a multi-level index, allows for setting indexes on multiple columns. In Pandas, this feature enables the creation of multiple levels of indexing on an axis, facilitating efficient handling of high-dimensional data in a lower-dimensional format.

For instance, consider the following scenario where indexes are set on the course number and student name columns. The names of these index columns are displayed on the left of the DataFrame. They appear at a lower level compared to the names of the other columns, such as "exam1".

```python
import numpy as np
import pandas as pd
np.random.seed(42)
rnd_score = pd.DataFrame(np.random.normal(80, 10, size=15).reshape((5, 3)),
                    index=[['CS101', 'CS101', 'CS201', 'CS201', 'CS201'],
                           ['lucy', 'lisa', 'scott', 'adam', 'lisa']],
                    columns=['exam1', 'exam2', 'exam3'])
rnd_score.round(0)
```

Output:

		exam1	exam2	exam3
CS101	lucy	85.0	79.0	86.0
	lisa	95.0	78.0	78.0
CS201	scott	96.0	88.0	75.0
	adam	85.0	75.0	75.0
	lisa	82.0	61.0	63.0

When working with a multi-level index, accessing data in the DataFrame requires using a combination of both the first and second level indexes, employing a list of tuples. The following code will display the content in the rnd_score index:

```
rnd_score.index
```

Output:

```
MultiIndex([('CS101',   'lucy'),
            ('CS101',   'lisa'),
            ('CS201',  'scott'),
            ('CS201',   'adam'),
            ('CS201',   'lisa')],
           )
```

To select specific subsets of data in hierarchical indexing, you can use the loc property:

```
rnd_score.loc['CS101']
```

Output:

	exam1	exam2	exam3
lucy	84.967142	78.617357	86.476885
lisa	95.230299	77.658466	77.658630

When selecting multiple indexes, you can pass a list of index values to the loc property:

```
rnd_score.loc[['CS101', 'CS201']]
```

Output:

		exam1	exam2	exam3
CS101	**lucy**	84.967142	78.617357	86.476885
	lisa	95.230299	77.658466	77.658630
CS201	**scott**	95.792128	87.674347	75.305256
	adam	85.425600	75.365823	75.342702
	lisa	82.419623	60.867198	62.750822

Additionally, you can select values based on an "inner" level of the index. The following code demonstrates selecting all values where the second index level is 'lisa' using the xs() method:

```
rnd_score.xs('lisa', level=1)
```

Output:

	exam1	exam2	exam3
CS101	95.230299	77.658466	77.658630
CS201	82.419623	60.867198	62.750822

Hierarchical indexing plays a crucial role in reshaping data and enables performing group-based operations such as creating pivot tables. You can pivot a level of the multi-indexed DataFrame's index labels into columns by using the unstack() method:

```
rnd_score['exam1'].unstack()
```

Output:

	adam	lisa	lucy	scott
CS101	NaN	95.230299	84.967142	NaN
CS201	85.4256	82.419623	NaN	95.792128

This operation transforms the data, converting the index values into columns, resulting in a reshaped DataFrame with a new structure. The inverse operation of unstack is *stack*. The stack() method in Pandas is used to reshape a DataFrame by converting columns into index levels. It allows you to restore the original structure of the DataFrame. By applying unstack() followed by stack() to rnd_score, you can obtain the initial DataFrame:

```
rnd_score.unstack().stack()
```

Output:

		exam1	exam2	exam3
CS101	lisa	95.230299	77.658466	77.658630
	lucy	84.967142	78.617357	86.476885
CS201	adam	85.425600	75.365823	75.342702
	lisa	82.419623	60.867198	62.750822
	scott	95.792128	87.674347	75.305256

In a DataFrame, it is possible to have a hierarchical index on either axis. For example:

```
np.random.seed(42)
rnd_score1 = pd.DataFrame(np.random.normal
    (80, 10, size=25).reshape((5, 5)),
    index=[['CS101', 'CS101', 'CS201', 'CS201', 'CS201'],
    ['lucy', 'lisa', 'scott', 'adam', 'lisa']],
    columns=[['Fall 2022', 'Fall 2022', 'Fall 2022',
    'Spring 2023', 'Spring 2023'],
    ['exam1', 'exam2', 'exam3', 'exam1', 'exam2']])
rnd_score1.round(0)
```
Output:

		Fall 2022			Spring 2023	
		exam1	exam2	exam3	exam1	exam2
CS101	lucy	85.0	79.0	86.0	95.0	78.0
	lisa	78.0	96.0	88.0	75.0	85.0
CS201	scott	75.0	75.0	82.0	61.0	63.0
	adam	74.0	70.0	83.0	71.0	66.0
	lisa	95.0	78.0	81.0	66.0	75.0

The hierarchical levels can have names assigned to them, which will be displayed in the output. For example:

```
rnd_score1.index.names = ['course', 'student']
```

```
rnd_score1.columns.names = ['semester', 'exam']
rnd_score1
```

Output:

course	student	semester		Fall 2022		Spring 2023	
		exam	exam1	exam2	exam3	exam1	exam2
CS101	lucy	84.967142	78.617357	86.476885	95.230299	77.658466
	lisa	77.658630	95.792128	87.674347	75.305256	85.425600
CS201	scott	75.365823	75.342702	82.419623	60.867198	62.750822
	adam	74.377125	69.871689	83.142473	70.919759	65.876963
	lisa	94.656488	77.742237	80.675282	65.752518	74.556173

In this example, please note that the index names 'course' and 'student' are not part of the row labels; they are only used for identification and clarity.

Partial column indexing involves selecting specific columns from a DataFrame using partial labels or a list of partial labels. This method helps you focus on particular columns or groups based on their names or hierarchical levels. For example:

```
rnd_score1['Fall 2022']
```

Output:

		exam1	exam2	exam3
CS101	lucy	84.967142	78.617357	86.476885
	lisa	77.658630	95.792128	87.674347
CS201	scott	75.365823	75.342702	82.419623
	adam	74.377125	69.871689	83.142473
	lisa	94.656488	77.742237	80.675282

Two operations can be used to rearrange the order of levels in a hierarchical index: *swaplevel* and *sort_index*.

The swaplevel() method swaps the positions of two levels in the index, creating a new object while keeping the data unchanged. For example:

```
rnd_score1.swaplevel('course', 'student').round(0)
```

Output:

student	course	semester		Fall 2022		Spring 2023	
		exam	exam1	exam2	exam3	exam1	exam2
lucy	CS101	85.0	79.0	86.0	95.0	78.0
lisa	CS101	78.0	96.0	88.0	75.0	85.0
scott	CS201	75.0	75.0	82.0	61.0	63.0
adam	CS201	74.0	70.0	83.0	71.0	66.0
lisa	CS201	95.0	78.0	81.0	66.0	75.0

On the other hand, the sort_index() method sorts the data based on the values in a single level of the index. It is often used in combination with swaplevel to achieve a lexicographically sorted result. For example:

```
rnd_score1.sort_index(level='student').round(0)
```

Output:

| semester | | Fall 2022 | | | Spring 2023 | |
course	student	exam1	exam2	exam3	exam1	exam2
CS201	adam	74.0	70.0	83.0	71.0	66.0
CS101	lisa	78.0	96.0	88.0	75.0	85.0
CS201	lisa	95.0	78.0	81.0	66.0	75.0
CS101	lucy	85.0	79.0	86.0	95.0	78.0
CS201	scott	75.0	75.0	82.0	61.0	63.0

In this case, the data is sorted based on the 'student' level.

Alternatively, you can use numerical indices and chain the swaplevel() and sort_index() methods together:

```
rnd_score1.swaplevel(0, 1).sort_index(level=0).round(0)
```

Output:

| semester | | Fall 2022 | | | Spring 2023 | |
student	course	exam1	exam2	exam3	exam1	exam2
adam	CS201	74.0	70.0	83.0	71.0	66.0
lisa	CS101	78.0	96.0	88.0	75.0	85.0
	CS201	95.0	78.0	81.0	66.0	75.0
lucy	CS101	85.0	79.0	86.0	95.0	78.0
scott	CS201	75.0	75.0	82.0	61.0	63.0

This approach achieves the same outcome of swapping and sorting the index levels.

The *reset_index()* method is used to remove the index from a DataFrame and replace it with the default numeric index. The original index values are moved to new columns in the DataFrame. Here are some examples to clarify its usage:

```
rnd_score.reset_index().round()
```

Output:

	level_0	level_1	exam1	exam2	exam3
0	CS101	lucy	85.0	79.0	86.0
1	CS101	lisa	95.0	78.0	78.0
2	CS201	scott	96.0	88.0	75.0
3	CS201	adam	85.0	75.0	75.0
4	CS201	lisa	82.0	61.0	63.0

If you just want to remove one level of index, add the level parameter to the reset_index() method. By specifying the level parameter as 1, you can remove only the second level of the index. The DataFrame is displayed with the second level of the index column named 'Level_1', and the original first level becomes part of the index:

```
rnd_score.reset_index(level=1).round()
```

Output:

	level_1	exam1	exam2	exam3
CS101	lucy	85.0	79.0	86.0
CS101	lisa	95.0	78.0	78.0
CS201	scott	96.0	88.0	75.0
CS201	adam	85.0	75.0	75.0
CS201	lisa	82.0	61.0	63.0

If you want a meaningful column name, the index must have a name before reset. In the next example, the index levels are assigned names using the index.names attribute. Then, the reset_index() method is used with the level parameter set to 'student' to remove that level of the index. The output displays the DataFrame with the 'student' level moved to a column:

```
rnd_score.index.names = ['course', 'student']
rnd_score.reset_index(level='student').round()
```

Output:

	student	exam1	exam2	exam3
course				
CS101	lucy	85.0	79.0	86.0
CS101	lisa	95.0	78.0	78.0
CS201	scott	96.0	88.0	75.0
CS201	adam	85.0	75.0	75.0
CS201	lisa	82.0	61.0	63.0

The DataFrame's *set_index()* method will create a new DataFrame using one or more of its columns as the index. This following code creates a new DataFrame rnd_score3 by resetting the index. Then, the set_index() method is used to set the columns 'course' and 'student' as the new index:

```
rnd_score3 = rnd_score.reset_index()
rnd_score3.set_index(['course', 'student']).round()
```

Output:

		exam1	exam2	exam3
course	**student**			
CS101	lucy	85.0	79.0	86.0
	lisa	95.0	78.0	78.0
CS201	scott	96.0	88.0	75.0
	adam	85.0	75.0	75.0
	lisa	82.0	61.0	63.0

By default the set_index() method removes the index columns from the DataFrame, though you can leave them in by passing drop=False to set_index(). Here, the reset_index() method is used on rnd_score3 to remove the current index. Then, set_index() is called to set the columns 'course' and 'student' as the index, while keeping the original index columns in the DataFrame:

```
rnd_score4 = rnd_score3.reset_index()
rnd_score4.set_index(['course', 'student'], drop=False).round()
```

Output:

course	student	index	course	student	exam1	exam2	exam3
CS101	lucy	0	CS101	lucy	85.0	79.0	86.0
	lisa	1	CS101	lisa	95.0	78.0	78.0
CS201	scott	2	CS201	scott	96.0	88.0	75.0
	adam	3	CS201	adam	85.0	75.0	75.0
	lisa	4	CS201	lisa	82.0	61.0	63.0

It's worth noting that the above examples do not use the inplace parameter, which avoids modifying the DataFrame in place. If you prefer to modify the DataFrame directly, you can set inplace=True as an argument in the respective methods.

Review Question 5.1
What is the purpose of Pandas hierarchical indexing tools and techniques?
a. To manipulate high-dimensional data
b. To perform statistical analysis
c. To visualize data
d. To clean data

Review Question 5.2
What is another term for hierarchical indexing in Pandas?
a. Multi-level index
b. Hierarchical sorting
c. Column reorganization
d. Pandas indexing

Review Question 5.3
How is data accessed in a DataFrame with a two-level index (multi-level index)?
a. By using the first level index only
b. By using the second level index only
c. By using a combination of both the first and second level indexes
d. By using a dictionary-like key

Review Question 5.4
Which library is used to create the DataFrame with a random normal sample?
```
random.normal(80, 10, size=15)
```
a. NumPy

b. Matplotlib
c. Seaborn
d. Scikit-learn

Review Question 5.5
What is the advantage of using hierarchical indexing in Pandas?
a. It reduces the memory usage of the DataFrame
b. It enables faster computation on the DataFrame
c. It improves the efficiency of data analysis
d. It simplifies the process of data visualization

Review Question 5.6
Suppose 'CS101' is a first level index value of a DataFrame, you can choose all values associated with the index 'CS101' by using the _______ property?
a. iloc
b. sx
c. loc
d. unstack

Review Question 5.7
How would you select multiple indexes of frist level, such as 'CS101' and 'CS201', from the DataFrame using hierarchical indexing?
a. rnd_score.iloc[['CS101', 'CS201']]
b. rnd_score.xs(['CS101', 'CS201'])
c. rnd_score.loc[['CS101', 'CS201']]
d. rnd_score.unstack(['CS101', 'CS201'])

Review Question 5.8
Suppose rnd_score DataFrame has hierarchical index, how would you select all values where the second index level is 'lisa'?
a. rnd_score.xs('lisa', level=1)
b. rnd_score.loc['lisa', level=2]
c. rnd_score.unstack('lisa', level=1)
d. rnd_score.iloc['lisa'].level(2)

Review Question 5.9
What is the purpose of the unstack method in Pandas?
a. To convert the index values into columns
b. To restore the original structure of the DataFrame
c. To select specific subsets of data based on labels
d. To convert columns into the index

Review Question 5.10
What is the output of the following code: rnd_score['exam1'].unstack()?
a. A reshaped DataFrame with index values as columns
b. A subset of data where the column is 'exam1'
c. A DataFrame with NaN values for missing data
d. A DataFrame with the index values intact

Review Question 5.11

What does the stack method do in Pandas?
a. Converts all columns into index levels
b. Rearranges the DataFrame by reshaping the data via converting columns into index levels.
c. Selects specific subsets of data based on labels
d. Restores the original structure of the DataFrame

Review Question 5.12
Which operation in Pandas is used to transform the data by converting the index values into columns?
a. unstack
b. stack
c. loc
d. xs

Review Question 5.13
Which property is used to assign names to the index levels of a DataFrame?
a. index.names
b. column.names
c. index.levels
d. column.levels

Review Question 5.14
What is the purpose of partial column indexing in Pandas?
a. To modify the values within the columns
b. To select specific rows based on partial label matches
c. To select a subset of columns based on partial label matches
d. To group columns together for computational purposes

Review Question 5.15
What is the output of the partial column indexing operation rnd_score1['Fall 2022']?
a. A DataFrame with all rows and columns labeled 'Fall 2022'
b. A DataFrame with only the 'Fall 2022' columns
c. An error because partial column indexing is not supported
d. Need double square brackets for the column name

Review Question 5.16
Which method swaps the positions of two levels in a hierarchical index?
a. sort_index()
b. reset_index()
c. swaplevel()
d. set_index()

Review Question 5.17
How do you sort the data in a DataFrame based on the values in the index?
a. sort_dataframe()
b. sort_data()
c. sort_index()
d. order_data()

Review Question 5.18
What is this called? `rnd_score1.swaplevel(0, 1).sort_index(level=0).round(0)`

a. swap and sort methods
b. chain methods
c. hierarchical methods
d. multi-level methods

Review Question 5.19
What does the reset_index() method do?
a. Swaps the positions of two levels in a hierarchical index
b. Sorts the data based on the values in a single level of the index
c. Removes the index from a DataFrame and replaces it with the default numeric index
d. Creates a new DataFrame using one or more columns as the index

Review Question 5.20
How can you remove only the second level of the index using reset_index()?
a. rnd_score.reset_index(level=0)
b. rnd_score.reset_index(level=1)
c. rnd_score.reset_index(level=2)
d. rnd_score.reset_index(level='student')

Review Question 5.21
How can you modify a DataFrame directly by using the set_index() method?
a. By setting inplace=True as an argument in the method
b. By using drop=False as an argument in the method
c. By chaining reset_index() and set_index() methods together
d. By specifying the index levels using the index.names attribute

Exercise 5.1

Run the following code to create a DataFrame with hierarchical indexing:

```python
import pandas as pd
import numpy as np

# Create a DataFrame
df = pd.DataFrame({
    'Population': [167500, 491918, 125904, 389255, 97456, 8336815, 1328],
    'Area': [82.31, 319.03, 61.47, 163.59, 21.4, 783.84, 45.51]},
    index=[['Missouri', 'Missouri', 'Kansas', 'Kansas', 'New York', 'New York', 'New York'],
    ['Springfield', 'Kansas City', 'Topeka', 'Wichita', 'Albany', 'New York City', 'Springfield']])
df
```

Task 1: Display the index of the DataFrame.
Task 2: Select a specific subset from the DataFrame. For example, select data for 'Missouri'.
Task 3: Select a subset based on an inner level of the index. For example, select data for 'Springfield'.
Task 4: Construct a pivot table where the rows represent states and the columns represent cities. The values in the table should reflect the population.
Task 5: Remove the index from a DataFrame and replace it with the default numeric index.
Task 6: Remove only the second level of index and display it as a column.
Task 7: Same as Task 6, but this time add a meaningful column name to this new column.
Task 8: First reset the index and then set the same index again.
Task 9: Same as Task 8, but this time, we want to keep all the original indexing columns.

5.2 Combining Datasets

A key part of the data preparation process involves combining data, which can be achieved in Pandas through various methods. These include merge(), join(), and concat(), each allowing for data combination. Before moving on to combining Pandas objects, it's important to understand SQL inner, outer, left, and right joins. The type of join determines which records are included in the final result set. Let's consider the example of a Student (left table) and an Advisor (right table):

StudentId	StudentName	AdvisorId
1	Alice	111
2	Bob	111
3	Chuck	222
4	Dan	Null

AdvisorId	AdvisorName
111	Xavier
222	Young
333	Zach

If you perform an INNER JOIN on these tables based on AdvisorId, you select the matching rows:

StudentId	StudentName	AdvisorId	AdvisorId	AdvisorName
1	Alice	111	111	Xavier
2	Alice	111	111	Xavier
3	Chuck	222	222	Young

In a LEFT JOIN, you keep everything from the left table and search for matching rows in the right table. Different from the INNER JOIN, if there are no matching rows from the right table, the rows from the left table are still included:

StudentId	StudentName	AdvisorId	AdvisorId	AdvisorName
1	Alice	111	111	Xavier
2	Alice	111	111	Xavier
3	Chuck	222	222	Young
4	Dan	Null	Null	Null

A RIGHT JOIN is similar to a LEFT JOIN, but the roles of the left and right tables are switched:

StudentId	StudentName	AdvisorId	AdvisorId	AdvisorName
1	Alice	111	111	Xavier
2	Alice	111	111	Xavier
3	Chuck	222	222	Young
Null	Null	Null	333	Zach

Finally, an OUTER JOIN keeps all matching rows like the INNER JOIN and includes the unmatched rows from both tables:

StudentId	StudentName	AdvisorId	AdvisorId	AdvisorName
1	Alice	111	111	Xavier
2	Alice	111	111	Xavier
3	Chuck	222	222	Young
4	Dan	Null	Null	Null
Null	Null	Null	333	Zach

The merge() function in Pandas is used for combining dataset horizontally. It requires two DataFrames with at least one common column. Let's start by creating the first dataset:

```python
score1 = pd.DataFrame({'student':
    ['adam', 'lucy', 'adam', 'scott'],
    'CS101 exam1': [79, 85, 81, 69],
    'CS101 exam2': [89, 95, 91, 74]})
score1
```

Output:

	student	CS101 exam1	CS101 exam2
0	adam	79	89
1	lucy	85	95
2	adam	81	91
3	scott	69	74

Next, let's create another DataFrame in a separate cell:

```python
score2 = pd.DataFrame({'student':
    ['adam', 'lucy', 'lisa'],
    'CS201 exam1': [69, 75, 82],
    'CS201 exam2': [82, 93, 90]})
score2
```

Output:

	student	CS201 exam1	CS201 exam2
0	adam	69	82
1	lucy	75	93
2	lisa	82	90

By default, the merge() function performs an INNER JOIN. Let's execute the following line in a new cell:

```python
pd.merge(score1, score2)
```

Output:

	student	CS101 exam1	CS101 exam2	CS201 exam1	CS201 exam2
0	adam	79	89	69	82
1	adam	81	91	69	82
2	lucy	85	95	75	93

In the above code, the common column between the two DataFrame objects is not explicitly specified. The merge() method uses the overlapping column names as the keys. However, it is considered good practice to specify the common column explicitly. If the two objects being joined have the same column with different names, you can use parameters in the merge() function to differentiate these columns. Let's see an example by creating a new DataFrame in a separate cell:

```
score3 = pd.DataFrame({'name':
    ['adam', 'lucy', 'lisa'],
    'CS201 exam1': [69, 75, 82],
    'CS201 exam2': [82, 93, 90]})
score3
```

Output:

	Name	CS201 exam1	CS201 exam2
0	Adam	69	82
1	Lucy	75	93
2	Lisa	82	90

If you try to merge score1 with score3 without specifying the common column, you will receive an error:

```
pd.merge(score1, score3)
```

Output:

```
MergeError: No common columns to perform merge on. Merge options: left_on=None, rig
ht_on=None, left_index=False, right_index=False
```

To fix this, use the left_on parameter to specify the column name in the left DataFrame and the right_on

parameter to specify the column name in the right DataFrame:

```
pd.merge(score1, score3, left_on='student',right_on='name')
```

Output:

	student	CS101 exam1	CS101 exam2	Name	CS201 exam1	CS201 exam2
0	adam	79	89	Adam	69	82
1	adam	81	91	Adam	69	82
2	lucy	85	95	lucy	75	93

If you have more than one common column between two DataFrames and you want to merge based on

only one column, you can use the on parameter. Let's create another DataFrame in a new cell:

```
score4 = pd.DataFrame({'student':
    ['adam', 'lucy', 'lisa'],
    'CS101 exam1': [69, 75, 82],
    'CS201 exam2': [82, 93, 90]})
score4
```
Output:

	student	CS101 exam1	CS201 exam2
0	Adam	69	82
1	lucy	75	93
2	lisa	82	90

Now, let's merge score1 with score4 based on the 'student' column only:

```
pd.merge(score1, score4, on='student')
```

Output:

	Student	CS101 exam1_x	CS101 exam2	CS101 exam1_y	CS201 exam2
0	Adam	79	89	69	82
1	Adam	81	91	69	82
2	Lucy	85	95	75	93

You may notice that the other column names for the common columns are added with suffixes to differentiate them. If you want to specify your own suffixes, you can use the suffixes parameter:

```
pd.merge(score1, score4, on='student', suffixes=('Spr', 'Fal'))
```

Output:

	Student	CS101 exam1Spr	CS101 exam2	CS101 exam1Fal	CS201 exam2
0	Adam	79	89	69	82
1	Adam	81	91	69	82
2	Lucy	85	95	75	93

By default, Pandas' merge() function performs an inner join. To perform a left join, use the how parameter:

```
pd.merge(score1, score2, how='left')
```

Output:

	student	CS101 exam1	CS101 exam2	CS201 exam1	CS201 exam2
0	adam	79	89	69.0	82.0
1	lucy	85	95	75.0	93.0
2	adam	81	91	69.0	82.0
3	scott	69	74	NaN	NaN

Similarly, to perform a right join, use the how parameter with the value 'right':

```
pd.merge(score1, score2, how='right')
```

Output:

	student	CS101 exam1	CS101 exam2	CS201 exam1	CS201 exam2
0	Adam	79.0	89.0	69	82
1	Adam	81.0	91.0	69	82
2	lucy	85.0	95.0	75	93
3	lisa	NaN	NaN	82	90

To perform a full outer join, you can use the value 'outer' for the how parameter:

```
pd.merge(score1, score2, how='outer')
```

Output:

	student	CS101 exam1	CS101 exam2	CS201 exam1	CS201 exam2
0	adam	79.0	89.0	69.0	82.0
1	adam	81.0	91.0	69.0	82.0
2	lucy	85.0	95.0	75.0	93.0
3	scott	69.0	74.0	NaN	NaN
4	lisa	NaN	NaN	82.0	90.0

To merge on multiple common columns, you can pass a list or tuple of column names to the on parameter.

Let's create two new DataFrame objects, score5 and score6:

```python
score5 = pd.DataFrame({
    'course': ['CS101', 'CS101', 'CS102', 'CS102'],
    'student': ['adam', 'lucy', 'adam', 'scott'],
    'exam1': [79, 85, 81, 69],
    'exam2': [89, 95, 91, 74]})
score5
```

Output:

	Course	student	exam1	exam2
0	CS101	adam	79	89
1	CS101	lucy	85	95
2	CS102	adam	81	91
3	CS102	scott	69	74

Here's the code for creating DataFrame object, score6:

```python
score6 = pd.DataFrame({
    'course': ['CS101', 'CS101', 'CS102'],
    'student': ['adam', 'lucy', 'lisa'],
    'exam3': [69, 75, 82],
    'exam4': [82, 93, 90]})
score6
```

Output:

	Course	student	exam3	exam4
0	CS101	adam	69	82
1	CS101	lucy	75	93
2	CS102	lisa	82	90

To combine the two DataFrames based on the same course and student, you can merge them using the *on* parameter:

```python
pd.merge(score5, score6, on=('course', 'student'))
```

Output:

	course	student	exam1	exam2	exam3	exam4
0	CS101	adam	79	89	69	82
1	CS101	lucy	85	95	75	93

Sometimes, it's convenient to know the source of each row, whether it's from the left DataFrame, right DataFrame, or both. You can use the *indicator* parameter to add a column named '_merge' that indicates the source of each row:

```python
pd.merge(score5, score6, how='outer', indicator=True)
```

Output:

	course	student	exam1	exam2	exam3	exam4	_merge
0	CS101	adam	79.0	89.0	69.0	82.0	both
1	CS101	lucy	85.0	95.0	75.0	93.0	both
2	CS102	adam	81.0	91.0	NaN	NaN	left_only
3	CS102	scott	69.0	74.0	NaN	NaN	left_only
4	CS102	lisa	NaN	NaN	82.0	90.0	right_only

You can also perform merging based on the index of DataFrame objects. In some cases, the column(s) used for merging in a DataFrame can be found in its index (row labels). To indicate that the index should be used as the merge key, you can set left_index=True or right_index=True (or both):

```python
score7 = pd.DataFrame({
    'student': ['adam', 'lucy', 'lisa'],
    'exam3': [69, 75, 82],
    'exam4': [82, 93, 90]},
    index=['CS101', 'CS103', 'CS102'])
score7
```
Output:

	Student	exam3	exam4
CS101	Adam	69	82
CS103	Lucy	75	93
CS102	Lisa	82	90

You can perform an inner join using the following code:

```python
pd.merge(score5, score7, left_on='course', right_index=True)
```

Output:

	course	student_x	exam1	exam2	student_y	exam3	exam4
0	CS101	adam	79	89	adam	69	82
1	CS101	lucy	85	95	adam	69	82
2	CS102	adam	81	91	lisa	82	90
3	CS102	scott	69	74	lisa	82	90

You can perform an outer join on the index using the following code:

```python
pd.merge(score5, score7, left_on='course', right_index=True, how='outer')
```

Output:

	Course	student_x	exam1	exam2	student_y	exam3	exam4
0.0	CS101	adam	79.0	89.0	adam	69	82
1.0	CS101	lucy	85.0	95.0	adam	69	82
2.0	CS102	adam	81.0	91.0	lisa	82	90
3.0	CS102	scott	69.0	74.0	lisa	82	90
NaN	CS103	NaN	NaN	NaN	lucy	75	93

In this case, you may see floating number indices and a NaN index because score5 has a range integer index, while score7 has a string index.

The *join()* method is used to horizontally join two DataFrame objects based on a common column name. It operates by combining objects using their index values. The join() method differs from the merge() method in a few ways. First, join() performs a left join by default, while merge() performs an inner join by default. Second, join() is a method of a DataFrame object, whereas merge() can be a function of the pandas module or a method of a DataFrame object.

To illustrate how the join() method works with the score1 and score2 objects created earlier in this section, you can use the following code in a new cell:

```
score1.join(score2, lsuffix='101', rsuffix='201')
```

Output:

	student101	CS101 exam1	CS101 exam2	student201	CS201 exam1	CS201 exam2
0	adam	79	89	adam	69.0	82.0
1	lucy	85	95	lucy	75.0	93.0
2	adam	81	91	lisa	82.0	90.0
3	scott	69	74	NaN	NaN	NaN

In the output, you can see that the join() method combines the two objects based on the common index values. The resulting DataFrame contains columns with suffixes '101' and '201' to differentiate between the columns from score1 and score2.

To combine or stack data along an axis, we can use the concat() function in pandas. This operation is also referred to as concatenation or stacking. For example, if we want to concatenate the score1 and score2 DataFrames, we can use the following code:

```
pd.concat([score1, score2])
```

Output:

	Student	CS101 exam1	CS101 exam2	CS201 exam1	CS201 exam2
0	Adam	79.0	89.0	NaN	NaN
1	Lucy	85.0	95.0	NaN	NaN
2	Adam	81.0	91.0	NaN	NaN
3	scott	69.0	74.0	NaN	NaN
0	Adam	NaN	NaN	69.0	82.0
1	Lucy	NaN	NaN	75.0	93.0
2	Lisa	NaN	NaN	82.0	90.0

By default, concat() works on the row axis and adds rows to the resulting DataFrame. We can also concatenate objects side by side along the column axis by specifying axis=1:

```
pd.concat([score1, score2], axis=1)
```

Output:

	student	CS101 exam1	CS101 exam2	student	CS201 exam1	CS201 exam2
0	adam	79	89	adam	69.0	82.0
1	lucy	85	95	lucy	75.0	93.0
2	adam	81	91	lisa	82.0	90.0
3	scott	69	74	NaN	NaN	NaN

By default, the concat() function performs an outer join, which returns all records from both objects.

To perform an inner join and include only the matching indices from both objects, we can specify join='inner':

```
pd.concat([score1, score2], axis=1, join='inner')
```

Output:

	Student	CS101 exam1	CS101 exam2	student	CS201 exam1	CS201 exam2
0	Adam	79	89	adam	69	82
1	lucy	85	95	lucy	75	93
2	Adam	81	91	lisa	82	90

Review Question 5.22
Which method in Pandas is used to connect rows in DataFrame objects based on common columns and perform inner join by default?
a. merge()
b. join()
c. concat()
d. append()

Review Question 5.23
Which method in Pandas is used to connect rows in DataFrame objects based on common columns and perform left join by default?
a. merge()
b. join()
c. concat()
d. append()

Review Question 5.24
Which type of join keeps everything from the left table and includes matching rows from the right table?
a. INNER JOIN
b. LEFT JOIN
c. RIGHT JOIN
d. OUTER JOIN

Review Question 5.25
In an INNER JOIN, the final result set includes:

a. Only the matching rows from both tables.
b. All rows from the left table and matching rows from the right table.
c. All rows from the right table and matching rows from the left table.
d. All matching rows from both tables, as well as unmatched rows from both tables.

Review Question 5.26
A RIGHT JOIN is similar to a LEFT JOIN, but:
a. It includes all matching rows from both tables.
b. It includes all unmatched rows from both tables.
c. It keeps everything from the right table and includes matching rows from the left table.
d. It keeps everything from the left table and includes matching rows from the right table.

Review Question 5.27
Which type of join keeps all matching rows and includes unmatched rows from both tables?
a. INNER JOIN
b. LEFT JOIN
c. RIGHT JOIN
d. OUTER JOIN

Review Question 5.28
When performing a LEFT JOIN, if there are no matching rows from the right table:
a. The rows from the left table are still included.
b. The rows from the left table are excluded.
c. The join operation fails and returns an error.
d. The join operation is not possible with a LEFT JOIN.

Review Question 5.29
How can you specify the common column explicitly when using the merge() function?
a. Using the common_column parameter
b. Using the merge_column parameter
c. Using the on parameter
d. Using the common_on parameter

Review Question 5.30
What happens if the common column between two DataFrame objects is not explicitly specified in the merge() function?
a. The merge operation fails.
b. An error is raised.
c. The merge is performed based on all overlapping column names.
d. The merge is performed based on the index of the DataFrames.

Review Question 5.31
How can you merge two DataFrame objects with different column names but the same attributes?
a. Use the rename() function to rename the columns inside the merge() function.
b. Use the merge_columns parameter in the merge() function.
c. Use the left_on and right_on parameters to specify the column names.
d. It is not possible to merge them without renaming the columns.

Review Question 5.32
Which parameter can be used to perform a left join with the merge() function?

a. left
b. left_join
c. how
d. on

Review Question 5.33
How can you merge two DataFrames with multiple common columns based on only one column?
a. Use the merge_columns parameter.
b. Use the merge_on parameter.
c. Use the on parameter.
d. It is not possible to merge based on only one column with multiple common columns.

Review Question 5.34
What happens if you merge two DataFrame objects that have a common column with different names by default?
a. An error is raised.
b. An inner join is performed by default.
c. A left join is performed by default.
d. A right join is performed by default.

Review Question 5.35
How can you add a column that indicates the source of each row when merging two DataFrames?
a. Using the indicator parameter with the value 'source'
b. Using the source_column parameter in the merge() function
c. Using the _merge parameter with the value 'source'
d. Using the indicator parameter with the value True

Review Question 5.36
Which parameter can be used to specify custom suffixes for the column names in case of overlapping columns?
a. column_suffixes
b. column_namesuffix
c. suffixes
d. column_suffix

Review Question 5.37
What does the following code do: pd.merge(score5, score7, left_on='course', right_index=True, how='outer') assuming score5 and score7 are two DataFrame objects?
a. Performs an inner join on the 'course' column of score5 and the index of score7.
b. Performs an outer join on the 'course' column of score5 and the index of score7.
c. Performs a left join on the 'course' column of score5 and the index of score7.
d. Performs a right join on the 'course' column of score5 and the index of score7.

Review Question 5.38
How can you indicate that the index should be used as the merge key in a merge operation?
a. Set left_index=True or right_index=True.
b. Set merge_index=True.
c. Use the index_key parameter.
d. Use the merge_key parameter.

Review Question 5.39
What does an outer join on the index include in the resulting DataFrame?
a. Only matching rows from both DataFrames.
b. Only matching rows from the left DataFrame.
c. Only matching rows from the right DataFrame.
d. All rows from both DataFrames, with NaN values for non-matching rows.

Review Question 5.40
Why may there be floating number indices and NaN indices in the output of a merge operation?
a. It is a bug in the merge() function.
b. The merge operation fails to align the indices properly.
c. One DataFrame has a range integer index, while the other has a string index.
d. The index keys were not specified correctly in the merge() function.

Review Question 5.41
How does the join() method differ from the merge() method?
a. join() performs an inner join, while merge() performs a left join.
b. join() is a method of a DataFrame object, while merge() can be a function or method.
c. join() combines objects based on their specified columns, while merge() combines objects based on index values.
d. join() can only be used with two DataFrame objects, while merge() can be used with any number of DataFrame objects.

Review Question 5.42
How does the join() method differ from the merge() method?
a. join() performs an inner join, while merge() performs a left join.
b. join() can be a function or method, while merge() is a method of a DataFrame object.
c. join() combines objects based on their index values, while merge() combines objects based on specified columns.
d. join() can only be used with two DataFrame objects, while merge() can be used with any number of DataFrame objects.

Review Question 5.43
What is the purpose of the concat() function in pandas?
a. To combine or stack data along an axis.
b. To perform inner joins between DataFrame objects.
c. To filter rows based on specified conditions.
d. To calculate summary statistics for DataFrame objects.

Review Question 5.44
By default, how does the concat() function work on DataFrame objects?
a. It adds columns to the resulting DataFrame.
b. It performs an inner join between the objects.
c. It adds rows to the resulting DataFrame.
d. It removes duplicates from the objects.

Review Question 5.45
How can we concatenate objects side by side along the column axis using concat() function?
a. By specifying axis=0 in the concat() function.
b. By specifying axis=1 in the concat() function.

c. By using the merge() function instead of concat().
d. By using the append() function instead of concat().

Review Question 5.46
What type of join does the concat() function perform by default with axis=1?
a. Inner join
b. Left join
c. Right join
d. Outer join

Review Question 5.47
How can we perform an inner join using the concat() function?
a. By specifying join='inner' and axis=1 in the concat() function.
b. By specifying inner=True and axis = 1 in the concat() function.
c. By using the merge() function instead of concat() because concat() won't do it.
d. By specifying axis=1 in the concat() function.

Exercise 5.2

Run the following code to create two DataFrames:

```python
import pandas as pd
# Create two dataframes
df1 = pd.DataFrame({
    'Name': ['John', 'Anna', 'Peter', 'Linda'],
    'Age': [28, 22, 35, 33],
    'City': ['New York', 'Los Angeles', 'Chicago', 'Houston']
})

df2 = pd.DataFrame({
    'Name': ['John', 'Anna', 'Michael', 'Sarah'],
    'Occupation': ['Engineer', 'Doctor', 'Teacher', 'Scientist'],
    'Birthplace': ['Houston', 'Houston', 'New York', 'Atlanta'],
    'Salary': [70000, 80000, 60000, 90000]
})
```

Next, proceed with the following tasks by using the merge() function:
Task 1: Combine the two dataframes by using inner join.
Task 2: Rename the "Name" column of df1 to "First Name" and save it to df3, then combine df3 and df2 by using inner join.
Task 3: Rename the "Birthplace" column of df2 to "City"and save it to df4, then combine the two dataframes using inner join based on the "Name" column.
Task 4: Same as Task 3, but this time, make sure the common column not used in the join has meaningful names in the result set.
Task 5: Same as Task 3, but this time specifically pick the "Name" and "City" columns to inner join.
Task 6: Perform a left join on the original two dataframes.
Task 7: Perform a right join on the original two dataframes.
Task 8: Perform a full outer join on the original two dataframes.
Task 9: Same as Task 8, but this time, add a column in the result set to indicate the source of each row in the result set.
Task 10: Perform an inner join on the original dataframes based on the index.

5.3 Reshape with Pivoting and Melting

In business data analytics, data often comes in various forms and structures that require transformation before analysis. One of the key strengths of the Pandas library in Python is its ability to reshape and manipulate data efficiently. Two powerful methods that enable analysts to restructure data in a Pandas DataFrame are *pivoting* and *melting*. These techniques help convert data between wide and long formats, which is crucial for tasks such as data visualization, aggregation, and reporting.

Wide format refers to a dataset where variables are spread across columns. Each subject or entity typically has a single row, with different attributes or measurements recorded in separate columns. For example, in a sales dataset, if each row represents a product, the columns might represent monthly sales data (e.g., "January Sales," "February Sales"), resulting in a wide table.

Product	January Sales	February Sales	March Sales
Product A	500	450	600
Product B	300	350	400

Long format, on the other hand, organizes the data so that each variable has its own row, and the attributes are stored in key-value pairs. In a long-format dataset, one column typically contains the variable names (e.g., 'Month'), and another column contains the corresponding values (e.g., 'Sales'). This structure allows for more flexibility in performing analysis, particularly for tasks like statistical modeling, time-series analysis, and plotting. In the same sales dataset, a long format would have separate rows for each product's sales in different months, with columns for 'Product', 'Month', and 'Sales'.

Product	Month	Sales
Product A	January	500
Product A	February	450
Product A	March	600
Product B	January	300
Product B	February	350
Product B	March	400

Pivoting involves restructuring data by rearranging rows and columns to create a new summary view. This is particularly useful when you need to aggregate or summarize data across different dimensions, such as time, categories, or other attributes.

In contrast to pivoting, melting involves transforming a wide-format DataFrame into a long-format one. This is essential when you need to restructure a DataFrame for certain types of analyses, such as statistical modeling, which often requires data in long format. Melting essentially unpivots a DataFrame, converting columns into rows to stack data vertically.

Both pivoting and melting are fundamental in business analytics because they allow you to restructure datasets to suit specific analytical tasks, making your data easier to manage and interpret.

In databases and CSV files, it is common to store multiple time series data in a format known as "long" or "stacked" format. In this format, each individual value is represented by a single row in the table, rather than having multiple values per row. Let's take a look at an example to better understand this:

```python
import pandas as pd
cs102 = pd.DataFrame({
    'year': [2022, 2022, 2023, 2023],
    'semester': ['Spr','Fal','Spr', 'Fal'],
    'hours': [19, 85, 81, 69],
    'gpa': [3.4, 2.9, 3.1, 3.9]})
cs102
```
Output:

	Year	semester	hours	gpa
0	2022	Spr	19	3.4
1	2022	Fal	85	2.9
2	2023	Spr	81	3.1
3	2023	Fal	69	3.9

In the provided example, we have a DataFrame called cs102, representing multiple time series data in the long or stacked format. Each row in the table represents a single observation, with individual values represented by a single row.

To convert the data from long to wide format, we can use the pivot() method of a DataFrame. By specifying the index as 'year', the columns as 'semester', and the values as 'hours', we reshape the data accordingly.

```python
cs102_hours_pivoted = cs102.pivot(
    index='year',
    columns='semester',
    values='hours')
cs102_hours_pivoted
```

Output:

semester	Fal	Spr
year		
2022	85	19
2023	69	81

A Pandas pivot table consists of three main elements: the index, the columns, and the values. The index determines the grouping at the row level, the columns determine the grouping at the column level, and the values are the numerical values that you want to summarize. In the example provided above, the index is the year, the column is the semester, and the value is the hours. If you want to obtain a DataFrame with hierarchical columns, you can omit the value parameter:

```
cs102_pivoted = cs102.pivot(
    index='year',
    columns='semester')
cs102_pivoted
```

Output:

semester	hours		gpa	
	Fal	Spr	Fal	Spr
year				
2022	85	19	2.9	3.4
2023	69	81	3.9	3.1

Another way to achieve the same result is by using set_index to create a hierarchical index, followed by calling unstack. This approach is equivalent to using the pivot method:

```
cs102.set_index(
    ['year',
    'semester']).unstack('semester')
```

Output:

semester	hours		Gpa	
	Fal	Spr	Fal	Spr
year				
2022	85	19	2.9	3.4
2023	69	81	3.9	3.1

Similar to the stack() method, the melt() method can be used to convert data from a wide format to a long format. The melt() method provides more flexibility by allowing customization of the output. For example:

```
dept = pd.DataFrame({
    'department': ['acct', 'finc', 'mktg', 'mgmt'],
    'student': [56,23,98, 77],
    'faculty': [6, 4, 6, 7]})
dept
```

Output:

	department	student	Faculty
0	acct	56	6
1	finc	23	4
2	mktg	98	6
3	mgmt	77	7

The dept DataFrame is currently in a wide format, where each row represents a department and there are separate columns for student and faculty counts.

To convert the DataFrame into a long format, we can use the melt() method without any arguments. This will transform all the columns into two columns: a variable column and a value column. The variable column will contain the column names, and the value column will contain the corresponding values:

```
dept.melt()
```

Output:

	Variable	value
0	Department	acct
1	Department	finc
2	Department	mktg
3	Department	mgmt
4	Student	56
5	Student	23
6	Student	98
7	Student	77
8	Faculty	6
9	faculty	4
10	faculty	6
11	faculty	7

To specify a group indicator column, use the `id_vars` parameter in the `melt()` method. This keeps the specified column(s) as identifiers while reshaping the data. For example:

```
dept.melt(id_vars='department')
```

Output:

	department	variable	Value
0	acct	student	56
1	finc	student	23
2	mktg	student	98
3	mgmt	student	77
4	acct	faculty	6
5	finc	faculty	4
6	mktg	faculty	6
7	mgmt	faculty	7

This command uses 'department' as the group indicator, creating a "long" DataFrame with a variable column and a corresponding value column.

To make the column names more meaningful, we can use the var_name and value_name parameters. By setting var_name to 'academic' and value_name to 'count', the column names in the melted DataFrame will be updated accordingly:

```
dept_melted = dept.melt(id_vars='department',
    var_name='academic', value_name='count')
dept_melted
```
Output:

	Department	academic	Count
0	Acct	student	56
1	Finc	student	23
2	Mktg	student	98
3	Mgmt.	student	77
4	Acct	faculty	6
5	Finc	faculty	4
6	Mktg	faculty	6
7	Mgmt.	faculty	7

In the example above, the melt() method is used with four variables:

The *id_vars*: These are the columns that we want to preserve in their current form and not reshape. In the given example, the department column is correctly structured and does not need to be reshaped.
The *value_vars*: These are the variables that we want to reshape into a single column. In the wide version of the dept DataFrame, there are separate columns for student and faculty, which represent values of a single column that we want to reshape.
The *var_name*: This parameter specifies the name of the new column that will be created during the reshaping process. In the example, we want to create a single column called "academic" with the values "student" and "faculty".
The *value_name*: This parameter specifies the name of the column that will contain the values corresponding to the reshaped column. The column "count" holds the values associated with the "academic" column.

By specifying these variables in the melt() method, we can reshape the data from a wide format to a long format, providing more flexibility in organizing and analyzing the data.

We can also use the pivot method to reshape the DataFrame back to its original layout. By specifying the index as 'department', columns as ['academic'], and values as 'count', we can obtain the original wide format DataFrame:

```
dept_back = dept_melted.pivot(index='department',
    columns=['academic'], values='count')
dept_back
```
Output:

academic	faculty	Student
department		
acct	6	56
finc	4	23
mgmt	7	77
mktg	6	98

Lastly, if we prefer to have the index as a column rather than the row label, we can use the reset_index() method. This will move the index into a separate column named 'index':

```
dept_back.columns.name=None
dept_back.reset_index()
```
Output:

	department	faculty	student
0	acct	6	56
1	finc	4	23
2	mgmt	7	77
3	mktg	6	98

Overall, the melt() method allows us to convert data from a wide format to a long format, while the pivot() method enables us to reshape the DataFrame from long to wide.

Review Question 5.48
The operations for rearranging tabular data are often referred to as _______?
a. transfer operations
b. downsize operations
c. reshape operations
d. resize operations

Review Question 5.49
Which method converts data into a wide format?
a. The stack() method
b. The melt() method
c. The pivot() method
d. The reshape() method

Review Question 5.50
How is the data stored in the "long" or "stacked" format?
a. Each value is represented by a single row in the table.
b. Each row represents multiple values.
c. Each column represents multiple values.
d. Each value is represented by a single column in the table.

Review Question 5.51
What are the three main elements of a pandas pivot table, or the pivot() method?
a. Index, columns, and values
b. Rows, columns, and values
c. Columns, values, and groups
d. Index, values, and groups

Review Question 5.52
How can you obtain a DataFrame with hierarchical columns using the pivot() method?

a. By omitting the value parameter
b. By specifying hierarchical=True
c. By calling the stack() method after pivot()
d. By using the melt() method instead of pivot()

Review Question 5.53
What is an equivalent approach to using the pivot() method?
a. Using the melt() method
b. Using the stack() method
c. Using the unstack() method
d. Using the set_index() method followed by unstack() method

Review Question 5.54
What is the purpose of transforming data from long to wide format?
a. To summarize numerical values
b. To convert hierarchical columns
c. To preserve the original structure
d. To aggregate or summarize data across different dimensions

Review Question 5.55
What is the purpose of converting data from a wide format to a long format?
a. To summarize numerical values
b. To create hierarchical columns
c. To facilitate analysis and visualization
d. To merge multiple columns into one

Review Question 5.56
Which method can be used to convert data from a wide format to a long format?
a. The pivot() method
b. The unstack() method
c. The melt() method
d. The unpivot() method

Review Question 5.57
Which column(s) are preserved without reshaping when using the melt() method?
a. All columns are reshaped.
b. Variable column is preserved.
c. Value column is preserved.
d. Id_vars column(s) are preserved.

Review Question 5.58
What is a "group indicator" column?
a. A column that identifies the groups or categories in the dataset.
b. A column that represents numerical values.
c. A column that is created during the reshaping process from long to wide.
d. A column that holds the values associated with all the numerical variable column.

Review Question 5.59
How can you specify the group indicator column in the melt() method?
a. By using the id_vars parameter

b. By using the var_name parameter
c. By using the value_name parameter
d. By using the columns parameter

Review Question 5.60
What does the var_name parameter specify in the melt() method?
a. Name of the value column
b. Name of the index column
c. Name of the variable column
d. Name of the group indicator column

Exercise 5.3

Consider the following DataFrame:

```
data = {
    'Date': ['2024-01-01', '2024-01-01', '2024-01-02', '2024-01-02', '2024-01-03', '2024-01-03'],
    'City': ['New York', 'Los Angeles', 'New York', 'Los Angeles', 'New York', 'Los Angeles'],
    'Temperature': [32, 75, 30, 77, 28, 76],
    'Humidity': [80, 10, 82, 15, 85, 10]
}
df = pd.DataFrame(data)
```

Task 1: Reshape the DataFrame such that 'Date' becomes the index, 'City' becomes the new columns of the DataFrame, and the values are represented by 'Temperature' readings.
Task 2: Similar to Task 1, reshape the DataFrame again. This time, create a DataFrame with hierarchical columns that include both 'Temperature' and 'Humidity' for each 'City'. The 'Date' should remain as the index.
Task 3: Obtain the same resultset as Task 2, but without using the pivot() method.

Exercise 5.4

Consider the following DataFrame:

```
data = {
    'Day': ['Monday', 'Tuesday', 'Wednesday', 'Thursday', 'Friday'],
    'New York': [32, 30, 28, 22, 30],
    'Los Angeles': [75, 77, 76, 78, 75],
    'Chicago': [20, 18, 15, 19, 17]
}
df = pd.DataFrame(data)
```

This DataFrame represents temperature data for New York, Los Angeles, and Chicago over five days.
Task 1: Reshape the DataFrame by transforming all the columns into two columns: a 'variable' column and a 'value' column. The 'variable' column should contain the column names, and the 'value' column should contain the corresponding values.
Task 2: Similar to Task 1, but this time, add a new column named "Day" as the first column in the reshaped DataFrame.
Task 3: This task is similar to Task 2, but the columns should be named as 'Day', 'City', and 'Temperature'.
Task 4: Reshape the DataFrame from Task 3 back to its original DataFrame.

5.4 Tidy Data

The concept of "tidy data," introduced by Hadley Wickham, refers to data that conforms to three key principles, as outlined in his paper [here](http://vita.had.co.nz/papers/tidy-data.pdf). These principles are:

1. Each column represents a distinct variable in the dataset.
2. Each row corresponds to a single observation.
3. Each table or dataset contains only one type of observational unit.

Converting data into a "long" format, which adheres to these principles, provides several advantages. It simplifies data manipulation, making it easier to add or retrieve information without concern for the data's structure. Additionally, long-format data is typically easier and faster to query and analyze.

It's important to distinguish between tidying data and data cleansing. Data cleansing involves addressing issues like missing values, redundant information, and incorrect data types. Tidying data, on the other hand, involves organizing the structure of the data to make it suitable for analysis. This process does not correct errors but restructures the data for easier use.

Let's consider an example. The following DataFrame is not in tidy format:

Progress	Adam	Lucy	Scott
Hours	12	78	120
GPA	4	3.9	3.3

While this table is readable, it violates the principles of tidy data for three main reasons:

1. The students' names are used as column headers, but they should be values in a column representing the "Name" variable.
2. "Hours" and "GPA" are treated as observations in rows, but they are distinct variables and should have their own columns.
3. The table mixes two different types of measurements: hours of study and GPA. These represent different units of observation and should be separated into different variables for a proper tidy format.

The above table can be tidied into the following format to ensure it is tidy and ready for analysis:

Name	Variable	Value
Adam	Hours	12
Lucy	Hours	78
Scott	Hours	120
Adam	GPA	4
Lucy	GPA	3.9
Scott	GPA	3.3

In this tidy format, each row represents a single observation (a student's progress in either "Hours" or "GPA"). The columns now adhere to the principles of tidy data:

1. Each column is a single variable: "Name," "Variable" (either Hours or GPA), and "Value."
2. Each row represents a single observation.
3. The table contains only one type of observational unit: student progress, measured either in study hours or GPA.

By restructuring the data in this way, it is easier to manipulate, analyze, and visualize. For example, if you wanted to calculate average hours spent studying or the average GPA for all students, this tidy structure would simplify the process.

This format is more flexible for common data manipulation tasks, such as filtering for specific variables or grouping by "Name" to summarize results. This tidy approach also works seamlessly with libraries like Pandas in Python, which are designed to handle and analyze data efficiently when it is in a tidy structure.

In this section, we will explore Pandas methods for converting a dataset to this structure:

```python
marks=pd.DataFrame({'statistics':[90,87,45],
    'English':[46,56,87],'Spanish':[95,74,45],
    'Physics':[75,65,33]},
    index=['adam','lucy','lisa'])
marks
```

Output:

	statistics	English	Spanish	Physics
adam	90	46	95	75
lucy	87	56	74	65
lisa	45	87	45	33

In this DataFrame, we can observe that it doesn't adhere to the principles of tidy data. The two primary variables (students and subjects) have not been identified as columns. Furthermore, the values representing subjects, such as statistics and physics, are observations and should not be treated as columns. We can address the anomalies in the "grades" DataFrame by utilizing the "stack" method, which moves all column names to the index. This method returns a new DataFrame or Series with a multilevel index:

```
marks_stacked = marks.stack()
marks_stacked
```

Output:

```
adam   statistics    90
       English       46
       Spanish       95
       Physics       75
lucy   statistics    87
       English       56
       Spanish       74
       Physics       65
lisa   statistics    45
       English       87
       Spanish       45
       Physics       33
dtype: int64
```

As observed in the output above, the DataFrame has been transformed from a wide format to a long format. Let's check the data type of this stacked object:

```
type(marks_stacked)
```

Output:

```
pandas.core.series.Series
```

To identify the two variables, "Name" and "Subject," as separate columns, use the "reset_index" method:

```
marks_stacked.reset_index()
```

Output:

	level_0	level_1	0
0	adam	statistics	90
1	adam	English	46
2	adam	Spanish	95
3	adam	Physics	75
4	lucy	statistics	87
5	lucy	English	56
6	lucy	Spanish	74
7	lucy	Physics	65
8	lisa	statistics	45
9	lisa	English	87
10	lisa	Spanish	45
11	lisa	Physics	33

We can change the column names using the "rename_axis" method and reset the index:

```
marks_stacked.rename_axis(['name',
    'subject']).reset_index(name='score')
```

Output:

	name	subject	score
0	adam	statistics	90
1	adam	English	46
2	adam	Spanish	95
3	adam	Physics	75
4	lucy	statistics	87
5	lucy	English	56
6	lucy	Spanish	74
7	lucy	Physics	65
8	lisa	statistics	45
9	lisa	English	87
10	lisa	Spanish	45
11	lisa	Physics	33

To revert this DataFrame back to its original (wide) format, we can use the "unstack" method:

```
marks_stacked.unstack()
```

Output:

	statistics	English	Spanish	Physics
Adam	90	46	95	75
Lucy	87	56	74	65
Lisa	45	87	45	33

Review Question 5.61

What are the three principles of tidy data?

a. Columns correspond to variables, rows contain observations, and each table contains one observational unit.

b. Each column represents an observation, rows correspond to variables, and each table contains multiple observational units.

c. Each column corresponds to a variable, rows contain variables, and each table contains one observational unit.

d. Each column represents a variable, rows contain observations, and each table contains multiple observational units.

Review Question 5.62

How is tidying data different from data cleansing?

a. Tidying data involves handling missing values, while data cleansing involves restructuring the data.

b. Tidying data involves rearranging the data, while data cleansing involves removing redundant information.

c. Tidying data involves restructuring the data, while data cleansing involves handling missing values and correcting inaccurate data types.

d. Tidying data involves removing filler characters, while data cleansing involves organizing the data correctly.

Review Question 5.63

In the example DataFrame given, why is it not considered tidy data?

Progress	Adam	Lucy	Scott
Hours	12	78	120
GPA	4	3.9	3.3

a. The DataFrame has too many filler characters.
b. The DataFrame contains multiple units of observation.
c. The DataFrame has incorrect data types.
d. The DataFrame has missing values.

Review Question 5.64

What is the benefit of converting data to the long format?
a. It simplifies data manipulation and facilitates data retrieval.
b. It reduces the number of variables in the dataset.
c. It improves data accuracy and removes redundant information.
d. It allows for more secure data storage.

Review Question 5.65

Which method can be used to convert a DataFrame to the long format?
a. stack()
b. unstack()
c. reshape()
d. pivot()

Review Question 5.66

What method can be used to convert a DataFrame back to its original (wide) format?
a. stack()
b. melt()
c. unstack()
d. pivot_table()

Review Question 5.67

What are the primary variables missing in the given DataFrame to adhere to tidy data principles?

	statistics	English	Spanish	Physics
adam	90	46	95	75
lucy	87	56	74	65
lisa	45	87	45	33

a. Age and Height
b. Name and Subject
c. Progress and GPA
d. Hours and 0-4 scale

5.5 Data Scaling

Data scaling prepares data for analytics. It involves transforming the data so that it fits within a specific

range or follows a specific distribution. This process is essential for many machine learning algorithms,

which perform better when the input data is scaled. In this section, we will cover the basics of data scaling, its importance, and the different techniques used to scale data.

Data scaling is a fundamental step in the data preparation process for several reasons. Firstly, it significantly *improves model performance*. Many machine learning algorithms, particularly those that rely on gradient descent, such as linear regression, logistic regression, and neural networks, require data to be scaled. When data is not scaled, the optimization process can become inefficient, leading to slower convergence and potentially suboptimal solutions. For example, consider a dataset with two features: age (ranging from 0 to 100) and income (ranging from $0 to $100,000). Without scaling, the income feature would dominate the age feature, making it difficult for the algorithm to learn effectively from the data.

Secondly, data scaling ensures *equal weighting of features*. In raw form, features with larger ranges can disproportionately influence the results of the analysis. By scaling the data, each feature contributes equally, preventing any single feature from skewing the results. For instance, in a dataset where one feature ranges from 1 to 1000 and another ranges from 0.01 to 0.1, the larger range feature could overshadow the smaller range feature, leading to biased model training. Scaling these features to a common range ensures that both have an equal impact on the model's learning process.

Additionally, scaling facilitates *comparison across different features and datasets*. When features are on a similar scale, it becomes easier to compare them directly, identify patterns, and draw meaningful insights. For example, in a healthcare dataset, comparing the impact of blood pressure (measured in mmHg) and cholesterol levels (measured in mg/dL) on heart disease risk is more straightforward when both features are scaled to a similar range.

Moreover, data scaling *reduces computational complexity*. Algorithms that involve distance calculations, such as k-nearest neighbors (KNN) and support vector machines (SVM), benefit significantly from scaled data. These algorithms compute distances between data points, and when the features are on different scales, the computation can become complex and inefficient. By scaling the data, we simplify these calculations, leading to faster and more efficient model training. For example, in a KNN algorithm, the distance between two data points with scaled features can be computed more accurately and quickly, improving the overall performance of the algorithm.

When preparing data for analysis, it is crucial to apply the appropriate scaling technique to ensure the data is in a suitable format for analytical needs. Various scaling techniques can be used depending on the nature of the data and the specific requirements of the analysis. Here, we will discuss four common data scaling techniques: Min-Max Scaling, Standardization, Robust Scaling, and Log Transformation.

Min-Max Scaling (Normalization) is a method that transforms data to fit within a specified range, usually [0, 1] or [-1, 1]. This technique is particularly useful when the data has a known minimum and maximum value. By using min-max scaling, each feature is rescaled proportionally to its original values, ensuring that all features are on a similar scale:

$$X' = \frac{X - X_{min}}{X_{max} - X_{min}}$$

Where X is the original value, X_{min} and X_{max} are the minimum and maximum values of the feature, respectively, and X' is the scaled value.

Min-Max Scaling is ideal when the data needs to be transformed to fit within a specific range, such as [0, 1] or [-1, 1]. This technique is particularly useful when the features in your dataset have similar scales. For instance, if you are working with a dataset where all features represent percentages or proportions, min-max scaling ensures that each feature is normalized to a common range, facilitating comparison and interpretation. This method is also beneficial when the algorithms are sensitive to the scale of the input data.

Standardization (Z-score Normalization) is another popular scaling technique that transforms the data to have a mean of zero and a standard deviation of one. This method is useful when the data follows a Gaussian distribution. Standardization ensures that each feature contributes equally to the model by centering the data around the mean and scaling it according to the standard deviation:

$$X' = \frac{X - \mu}{\sigma}$$

Where X is the original value, μ is the mean of the feature, σ is the standard deviation of the feature, and X' is the scaled value.

Standardization is the go-to technique when the data follows a Gaussian distribution, meaning it is normally distributed. Standardization transforms the data so that it has a mean of zero and a standard deviation of one. This technique is particularly useful for machine learning algorithms that assume normally distributed data, such as linear regression, logistic regression, and principal component analysis (PCA). For example, in linear regression, standardizing the input features ensures that each feature contributes equally to the model, preventing features with larger ranges from dominating the analysis. Additionally, standardization is beneficial when you need to compare features that have different units of measurement, such as height (in centimeters) and weight (in kilograms).

Robust Scaling is a technique that uses the median and the interquartile range (IQR) to scale the data. This method is less sensitive to outliers, making it ideal for datasets with significant outliers. By focusing on the median and IQR, robust scaling ensures that the scaled data is not overly influenced by extreme values:

$$X' = \frac{X - median}{IQR}$$

Where X is the original value, *median* is the median of the feature, IQR is the interquartile range of the feature, and X' is the scaled value.

Robust Scaling is suitable for datasets that contain outliers, which are extreme values that can skew the results of other scaling methods. Robust scaling uses the median and the interquartile range (IQR) to scale the data, making it less sensitive to outliers. This technique is ideal when you have features with significant outliers that you do not want to remove but need to account for in your analysis. For example, in a financial dataset where some transactions are exceptionally large compared to the rest, robust scaling ensures that these outliers do not disproportionately affect the scaling of the data. By focusing on the median and IQR, robust scaling provides a more accurate representation of the central tendency and spread of the data.

Log Transformation is a technique that applies the logarithm function to the data. This method can help manage skewed data and reduce the impact of outliers. By transforming the data logarithmically, the scale of the data is compressed, which can make patterns in the data more apparent and easier to analyze:

$$X' = \log(X + 1)$$

Where X is the original value, and X' is the transformed value.

Log Transformation is appropriate for data that is highly skewed, meaning it has a long tail on one side of the distribution. This technique applies the logarithm function to the data, compressing the scale and reducing the impact of large values. Log transformation is particularly useful when you want to manage skewed data and make patterns more apparent. For example, in a dataset containing household incomes, where a small number of households have significantly higher incomes than the rest, log transformation can help reduce the skewness and highlight underlying trends. Additionally, log transformation is beneficial when working with multiplicative relationships, such as growth rates or ratios, as it can linearize exponential growth patterns.

Each of these data scaling techniques has its advantages and is suited for different scenarios. Selecting the appropriate data scaling technique depends on the characteristics of your dataset and the requirements of your analytical model. Min-max scaling is useful for bringing features within a specific range, standardization is ideal for normally distributed data, robust scaling handles outliers effectively, and log transformation manages skewed data. Understanding when to use each technique ensures that your data is well-prepared for analysis, leading to more accurate and reliable results.

Example 5.1

Let's consider a dataset with the following values for a single feature:

$\{10, 20, 30, 40, 50\}$

1. Min-Max Scaling (Normalization):

$$X' = \frac{X - X_{min}}{X_{max} - X_{min}} = \frac{X - 10}{50 - 10}$$

Scaled values: $\{0, 0.25, 0.5, 0.75, 1\}$

2. Standardization (Z-score Normalization):

Mean (μ) = 30, Standard deviation (σ) = 15.81

$$X' = \frac{X - \mu}{\sigma} = \frac{X - 30}{15.81}$$

Scaled values: $\{-1.27, -0.63, 0, 0.63, 1.27\}$

3. Robust Scaling:

Median = 30, IQR = 20

$$X' = \frac{X - median}{IQR} = \frac{X - 30}{20}$$

Scaled values: $\{-1, -0.5, 0, 0.5, 1\}$

4. Log Transformation:

$$X' = \log(X + 1)$$

Scaled values: $\{2.40, 3.04, 3.43, 3.71, 3.92\}$

Review Question 5.68

What is the primary purpose of data scaling in data preparation for analytics?
a. To transform data into categorical values
b. To fit data within a specific range or follow a specific distribution
c. To eliminate missing values
d. To convert data into binary format

Review Question 5.69
Why is data scaling particularly important for machine learning algorithms like linear regression and neural networks?
a. It increases the size of the dataset
b. It improves model performance by ensuring efficient optimization
c. It converts categorical data into numerical data
d. It removes outliers from the dataset

Review Question 5.70
In the context of data scaling, what does "equal weighting of features" mean?
a. Ensuring all features have the same number of missing values
b. Making sure all features are equally important in the analysis
c. Ensuring all features have the same range of values
d. Making sure all features have the same data type

Review Question 5.71
How does scaling facilitate comparison across different features and datasets?
a. By converting all data to categorical values
b. By standardizing all features to the same unit of measurement
c. By making features easier to compare directly and identify patterns
d. By removing outliers from the dataset

Review Question 5.72
Which of the following algorithms benefit significantly from scaled data due to their reliance on distance calculations?
a. Decision trees
b. K-nearest neighbors (KNN) and support vector machines (SVM)
c. Naive Bayes
d. Random forests

Review Question 5.73
What is the primary advantage of Min-Max Scaling (Normalization)?
a. It reduces the number of features in the dataset
b. It transforms data to fit within a specified range, usually [0, 1] or [-1, 1]
c. It removes duplicate entries from the dataset
d. It converts categorical data into numerical data

Review Question 5.74
For which type of dataset is Min-Max Scaling particularly useful?
a. Datasets with categorical variables
b. Datasets where all features represent percentages or proportions
c. Datasets with significant outliers
d. Datasets with missing values

Review Question 5.75
When is Standardization (Z-score Normalization) most appropriate?
a. When the data follows a Gaussian distribution
b. When the dataset contains only categorical variables
c. When the features have a large number of missing values
d. When the dataset is very small

Review Question 5.76
If the original dataset is {10, 20, 30, 40, 50} and the scaled dataset is {-1.27, -0.63, 0, 0.63, 1.27}, which scaling technique is used?
a. Min-Max Scaling (Normalization)
b. Standardization (Z-score Normalization)
c. Robust Scaling
d. Log Transformation

Review Question 5.77
Which scaling technique uses the median and interquartile range (IQR) to scale the data?
a. Min-Max Scaling
b. Standardization
c. Robust Scaling
d. Log Transformation

Review Question 5.78
Why is Robust Scaling particularly suitable for datasets with outliers?
a. It converts outliers to categorical values
b. It uses the median and IQR, making it less influenced by extreme values
c. It removes outliers from the dataset
d. It transforms data to fit within a specific range

Review Question 5.79
In which scenario is Log Transformation most beneficial?
a. When the data is highly skewed
b. When the data follows a Gaussian distribution
c. When the dataset contains only categorical variables
d. When the dataset has no outliers

Review Question 5.80
What is the primary purpose of applying the logarithm function to the data in Log Transformation?
a. To convert data into binary format
b. To handle skewed data and reduce the impact of outliers
c. To remove missing values from the dataset
d. To increase the number of features in the dataset

Review Question 5.81
If the original dataset is {10, 20, 30, 40, 50} and the scaled dataset is {-1, -0.5, 0, 0.5, 1}, which scaling technique is used?
a. Min-Max Scaling (Normalization)
b. Standardization (Z-score Normalization)
c. Robust Scaling
d. Log Transformation

Review Question 5.82
What does Robust Scaling focus on to ensure it is less influenced by outliers?
a. Mean and standard deviation
b. Minimum and maximum values
c. Median and interquartile range (IQR)
d. Logarithmic values

Review Question 5.83
Why is it important to select the appropriate data scaling technique?
a. To reduce the size of the dataset
b. To ensure the data is in a suitable format for analysis
c. To remove duplicate entries
d. To convert all data to categorical values

Review Question 5.84
Which data scaling technique is ideal for managing skewed data?
a. Min-Max Scaling
b. Standardization
c. Robust Scaling
d. Log Transformation

Review Question 5.85
Which technique is beneficial when working with features that have different units of measurement?
a. Min-Max Scaling
b. Standardization
c. Robust Scaling
d. Log Transformation

Exercise 5.5

Task 1: Given a dataset with the values {5, 10, 15, 20, 25}, apply min-max scaling to transform the data to the range [0, 1].
Task 2. Standardize the dataset {2, 4, 6, 8, 10} and calculate the mean and standard deviation of the scaled data.
Task 3. Apply robust scaling to the dataset {100, 200, 300, 400, 500} and compare the results with standardization.
Task 4. Use log transformation on the dataset {1, 10, 100, 1000, 10000} and interpret the results.

5.6 Chapter Summary

In this chapter, you learned data preparation, including hierarchical indexing for scattered data and data combination methods like merge(), join(), concat(), and append(). Pivoting and Melting were introduced for reshaping data. The concept of tidy data was emphasized, underscoring the importance of well-structured data for analysis. Lastly, the chapter highlighted data scaling, a crucial aspect of data preparation that ensures the data range is suitable for various algorithms, contributing to more accurate and efficient models.

5.7 Solutions to the Review Questions

5.1 A; 5.2 A; 5.3 C; 5.4 A; 5.5 C; 5.6 C; 5.7 C; 5.8 A; 5.9 A; 5.10 A; 5.11 B; 5.12 A; 5.13 A; 5.14 C; 5.15 B; 5.16 C; 5.17 C; 5.18 B; 5.19 C; 5.20 B; 5.21 A; 5.22 A; 5.23 B; 5.24 B; 5.25 A; 5.26 C; 5.27 D; 5.28 A; 5.29 C; 5.30 C; 5.31 C; 5.32 C; 5.33 C; 5.34 A; 5.35 D; 5.36 C; 5.37 B; 5.38 A; 5.39 D; 5.40 C; 5.41 B; 5.42 C; 5.43 A; 5.44 C; 5.45 B; 5.46 D; 5.47 A; 5.48 C; 5.49 C; 5.50 A; 5.51 A; 5.52 A; 5.53 D; 5.54 D; 5.55 C; 5.56 C; 5.57 D; 5.58 A; 5.59 A; 5.60 C; 5.61 A; 5.62 C; 5.63 B; 5.64 A; 5.65 A; 5.66 C; 5.67 B; 5.68 B; 5.69 B; 5.70 C; 5.71 C; 5.72 B; 5.73 B; 5.74 B; 5.75 A; 5.76 B; 5.77 C; 5.78 B; 5.79 A; 5.80 B; 5.81 C; 5.82 C; 5.83 B; 5.84 D; 5.85 B;

Chapter 6: Data Aggregation

Chapter Learning Objectives

6.1 Explain Pandas group operations
6.2 Utilize the 'Split-Apply-Combine' methodology for conducting data analysis
6.3 Demonstrate aggregation with data transformation
6.4 Perform custom operations with apply() method
6.5 Summarize data with pivot tables and cross-tabulations
6.6 Generate descriptive and summary statistics

6.1 Introduction

Data analytics often involves analyzing and summarizing large datasets to extract meaningful insights. One task in this process is data aggregation, which combines multiple data points into a single value or summary statistics. Pandas provides efficient tools for performing data aggregation.

Pandas provides a powerful framework for structured data analysis through Series and DataFrame structures. Its aggregation capabilities simplify the process of grouping data and computing summary statistics for each group. With Pandas, handling large datasets and performing grouping and summarization based on specific criteria is straightforward. You can easily calculate various statistical measures, such as mean, sum, count, and more, within distinct groups using Pandas' flexible and efficient methods. Additionally, you can apply custom aggregation functions using the agg() method, providing even more flexibility in your analysis.

Pandas provides the groupby() function, allowing you to group the data based on one or more variables of interest. This function creates a GroupBy object, which contains individual groups, each representing a specific grouping criterion. Once the data is grouped, you can apply various aggregation functions to compute summary statistics for each group.

After performing the aggregation, you can further refine and transform the resulting data using Pandas' rich set of data manipulation methods. This includes sorting the aggregated data, filtering specific groups based on conditions, merging groups, or creating new columns derived from the aggregated values.

In addition to data aggregation, Pandas provides two other important group operations: transformation and filtering. Transformation involves applying operations to individual data points within each group, enabling data modification while preserving the original structure. Filtering allows for selecting specific groups or subsets of data based on defined conditions, enabling focused analysis and targeted observations. By combining aggregation, transformation, and filtering, Pandas offers a comprehensive toolkit for exploring and analyzing grouped data, empowering data scientists to derive valuable insights and make data-driven decisions.

Let's illustrate aggregation, transformation, and filtering using Pandas:

Aggregation involves computing a summary statistic (like mean, sum, or count) for each group in the data.

```python
import pandas as pd
# Sample DataFrame
data = {
    'Category': ['A', 'B', 'A', 'B', 'A', 'B'],
    'Value': [10, 20, 30, 40, 50, 60]
}
df = pd.DataFrame(data)
# Aggregating by 'Category', calculating the mean of 'Value'
aggregated_df = df.groupby('Category').agg({'Value': 'mean'})
aggregated_df
```

Output:

	Value
Category	
A	30.0
B	40.0

Transformation applies a function to each group, but returns an object that is the same size as the original.

```python
# Applying a transformation to normalize the 'Value' column by group
df['Transformed_Value'] =
df.groupby('Category')['Value'].transform(lambda x: (x - x.mean()))
df
```

Output:

	Category	Value	Transformed_Value
0	A	10	-20.0
1	B	20	-20.0
2	A	30	0.0
3	B	40	0.0
4	A	50	20.0
5	B	60	20.0

The transform function normalizes the Value column by subtracting the mean of each group from the values.

Filtering selects specific groups or subsets of data that meet certain criteria.

```
# Filtering groups where the mean 'Value' is greater than 35
f_df = df.groupby('Category').filter(lambda x: x['Value'].mean() > 35)
f_df
```

Output:

	Category	Value	Transformed_Value
1	B	20	-20.0
3	B	40	0.0
5	B	60	20.0

This example filters out the rows where the mean of Value in each group is greater than 35. Only Category B meets the condition.

The *filter()* method of DataFrame in Pandas allows us to selectively include or exclude data based on specific conditions. When used with groupby(), unlike the aggregate() method, which returns a single value for each group, the filter() method retrieves all rows from each group depending on whether the group-wise condition is met. This is similar to the HAVING clause in SQL, which filters on aggregated results.

Review Question 6.1
What is the purpose of data aggregation in business data analytics?
a. To extract meaningful insights from large datasets.
b. To organize data in a tabular format.
c. To explore the structure of the dataset.
d. To load data into a Pandas DataFrame.

Review Question 6.2
Which of the following structures does Pandas provide for structured data analysis?
a. Array and List
b. Series and DataFrame
c. Dictionary and Tuple
d. Set and Queue

Review Question 6.3
What can you do with Pandas' aggregation capabilities?
a. Perform data grouping and summarizing.
b. Load data into a Pandas DataFrame.
c. Explore the structure of the dataset.

d. Organize data in a tabular format.

Review Question 6.4
What is the purpose of the groupby() function in Pandas?
a. To apply aggregation functions to the data.
b. To filter specific groups based on conditions.
c. To transform individual data points within each group.
d. To group the data based on variables of interest.

Review Question 6.5
Which of the following is an example of an aggregation function in Pandas?
a. sort()
b. filter()
c. transform()
d. sum()

Review Question 6.6
What method can be used in Pandas to apply custom aggregation functions?
a. agg()
b. sort()
c. filter()
d. transform()

Review Question 6.7
What can't you do with the aggregated data in Pandas?
a. Sort the aggregated data.
b. Filter specific groups based on conditions.
c. Merge groups.
d. Select rows that meet certain conditions.

Review Question 6.8
What is the purpose of transformation in Pandas' group operations?
a. To apply aggregation functions to the data.
b. To filter specific groups based on conditions.
c. To modify individual data points within each group.
d. To merge groups.

Review Question 6.9
What is the purpose of filtering in Pandas' group operations?
a. To apply aggregation functions to the data.
b. To modify individual data points within each group.
c. To select specific groups or subsets of data based on conditions.
d. To merge groups.

Review Question 6.10
What are the three important group operations provided by Pandas?
a. Aggregation, filtering, and merging.
b. Aggregation, transformation, and filtering.
c. Aggregation, transformation, and sorting.
d. Filtering, transformation, and merging.

Review Question 6.11
What does Pandas' comprehensive toolkit for grouped data analysis empower data scientists to do?
a. Perform data aggregation and transformation only.
b. Perform data filtering and sorting only.
c. Derive valuable insights and make data-driven decisions.
d. None of the options is correct.

Review Question 6.12
What is the purpose of the filter() method in pandas?
a. To calculate the average value for each group
b. To retrieve rows from each group based on specific conditions
c. To sort the data within each group
d. To combine multiple groups into a single group

Review Question 6.13
In the given example, what is x used in the filter() method?
```
grouped_course.filter(lambda x:x['act'].mean()>30.5)
```
a. an unknown value
b. the mean act value
c. a row in grouped_course
d. a column in grouped_course

Review Question 6.14
What does the filter() method return?
a. The average value for each group
b. The total sum of each group
c. The filtered rows from each group based on the condition
d. The first row from each group

Review Question 6.15
What is the main difference between the filter() and transform() methods in Pandas?
a. The filter() method modifies the values within a group, while the transform() method reduces the number of records.
b. The filter() method reduces the number of records, while the transform() method maintains the same number of records as the input.
c. The filter() method requires the output to have the same shape as the input, while the transform() method can return an object of any shape.
d. The filter() method applies a function to each value within a group, while the transform() method retrieves rows based on specific conditions.

Review Question 6.16
In the given example, what transformation is applied using the transform() method?
```
grouped_score['grade'].transform(lambda x:x/20)
```
a. Converting grades to a scale of 1 to 20.
b. Converting grades to a scale of 1 to 5 by dividing each value by 20.
c. Replacing missing values with the value 0.
d. Calculating the total count of missing values in each group.

6.2 Group Operations

Aggregation summarizes a group of values into a single result. The "Split-Apply-Combine" methodology, introduced by Hadley Wickham, provides an efficient approach for this process, consisting of three steps:

Step 1. Splitting the Data

Use Pandas' groupby() method to divide the data into smaller groups based on one or more variables. This can be done along rows (`axis=0`) or columns (`axis=1`).

Step 2. Applying Functions to Each Group

After splitting, apply aggregation functions to each group. Pandas offers built-in options like `min()`, `max()`, `mean()`, `sum()`, `count()`, `std()`, and `var()`, among others. You can also define custom functions for more flexible analysis.

Step 3. Combining the Results

Finally, the aggregated results are combined into a single Pandas DataFrame or Series. This new object is typically smaller than the original dataset, representing the final outcome of the aggregation process.

For more on the "Split-Apply-Combine" approach, see Hadley Wickham's paper: [The Split-Apply-Combine Strategy for Data Analysis](https://www.jstatsoft.org/article/view/v040i01/v40i01.pdf).

To understand group operations, let's work through an example. First set up the DataFrame:

```python
score = pd.DataFrame({
    'course':['CS101', 'CS101', 'CS201', 'CS201', 'CS101'],
    'student':['12345', '12346', '12345', '12347', '12345'],
    'grade':[65, 89, 74, 85, 92],
    'absence':[8, 4, 5, 5, 2] })
score
```

Output:

	course	student	grade	absence
0	CS101	12345	65	8
1	CS101	12346	89	4
2	CS201	12345	74	5
3	CS201	12347	85	5
4	CS101	12345	92	2

Suppose we want to compute the mean grade and absence using the course labels. We can group the DataFrame by the 'course' column:

```
grouped = score.groupby('course')
grouped
```

Output:

```
<pandas.core.groupby.generic.DataFrameGroupBy object at 0x0430190E02405E0>
```

The `grouped` variable holds a GroupBy object, which is essentially a blueprint for how the data should be grouped. At this stage, no computations have occurred on the data itself—just like a SQL view, which defines a query but doesn't execute it or store data. Instead, the GroupBy object stores information about how the grouping should occur (based on the 'course' column) and waits for an operation to be applied, such as aggregation, transformation, or filtering. This makes it similar to a "view" in SQL, which defines an operation but doesn't immediately compute or store results until queried. The purpose of this object is to provide the necessary information to apply operations to each group.

Examining the properties of the groupby object, we can access the data type using the type() function:

```
type(grouped)
```

Output:

```
pandas.core.groupby.generic.DataFrameGroupBy
```

Each group within the groupby object is a separate DataFrame. We can obtain the names of the groups using the groups attribute, which returns a dictionary with the group names as keys:

```
grouped.groups.keys()
```

Output:

```
dict_keys(['CS101', 'CS201'])
```

To retrieve specific records based on their position in each group, we can use the nth() method. For example, to see the details of the second score belonging to each course:

```
grouped.nth(1)
```

Output:

	Student	grade	absence
course			
CS101	12346	89	4
CS201	12347	85	5

To access all the data for a particular group, we can use the get_group() method. Here, we retrieve all data for the 'CS101' group:

```
grouped.get_group('CS101')
```
Output:

	course	student	grade	Absence
0	CS101	12345	65	8
1	CS101	12346	89	4
4	CS101	12345	92	2

To compute group means, we can use the mean method on the GroupBy object:

```
grouped[['grade', 'absence']].mean()
```
Output:

	grade	Absence
course		
CS101	82.0	4.666667
CS201	79.5	5.000000

By applying the mean() method to the "grade" and "absence" columns of the grouped, providing us with a summary measure of the students' performance and attendance within each course group. Thirteen aggregate functions can be applied to groups, including sum(), max(), min(), std(), var(), mean(), count(), size(), sem(), first(), last(), describe(), and nth().

If multiple keys are passed as a list, the resulting DataFrame will have a hierarchical index consisting of unique pairs of keys:

```
grouped2 = score.groupby(['course', 'student'])
grouped2.mean()
```

Output:

		grade	Absence
course	**student**		
CS101	**12345**	65.0	8.0
	12346	89.0	4.0
CS201	**12345**	74.0	5.0
	12347	85.0	5.0

Here we grouped the data using two keys (course and student), and the resulting DataFrame now has a hierarchical index consisting of the unique pairs of keys observed. To unstack the hierarchical index, we can use the unstack() method:

```
grouped2.mean().unstack()
```

Output:

student	grade			Absence		
	12345	12346	12347	12345	12346	12347
course						
CS101	78.5	89.0	NaN	5.0	4.0	NaN
CS201	74.0	NaN	85.0	5.0	NaN	5.0

Another useful GroupBy method is size, which returns a Series containing group sizes:

```
score.groupby(['course', 'student']).size()
```

Output:

```
course  student
CS101   12345      2
        12346      1
CS201   12345      1
        12347      1
dtype: int64
```

Note that missing values in a group key are excluded from the result by default. To include them, you can pass dropna=False to the groupby method. First, drop a student name:

```
score.loc[4, 'student'] = None
score
```

Output:

	course	student	grade	Absence
0	CS101	12345	65	8
1	CS101	12346	89	4
2	CS201	12345	74	5
3	CS201	12347	85	5
4	CS101	None	92	2

Now, try the size again:

```
score.groupby(['course', 'student']).size()
```

Output:

```
course  student
CS101   12345      1
        12346      1
CS201   12345      1
        12347      1
dtype: int64
```

This behavior can be disabled by passing dropna=False to groupby:

```
score.groupby(['course', 'student'], dropna=False).size()
```

Output:

```
course   student
CS101    12345        1
         12346        1
         NaN          1
CS201    12345        1
         12347        1
dtype: int64
```

The groupby object allows for iteration, enabling you to iterate over groups and retrieve a sequence of 2-tuples. Each tuple contains the group name and the corresponding chunk of data. Consider the example:

```
for name, group_df in grouped:
    print(name)
    print(group_df)
```

Output:

```
CS101
   course student   grade   absence
0   CS101    12345      65         8
1   CS101    12346      89         4
4   CS101     None      92         2
CS201
   course student   grade   absence
2   CS201    12345      74         5
3   CS201    12347      85         5
```

When multiple keys are used, the first element in the tuple will be a tuple of key values. For example:

```
for (c, s), group_df in grouped2:
    print((c, s))
    print(group_df)
```

Output:

```
('CS101', '12345')
   course student   grade   absence
0   CS101    12345      65         8
4   CS101     None      92         2
('CS101', '12346')
   course student   grade   absence
1   CS101    12346      89         4
('CS201', '12345')
   course student   grade   absence
2   CS201    12345      74         5
('CS201', '12347')
   course student   grade   absence
3   CS201    12347      85         5
```

You can also select a column or subset of columns from a groupby object. Indexing a GroupBy object created from a DataFrame with a column name or array of column names allows you to subset columns for aggregation. For example, to compute means for just the "grade" column in the previous dataset, you can use either of the following lines, which will yield the same result:

```
score.groupby('course')['grade'].mean()
```
Or:

```
score['grade'].groupby(score['course']).mean()
```

Output:

```
course
CS101    82.0
CS201    79.5
Name: grade, dtype: float64
```

Review Question 6.17
What is the purpose of aggregation in data analytics?
a. To split the data into smaller groups.
b. To combine individual groups into a single object.
c. To summarize a group of values into a single value.
d. To apply functions to each group individually.

Review Question 6.18
What is the first step in the "Split-Apply-Combine" methodology?
a. Applying functions to each group.
b. Combining the results into a single object.
c. Splitting the data into smaller, manageable groups.
d. Defining custom aggregation functions.

Review Question 6.19
What does the groupby() method in Pandas allow you to do?
a. Combine individual groups into a single object.
b. Define custom aggregation functions.
c. Split the data into smaller groups based on variables.
d. Apply built-in aggregation functions to each group.

Review Question 6.20
What is the second step in the "Split-Apply-Combine" methodology?
a. Splitting the data into smaller, manageable groups.
b. Defining custom aggregation functions.
c. Combining the results into a single object.
d. Applying functions to each group individually.

Review Question 6.21
Which of the following is NOT a built-in aggregation function in Pandas?
a. min()
b. max()
c. average()
d. count()

Review Question 6.22
What is the purpose of combining the results in the "Split-Apply-Combine" methodology?

a. To split the data into smaller groups.
b. To combine individual groups into a single object.
c. To apply functions to each group individually.
d. To summarize the aggregate values from each group.

Review Question 6.23
What does the combined result of the "Split-Apply-Combine" methodology represent?
a. Individual groups from the original dataset.
b. Custom aggregation functions applied to each group.
c. A unified output capturing key information from each group.
d. Aggregated values for the entire dataset.

Review Question 6.24
What does the "Split-Apply-Combine" methodology enable in data analysis?
a. Extraction of meaningful insights and patterns.
b. Sorting and filtering of the original dataset.
c. Defining custom aggregation functions.
d. Combining multiple datasets into a single object.

Review Question 6.25
What is the purpose of group operations in pandas?
a. To divide the data into rows and columns.
b. To split the data into groups based on provided keys.
c. To calculate the mean and sum for each individual value.
d. To combine the results into a single result object.

Review Question 6.26
What is the next step after splitting the data into groups in group operations?
a. Dividing the data into rows and columns.
b. Applying a function to each individual group.
c. Combining the results into a result object.
d. Calculating the mean and sum for each individual value.

Review Question 6.27
What does the result object of the third step in "Split-Apply-Combine" methodology represent?
a. The original dataset with grouped data.
b. The function applied to each individual group.
c. A combined object capturing results from each group.
d. The summary statistics for each individual value.

Review Question 6.28
How can we access specific records based on their position in each group?
a. Using the get_group() method.
b. Using the mean() method.
c. Using the nth() method.
d. Using the groups attribute.

Review Question 6.29
What is the result when grouping the data using multiple keys?
a. The data is split into rows and columns.

b. The result is a DataFrame indexed by unique values in the grouping column.
c. The data is unstacked to remove the hierarchical index.
d. Non-numeric columns are excluded from the result.

Review Question 6.30
How can the hierarchical index be rearranged to produce a reshaped(wider) DataFrame in Pandas?
a. By using the unstack() method.
b. By using the describe() method.
c. By using the size() method.
d. By using the nth() method.

Review Question 6.31
What happens to non-numeric columns in the aggregation result by default?
a. They are included in the result which may result in an error.
b. They are excluded from the result.
c. They are converted to numeric values.
d. They are transformed using the nth() method.

Review Question 6.32
Which method returns a Series containing group sizes?
a. sum()
b. size()
c. max()
d. mean()

Review Question 6.33
How can missing values in a group key be included in the result?
a. By passing dropna=True to the groupby method.
b. By passing dropna=False to the groupby method.
c. By using the describe() method.
d. By using the first() method.

Review Question 6.34
Filtering operation on groups will result in a DataFrame that has ________.
a. less rows than the original DataFrame
b. number of rows equal to the number of groups
c. bigger number of rows than the original DataFrame
d. smaller or the same number of rows compared the original DataFrame

Review Question 6.35
Given:
```python
df = pd.DataFrame({'a': [4,3,3],'b': [1, 4, 1],'c': [5,4,2]})
```
The following code:
```python
for name, group_df in df.groupby('b'):
    print(name)
```
Will it result in how many loop iterations?
a. 1
b. 2
c. 3
d. 4

Exercise 6.1

Consider the following DataFrame:

```python
from datetime import datetime
df = pd.DataFrame({
    'OrderID': [1, 2, 3, 4, 5],
    'Product': ['Product A', 'Product B', 'Product B', 'Product A', 'Product B'],
    'Quantity': [2, 1, 5, 3, 1],
    'UnitPrice': [10.0, 20.0, 15.0, 10.0, 20.0],
    'OrderDate': [datetime(2024, 1, 1), datetime(2024, 1, 2), datetime(2024, 1, 2),
datetime(2024, 1, 3), datetime(2024, 1, 3)],
    'CustomerID': [1, 2, 2, 3, 3]
})
```

The DataFrame represents sales records of a small business

Task 1: Calculate the total quantity sold for each product.

Task 2: List all the unique products in the DataFrame.

Task 3: Assuming the records are in chronological order, find the first sale record for each product.

Task 4: Find the first sale record for each product without assuming chronological order.

Task 5: Identify the most recent sale record for each product.

Task 6: Retrieve all sale records for 'Product B'.

Task 7: Count the number of sale records for each product.

6.3 Data Aggregation

Aggregations involve transforming data arrays into scalar values. The previous examples have demonstrated various aggregations, such as mean, count, min, and sum. There are more such aggregations and you can even use your custom aggregations.

For instance, the nsmallest() method from the Series selects the requested number of smallest values from the data. Consider the following example:

```python
score = pd.DataFrame({
    'course':['CS101', 'CS101', 'CS201', 'CS201', 'CS101'],
    'student':['12345', '12346', '12345', '12347', '12345'],
    'grade':[65, 89, 74, 85, 92],
    'absence':[8, 4, 5, 5, 2] })
score
```

Output:

	course	student	Grade	absence
0	CS101	12345	65	8
1	CS101	12346	89	4
2	CS201	12345	74	5
3	CS201	12347	85	5
4	CS101	12345	92	2

In a new cell, you can use the following code to display the two smallest in each group:

```
score.groupby('course')['grade'].nsmallest(2)
```

Output:

```
course
CS101    0    65
         1    89
CS201    2    74
         3    85
Name: grade, dtype: int64
```

To use custom aggregation functions, you can pass any function that aggregates an array to the aggregate or agg() method. For example:

```
def variability(series):
    return series.max() - series.min()
```

This variability() function computes the range of a series by subtracting the minimum value from the maximum value. To apply this function, you can use the following code in a new cell:

```
score.groupby('course')[['grade', 'absence']].agg(variability)
```

Output:

Course	grade	absence
CS101	27	6
CS201	11	0

You may notice that certain methods like describe also work, even though they are not strictly considered aggregations. For instance:

```
score.groupby('course').describe()
```
Output:

course	grade								absence							
	count	mean	std	min	25%	50%	75%	max	count	mean	std	min	25%	50%	75%	max
CS101	3.0	82.0	14.8	65.0	77.00	89.0	90.50	92.0	3.0	4.67	3.06	2.0	3.0	4.0	6.0	8.0
CS201	2.0	79.5	7.8	74.0	76.75	79.5	82.25	85.0	2.0	5.00	0.00	5.0	5.0	5.0	5.0	5.0

You can apply multiple functions to a dataset column-wise. By passing a list of functions or function names, you will receive a DataFrame with column names derived from the functions:

```
score.groupby('course')[['grade', 'absence']].agg(['mean', variability])
```

Output:

	grade		absence	
	mean	variability	mean	variability
Course				
CS101	82.0	27	4.666667	6
CS201	79.5	11	5.000000	0

You have the flexibility to customize the column names when applying functions to a DataFrame using GroupBy. Instead of relying on the default column names provided by GroupBy, you can pass a list of (name, function) tuples. The first element of each tuple will be used as the column names in the resulting DataFrame. This can be viewed as an ordered mapping between the specified names and the corresponding functions:

```
list = [('average', 'mean'), ('range', variability)]
score.groupby('course')[['grade', 'absence']].agg(list)
```

Output:

	grade		absence	
	average	range	average	range
course				
CS101	82.0	27	4.666667	6
CS201	79.5	11	5.000000	0

When working with a DataFrame, you have more flexibility in applying functions to columns within a GroupBy operation. There are two approaches you can take: applying a list of functions to all columns or specifying different functions for each column.

To apply a list of functions to a specific column, you can use the agg method on the grouped DataFrame. For example:

```
score.groupby('course')['grade'].agg(list)
```

Output:

	average	Range
course		
CS101	82.0	27
CS201	79.5	11

In this case, the agg() method is used on the GroupBy object, targeting the 'grade' column. The list of functions (list) is applied to the selected column, resulting in the computation of the average and range.

If you want to apply potentially different functions to one or more columns, you can pass a dictionary to the agg method. The dictionary should map column names to the desired function specifications. For example:

```
func_dict = {'grade':'mean', 'absence':'max'}
```

```python
score.groupby('course').agg(func_dict)
```

Output:

	grade	absence
Course		
CS101	82.0	8
CS201	79.5	5

In this case, the agg() method takes a dictionary (func_dict) specifying different functions for each column. The 'grade' column is aggregated using the 'mean' function, while the 'absence' column is aggregated using the 'max' function.

You also have the option to provide custom column names for the aggregated results. To do this, you can use a dictionary where the keys are the original column names, and the values can either be a list of tuples (each containing a new column name and a function) or a string representing a function name. For example:

```python
custom_dict = {'grade':[('average','mean')], 'absence':'max'}
score.groupby('course').agg(custom_dict)
```

Output:

	grade	absence
	average	max
course		
CS101	82.0	8
CS201	79.5	5

In this case, the 'grade' column is renamed to 'average', and the 'absence' column retains the name 'max'.

Review Question 6.36
What does the nsmallest() method do in the given code example?

```python
score.groupby('course')['grade'].nsmallest(2)
```

a. Selects the 2 largest values from each group of the 'grade' column
b. Selects the 2 smallest values from each group of the 'grade' column
c. Calculates the mean of the 'grade' column in each group
d. Counts the number of unique values in the 'grade' column for each group

Review Question 6.37
What is the purpose of the groupby() function in the given code example?

```python
score.groupby('course')['grade'].nsmallest(2)
```

a. Split the data into smaller groups based on the 'course' column
b. Split the data into smaller groups based on the 'course' and the 'grade' columns
c. Filter out rows with missing values in the 'course' column
d. Sort the data in ascending order based on the 'grade' column

Review Question 6.38
What does the x() function calculate in the given code example?
```
def x(series):
    return series.max() - series.min()
```
a. Mean of the series
b. Standard deviation of the series
c. Range of the series (maximum value minus minimum value)
d. Sum of the series

Review Question 6.39
What is the output of **score.groupby('course').agg(x)** given:
```
def x(series):
    return series.max() - series.min()?
```
a. Mean and standard deviation of the 'grade' and 'absence' columns for each group
b. Maximum and minimum values of the 'grade' and 'absence' columns for each group
c. Range (maximum value minus minimum value) of the columns for each group
d. Count, mean, standard deviation, minimum, and maximum values of the 'grade' and 'absence' columns for each group

Review Question 6.40
What does the describe() method provide in the given code example assuming the score contains grade and absence columns?
```
score.groupby('course').describe()
```
a. Count, mean, and standard deviation of the 'grade' and 'absence' columns for each group
b. Maximum and minimum values of the 'grade' and 'absence' columns for each group
c. Range (maximum value minus minimum value) of the 'grade' and 'absence' columns for each group
d. Count, mean, standard deviation, minimum, and maximum values of the 'grade' and 'absence' columns for each group

Review Question 6.41
How can you specify different functions for each column when using the agg() method?
a. By passing a list of functions to the agg() method
b. By providing a dictionary mapping column names to function specifications
c. By using a custom function for each column
d. By applying the agg() method multiple times with different functions

Review Question 6.42
What does the following code output?
```
func_dict = {'grade':'mean', 'absence':'max'}
score.groupby('course').agg(func_dict)
```
a. The mean value of the 'grade' column and the maximum values of the 'absence' column for each course
b. The sum and maximum values of the 'grade' column for each course
c. The mean values of the 'absence' column and the maximum values of the 'grade' column for each course
d. The sum and maximum values of the 'absence' column for each course

Review Question 6.43
What is the purpose of using a dictionary with tuples when applying custom column names to the aggregated results?
a. To specify the desired functions for each column

b. To provide custom column names for the aggregated results
c. To filter the rows in the DataFrame based on specific conditions
d. To sort the DataFrame based on column values

Exercise 6.2

Given the same DataFrame as in Exercise 6.1, complete the following tasks:
Task 1: Display the two largest quantities of each product.
Task 2: Create a function called iqr() that will calculate the inter-quartile range for a Series.
Task 3: Apply iqr() to the 'Quantity' and 'UnitPrice' columns of each product.
Task 4: Calculate the median and inter-quartile range (IQR) for the 'Quantity' and 'UnitPrice' of each product.
Task 5: Repeat Task 4, but the column headers should be named 'middle' and 'inter-quartile range'. Do not rename the column headers after the results in Task 4.
Task 6: Apply the 'median' function to the 'Quantity' and iqr() to the 'UnitPrice'.
Task 7: Repeat Task 6, but provide custom column names for the result set. Use 'middle' for the 'Quantity', and 'iqr' for the 'UnitPrice'. Do not rename the column headers after the results in Task 6.

6.4 The *apply()* Method on GroupBy

You have seen how apply() applies a function to rows or columns. The apply() method also allows you to perform custom operations on grouped data. It splits the dataset into smaller pieces based on the grouping criteria, applies a specified function to each piece, and then combines the results. For example, let's consider the following code:

```
score.groupby('course')[['grade', 'absence']].apply(variability)
```

Output:

course	grade	absence
CS101	27	6
CS201	11	0

In this case, we are grouping the score DataFrame by the 'course' column and selecting the 'grade' and 'absence' columns for analysis. We then apply a custom function called variability() to calculate the variability of each column within each group.

The apply() method applies the variability() function to each group separately and returns the computed results as a DataFrame. The resulting DataFrame has the group names as the index (i.e., 'CS101' and 'CS201' in this case) and the columns 'grade' and 'absence'. The values represent the variability of grades and absences within each group (course in this case).

At this time, you may wonder about the differences between agg() and apply(). The agg() applies one or more aggregation functions to the grouped data. The apply() applies a function along an axis of the DataFrame or a grouped object. It is more general-purpose and can be used for applying any custom function, not limited to aggregation. It allows for more flexibility in applying complex operations.

You can perform quantile and bucket analysis with apply() method. In previous chapters on data wrangling, you learned about tools in Pandas such as cut() and qcut() that allow you to divide data into bins or quantiles. When combined with the groupby operation, these functions become handy for performing bucket or quantile analysis on datasets. Let's start with a simple dataset called score1:

```
score1 = pd.DataFrame({
    'grade':[65, 89, 74, 85, 92, 99],
    'absence':[8, 4, 5, 5, 2, 1] })
score1
```

Output:

	grade	Absence
0	65	8
1	89	4
2	74	5
3	85	5
4	92	2
5	99	1

Let's create two equal-length buckets based on the grade column:

```
buckets = pd.cut(score1.grade, 2)
buckets
```

Output:

```
0       (64.966, 82.0]
1         (82.0, 99.0]
2       (64.966, 82.0]
3         (82.0, 99.0]
4         (82.0, 99.0]
5         (82.0, 99.0]
Name: grade, dtype: category
Categories (2, interval[float64, right]): [(64.966, 82.0] < (82.0, 99.0]]
```

Now, let's define a function get_stats that computes statistics for a given column:

```
def get_stats(column):
    return pd.DataFrame({'min':column.min(),
                         'max':column.max(),
                         'count':column.count()})
```

We can directly pass the categorical object buckets returned by cut to groupby(). This allows us to compute group statistics for the quartiles:

```
score1.groupby(buckets).apply(get_stats)
```
Output:

grade		min	Max	Count
(64.966, 82.0]	grade	65	74	2
	absence	5	8	2
(82.0, 99.0]	grade	85	99	4
	absence	1	5	4

In the above example, we divided the data into equal-length buckets based on the grades. We then applied the get_stats() function to each bucket, which computed the minimum, maximum, and count for both the grade and absence columns within each bucket.

Alternatively, we can use qcut to create equal-size buckets based on sample quantiles:

```
buckets2 = pd.qcut(score1.grade, 2)
buckets2
```

Output:

```
0    (64.999, 87.0]
1      (87.0, 99.0]
2    (64.999, 87.0]
3    (64.999, 87.0]
4      (87.0, 99.0]
5      (87.0, 99.0]
Name: grade, dtype: category
Categories (2, interval[float64, right]): [(64.999, 87.0] < (87.0, 99.0]]
```

We can then apply the get_stats function to these buckets:

```
score1.groupby(buckets2).apply(get_stats)
```
Output:

grade		min	max	Count
(64.999, 87.0]	grade	65	85	3
	absence	5	8	3
(87.0, 99.0]	grade	89	99	3
	absence	1	4	3

In this case, the data was divided into two equal-sized buckets based on sample quantiles. The get_stats() function was then applied to each bucket, providing statistics on the grade and absence columns.

By combining the cut() or qcut() functions with groupby(), you can perform bucket or quantile analysis on datasets and gain insights into different segments or ranges of your data.

In the remaining part of the section, let's explore an example of filling missing values with group-specific values. When dealing with missing data, there are cases where you might want to replace the null (NA) values with a fixed value or a value derived from the data. The fillna() function is the right tool to use for such scenarios. Let's walk through an example to understand how it works. First, a DataFrame called score2:

```python
score2 = pd.DataFrame({
    'course':['CS101', 'CS201', 'CS201', 'CS101', 'CS101', 'CS101'],
    'grade':[65, 89, 74, 85, None, 99],
    'absence':[8, 4, None, 6, 2, 1] })
score2
```

Output:

	course	grade	absence
0	CS101	65.0	8.0
1	CS201	89.0	4.0
2	CS201	74.0	NaN
3	CS101	85.0	6.0
4	CS101	NaN	2.0
5	CS101	99.0	1.0

Take a look at the mean of grade and absence columns:

```python
score2[['grade', 'absence']].mean()
```
Output:

```
grade       82.4
absence      4.2
dtype: float64
```

As you can see, there are missing values represented as NaN in the DataFrame. To fill in these missing values with the mean of their respective columns, we can use the fillna() function:

```python
score2.fillna(score2[['grade', 'absence']].mean())
```
Output:

	course	grade	absence
0	CS101	65.0	8.0
1	CS201	89.0	4.0
2	CS201	74.0	4.2
3	CS101	85.0	6.0
4	CS101	82.4	2.0
5	CS101	99.0	1.0

In some cases, you may want to fill missing values with a value that varies based on the group. To achieve this, you can first calculate the mean for each group, then replace missing values within each group using the group-specific mean. Let's calculate the group mean for verification purpose:

```python
course_mean = score2.groupby('course').mean()
course_mean
```

Output:

course	grade	absence
CS101	83.0	4.25
CS201	81.5	4.00

Now, instead of manually filling missing values, we can apply the mean value for each group to the corresponding rows in the DataFrame using `groupby` and the `transform` method. The `transform('mean')` function computes the group-specific mean and broadcasts it to the original DataFrame, allowing us to use it with `fillna`:

```
grouped2 = score2.groupby('course')
score2.fillna(grouped2.transform('mean'))
```

Output:

	course	grade	absence
0	CS101	65.0	8.0
1	CS201	89.0	4.0
2	CS201	74.0	4.0
3	CS101	85.0	6.0
4	CS101	83.0	2.0
5	CS101	99.0	1.0

As shown, the missing values in each group have been replaced with the mean value of their respective groups. For example, the missing grade in index 4 has been filled with the group mean of 83.0 for the `CS101` course.

Review Question 6.44
What does the apply() method in Pandas' GroupBy allow you to do?
a. Split the dataset into smaller pieces based on grouping criteria
b. Calculate the mean and standard deviation of each column within each group
c. Combine the results from different groups into a single output
d. Apply custom operations or functions to the grouped data

Review Question 6.45
Suppose x is a function for the range of a series. , How to calculate the range of the 'grade' and 'absence' columns for each course?
a. `score.groupby('course')[['grade', 'absence']].compute(x)`
b. `score.groupby('course')['grade', 'absence'].apply(x)`
c. `score.groupby('course')[['grade', 'absence']].apply(x)`
d. `score.groupby('course')['grade', 'absence'].compute(x)`

Review Question 6.46
Which method can be used to perform quantile and bucket analysis on datasets?
a. groupby()
b. cut() and qcut()
c. apply()
d. DataFrame()

Review Question 6.47
What does the output of the code snippet buckets represent?
```
Buckets = pd.cut(score1.grade, 2)
```
a. The count of values in each bucket
b. The minimum and maximum values in each bucket
c. The intervals representing the buckets
d. The average grade in each bucket

Review Question 6.48
What is the difference between using cut() and qcut() functions for creating buckets?
a. cut() creates equal-length buckets, while qcut() creates equal-size buckets based on sample quantiles.
b. cut() creates equal-size buckets, while qcut() creates equal-length buckets based on sample quantiles.
c. cut() creates equal-length buckets, while qcut() creates equal-size buckets based on the mean values.
d. cut() and qcut() are two different names for the same function.

Review Question 6.49
What is the purpose of the fillna() function in Pandas?
a. To remove missing values from a DataFrame.
b. To replace missing values with a fixed value.
c. To calculate the mean value of a column.
d. To create a new DataFrame with missing values.

Review Question 6.50
Given score2 is a DataFrame and grouped2 is a grouped object of it, how to replace missing values with the mean value of their respective columns?
```
a. score2.fillna(grouped2.transform('mean'))
b. score2.fillna(grouped2.column.transform('mean'))
c. score2.fillna(score2[['grade', 'absence']].mean())
d. score2.fillna(score2.column.mean())
```

Review Question 6.51
Suppose score2 is a DataFrame. What is the output of score2.mean() assuming there is no errors?
a. The mean value of each row in the DataFrame.
b. The mean value of each column in the DataFrame.
c. The mean value of all data points in the DataFrame.
d. The mean value of all numeric data points in the DataFrame.

Review Question 6.52
Given score2 is a DataFrame and grouped2 is a grouped object of it, how to replace each missing value with the mean value of its corresponding group.?
```
a. score2.fillna(grouped2.transform('mean'))
b. score2.fillna(grouped2.column.transform('mean'))
c. score2.fillna(score2.mean())
```

d. `score2.fillna(score2.column.mean())`

Review Question 6.53
What is one advantage of the apply() method over the transform() method?
a. The apply() method can return an object of different shape, while the transform() method requires the output to have the same shape as the input.
b. The apply() method reduces the number of records, while the transform() method maintains the same number of records as the input.
c. The apply() method allows for selective retrieval of rows based on conditions, while the transform() method applies a function to each value within a group.
d. The apply() method can fill missing values, while the transform() method can only modify existing values.

Exercise 6.3

Given the DataFrame from Exercise 6.1, complete the following tasks:
Task 1: Create two buckets of equal length based on the 'Quantity' column.
Task 2: Define a Python function named get_central_tendency(). This function should return the mean and median of a DataFrame column.
Task 3: Calculate the central tendency for each bucket (for both 'Quantity' and 'UnitPrice') that you defined in Task 1.
Task 4: Similar to Task 1, but this time, create two buckets that are roughly equal in size based on the 'Quantity' column.
Task 5: Repeat Task 3, but use the buckets defined in Task 4.
Task 6: Remove the 'Quantity' for OrderId=1 and 'UnitPrice' for OrderId=5 from the DataFrame. Save the resulting DataFrame as df1.
Task 7: Using df1 from Task 6, replace the null 'Quantity' and 'UnitPrice' values with the mean of the same product (do not assume there are only 5 orders).
Task 8: Provide a written explanation and code to verify that the two values you inserted in Task 7 are correct.

6.5 Pivot Tables

We first introduced the pivot() method when discussing how to reshape DataFrames in an earlier chapter. A pivot table is a powerful data summarization and analysis tool, commonly found in spreadsheet software like Excel or Google Sheets. It enables you to transform and reorganize large datasets into a more manageable and insightful format. Pivot tables provide a flexible way to aggregate, summarize, and analyze data from multiple perspectives, creating a multidimensional view of the dataset.

In a pivot table, you define the table's structure by selecting columns from your dataset to serve as "row fields," "column fields," and "value fields." The row fields determine the rows of the table, the column fields define the columns, and the value fields contain the summarized data.

The pivot table then performs calculations on the values based on the specified aggregation functions, such as sum, count, average, maximum, or minimum. This allows you to analyze and summarize large datasets by grouping and aggregating data across different variables.

Let's consider an example to illustrate the concept of a pivot table. Suppose you have a dataset containing information about sales transactions in an online store. The dataset has the following columns: "Product Category," "Region," "Salesperson," and "Sales Amount." Each row represents a specific sale, and the columns capture different attributes of each transaction. Here's a small portion of the dataset:

Product Category	Region	Salesperson	Sales Amount
Electronics	East	John	$500
Clothing	West	Sarah	$300
Electronics	East	Emma	$700
Clothing	West	John	$200
Electronics	West	Sarah	$600

Now, let's say we want to gain insights into the total sales amount for each product category across different regions. We can use a pivot table to achieve this:

Product Category	East	West
Electronics	$1,200	$600
Clothing	$0	$500

This pivot table summarizes the data, showing the total sales amount for each product category by region. In this example, we can see that Electronics has higher sales in the East region, while Clothing has higher sales in the West region.

You can further explore the data by adding additional variables. For instance, you could include the "Salesperson" field as a secondary column field to analyze the performance of salespersons within each product category and region. The pivot table would then look like this:

Product Category	East	West
Electronics	$1,200	$600
John	$500	$0
Emma	$700	$0
Sarah	$0	$600
Clothing	$0	$500
Sarah	$0	$300
John	$0	$200

Now, we can analyze the sales performance of each salesperson within the product categories and regions. The pivot table shows, for example, that John has made electronics sales only in the East region.

In Pandas, you can create pivot tables using a combination of the `groupby` operation and reshaping through hierarchical indexing. The DataFrame class in Pandas has a built-in `pivot_table()` method, and there is also a top-level function called `pandas.pivot_table()` that can be used for the same purpose.

Let's explore an example. Suppose we want to calculate the average grade and ACT scores, grouped by the course and absence levels. To do this, we can use the pivot_table() method with the index parameter set to the desired grouping columns. Here's the dataset:

```python
score3 = pd.DataFrame({
    'course':['CS101', 'CS201', 'CS201', 'CS101', 'CS101', 'CS101'],
    'grade':[65, 89, 74, 85, 91, 99],
    'absence':[2, 4, 4, 3, 2, 1],
    'act':[28, 31, 30, 32, 30, 33]})
score3
```

Output:

	Course	grade	absence	act
0	CS101	65	2	28
1	CS201	89	4	31
2	CS201	74	4	30
3	CS101	85	3	32
4	CS101	91	2	30
5	CS101	99	1	33

We can create the pivot table by specifying the index parameter as a list of columns to group by:

```python
score3.pivot_table(index=['course', 'absence'])
```
Output:

course	absence	Act	Grade
CS101	1	33.0	99.0
	2	29.0	78.0
	3	32.0	85.0
CS201	4	30.5	81.5

The resulting pivot table displays the average act and grade values for each combination of course and absence. The index consists of two levels, with the course and absence values serving as the row identifiers.

Pivot tables provide a convenient way to summarize and analyze data, allowing you to gain insights by organizing information in a structured manner. They can be customized further to include additional aggregations, calculations, and other parameters as needed. The previous pivot_table() example can also be achieved using the groupby() method directly:

```python
score3.groupby(by=['course','absence']).mean()[['act', 'grade']]
```

Now, let's consider another scenario. Suppose we want to calculate the average of only the 'grade' column while grouping by 'course' and 'absence'. Additionally, we want to create subgroups based on the 'act' values, with 'course' and 'absence' as the row and 'act' as the column:

```
score3.pivot_table(index=['course', 'absence'], columns='act')
```

Output:

				grade		
	act	28	30	31	32	33
course	absence					
CS101	1	NaN	NaN	NaN	NaN	99.0
	2	65.0	91.0	NaN	NaN	NaN
	3	NaN	NaN	NaN	85.0	NaN
CS201	4	NaN	74.0	89.0	NaN	NaN

The resulting pivot table displays the average 'grade' values for each combination of 'course', 'absence', and 'act'. Missing values are represented as NaN (Not a Number).

We can further enhance this table by adding partial totals using the margins=True parameter. This will include an "All" row and column, displaying the group statistics for all the data within a single tier:

```
score3.pivot_table(index=['course', 'absence'],
                   columns='act', margins=True)
```

Output:

						Grade	
	act	28	30	31	32	33	All
course	absence						
CS101	1	NaN	NaN	NaN	NaN	99.0	99.000000
	2	65.0	91.0	NaN	NaN	NaN	78.000000
	3	NaN	NaN	NaN	85.0	NaN	85.000000
CS201	4	NaN	74.0	89.0	NaN	NaN	81.500000
All		65.0	82.5	89.0	85.0	99.0	83.833333

To use an aggregation function other than mean, you can pass it to the aggfunc keyword argument:

```
score3.pivot_table(index=['course', 'absence'],
                   columns='act', margins=True,
                   aggfunc='min')
```

Output:

					grade		
	act	28	30	31	32	33	All
course	absence						
CS101	1	NaN	NaN	NaN	NaN	99.0	99
	2	65.0	91.0	NaN	NaN	NaN	65
	3	NaN	NaN	NaN	85.0	NaN	85
CS201	4	NaN	74.0	89.0	NaN	NaN	74
All		65.0	74.0	89.0	85.0	99.0	65

Here, the pivot table shows the minimum 'grade' values for each combination of 'course', 'absence', and 'act', along with the corresponding "All" values representing the minimum value within each tier.

In situations where certain combinations of groups have missing values or NaN (Not a Number), you can specify a fill value to replace those empty entries. This can be achieved by using the fill_value parameter in the pivot_table() function. Let's consider an example:

```
score3.pivot_table(index=['course', 'absence'],
                   columns='act', margins=True,
                   aggfunc='min', fill_value=0)
```

Output:

			grade					
	act	28	30	31	32	33	All
course	absence						
CS101	1	0	0	0	0	99	99
	2	65	91	0	0	0	65
	3	0	0	0	85	0	85
CS201	4	0	74	89	0	0	74
All		65	74	89	85	99	65

In this updated pivot table, we have specified fill_value=0. Now, any empty or NaN entries are replaced with zeros. For example, in the row where 'course' is CS101 and 'absence' is 1, all 'act' values are zero except for '33', which remains as 99. Similarly, other empty entries are filled with zeros accordingly.

Review Question 6.54
What is the purpose of a pivot table?
a. To create row fields, column fields, and value fields
b. To perform calculations on values based on aggregation functions
c. To summarize and analyze large datasets from multiple perspectives
d. All of the other options are correct

Review Question 6.55
In a pivot table, you can define the layout of the table by selecting _______ from your dataset to serve as the "row fields," "column fields," and "value fields."
a. rows
b. columns
c. rows and columns
d. rows, columns, and values

Review Question 6.56
What types of calculations can be performed in a pivot table?
a. Sorting and filtering
b. Counting and summing

c. Formatting and styling
d. Importing and exporting

Review Question 6.57
How can you drill down into the data in a pivot table (not in Pandas coding)?
a. By adding additional variables as row fields
b. By adding additional variables as row and column fields
c. By adding additional variables as value fields
d. By adding additional variables as filter fields

Review Question 6.58
What are the row identifiers in the pivot table?

course	absence	Act	Grade
CS101	1	33.0	99.0
	2	29.0	78.0
	3	32.0	85.0
CS201	4	30.5	81.5

a. act values
b. grade values
c. course and absence values
d. absence values

Review Question 6.59
How can the following pivot_table() example be achieved using the groupby() method?

```
score3.pivot_table(index=['course', 'absence'])
```

a. score3.groupby(by='course').mean()
b. score3.groupby(by='absence').mean()
c. score3.groupby(by=['course', 'absence']).mean()
d. score3.groupby(by=['act', 'grade']).mean()

Review Question 6.60
Given a DataFrame with four columns: course, grade, absence, and act. What does the pivot table with index=['course', 'absence'] and columns='act' represent?
a. Average 'grade' values for each combination of 'course' and 'absence'
b. Average 'act' values for each combination of 'course' and 'absence'
c. Average 'grade' values for each 'act' value within 'course' and 'absence' groups
d. Average 'act' values for each 'grade' value within 'course' and 'absence' groups

Review Question 6.61
What does the margins=True parameter do in the pivot_table() function?
a. Adds partial totals for each group within a single tier
b. Sorts the values in ascending order
c. Filters the data based on specific criteria
d. Excludes missing values from the calculation

Review Question 6.62
What does the fill_value parameter in the pivot_table() function allow you to do?
a. Exclude rows with missing values from the analysis
b. Replace NaN entries with custom values

c. Remove empty columns from the pivot table
d. Filter the data based on specific criteria

Exercise 6.4

Given the following DataFrame:

```python
data = {
    'Date': ['2024-01-01', '2024-01-02', '2024-01-03', '2024-01-04', '2024-01-05', '2024-01-06'],
    'Product': ['Apples', 'Oranges', 'Bananas', 'Apples', 'Bananas', 'Bananas'],
    'Location': ['Store 1', 'Store 1', 'Store 2', 'Store 2', 'Store 1', 'Store 2'],
    'Quantity': [5, 3, 6, 7, 8, 2],
    'Price': [1.0, 0.5, 0.25, 1.0, 0.25, 0.25]
}
df = pd.DataFrame(data)
```

Task 1: Reshape the DataFrame with 'Location', 'Product', and 'Date' as indices.
Task 2: Compute the average of the 'Quantity' column, grouped by the 'Price' column.
Task 3: Similar to Task 2, but include an 'All' row and column that display the group statistics for all data within a single tier.
Task 4: For Task 3, replace the default aggregation function 'mean' with 'sum'.
Task 5: Similar to Task 4, but replace 'NaN' values with 0.

6.6 Cross-Tabulations: Crosstab

A cross-tabulation, commonly known as a crosstab, is a statistical tool used to analyze the relationship between two or more categorical variables. It creates a contingency table that displays the frequency distribution of these variables, allowing you to easily visualize and interpret complex data patterns.

For example, a marketing team might use a crosstab to examine the relationship between customer age groups and product preferences. This could help tailor marketing strategies for specific demographics.

Crosstabs are particularly valuable in fields such as market research, social sciences, and business analytics, where understanding the interplay between multiple factors is crucial. They provide a foundation for more advanced statistical analyses, including chi-square tests for independence and association measures like Cramer's V.

While crosstabs excel at summarizing categorical data, it's important to note that they don't establish causation. Instead, they offer insights into potential relationships that may warrant further investigation.

Let's explore an example. First, the data:

```python
score4 = pd.DataFrame({
    'course':['CS101', 'CS201', 'CS201', 'CS101', 'CS101', 'CS101'],
    'class':['FR', 'FR', 'FR', 'FR', 'SO', 'SO'],
    'grade':[65, 89, 74, 85, 91, 99],
    'absence':[2, 4, 4, 3, 2, 1],
    'act':[28, 31, 30, 32, 30, 33]})
score4
```

Output:

	course	class	Grade	absence	act
0	CS101	FR	65	2	28
1	CS201	FR	89	4	31
2	CS201	FR	74	4	30
3	CS101	FR	85	3	32
4	CS101	SO	91	2	30
5	CS101	SO	99	1	33

Let's say we're interested in the distribution of students across different classes and courses. We can use the crosstab() function in pandas, specifying 'course' as the index and 'class' as the columns:

```python
pd.crosstab(index=score4['course'], columns=score4['class'])
```

Output:

class	FR	SO
course		
CS101	2	2
CS201	2	0

Each cell in this table represents the number of students in a particular course and class. For instance, there are no sophomore students in CS201.

If you're conducting a survey and need to summarize absence data by course and class, you can use the pd.crosstab() function again, this time with the 'values' and 'aggfunc' parameters:

```python
pd.crosstab(score4['course'], score4['class'],
            values=score4['absence'], aggfunc='sum')
```

Output:

Class	FR	SO
Course		
CS101	5.0	3.0
CS201	8.0	NaN

Alternatively, you can achieve the same result using the pivot_table() function:

```python
score4.pivot_table(index='course', columns='class',
                   values='absence', aggfunc='sum')
```

Review Question 6.63
What is the purpose of a cross-tabulation (crosstab) technique?
a. To compute group frequencies based on different categories
b. To compute the mean value of a dataset
c. To calculate the total sum of a column in a dataset
d. To filter data based on specific criteria

Review Question 6.64
Which function can be used to compute cross-tabulations in pandas?
a. pd.groupby()
b. pd.tabulation()
c. pd.crosstab()
d. pd.aggregate()

Exercise 6.5

Using the same DataFrame as in Exercise 6.4, please complete the following tasks:
Task 1: Determine the distribution of sales across various locations and products.
Task 2: Calculate the total sales of different products across various locations.
Task 3: Select all rows for products where the average sales value is greater than 6.
Task 4: Update the 'Price' column to reflect a 10% increase.

6.7 Summary Statistics

Descriptive and summary statistics are fundamental in descriptive data analysis, providing valuable insights into the characteristics of a dataset. In Chapter 2, you learned descriptive statistics. In this section, we will explore how to calculate and interpret summary statistics on a DataFrame.

Let's consider a fictitious example of a retail store chain that operates in multiple locations across different cities. The company wants to analyze its sales data and gain insights into the performance of each store location and product category. By calculating descriptive and summary statistics, the company can identify top-performing stores, popular product categories, and trends in customer behavior.

```python
import numpy as np
# Create a DataFrame with sales data
np.random.seed(42)
data = {
    'Store Location': ['New York', 'Los Angeles', 'Chicago', 'Houston', 'Miami'],
    'Product Category': ['Electronics', 'Clothing', 'Electronics', 'Furniture', 'Clothing'],
    'Sales': np.random.randint(1000, 5000, size=5),
    'Products Sold': np.random.randint(50, 200, size=5),
    'Customers Served': np.random.randint(20, 100, size=5)
}
sales_df = pd.DataFrame(data)
sales_df
```

Output:

	Store Location	Product Category	Sales	Products Sold	Customers Served
0	New York	Electronics	4174	121	94
1	Los Angeles	Clothing	4507	70	43
2	Chicago	Electronics	1860	152	22
3	Houston	Furniture	2294	171	41
4	Miami	Clothing	2130	124	72

We can perform descriptive and summary statistics, such as grouping by store location:

```
# Grouping by Store Location
store_stats = sales_df.groupby('Store Location').agg(
    TotalSales=('Sales', 'sum'),
    AvgProductsSold=('Products Sold', 'mean'),
    MaxCustomers=('Customers Served', 'max')
)
store_stats
```

Output:

Store Location	TotalSales	AvgProductsSold	MaxCustomers
Chicago	1860	152.0	22
Houston	2294	171.0	41
Los Angeles	4507	70.0	43
Miami	2130	124.0	72
New York	4174	121.0	94

Next, we show an example of grouping by product category based on the same data:

```
# Grouping by Product Category
category_stats = sales_df.groupby('Product Category').agg(
    TotalSales=('Sales', 'sum'),
    AvgSales=('Sales', 'mean'),
    MinProductsSold=('Products Sold', 'min')
)
category_stats
```

Output:

Product Category	TotalSales	AvgSales	MinProductsSold
Clothing	6637	3318.5	70
Electronics	6034	3017.0	121
Furniture	2294	2294.0	171

Here's another example of fictitious sales data for a retail store chain that includes information about customer segments. We can use this data to demonstrate grouping by customer segments.

```python
# Create a DataFrame with sales data and customer segments
np.random.seed(42)
data = {
    'CustomerID': range(1, 101),
    'CustomerSegment': np.random.choice(['Segment A', 'Segment B', 'Segment C'], size=100),
    'Store Location': np.random.choice(['New York', 'Los Angeles', 'Chicago'], size=100),
    'Product Category': np.random.choice(['Electronics', 'Clothing', 'Furniture'], size=100),
    'Sales': np.random.randint(100, 1000, size=100),
    'Products Sold': np.random.randint(10, 50, size=100),
}
sales_df = pd.DataFrame(data)
sales_df.head()
```

Output:

	CustomerID	CustomerSegment	Store Location	Product Category	Sales	Products Sold
0	1	Segment C	Chicago	Electronics	262	38
1	2	Segment A	Chicago	Clothing	819	35
2	3	Segment C	Chicago	Electronics	780	44
3	4	Segment C	New York	Clothing	260	34
4	5	Segment A	Chicago	Clothing	679	33

Now, we can group the data by different customer segments using the groupby function. Here's an example:

```python
# Grouping by customer segment
segment_sales = sales_df.drop(['Store Location', 'Product Category'],
axis=1).groupby('CustomerSegment').sum()
segment_sales
```

Output:

	CustomerID	Sales	Products Sold
CustomerSegment			
Segment A	1868	17522	935
Segment B	1891	16640	1044
Segment C	1291	18903	1014

By grouping the data by customer segments, you can analyze the sales performance of each segment separately. Feel free to modify the code and explore other statistics or add more variables to gain further insights into the retail store's customer segments.

Summary statistics by levels involve calculating aggregate metrics like mean, median, sum, count, and standard deviation for subsets of data defined by one or more categorical variables. This is particularly useful for identifying trends and patterns within specific groups.

You can also group by multiple columns to get more granular insights. For example, let's calculate the total sales and average products sold by both customer segment and store location (output omitted for brevity):

```python
# Grouping by customer segment and store location
```

```
segment_sales = sales_df.drop(['Product Category', 'CustomerID'],
axis=1).groupby(['CustomerSegment', 'Store Location']).agg({'Sales':
'sum', 'Products Sold': lambda x: round(x.mean(), 2)}).reset_index()
segment_sales
```

Review Question 6.65
What is the purpose of performing descriptive and summary statistics by level?
a. To identify top-performing products in each store location.
b. To analyze sales data across different cities.
c. To uncover patterns and trends within subsets of the dataset.
d. To calculate the total sales for each store location.

Review Question 6.66
What is the purpose of grouping the data by customer segment in the example?
```
segment_sales = sales_df.groupby('CustomerSegment').sum()
```
a. To analyze the sales performance of each customer segment separately.
b. To identify patterns and trends within subsets of the dataset.
c. To calculate the total sales and products sold for each customer segment.
d. To compare the customer ID and sales for each customer segment.

Exercise 6.6

Using the same DataFrame as in Exercise 6.4, please complete the following tasks:
Task 1: Display the 'total products sold', 'average units of each product sold', and 'maximum price' for each store.
Task 2: Display the 'total units sold', 'average units of each product sold', and 'minimum price' for each product.
Task 3: Display the total units sold, broken down by both store and product.

Exercise 6.7
Given the following DataFrame, perform the tasks below:
```
data = {
    'CustomerID': [1, 2, 3, 4, 5, 6, 7, 8],
    'Country': ['US', 'UK', 'US', 'UK', 'US', 'UK', 'US', 'UK'],
    'Category': ['Electronics', 'Clothing', 'Clothing', 'Electronics',
'Clothing', 'Electronics', 'Electronics', 'Clothing'],
    'Sales': [200, 150, 100, 300, 250, 400, 100, 200],
    'Quantity': [2, 3, 1, 4, 2, 5, 1, 2]
}
df = pd.DataFrame(data)
```
Task 1: Calculate the total sales and average quantity sold by country.
Task 2: Determine the total sales and average quantity sold by category and country.
Task 3: Display the sum of sales and average quantity for each country-category combination.

6.8 Chapter Summary

In this chapter, we explored data aggregation, focusing on the "Split-Apply-Combine" methodology. The versatile groupby() method facilitated data grouping based on criteria, enabling comprehensive analyses. Integration with cut() and qcut() enhanced our analyses, providing insights into segments and categories. We delved into pivot tables and cross-tabulation, summarizing and exploring data across dimensions to discern relationships. A practical example showcased summary statistics at different levels, revealing insights into store performance and customer patterns.

6.9 Solutions to the Review Questions

6.1 A; 6.2 B; 6.3 A; 6.4 D; 6.5 D; 6.6 A; 6.7 C; 6.8 C; 6.9 C; 6.10 B; 6.11 C; 6.12 B; 6.13 C; 6.14 C; 6.15 B; 6.16 B; 6.17 C; 6.18 C; 6.19 C; 6.20 D; 6.21 C; 6.22 D; 6.23 C; 6.24 A; 6.25 B; 6.26 B; 6.27 C; 6.28 C; 6.29 B; 6.30 A; 6.31 A; 6.32 B; 6.33 B; 6.34 D; 6.35 B; 6.36 B; 6.37 A; 6.38 C; 6.39 C; 6.40 D; 6.41 B; 6.42 A; 6.43 B; 6.44 D; 6.45 C; 6.46 B; 6.47 C; 6.48 A; 6.49 B; 6.50 C; 6.51 B; 6.52 A; 6.53 A; 6.54 C; 6.55 B; 6.56 B; 6.57 B; 6.58 C; 6.59 C; 6.60 C; 6.61 A; 6.62 B; 6.63 A; 6.64 C; 6.65 C; 6.66 A;

Chapter 7: Data Visualization

Chapter Learning Objectives

7.1 Plot simple graphic with Pandas
7.2 Distinct among Pandas, Matplotlib, and Seaborn modules for graphing
7.3 Plot more advanced graphic with Seaborn
7.4 Differentiate general and specific plotting method in Seaborn

7.1 Introduction

Data visualization simplifies data analysis and communicates insights to decision-makers effectively. It helps reveal relationships between variables that might otherwise be difficult to detect. By visualizing data, we can better understand complex patterns, identify anomalies, and present findings in a way that resonates with diverse audiences. This approach eliminates the need for manual data inspection and allows us to quickly derive valuable insights.

A key component of data analysis is *Exploratory Data Analysis (EDA)*, which involves summarizing a dataset's main features using visual methods. EDA is crucial for identifying trends, spotting outliers, forming hypotheses, and validating assumptions through both summary statistics and graphical representations.

Another important element of data visualization is *storytelling with data*. This technique involves building a narrative around the data to make it more engaging and accessible to the audience. Effective data storytelling goes beyond charts and graphs—it crafts a coherent story that emphasizes key insights and findings. When done well, data storytelling transforms complex datasets into compelling narratives that drive action and decision-making.

In this chapter, we will explore three key libraries for data visualization: pandas, matplotlib, and seaborn. The pandas library integrates with matplotlib to produce basic visualizations, while seaborn, built on top of matplotlib, offers advanced statistical graphics. We will cover various plot types frequently used in exploratory and descriptive data analysis, such as line plots, bar charts, pie charts, histograms, scatter plots, box plots, and heatmaps. Each type of plot is designed to help us understand and present data effectively for specific purposes.

Review Question 7.1
What is the primary purpose of data visualization?
a. To eliminate outliers in the data
b. To present data analytics to decision makers
c. To identify complex patterns in the data and solve the problem
d. To manually sift through data efficiently

Review Question 7.2
How does data visualization help in understanding data patterns?
a. By eliminating outliers in the data
b. By providing advanced statistical analysis
c. By visualizing relationships between variables
d. By automating data sifting processes

Review Question 7.3
Which libraries/modules will be explored for data visualization in this book?
a. pandas, numpy, and scikit-learn
b. seaborn, matplotlib, and plotly
c. pandas, matplotlib, and seaborn
d. matplotlib, ggplot, and d3.js

Review Question 7.4
What is the benefit of data visualization in data analysis?
a. Eliminates the need for data cleaning
b. Automates the process of data analysis
c. Enables effective communication of insights
d. Replaces the need for statistical analysis

Review Question 7.5
What does data visualization eliminate in the data analysis process?
a. Outliers in the data
b. Manual data sifting
c. Statistical analysis
d. Data cleaning tasks

7.2 Pandas for Data Visualization

The *Matplotlib* package is a popular and widely-used data visualization library in Python. It provides a comprehensive set of functions and classes for creating high-quality static, animated, and interactive visualizations. Matplotlib is designed to facilitate the creation of various types of plots, charts, and figures, making it an essential tool for data analysis, scientific research, and data visualization tasks.

The Pandas library seamlessly utilizes the Matplotlib library for visualizations, providing a more intuitive and user-friendly experience when plotting graphs. Pandas' plot function, which is based on the Matplotlib plot function, offers a straightforward way to create a wide range of plots by specifying the desired type of plot using the "kind" parameter. This showcases the concept of polymorphism in object-oriented programming, where the same method can be used to perform different tasks based on the provided parameters.

Pandas is a flexible tool that can handle both long and wide data formats effectively. Its primary data structures, Series and DataFrame, are versatile and can work with data in various shapes. For many operations and visualizations, Pandas can work directly with wide data without requiring reshaping.

Unlike Pandas, which is primarily for data manipulation and analysis with some plotting features, Seaborn is designed specifically for creating attractive and informative statistical graphics. The API of Seaborn expects data to be in a long format where each row represents an observation, which aligns well with Pandas DataFrames. This makes Seaborn particularly powerful when used in conjunction with Pandas, as it can directly utilize Pandas DataFrames to create complex visualizations with minimal code. While Pandas is suitable for quick, simple plots, Seaborn offers more sophisticated and aesthetically pleasing visualizations for statistical analysis and exploration. For simplicity, add the following lines before you practice the code in this chapter:

```python
import matplotlib.pyplot as plt
import seaborn as sns
```

Review Question 7.6
What is the Matplotlib package?
a. A data manipulation library in Python.
b. A library for statistical analysis.
c. A popular data visualization library in Python.
d. A library for machine learning algorithms.

Review Question 7.7
How does Pandas utilize the Matplotlib library?
a. By incorporating it into the data manipulation process.
b. By providing an alternative to Matplotlib for visualizations.
c. By automatically generating visualizations from Pandas objects.
d. By offering a more powerful interface for plotting graphs.

Review Question 7.8

What is the purpose of the "kind" parameter in the Pandas plot() method?
a. It specifies the type of visualization to create.
b. It determines the size of the plot.
c. It controls the color palette used in the plot.
d. It adjusts the scaling of the x-axis and y-axis.

Review Question 7.9
How does the Pandas plot() method handle wide data?
a. It automatically reshapes wide data into long format.
b. It is not suitable for visualizing wide data.
c. It requires additional preprocessing of wide data.
d. It is particularly well-suited for visualizing wide data.

Review Question 7.10
What is the main difference between Pandas and Seaborn in terms of data visualization?
a. Pandas can only handle short data, while Seaborn works with long data
b. Seaborn is primarily for data manipulation, while Pandas is for visualization
c. Pandas offers basic plotting capabilities, while Seaborn specializes in statistical visualization
d. Seaborn can't work with Pandas DataFrames, but Pandas can

Review Question 7.11
Which statement best describes the relationship between Pandas and Seaborn?
a. They are completely independent and cannot be used together
b. Seaborn can only work with data that has been preprocessed by Pandas
c. Pandas can create more complex visualizations than Seaborn
d. Seaborn can directly utilize Pandas DataFrames to create complex visualizations

7.2.1 Line Plots

A line plot displays information as a series of data points connected by straight line segments. Line plots are useful for showing trends over time. They can be created using the plot() method of pandas Series and DataFrame objects. By default, the plot() method generates line plots. When applied to a DataFrame, the plot method plots each column as a separate line on the same subplot and automatically generates a legend.

Let's consider a DataFrame called score_df containing student IDs and scores for three exams (exam1, exam2, and exam3). The DataFrame looks like this:

```
import pandas as pd
data = {'studentID':['12345', '12346', '12347', '12348', '12349'],
        'exam1':[56, 74, 80, 88, 91],
        'exam2':[98, 88, 85, 89, 92],
        'exam3':[95, 85, 56, 79, 88]}
score_df=pd.DataFrame(data)
score_df
```
Output:

	studentID	exam1	exam2	exam3
0	12345	56	98	95
1	12346	74	88	85
2	12347	80	85	56
3	12348	88	89	79
4	12349	91	92	88

To create a line plot using the default behavior, you can simply call the plot() method on the DataFrame:

```
score_df.plot()
```

Output:

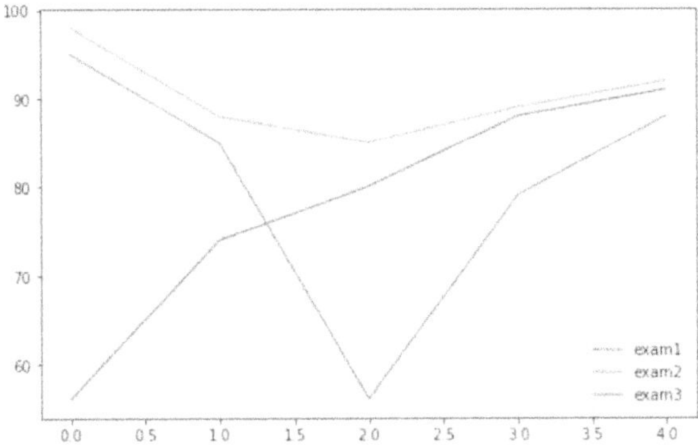

This will generate a line plot with the values of the index column (by default, the DataFrame's index) on the x-axis and all the numeric columns on the y-axis.

If you want to customize the x-axis or select specific columns for the y-axis, you can use the x and y parameters. For example, to plot the student ID on the x-axis and only the 'exam2' and 'exam3' columns on the y-axis, you can do the following (df.plot() is equivalent to df.plot.line()):

```
score_df.plot.line(x='studentID', y=['exam2', 'exam3'])
```

Output:

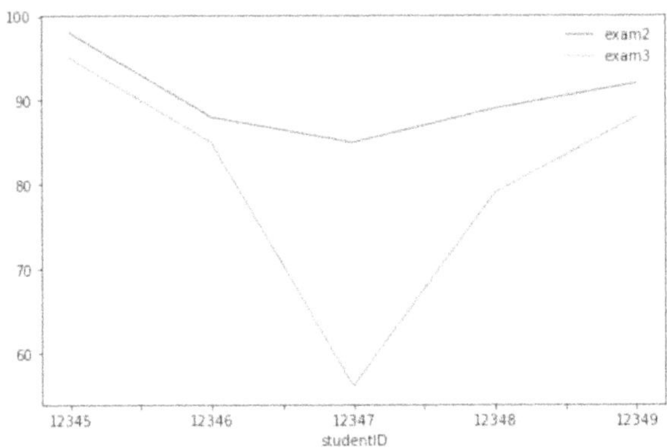

Review Question 7.12
What type of visualization is created using the plot() method of pandas DataFrame objects by default?

a. Bar plots
b. Line plots
c. Pie charts
d. Scatter plots

Review Question 7.13
What does the plot() method of a DataFrame do by default?
a. Creates scatter plots
b. Generates bar plots
c. Plots each numeric column as a separate line on the same subplot
d. Plots a single line with data from all numeric columns

Review Question 7.14
How can you customize the x-axis and select specific columns for the y-axis in a line plot?
a. By using the plot() method without any additional parameters
b. By specifying the desired columns as arguments to the plot() method
c. By using the kind parameter in the plot() method
d. By calling the plot.line() method instead of plot()

Review Question 7.15
Which method is equivalent to df.plot.line()?
a. df.plot.bar()
b. df.plot.scatter()
c. df.plot.pie()
d. df.plot()

Review Question 7.16
What allows you to choose the appropriate method for creating a specific type of visualization?
a. The plot attribute of pandas Series and DataFrame objects
b. The x and y parameters of the plot() method
c. The family of methods within the plot attribute
d. The kind parameter in the plot() method

7.2.2 Area plots

Area plots provide a different perspective compared to line plots. While line plots show the trend of data along the x-axis, area plots take it a step further by stacking the data from different columns on top of each other. Each layer represents a different column and is filled with a distinct color, creating a visual representation of the cumulative data. In the case of the DataFrame score_df, an area plot can be generated by calling the plot.area() method on the DataFrame (equivalent to score_df.plot(kind='area')):

```
score_df.plot.area()
```

Output:

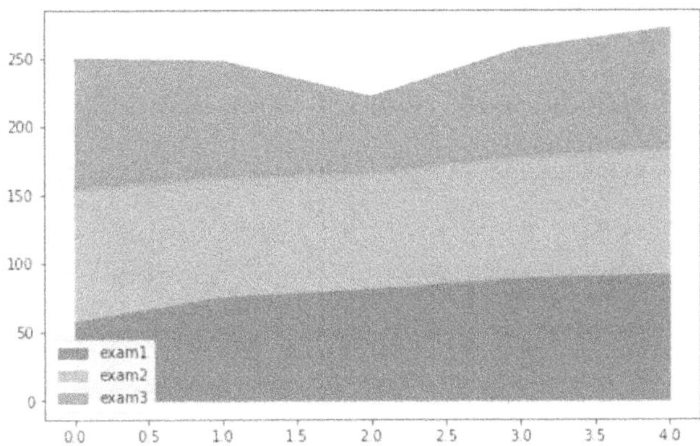

The resulting plot shows the total score for each student, as well as the individual components of that score (exam1, exam2, and exam3). By visually stacking the data, area plots allow us to observe the overall magnitude of the scores and how each component contributes to the total. They provide a comprehensive view of the data's composition and changes along the x-axis.

Area plots, also known as area charts, are particularly useful when comparing two or more quantities to understand their correlation and how they contribute to the total amount. For instance, an area plot can be used to visualize the distribution of a company's market share or the breakdown of a population by age group over time. By providing a sense of magnitude and trend, area plots help analysts to gain insights into the larger picture of the data.

Review Question 7.17
What is the main difference between area plots and line plots?
a. Area plots display cumulative data, while line plots show individual data points.
b. Area plots show trends along the y-axis, while line plots show trends along the x-axis.
c. Area plots use distinct colors for each column, while line plots use different line styles.
d. Area plots stack data from different columns, while line plots show the average.

Review Question 7.18
Given a DataFrame of student with 3 exam scores, what does each layer in an area plot represent?
a. Each layer represents a different student in the dataset.
b. Each layer represents a different exam in the dataset.
c. Each layer represents a different score category in the dataset.
d. Each layer represents a different color used in the plot.

Review Question 7.19
How can an area plot be generated for the DataFrame score_df?
a. By calling the area() method on the DataFrame.
b. By calling the plot.area() method on the DataFrame.
c. By calling the plot.kind.area() method on the DataFrame.
d. By calling the plot(kind= 'area') or plot.area() method on the DataFrame.

Review Question 7.20
Given a DataFrame of student with 3 exam scores, what information can be observed from an area plot?
a. The correlation between different columns in the dataset.
b. The outliers in the data points.
c. The overall magnitude of the scores and their composition.
d. The statistical summary of the dataset.

7.2.3 Bar Plots

Bar plots can be created using the plot.bar() and plot.barh() methods. The plot.bar() method generates vertical bar plots, while the plot.barh() method creates horizontal bar plots. By default, the index of the Series or DataFrame is used as the ticks on the x-axis for bar plots and on the y-axis for horizontal bar plots.

Bar plots are useful for visualizing categorical data. They represent different categories as bars, where the width or height of each bar corresponds to the value associated with that category. This allows for easy comparison and analysis of data across different categories.

When applied to a DataFrame, the bar plots group the values in each column together and display them as grouped bars, side by side, for each value. This provides a clear visual representation of how the values in each column compare to one another:

```
score_df.plot.bar()
```

Output:

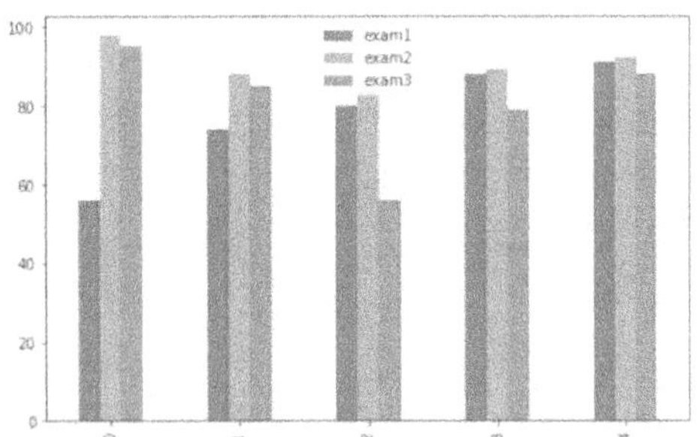

It's important to note that the legend in the plot is automatically titled based on the column names in the DataFrame, in this case, "Exam". This helps in identifying and interpreting the bars in the plot.

Stacked bar plots can be created from a DataFrame by setting the parameter stacked=True. This results in the values in each column being stacked on top of each other in the plot. To generate a stacked horizontal bar plot from the score_df DataFrame, you can use the plot.barh(stacked=True) method:

```
score_df.plot.barh(stacked=True)
```

Output:

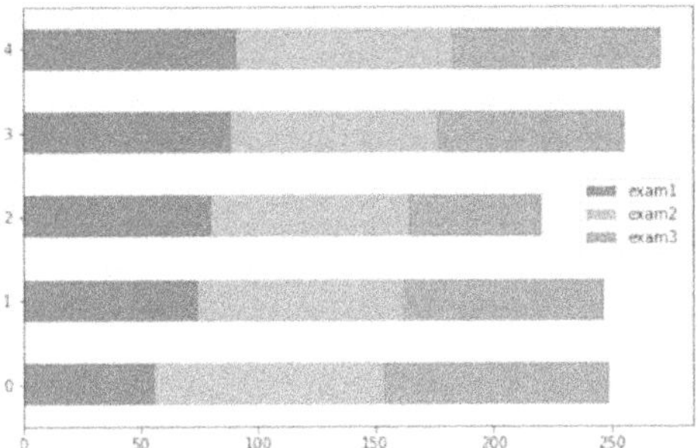

The bar charts are commonly used to display the frequency or count of a categorical variable. To demonstrate this, let's convert the numeric scores into letter grades. We can define a Python function called letterGrade that maps each score to a corresponding letter grade:

```python
def letterGrade(score):
    if score >=90:
        return 'A'
    elif score >= 80:
        return 'B'
    elif score >= 70:
        return 'C'
    elif score >= 60:
        return 'D'
    else:
        return 'F'
```

A useful approach for bar plots is to visualize the value frequency of a Series using the value_counts() method, and then chain it with the bar() plot method. For example, to plot the frequency of letter grades for exam1, you can do the following:

```python
score_df.exam1.apply(letterGrade).value_counts().plot.bar()
```

Output:

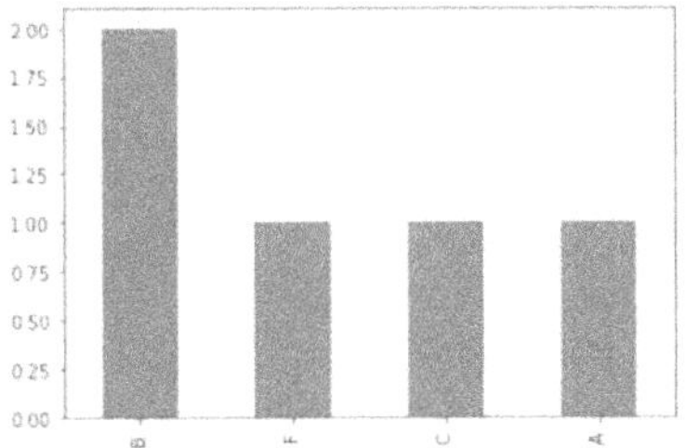

You can use the following code to display all three exams by a for loop:

```python
for exam in score_df.drop('studentID', axis=1).columns:
    score_df[exam].apply(letterGrade).value_counts().plot.bar()
    plt.title(f'Letter Grades for {exam}')
    plt.show()
```

Another useful technique for creating bar plots involves first creating a cross-tabulation or contingency table from a DataFrame. To demonstrate this, we can reshape the score_df DataFrame into a long format using the melt() method:

```python
score_df_long = score_df.melt(
    value_vars=['exam1', 'exam2', 'exam3'],
    var_name='exam', value_name='score')
score_df_long
```

Output:

	exam	Score
0	exam1	56
1	exam1	74
2	exam1	80
3	exam1	88
4	exam1	91
5	exam2	98
6	exam2	88
7	exam2	85
8	exam2	89
9	exam2	92
10	exam3	95
11	exam3	85
12	exam3	56
13	exam3	79
14	exam3	88

We can add a new column called 'letterGrade' by applying the letterGrade function to the 'score' column:

```python
score_df_long['letterGrade'] = score_df_long.score.apply(letterGrade)
score_df_long
```

Output:

	exam	Score	letterGrade
0	exam1	56	F
1	exam1	74	C
2	exam1	80	B
3	exam1	88	B
4	exam1	91	A
5	exam2	98	A
6	exam2	88	B
7	exam2	85	B
8	exam2	89	B
9	exam2	92	A
10	exam3	95	A
11	exam3	85	B
12	exam3	56	F
13	exam3	79	C
14	exam3	88	B

To count the number of students receiving each letter grade for each exam, we can use the crosstab() function from Pandas:

```python
grade_counts = pd.crosstab(score_df_long.exam, score_df_long.letterGrade)
```

`grade_counts`
Output:

letterGrade	A	B	C	F
exam				
exam1	1	2	1	1
exam2	2	3	0	0
exam3	1	2	1	1

Finally, we can plot the counts using the plot.bar() method, specifying rot=45 to rotate the x-axis labels for better readability:

`grade_counts.plot.bar(rot=45)`
Output:

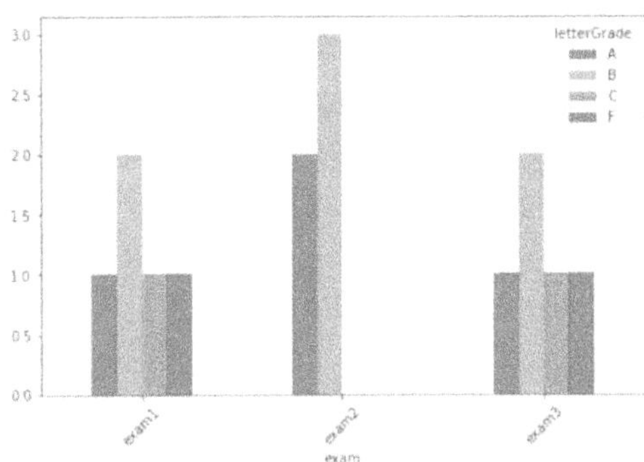

Review Question 7.21
What is the default orientation of the bars in the plot generated by the plot.bar() method?
a. Vertical
b. Horizontal
c. Diagonal
d. Circular

Review Question 7.22
What type of data are bar plots particularly useful for visualizing?
a. Numerical data
b. Continuous data
c. Categorical data
d. Time series data

Review Question 7.23
By default, how are values in each column represented in a bar plot when applied to a DataFrame?
a. They are shown as individual bars grouped together
b. They are stacked on top of each other
c. They are connected by a line
d. They are displayed as scatter points

Review Question 7.24
What parameter can be set to create a stacked bar plot from a DataFrame?
a. stacked=True
b. stacked=False

c. stacked_plot=True
d. stacked_plot=False

Review Question 7.25
What does the value_counts() method combined with the bar() plot method visualize?
a. Correlation between two variables
b. Statistical summary of a dataset
c. Frequency or count of a categorical variable
d. Trend of a continuous variable

Review Question 7.26
What function can be used to create a cross-tabulation or contingency table from a DataFrame?
a. melt()
b. letterGrade()
c. value_counts()
d. crosstab()

Exercise 7.1

Given the following dataframe, complete the tasks below:

```python
grades_df = pd.DataFrame({
    'math': [89, 94, 77, 85, 92, 88, 76, 95, 87, 90],
    'english': [85, 88, 92, 78, 87, 93, 80, 90, 86, 94],
    'science': [91, 85, 88, 92, 86, 89, 93, 87, 90, 94]
})
```

Task 1: Plot vertical bar chart comparing each student's grades.
Task 2: Plot stacked horizontal bar chart.
Task 3: Define function to convert scores to letter grades, apply function to each column and plot frequency of letter grades.
Task 4: Reshape DataFrame into long format, add 'letterGrade' column, create cross-tabulation, and plot the counts.

7.2.4 Pie charts

A pie chart displays distinct values of a variable as sectors within a circle. It is commonly used when working with categorical variables. The primary purpose of using a pie chart is to show proportions and percentages. Each sector of the pie chart represents a proportion of the whole, allowing for an immediate visual comparison between categories. This makes it easier to understand the distribution of a single categorical variable and the relationship of each category to the total. However, pie charts are most effective when there are a limited number of categories, as too many slices can make the chart difficult to interpret.

In Pandas, when creating a pie chart, you need to use the value_counts() or sum() function to calculate the number of values in each category. This is because Pandas does not perform the aggregation automatically during plotting. However, you can easily chain the necessary methods together.

For example, using score_df_long and creating a pie chart showing the sum of absences grouped by the 'exam' column, we can use the following code:

```
absence = [10, 8, 6, 5, 2, 1, 2, 3, 0, 0, 1, 5, 8, 5, 4]
score_df_long['absence'] = absence
score_df_long.groupby('exam')['absence'].sum().plot.pie()
```
Output:

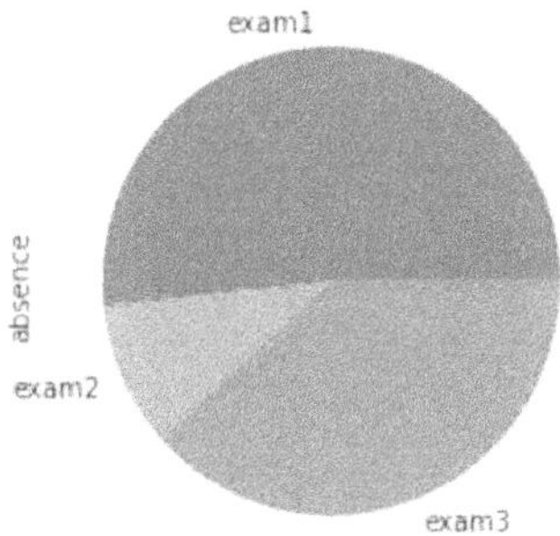

The resulting output is a pie chart displaying the distribution of absences for each exam. Note that the legend in the plot will automatically indicate the categories based on the 'exam' column values.

Review Question 7.27
What does a pie chart visually represent?
a. Distinct values of a variable as sectors within a circle
b. Trend of data along the x-axis
c. Stacked data from different columns
d. Magnitude of scores and their components

Review Question 7.28
Why is the value_counts() function often used when creating a pie chart in Pandas?
a. To perform automatic aggregation during plotting
b. To calculate the number of values in each category
c. To display the legend in the plot
d. To chain necessary methods together

7.2.5 Histograms and Density Plots

A histogram is a type of bar plot that provides a visual representation of the frequency distribution of a dataset. It divides the data into discrete, evenly spaced intervals called bins and plots the number of data points falling within each bin. Histograms are useful for gaining insights into the distribution and range of the data.

When creating a histogram using Pandas, you can use the plot.hist() method. For example, using the same DataFrame score_df_long to visualize the frequency distribution of the 'score' column, we can use the following code:

```
score_df_long['score'].plot.hist()
```

Output:

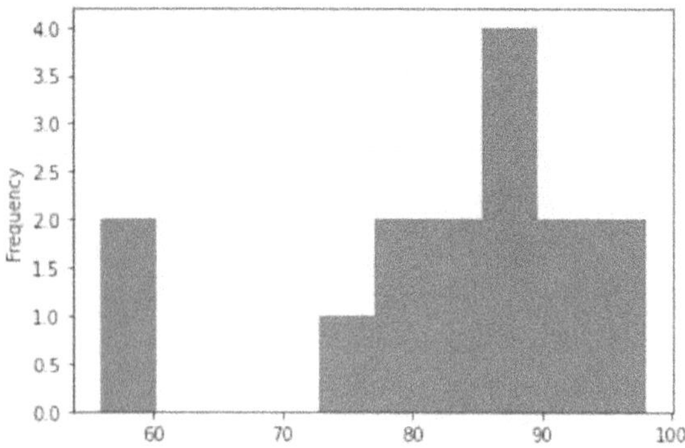

Additionally, you can specify the number of bins to use in the histogram by providing the 'bins' parameter. This determines the granularity of the intervals. For example:

```
score_df_long['score'].plot.hist(bins=20)
```

Output:

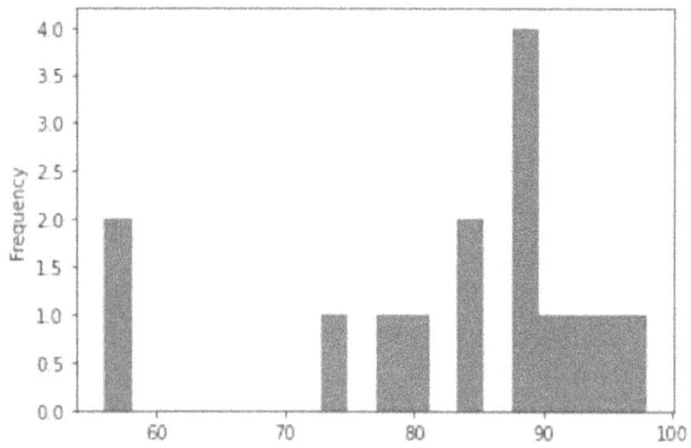

In this case, the histogram will be divided into 20 bins, providing a more detailed view of the distribution.

By examining a histogram, you can identify the central tendency, spread, and shape of the data, as well as any outliers or unusual patterns. It allows you to quickly grasp the overall characteristics of the dataset and make informed decisions based on the distribution of values.

A *density plot* provides a smooth estimate of the probability density function (PDF) of a continuous variable.

It is similar to a histogram but uses a kernel density estimate (KDE) to create a smooth curve. When creating a density plot using Pandas, you can use the plot.density() method. For example:

```
score_df_long['score'].plot.density()
```

Output:

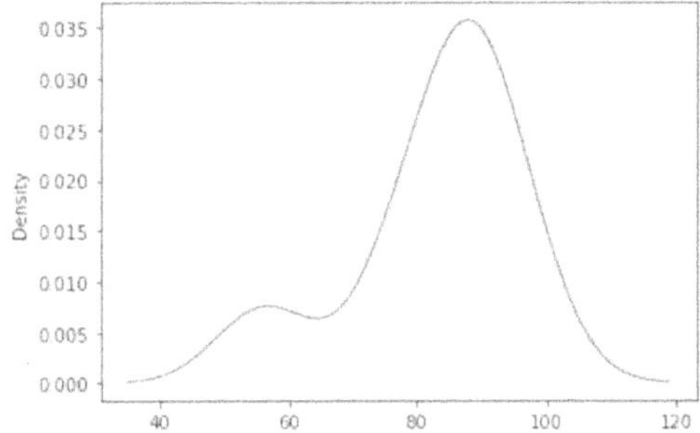

Compared to the histogram, The density plot displays a smooth curve that represents the estimated probability density function of the scores.

Unlike a histogram, where the y-axis represents the frequency or count of data points in each bin, the y-axis in a density plot represents the probability of a data point occurring. The values on the y-axis are derived from the KDE, which calculates the density of data points at each location along the density line.

The KDE is calculated by assigning weights to the distances of data points for each location on the density line. Locations with a higher density of data points will have a higher KDE, indicating a higher probability of observing a data point in that location.

Density plots are particularly useful for visualizing the shape and distribution of continuous data. They provide a smooth representation of the underlying PDF and can reveal patterns such as modes, skewness, and multimodality in the data. By examining a density plot, you can gain insights into the concentration of data points and the relative likelihood of observing data values at different locations along the distribution.

Review Question 7.29
What is the purpose of a histogram?
a. To display categorical data
b. To visualize the frequency distribution of a dataset
c. To represent continuous probability density functions
d. To compare multiple datasets

Review Question 7.30
How can you create a histogram using Pandas?

a. By using the plot.histogram() method
b. By using the plot.histog() method
c. By using the plot.hist() method
d. By using the plot.hi() method

Review Question 7.31
What does each bar in a histogram represent?
a. The range of data points
b. The frequency of data points within an interval
c. The average of data points within an interval
d. The sum of data points within an interval

Review Question 7.32
How can you adjust the level of detail in a histogram?
a. By changing the color of the bars
b. By specifying the number of bins
c. By adjusting the height of the bars
d. By changing the axis labels

Review Question 7.33
What insights can you gain from examining a histogram?
a. The central tendency and spread of the data
b. The probability density function of the data
c. The correlation between variables
d. The data history

Review Question 7.34
What is the main advantage of using a histogram?
a. It displays categorical data more effectively than other plots.
b. It provides a visual representation of continuous probability density functions.
c. It allows for direct comparison of multiple datasets.
d. It quickly reveals the frequency distribution and range of the data.

Review Question 7.35
What is the main purpose of a density plot?
a. To visualize the frequency distribution of a dataset
b. To display categorical variables as sectors within a circle
c. To estimate the probability density function of a continuous variable
d. To compare multiple datasets

Review Question 7.36
How does a density plot differ from a histogram?
a. A density plot shows categorical variables, while a histogram shows continuous variables.
b. A density plot represents the probability density function, while a histogram represents frequency counts.
c. A density plot uses bars to display data, while a histogram uses a smooth curve.
d. A density plot requires the use of kernel density estimate (KDE), while a histogram does not.

Review Question 7.37
What does the y-axis represent in a density plot?
a. Frequency counts of data points

b. Probability density of data points
c. Bins or intervals of the data
d. Kernel density estimate (KDE) values

Review Question 7.38
What patterns can be identified by examining a density plot?
a. Central tendency and frequency of the data
b. Frequency distribution and range of the data
c. Modes, skewness, and multimodality of the data
d. Outliers or density in the data

Review Question 7.39
What insights can be gained from a density plot?
a. Concentration of data points and relative likelihood at different locations
b. Correlation between variables and their interactions
c. Frequency counts of data points in each bin
d. Average and standard deviation of the data

7.2.6 Box Plots

A box plot summarizes the distribution of a continuous variable using five key statistical measures:

Minimum value (whiskers): The lower whisker represents the minimum value observed in the dataset, excluding any outliers.
25th percentile: Also known as the lower quartile, this value marks the point below which 25% of the data falls. It indicates the boundary of the lower quartile or the first quartile.
Median (50th percentile): The median is the middle value of the dataset when it is sorted. It represents the midpoint of the distribution, separating the lower 50% from the upper 50%.
75th percentile: Also known as the upper quartile, this value marks the point below which 75% of the data falls. It indicates the boundary of the upper quartile or the third quartile.
Maximum value (whiskers): The upper whisker represents the maximum value observed in the dataset, excluding any outliers.

In a box plot, the box itself represents the interquartile range (IQR), which is the range between the 25th and 75th percentiles. The length of the box indicates the spread or variability of the data within this middle 50% range. Additionally, the box plot can also reveal any outliers or extreme values in the dataset. These outliers, which lie outside the whiskers, are denoted by small circles or dots in the plot.

A box plot is commonly used for continuous variables, such as ratio or interval variables. However, it can also be used for certain categorical variables, particularly ordinal variables that have a natural ordering. By examining a box plot, you can quickly grasp important statistical information about the dataset, including the range, median, quartiles, and presence of outliers. It provides a concise summary of the data's distribution and aids in comparing multiple groups or variables plotted side-by-side.

To create a box plot using Pandas, you can use the plot.box() method. For example:

```
score_df_long['score'].plot.box()
```

Output:

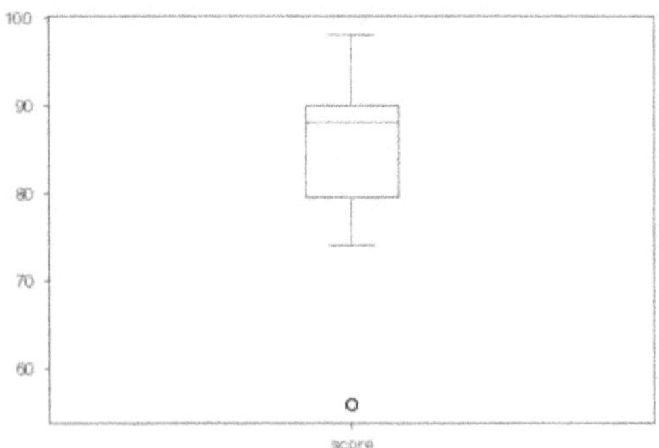

The box plot displaying the statistical measures and outliers associated with the 'score' column.

Review Question 7.40
Which of the following statistical measures is represented by the lower whisker in a box plot?
a. 25th percentile
b. Median
c. 75th percentile
d. Minimum value

Review Question 7.41
What does the box in a box plot represent?
a. The range of the data
b. The median value
c. The interquartile range
d. The standard deviation

Review Question 7.42
How many statistical measures are displayed in a box plot?
a. 3
b. 4
c. 5
d. 6

Review Question 7.43
Which of the following is NOT a purpose of using a box plot?
a. Identifying outliers
b. Comparing multiple groups or variables
c. Showing the exact distribution of data points
d. Understanding the range and quartiles of the data

Review Question 7.44

Which type of variables are commonly used with box plots?
a. Nominal variables
b. Continuous variables
c. Binary variables
d. Categorical variables

Review Question 7.45
What do outliers in a box plot represent?
a. Errors in the data collection process
b. Extreme values in the dataset
c. Missing data points
d. Inconsistent variable types

7.2.7 Scatter or Point Plots

A scatter plot allows us to examine the relationship between two continuous variables by plotting their values as points on a Cartesian coordinate system. It helps us determine whether there is a correlation or association between the variables. Scatter plots are a useful tool for understanding the relationship between two variables. They can reveal patterns, trends, clusters, or the absence of any clear relationship. By examining the distribution of points, we can gain insights into the *strength* and *direction* of the relationship.

To create a scatter plot in Pandas, we need to specify the independent variable (x-axis) and the dependent variable (y-axis). This can be done by providing the respective column names as the x and y parameters. Let's consider an example where we want to investigate the relationship between the 'absence' variable and the 'score' variable in the score_df_long:

```
score_df_long.plot.scatter(x='absence', y='score')
```

Output:

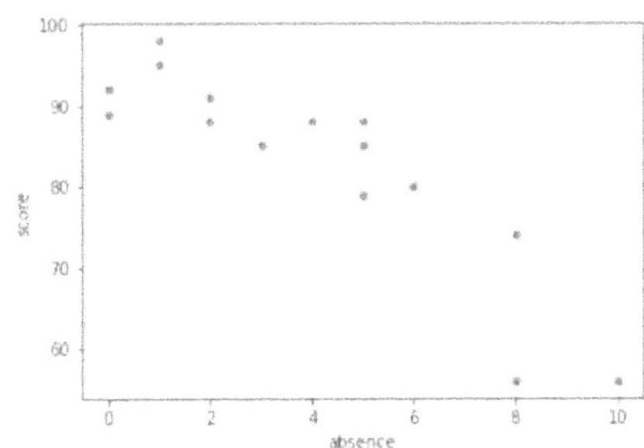

However, a potential issue with this plot is that it does not differentiate between the exams. There are three instances where 'absence' is 5, but we cannot determine which exam each point corresponds to. To address this, we can use the seaborn module, which provides additional functionalities for data visualization. By using the sns.scatterplot() function from seaborn and specifying the 'hue' parameter as 'exam', we can differentiate the points for each exam in the scatter plot:

```
sns.scatterplot(data=score_df_long, x='absence', y='score', hue='exam')
```

Output:

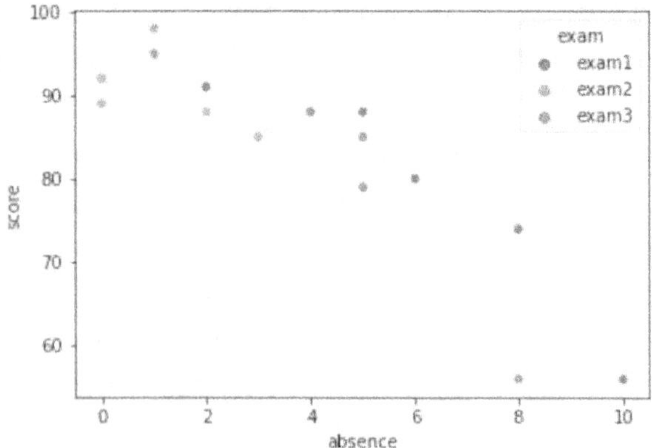

This scatter plot has different colors or markers representing each exam, allowing for better differentiation and understanding of the data.

Review Question 7.46
What is the purpose of a scatter plot?
a. To display categorical data
b. To visualize the relationship between two continuous variables
c. To represent the frequency distribution of a dataset
d. To compare multiple groups or variables

Review Question 7.47
What insights can be gained from a scatter plot?
a. The statistical measures of a dataset
b. The frequency of data points in each interval
c. The correlation or association between two variables
d. The spread or variability of the data

Review Question 7.48
How do we specify the variables for a scatter plot in Pandas?
a. By providing the column names as x and y parameters
b. By assigning values to the independent and dependent variables
c. By using the scatterplot() function from seaborn
d. By specifying the hue parameter as 'exam'

Review Question 7.49
What issue can arise when creating a scatter plot without differentiation?
a. The inability to display categorical data
b. The loss of statistical measures in the plot
c. Difficulty in identifying relationships specific to different groups
d. Inaccurate representation of the frequency distribution

Review Question 7.50
How can we address the issue of differentiation in a scatter plot using seaborn?
a. By specifying the column names as x and y parameters
b. By assigning values to the independent and dependent variables
c. By using the scatterplot() function from seaborn
d. By specifying the hue parameter

Review Question 7.51
What advantage does adding the 'hue' parameter provide in a scatter plot using seaborn?
a. It allows for the representation of categorical data.
b. It enhances the statistical measures in the plot.
c. It improves the accuracy of the frequency distribution.
d. It enables differentiation and understanding of relationships specific to each group.

7.2.8 Subplot

Subplots allows you to create separate plots for different columns, making it easier to observe the variations in data for each group. To enable subplots, you simply need to set the subplots parameter to True when using the plot function. Here's an example code snippet:

```
score_df.plot.bar(subplots=True)
```

Output:

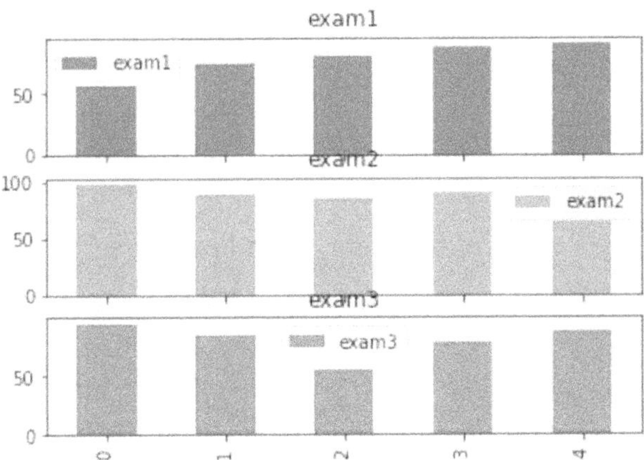

The output includes three subplots, with each subplot representing a different exam.

Now, let's explore a more comprehensive example that includes additional parameters to customize the layout and appearance of the subplots:

```
score_df.plot.bar(subplots=True,
            title=['Exam One', 'Exam Two', 'Exam Three'],
            ylabel='scores out of 100',
            sharey=True,
            layout=(2, 2),
            figsize=(10, 7),
```

```
legend=False
)
```

Output:

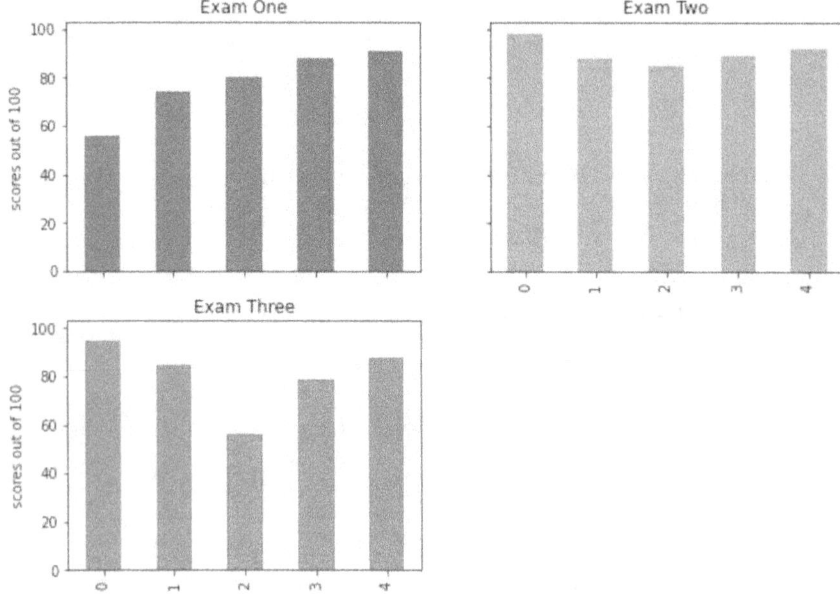

In this code snippet, we've provided a list of titles for each subplot using the title parameter. To ensure that the legend doesn't interfere with the subplots, we set the legend parameter to False. The layout parameter allows us to specify the desired arrangement of the subplots by indicating the number of rows and columns. In this case, we have specified a layout of 2 rows and 2 columns. Furthermore, we've adjusted the size of the figure using the figsize parameter to make it more suitable for display.

It's worth noting that when using a list for the title parameter, it's essential to set the legend parameter to False. Additionally, you can utilize the sharey parameter to ensure that the y-axis label is shared across all the subplots, making it easier to compare the scores.

Review Question 7.52
What is the purpose of using subplots in data visualization?
a. To create separate plots for different rows and columns
b. To customize the layout and appearance of the plots
c. To enable sharing of the y-axis label across all plots
d. To generate clear visual representations of data for each group

Review Question 7.53
How can you enable subplots in the plot function?
a. It is by default
b. Use the sharey parameter to True

c. Specify the desired layout with the layout parameter
d. Set the subplots parameter to True

Review Question 7.54
Which parameter can be used to customize the layout and appearance of subplots?
a. figsize
b. ylabel
c. title
d. legend

Review Question 7.55
Why is it important to set the legend parameter to False when using a list for the title parameter?
a. It ensures the y-axis label is shared across all subplots.
b. It avoids interference between the legend and subplots.
c. It provides clear visual representations of data for each exam.
d. It specifies the desired arrangement of the subplots.

Review Question 7.56
What does the sharey parameter do in subplots?
a. Sets the title for each subplot
b. Adjusts the size of the figure
c. Shares the y-axis label across all subplots
d. Specifies the number of rows and columns in the layout

7.3 Matplotlib

Matplotlib is a powerful and versatile data visualization library for Python, widely used in business data analytics. It provides a MATLAB-like interface for creating a wide variety of static, animated, and interactive plots and charts. Matplotlib allows analysts to transform raw data into meaningful visual representations, making it easier to identify trends, patterns, and insights crucial for informed decision-making. With its extensive customization options, Matplotlib enables users to create publication-quality figures suitable for reports and presentations. From simple line graphs to complex multi-panel visualizations, Matplotlib offers the flexibility and functionality needed to effectively communicate data-driven stories in business contexts. Its integration with other popular data analysis libraries like NumPy and pandas makes it an essential tool for any business analyst working with Python.

7.3.1 Matplotlib and Pandas

While Pandas offers a convenient and user-friendly API for plotting directly from DataFrames, it relies heavily on Matplotlib behind the scenes. The Pandas plotting functionality is essentially a simplified interface built on top of Matplotlib, which handles the intricate details of plot creation. Even though Pandas enables quick and easy visualizations, having a solid grasp of Matplotlib is still important, especially for advanced customizations that go beyond what Pandas offers.

For instance, Pandas' plotting methods often accept an optional `ax` parameter, allowing you to pass a Matplotlib `subplot` object. This feature is particularly useful for fine-tuning and controlling the layout of your subplots when you need more advanced designs:

```
# Sample data for two data sets
data1 = {'Month': ['Jan', 'Feb', 'Mar', 'Apr', 'May'],
         'Sales': [200, 150, 300, 250, 400]}
data2 = {'Month': ['Jan', 'Feb', 'Mar', 'Apr', 'May'],
         'Expenses': [180, 130, 280, 220, 360]}
# Creating Pandas DataFrames
df_sales = pd.DataFrame(data1)
df_expenses = pd.DataFrame(data2)
# Create subplots
fig, (ax1, ax2) = plt.subplots(2, 1, figsize=(8, 10))
# Plot Sales on the first subplot
df_sales.plot(x='Month', y='Sales', kind='bar', ax=ax1, title='Monthly
Sales')
# Plot Expenses on the second subplot
df_expenses.plot(x='Month', y='Expenses', kind='bar', ax=ax2,
title='Monthly Expenses')
```

With Matplotlib, you can arrange multiple plots within a single figure in various layouts (e.g., side-by-side, in a grid, etc.). In the Pandas-only example, you lose the ability to arrange the plots in a controlled layout. Additionaly, in the Matplotlib version, you explicitly created two subplots (ax1 and ax2), allowing you to place multiple plots together, offering better control over the design and spacing:

```
# Create a figure with two subplots
fig, (ax1, ax2) = plt.subplots(1, 2, figsize=(10, 4))
# Plot Sales on the first subplot using the ax parameter
df_sales.plot(x='Month', y='Sales', kind='bar', ax=ax1,
color='skyblue')
ax1.set_title('Monthly Sales')
ax1.set_xlabel('Month')
ax1.set_ylabel('Sales')
# Plot Expenses on the second subplot using the ax parameter
df_expenses.plot(x='Month', y='Expenses', kind='bar', ax=ax2,
color='salmon')
ax2.set_title('Monthly Expenses')
ax2.set_xlabel('Month')
ax2.set_ylabel('Expenses')
# Adjust layout for better spacing
plt.tight_layout()
```

```
# Display the plots
plt.show()
```

The plotting capabilities of Pandas are designed to provide quick insights without much configuration. However, it's important to recognize that Pandas is leveraging Matplotlib behind the scenes. This means that learning Matplotlib not only gives you a deeper understanding of how Pandas' plots work but also enables you to extend and customize those plots. If you need to change colors, tweak axes, or even create complex multi-figure layouts, Matplotlib is your go-to.

Here's an example: Pandas allows you to create a line plot with just `df.plot()`, but if you need to customize the figure size or adjust the aspect ratio, you may have to use Matplotlib directly. By learning Matplotlib, you gain access to these lower-level controls, offering more flexibility in your visualizations:

```
# Sample data
data = {'Month': ['Jan', 'Feb', 'Mar', 'Apr', 'May'],
        'Sales': [200, 150, 300, 250, 400]}
df = pd.DataFrame(data)
# Basic line plot with Pandas
df.plot(x='Month', y='Sales', kind='line', title='Monthly Sales')
plt.show()
# Customized line plot with Matplotlib
fig, ax = plt.subplots(figsize=(12, 8))  # Custom figure size
# Plotting with customizations
df.plot(x='Month', y='Sales', kind='line', ax=ax, title='Monthly
Sales', color='blue', linestyle='--', marker='o')
# Adding grid lines
ax.grid(True, which='both', linestyle='--', linewidth=0.5)
# Customizing the legend
ax.legend(['Sales'], loc='upper left', fontsize='large')
# Annotating specific points
for i, txt in enumerate(df['Sales']):
    ax.annotate(txt, (i, df['Sales'][i]), textcoords="offset points",
xytext=(0,10), ha='center')
# Adding labels and title
ax.set_xlabel('Month', fontsize=12)
ax.set_ylabel('Sales', fontsize=12)
ax.set_title('Monthly Sales with Customizations', fontsize=16)
# Customizing the aspect ratio
ax.set_aspect(aspect='auto')
# Show the customized plot
plt.show()
```

Review Question 7.57

What is Matplotlib primarily used for in business data analytics?
a. Database management
b. Data visualization
c. Machine learning algorithms
d. Web development

Review Question 7.58
What type of interface does Matplotlib provide?
a. R-like interface
b. MATLAB-like interface
c. SQL-like interface
d. Java-like interface

Review Question 7.59
What is the relationship between Pandas and Matplotlib for plotting?
a. Pandas replaces Matplotlib completely
b. Pandas and Matplotlib are entirely separate
c. Pandas relies on Matplotlib for its plotting functionality
d. Matplotlib is built on top of Pandas

Review Question 7.60
Which of the following is an advantage of using Matplotlib directly over Pandas for plotting?
a. Simpler syntax
b. Faster execution
c. More customization options
d. Automatic data cleaning

7.3.2 Matplotlib and Seaborn

Following our discussion on Pandas and Matplotlib, it's essential to recognize another powerful library in the Python data visualization ecosystem: Seaborn. Built on top of Matplotlib, Seaborn simplifies the process of creating statistical visualizations and comes with aesthetically pleasing, publication-ready themes. It provides higher-level interfaces for drawing attractive and informative statistical graphics, making it easier to create more complex plots such as pair plots, heatmaps, and regression plots.

While Seaborn simplifies many types of visualizations, it's built on the robust foundation of Matplotlib, making it easier to perform statistical data analysis and plot attractive graphics with minimal code. However, Seaborn itself is not a replacement for Matplotlib but rather a complementary tool. Many of the plots you generate with Seaborn can be further customized using Matplotlib functions.

For example, if you create a heatmap in Seaborn but need to adjust the layout of subplots or customize colors beyond Seaborn's built-in themes, you'll still need Matplotlib. Thus, Seaborn accelerates the creation of sophisticated statistical plots, while Matplotlib provides the flexibility to customize and fine-tune the visual output.

In business data analytics, where visual clarity and precision are crucial for decision-making, being proficient in Matplotlib ensures that you can create tailored visualizations that meet the specific needs of stakeholders. While Seaborn is an excellent tool for quickly generating insightful plots, Matplotlib gives you the ability to modify and enhance these plots to better communicate your findings.

Since Matplotlib comes pre-installed with Anaconda, there's no need for additional installations. Mastering Matplotlib not only gives you control over visualizations created with Pandas and Seaborn but also prepares you for working with a variety of other Python data visualization libraries. In the next section, we'll dive deeper into Seaborn, exploring its features and how it simplifies the process of creating statistical visualizations that are both informative and aesthetically pleasing.

Review Question 7.61
What is the primary advantage of Seaborn over Matplotlib?
a. It replaces Matplotlib entirely
b. It simplifies the creation of statistical visualizations
c. It offers more customization options
d. It's faster in processing large datasets

Review Question 7.62
How does Seaborn relate to Matplotlib?
a. Seaborn is a completely independent library
b. Seaborn is built on top of Matplotlib
c. Matplotlib is built on top of Seaborn
d. They are competing libraries with no relation

Review Question 7.63
In what scenario might you still need to use Matplotlib when working with Seaborn?
a. When creating basic plots
b. When working with pandas DataFrames
c. When adjusting subplot layouts or customizing colors beyond Seaborn's themes
d. When generating heatmaps

Review Question 7.64
What is the relationship between Seaborn and Matplotlib in terms of functionality?
a) Seaborn completely replaces Matplotlib
b) Seaborn is a subset of Matplotlib
c) Seaborn is complementary to Matplotlib
d) Seaborn and Matplotlib are identical in functionality

Review Question 7.65
Why is proficiency in Matplotlib important for business data analytics?
a. It's the only tool available for data visualization
b. It allows for creation of tailored visualizations to meet specific stakeholder needs
c. It's faster than Seaborn for all types of plots
d. It's required to use Seaborn

Review Question 7.66
What is an advantage of mastering Matplotlib beyond working with Seaborn?
a. It allows you to create 3D visualizations
b. It prepares you for working with other Python data visualization libraries
c. It's necessary for machine learning tasks
d. It enables real-time data plotting

7.4 Seaborn

While Pandas is excellent for generating quick, functional plots for personal use, professional settings like presentations and reports demand a higher level of clarity and aesthetic appeal. This is where Seaborn excels. Seaborn is a Python-based data visualization library designed to enhance both the readability and visual quality of your plots. It modifies the default styles and color schemes of Matplotlib, making it easier to create polished, publication-quality graphics.

Even if you don't directly use the Seaborn API, simply importing Seaborn can improve the aesthetics of your Matplotlib plots by updating the default color palettes and plot styles. Seaborn also introduces conveniences like automatic aggregation for categorical data, helping you simplify your plotting code while achieving more attractive results.

While Matplotlib offers detailed, fine-grained control over every aspect of a plot, Seaborn focuses on making complex visualizations easy to create with less code. Seaborn is particularly well-suited for producing intricate, multi-dimensional plots, such as pair plots, heatmaps, and facet grids, which can be cumbersome to create in Matplotlib alone. Seaborn abstracts much of the complexity, allowing you to focus more on analysis and less on plot configuration.

Despite its strengths, Seaborn's customizations are more limited compared to Matplotlib. For advanced visualizations that require full control over axes, labels, or annotations, Matplotlib remains indispensable. However, for many business data analytics tasks, Seaborn provides an optimal balance of simplicity and aesthetics.

Seaborn offers three types of plots. The first type is relational plots, which depict the relationship between two variables. Specific methods like scatterplot and lineplot are available, or you can use the general method, relplot, by setting the "kind" parameter. Scatter plots are suitable for visualizing relationships between numeric variables, while line plots are effective for identifying trends and changes over time.

General method	Specific method
relplot()	scatterplot()
	lineplot()

The second type is categorical plots, which are ideal for categorical data. Seaborn provides eight specific methods, such as barplot, boxplot, stripplot, swarmplot, pointplot, boxenplot, violinplot, and countplot, along with a general method called catplot.

General method	Specific method
catplot()	barplot()
	boxplot()
	stripplot()
	swarmplot()
	pointplot()
	boxenplot()
	violinplot()
	countplot()

Lastly, distribution plots are used to examine how numeric data is distributed across a range of values. Seaborn offers three specific methods: histplot for histograms, kdeplot for kernel density estimate plots, and ecdfplot for empirical cumulative distribution function plots. The general method, displot, encompasses all three.

General method	Specific method
displot()	histplot()
	kdeplot()
	ecdfplot()

The seaborn library complements matplotlib by improving the default settings and offering simplified options for creating visually appealing plots. It provides specialized methods for different plot types, allowing you to effectively visualize relationships, categorical data, and data distributions.

Review Question 7.67
Which type of plot is suitable for visualizing the relationship between two numeric variables?
a. Scatter plot
b. Bar plot
c. Histogram
d. Box plot

Review Question 7.68
Which type of plot is ideal for categorical data in seaborn?
a. catplot()
b. scatterplot()
c. lineplot()
d. histplot()

Review Question 7.69
Which seaborn method is NOT suitable for examining how numeric data is distributed across a range of values?
a. catplot()
b. histplot()
c. kdeplot()
d. ecdfplot()

Review Question 7.70
Which general method in seaborn encompasses the creation of histograms, kernel density estimate plots, and empirical cumulative distribution function plots?
a. relplot()
b. catplot()
c. displot()
d. scatterplot()

7.4.1 General Method vs. Specific Method

Seaborn allows plot creation using either general or specific methods. Here's how to create a line plot with both: First, we use the general method relplot(), specifying 'line' as the kind parameter. We set the x and y parameters to the 'absence' and 'score' columns, respectively. The hue parameter groups the data by the 'exam' column, representing three exam groups.

```
sns.relplot(data=score_df_long, kind='line', x='absence', y='score', hue='exam')
```
Output:

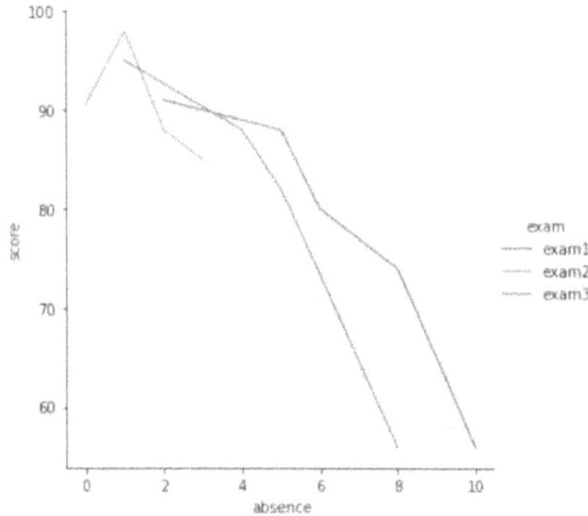

Next, we create the same plot using the specific method lineplot(). The only difference is that the kind parameter isn't required.

```
sns.lineplot(data=score_df_long,x='absence', y='score', hue='exam')
```

Both methods produce similar information, but with visual differences. Specific method plots are often wider and shorter, have a border, and place the legend within the border. General methods can create plots with subplots and offer more flexibility.

Review Question 7.71
What is the purpose of the "kind" parameter in the relplot() method?
a. It specifies the type of plot to be created.
b. It determines the color palette to be used.
c. It sets the x-axis label.
d. It controls the size of the plot.

Review Question 7.72
What advantage do general methods have over specific methods in seaborn?
a. General methods create wider and shorter plots.
b. General methods allow for subplots.
c. General methods offer more color customization options.
d. General methods provide a different set of plot types.

7.4.2 Relational Plots in Seaborn

To create a scatter plot in Seaborn, you can set the kind parameter of the relplot() method to 'scatter':

```
sns.relplot(data=score_df_long, kind='scatter', x='absence', y='score', hue='exam')
```

Output:

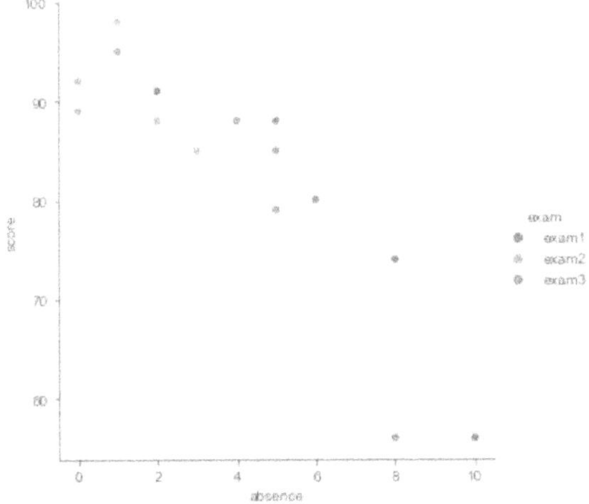

You can also incorporate the size of the dots in a scatter plot to display additional information. The size parameter is used to set the dot size based on the values in a specific column. By using the sizes parameter, you can control the variance in dot sizes. In the following example, the tuple (10, 100) specifies that the dot sizes should range from 10 to 100, with the largest dots being ten times larger than the smallest dots:

```
gpa = [3.5, 2.8, 4.0, 3.6, 1.7, 2.9, 3.3, 3.4, 3.9, 2.7, 2.0, 3.1, 3.0, 3.3, 3.4]
score_df_long['gpa'] = gpa
g = sns.relplot(data=score_df_long, kind='scatter',
          x='absence', y='score', hue='exam', size='gpa', sizes=(10,100))
for ax in g.axes.flat:
    ax.set(xticks=[x for x in range(0,11)])
```

Output:

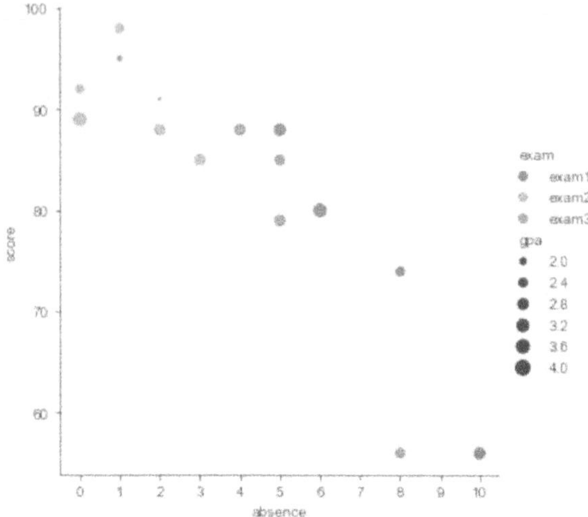

To create individual plots for each exam, use the sns.relplot() function with the col parameter set to 'exam'. This creates a subplot for each exam. Limit the number of subplots per row with col_wrap. Disable subplot titles by setting legend to False. Here's an example:

```
sns.relplot(data=score_df_long,kind='line', x='absence', y='score',
     hue='exam', height=4, aspect=1.25,col='exam', col_wrap=2, legend=False)
```

Recall that seaborn offers two main ways to create plots: specific methods like sns.lineplot() and general methods like sns.relplot(). The former returns a single *Axes* object, which can be customized by calling methods like set(). The latter returns a *FacetGrid* object containing multiple Axes objects. Customize each subplot by looping through the Axes objects in the FacetGrid using axes.flat and calling set() on each.

Axes is a class from Matplotlib, which is a lower-level plotting library. An Axes object represents a single plot with its own coordinate system, labels, title, and other features. On the other hand, FacetGrid is a class from Seaborn, which is a higher-level interface built on top of Matplotlib. It is used to create a grid of multiple plots by mapping dataset variables to the rows and columns of the grid, allowing you to explore complex data relationships.

The Axes class is used when you need a single plot, or when you are customizing individual plots in detail.

The FacetGrid class is useful when you want to create a series of plots that share common axes but show different subsets of the data, making it easier to compare these subsets side by side:

```python
# Specific method:
ax = sns.lineplot(data=score_df_long,
    x='absence', y='score',
    hue='exam')
ax.set(title='Scores by Exam', ylabel='Score out of 100')
```
Output:

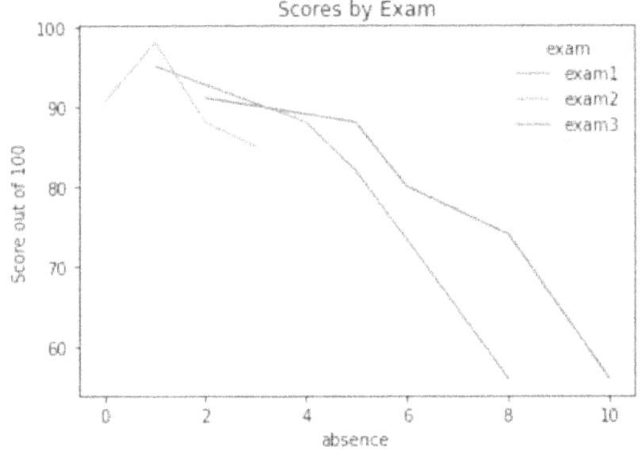

```python
# General method:
g = sns.relplot(data=score_df_long,
    kind='line', x='absence', y='score',
    hue='exam')
for ax in g.axes.flat:
    ax.set(title='Scores by Exam', ylabel='Score out of 100')
```
Output:

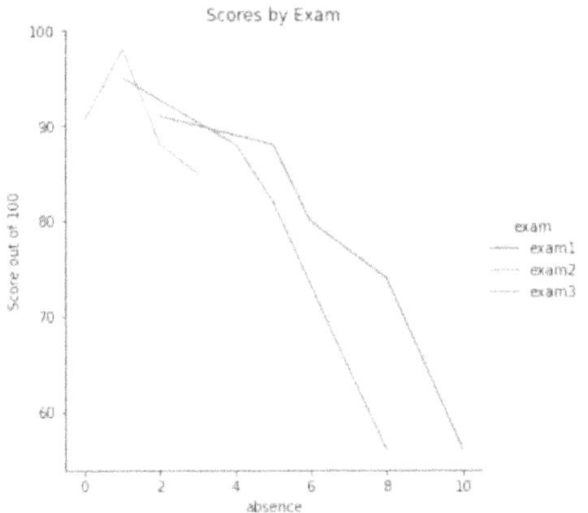

You can enhance plots by using parameters like xticks and yticks to set specific tick values, xlim and ylim to limit the data range, and tick_params() to rotate tick labels. For general methods, use the g.axes.flat accessor to loop through the Axes objects.

```python
g = sns.relplot(data=score_df_long,
```

```
    kind='line', x='absence', y='score',
    hue='exam', aspect=1.25)
for ax in g.axes.flat:
    ax.set(title='High score by absence',
           ylabel='Score out of 100',
           xticks=[x for x in range(0, 6, 1)],
           xlim=(0,5), ylim=(80,100)),
    ax.tick_params('x', labelrotation=30)
```

Output:

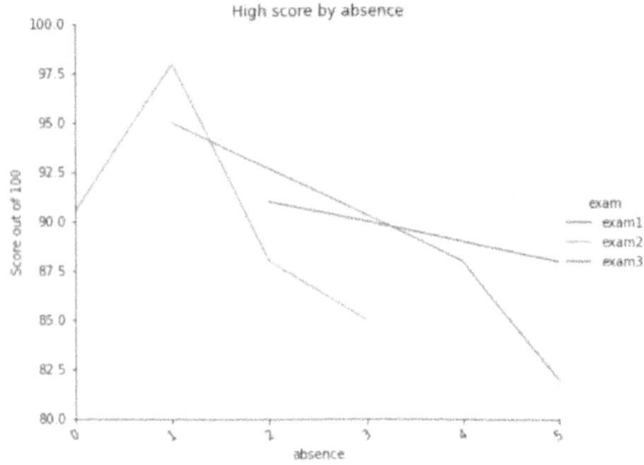

For specific methods, the enhancements are similar, but you don't need to loop through a FacetGrid object:

```
ax = sns.lineplot(data=score_df_long,
    x='absence', y='score', hue='exam')
ax.set(title='High score by absence',
    ylabel='Score out of 100',
    xticks=[x for x in range(0, 6, 1)],
    xlim=(0,5), ylim=(80,100))
ax.tick_params('x', labelrotation=30)
```
Output:

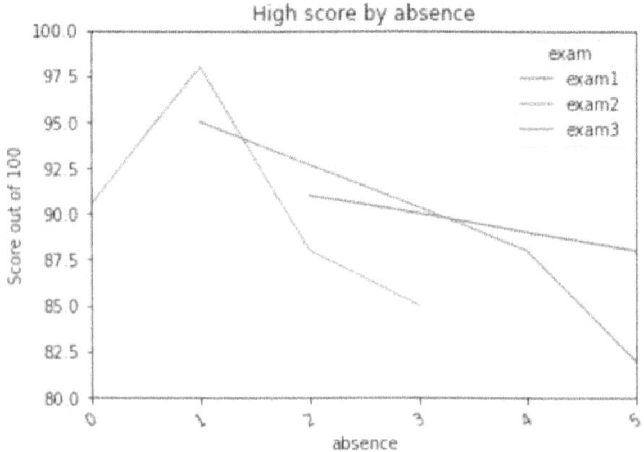

The aspect parameter is not applicable for axes-level functions like lineplot. Instead, the figure size should be controlled through Matplotlib's figure creation, using the figsize parameter:

```
ax = plt.subplots(figsize=(10, 8))
```

Use sns.set_style() to set the background style for a plot. There are five preset styles: 'ticks' (default), 'white', 'dark', 'whitegrid', and 'darkgrid'. Once set, the style remains in effect until changed. To return to the default style, use "sns.set_style('ticks')".

```
sns.set_style('darkgrid')
sns.relplot(data=score_df_long, kind='line',
            x='absence', y='score', hue='exam')
```

Output:

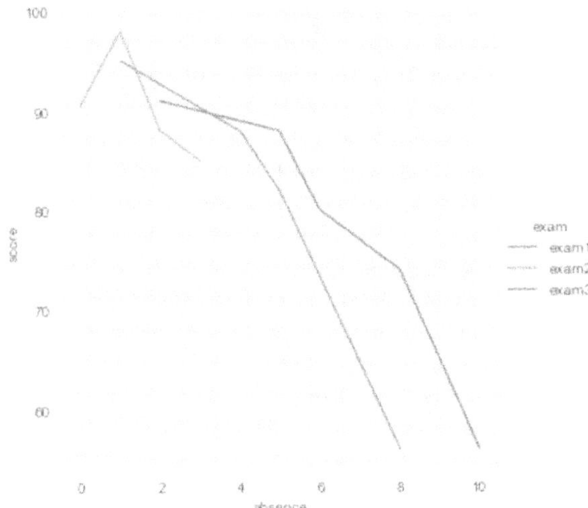

Review Question 7.73
Given the score_df_long in the book, when separating the three exam line plots into individual plots, which parameter should be used?
a. hue
b. aspect
c. col
d. legend

Review Question 7.74
What does the legend parameter do in the code example?
```
sns.relplot(data=score_df_long, kind='line', x='absence', y='score',
    hue='exam',height=4,aspect=1.25,col='exam',col_wrap=2, legend=False)
```
a. Enables grid lines for each tick
b. Sets the background style for the plot
c. Controls the number of subplots per row
d. Disables the automatically generated subplot titles

Review Question 7.75
Which object is returned when using a specific method to create a plot in Seaborn?
a. Axes object
b. FacetGrid object
c. Plot object
d. Grid object

Review Question 7.76
How can you add a title and y-label to a plot created with a general method?
a. Call the set() method directly on the FacetGrid object.
b. Loop through the Axes objects in the FacetGrid object and call the set() method on each.
c. Use the title() and ylabel() functions.
d. Access the Axes object using the get_axes() method.

Review Question 7.77
What is the purpose of the set_style() method in Seaborn?
a. Sets the background style for the plot
b. Changes the color palette of the plot
c. Adjusts the size of the plot
d. Adds grid lines to the plot

Exercise 7.2

Given the following DataFrame:

```
products_df = pd.DataFrame({
    'product1': [169, 161, 115, 120, 152],
    'product2': [85, 168, 162, 178, 157],
    'product3': [121, 135, 168, 132, 146],
})
```

Complete the following tasks:

Task 1: Convert the DataFrame to long format with 'product' and 'quantity' columns, similar to score_df_long in the chapter.

Task 2: Add prices to the long format and draw a scatter plot to show the relationship between quantity and price (price is independent variable). prices = [16.38, 18.63, 23.65, 20.26, 19.85, 22.69, 19.43, 17.85, 15.99, 20.96, 23.18, 19.21, 17.41, 20.11, 18.55]

Task 3: Add 'days_in_inventory' to the long format and draw a scatter plot with dot size indicating days in inventory. dii = [5, 18, 6, 20, 12, 56, 19, 10, 120, 20, 23, 19, 53, 70.11, 18]

Task 4: Create individual line plots for each product as subplots with a limit of two plots per row.

Task 5: Use seaborn's specific method to create a line chart between price and quantity for all products.

Task 6: Do the same(similarly) as Task 5 with seaborn's general method.

Task 7: Enhance the plots in Task 6 by setting specific tick values, data range limits, rotating tick labels, and adjusting the aspect ratio similar to the example in the chapter with general method.

Task 8: Use seaborn's specific method with enhancements for Task 7.

Task 9: Set the background style to "whitegrid" and and conduct Task 2 again.

Task 10: Reset the background to the default as explained in the chapter and conduct Task 2 again.

7.4.3 Save a Plot

To save a plot, use the savefig() method in the FacetGrid object. The file extension determines the format. You can specify both a filename and path. In the example below, the plot is saved as 'scoresbyexam.png', 'scoresbyexam.svg', and 'scoresbyexam.pdf' in the current directory. The PNG format is commonly used, but if you want to zoom in without losing quality or embed the graph on the web, consider using the SVG format, which is a vector graphics format. Here's an example:

```python
g = sns.relplot(data=score_df_long, kind='line', x='absence',y='score',
    hue='exam',legend=False, col='exam', col_wrap=2, height=4)
g.fig.suptitle('Scores by Exam', y=1.05)
for ax in g.axes.flat:
    ax.set(ylabel='Scores out of 100', xticks=[x for x in range(0,11)])
g.savefig('scoresbyexam.png')
g.savefig('scoresbyexam.svg')
g.savefig('scoresbyexam.pdf')
```
Output:

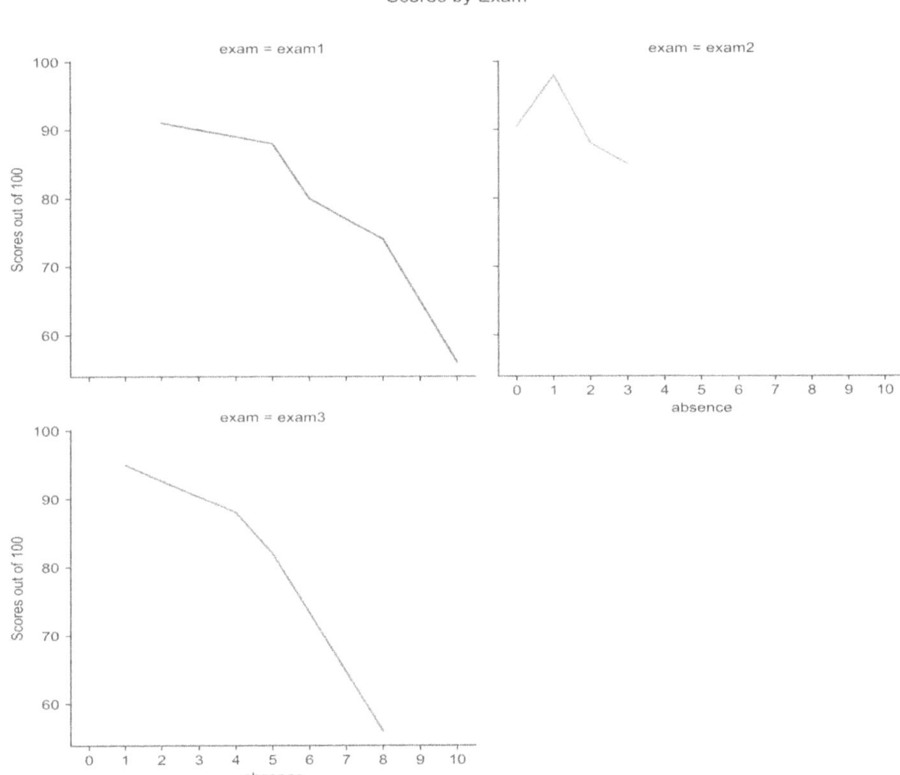

To save a plot in Axes class, call the get_figure() method from the Axes object and chain it with the savefig()

method. This allows you to save the plot in different file formats:

```python
g = sns.relplot(data=score_df_long, kind='line',
    x='absence', y='score', hue='exam',
    legend=False, col='exam', col_wrap=2, height=4)
g.fig.suptitle('Scores by Exam', y=1.05)
for ax in g.axes.flat:
    ax.set(ylabel='Scores out of 100',
          xticks=[x for x in range(0,11)],
        #  ylim=(50,100)
          )
ax.get_figure().savefig('scores.png')
ax.get_figure().savefig('scores.svg')
ax.get_figure().savefig('scores.pdf')
```

The output is the same as the FacetGrid approach mentioned earlier. Note: Uncomment the ylim parameter in the code if you want to set specific limits for the y-axis. If you don't include the hue parameter, the plot will display the average score for the three exams as a single line. Additionally, a confidence interval will be generated and indicated by shaded areas above and below the plot line. By default, the confidence interval is set to 95%, meaning that if we were to repeat the sampling process multiple times and construct confidence intervals from the data, approximately 95% of those intervals would contain the true population parameter. The presence of a confidence interval in a line plot suggests that there is a range of values, determined from the sample data, which is likely to contain the fixed true mean of the population. The line itself represents the estimated mean based on the sample, and the confidence interval indicates the precision of this estimate. Here's an example without the hue parameter:

```
sns.relplot(data=score_df_long, kind='line', x='absence', y='score')
```

Output:

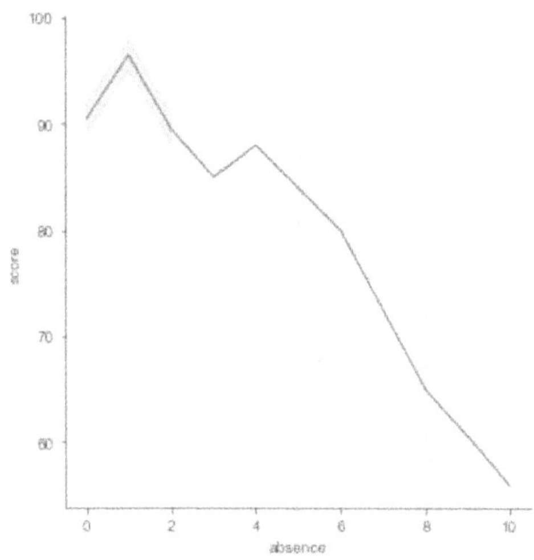

Review Question 7.78
How can you save a plot created with a general method in Seaborn?
a. Call the savefig() method directly on the Axes object.
b. Call the savefig() method of the FacetGrid object.
c. Use the saveplot() function from the seaborn library.
d. Specify the desired file format in the relplot() function.

Review Question 7.79
How can you save a plot created with a specific method in Seaborn?
a. Use the savefig() function from the seaborn library.
b. Call the savefig() method directly on the FacetGrid object.
c. Call the get_figure() method on the Axes object and then call savefig() on the returned figure object.
d. Specify the desired file format in the lineplot() function.

Review Question 7.80
What is the advantage of using the SVG file format when saving a plot?
a. It provides scalability without losing quality.
b. It reduces the file size compared to other formats.
c. It supports advanced animations.
d. It allows for faster rendering in web browsers.

Review Question 7.81
What does the presence of a confidence interval indicate in a line plot?
a. The range of data points for each exam
b. The standard deviation of the data points
c. The range of plausible values for the true mean of the population from which the sample was drawn
d. The margin of error for the plotted line

Review Question 7.82
Which format should be used when exporting Seaborn plots in order to embed them on a website?
a. TIFF
b. PNG
c. SVG
d. RAW

7.4.4 Pair Plots

A pair plot displays the relationships between all possible pairs of variables within a dataset. It's an invaluable asset in exploratory data analysis, allowing us to inspect scatter plots among a set of variables, also known as a pairs plot or scatter plot matrix.

In Seaborn, while specific plot functions like lineplot() have corresponding general methods like relplot(), the pairplot() function is a bit different. It does not have a direct general method equivalent. Instead, pairplot() is a high-level interface for creating pairwise relationship plots and is built on top of the PairGrid class, which provides the flexibility to create a wide variety of multi-plot grids.

When creating a pair plot, there's no need to specify the column names as arguments. This is because all variables in the dataset are automatically considered for plotting. The only parameter you need to provide is the DataFrame's name.

In a pair plot, when a variable is plotted against itself, it results in a redundant straight line along the diagonal. To make better use of this space, Seaborn's pairplot() function can replace these diagonal plots with informative univariate distribution plots. You can include histograms or density estimates along the diagonal. For instance, by setting diag_kind='kde', you can display kernel density estimates instead of histograms for each variable. Here's an example:

```
sns.pairplot(score_df_long, diag_kind='kde')
```

This code generates a pair plot that displays the bivariate relationships between all possible pairs of variables in the score_df_long DataFrame. Along the diagonal, you'll see the kernel density estimates (kde) or histograms of each variable.

Output:

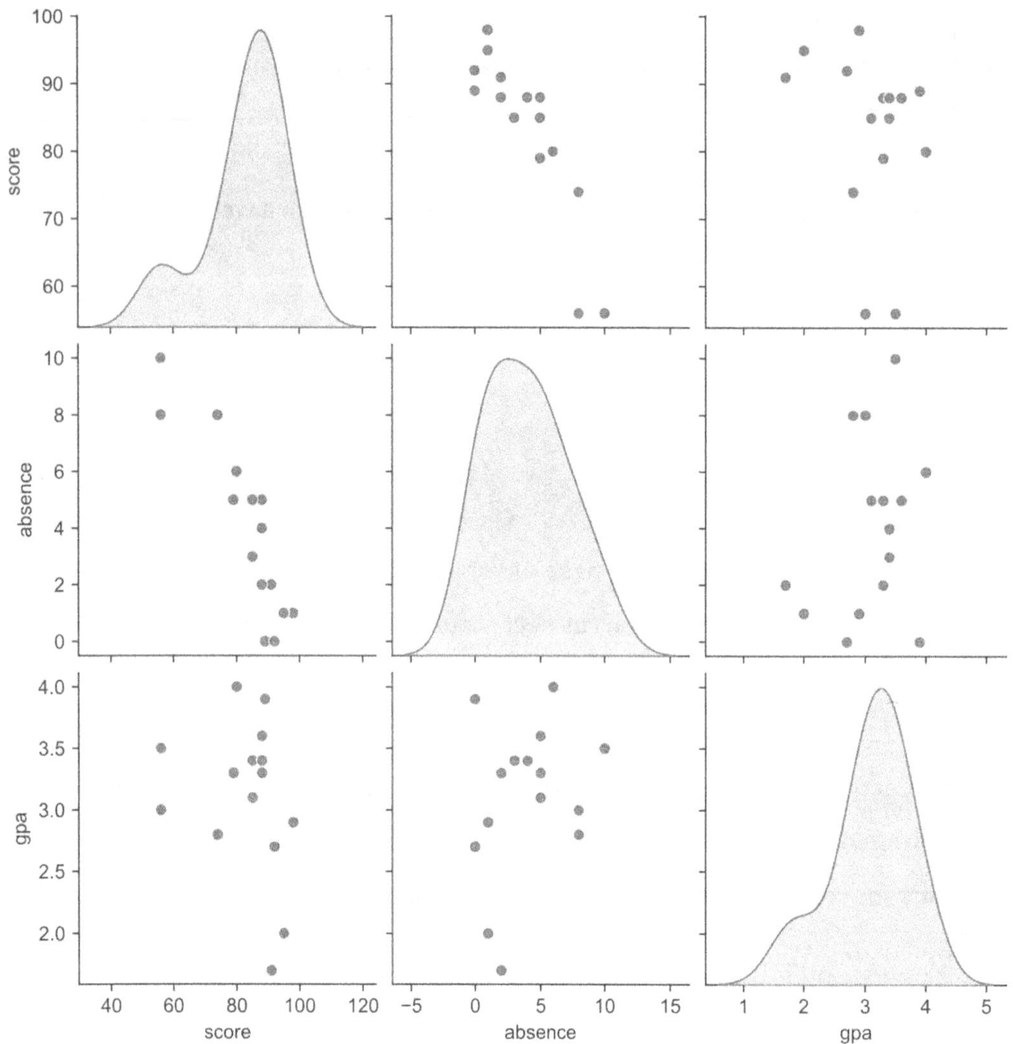

Review Question 7.83

What does a pair plot visualize?

a. Relationships between variables
b. Distribution of a single variable
c. Summary statistics of a dataset
d. Correlation coefficients between variables

Review Question 7.84
When creating a pair plot, do you need to specify column names as arguments?
a. Yes, you need to provide column names.
b. No, column names are automatically considered for plotting.
c. Only some column names need to be specified.
d. Only one column name is required for a pair plot.

Review Question 7.85
What information do the diagonal plots in a pair plot provide?
a. Relationships between variables
b. Correlation coefficients between variables
c. Distribution of individual variables
d. Summary statistics of a dataset

Review Question 7.86
The pairplot() function in Seaborn allows you to enhance the pair plot output _______ along the diagonal.
a. By adding color gradients to the scatter plots
b. By including additional variables in the plot
c. By specifying column names for plotting
d. By including histograms or density estimates

Review Question 7.87
What does setting diag_kind='kde' do in the pairplot() function?
a. It changes the color scheme of the scatter plots.
b. It includes additional variables in the plot.
c. It displays kernel density estimates instead of histograms.
d. It calculates correlation coefficients between variables.

Exercise 7.3

Prerequisite: Utilize the DataFrame from Exercise 7.2.
Task 1: Export the figure created in Task 5 of Exercise 7.2 into three different file formats: PNG, SVG, and PDF. Implement this task using the FacetGrid class from Seaborn.
Task 2: Replicate Task 1, but this time, employ the Axes class from Matplotlib for the figure creation and exporting process.
Task 3: Generate a pairplot using the DataFrame that you modified in Task 3 of Exercise 7.2. This will help visualize pairwise relationships in the dataset.

7.4.5 Categorical Plots in Seaborn

Previously, we looked at various categorical plots using pandas. Now let's further explore categorical

plotting, this time using Seaborn. We'll begin with the bar plot:

```
sns.catplot(data=score_df_long, kind='bar', x='exam', y='score')
```

Output:

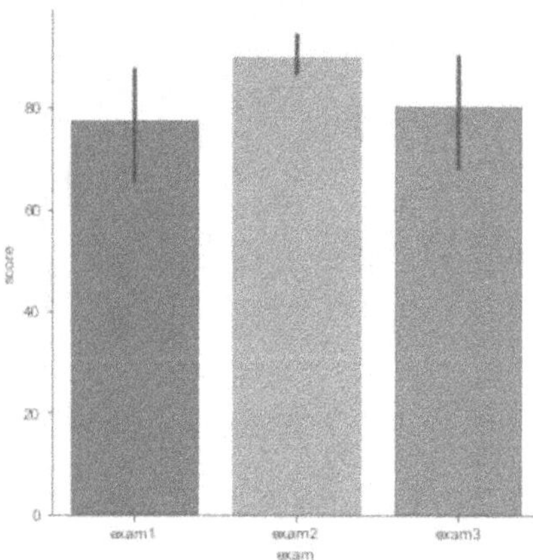

The vertical lines on top of each bar in the output of your seaborn bar plot are called *error bars*. Error bars are graphical representations of the variability of data and are used on graphs to indicate the error, or uncertainty in a reported measurement. They give a general idea of how precise a measurement is, or conversely, how far from the reported value the true (error free) value might be. In the context of a seaborn bar plot, these error bars represent the confidence interval around the estimate. By default, seaborn uses bootstrapping to compute confidence intervals, which can be computationally expensive with large datasets. If you want to remove these error bars, you can set the errorbar parameter to None in your catplot function:

```
sns.catplot(data=score_df_long, kind='bar', x='exam', y='score',errorbar=None)
```

This will generate a bar plot without any error bars. Please note that removing error bars might make the plot less informative as it no longer displays the variability of the data.

You can enhance the bar plot by using additional parameters. For example, you can add the hue parameter to group the bars based on another variable (e.g., gender). Additionally, you can modify the orientation of the plot using the orient parameter. If you switch the orientation, you also need to switch the x and y values accordingly. This allows you to create more informative and visually appealing bar plots:

```
gender = ['F', 'F', 'M', 'M', 'M', 'F', 'M', 'F', 'F', 'F', 'M', 'F', 'M', 'M', 'M']
score_df_long['gender'] = gender
sns.catplot(data=score_df_long,kind='bar',x='score',y='exam',hue='gender', orient='h')
```
Output:

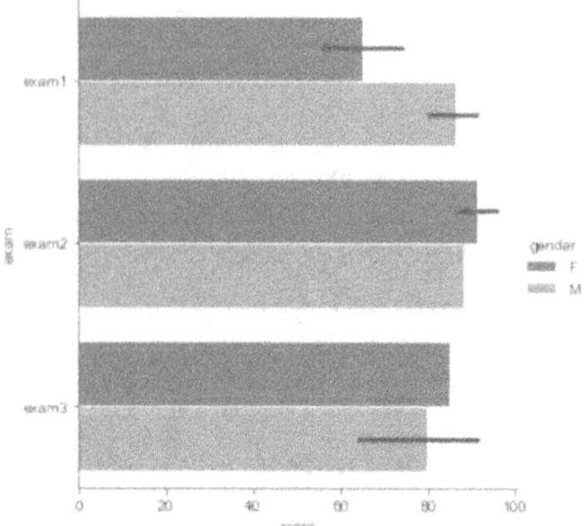

Next, let's discuss the box plot. A box plot provides valuable information about the distribution and skewness of a variable. It is created using the sns.catplot() function with the kind parameter set to 'box'.

```
sns.catplot(data=score_df_long, kind='box', x='gender', y='score')
```

Output:

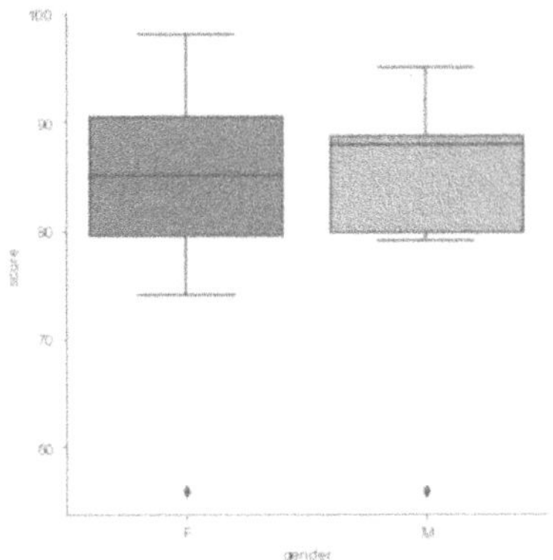

Moving on to the strip plot. A strip plot is similar to a scatter plot, but it is specifically used when one variable is categorical and the other is continuous, allowing for a clear visualization of the distribution of the continuous variable across different categories, which can be particularly useful for identifying patterns or outliers within each category. It is created using the catplot() function with the kind parameter set to 'strip'. The x-axis represents the categorical variable (e.g., gender), and the y-axis represents the continuous variable (e.g., score):

```
sns.catplot(x='gender',y='score', kind='strip', data=score_df_long)
```
Output:

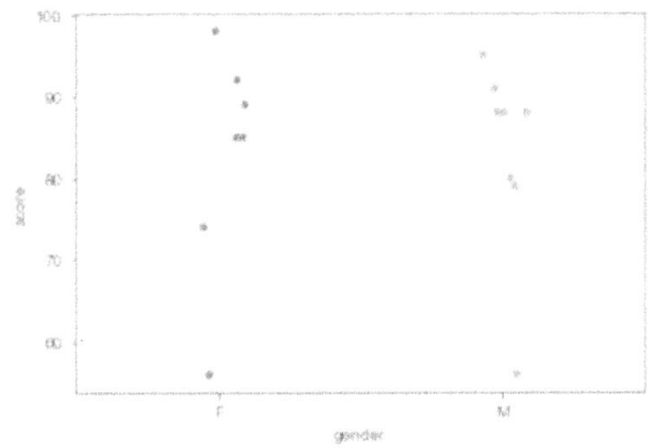

Finally, we have count plots. Count plots are used to display the frequency or count of each unique value in a categorical variable. You can create a count plot using the countplot() function. Simply specify the variable you want to plot (e.g., the letter grades in the score_df_long data frame), and the function will generate a bar plot where the length of each bar represents the count of observations for that particular value.

```
sns.countplot(data=score_df_long, x='letterGrade')
```
Output:

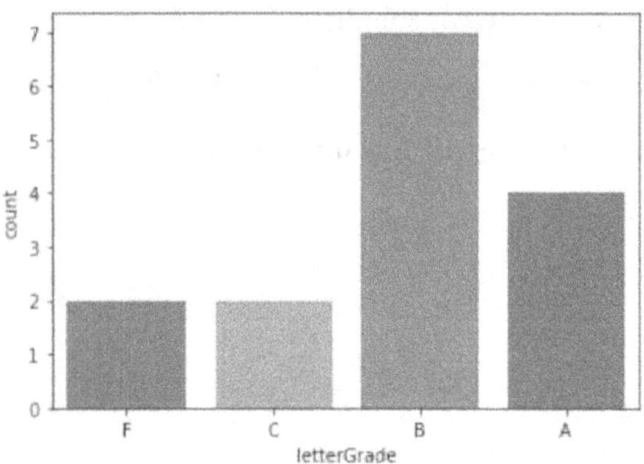

These different types of categorical plots in Seaborn provide a variety of options to visualize and analyze data with categorical and continuous variables. They help beginners gain insights into their datasets and communicate their findings effectively.

Review Question 7.88
What function is used to create a bar plot in Seaborn?
a. sns.scatterplot()
b. sns.boxplot()
c. sns.catplot()
d. two sns.lineplot() functions

Review Question 7.89
You can group the bars based on another variable _______ to the sns.catplot() function.
a. By setting the kind parameter to 'bar'
b. By specifying the variable in the x-axis
c. By adding the hue parameter
d. By modifying the orientation using the orient parameter

Review Question 7.90
What information does a box plot provide?
a. Frequency distribution of categorical variables
b. Correlation between two continuous variables
c. Distribution and skewness of a variable
d. Relationship between two categorical variables

Review Question 7.91
Which plot is usually NOT used when one variable is categorical and the other is continuous?
a. Bar plot
b. Box plot
c. Strip plot
d. Line plot

Review Question 7.92
What does a count plot represent?
a. Distribution and skewness of a variable

b. Frequency or count of each unique value in a categorical variable
c. Relationship between two continuous variables
d. Grouping of bars based on another variable

Exercise 7.4

Given the following dataset:
```
data = {
    'Student': ['Alice', 'Bob', 'Charlie', 'David', 'Eva', 'Frank', 'Grace', 'Hannah', 'Ian', 'Jane'],
    'Grade': ['A', 'B', 'C', 'A', 'B', 'C', 'A', 'B', 'C', 'A'],
    'Age': [22, 23, 21, 22, 20, 21, 23, 22, 20, 21],
    'StudyHours': [10, 8, 6, 9, 7, 5, 10, 8, 6, 9]
}
df = pd.DataFrame(data)
```
Complete the following tasks with seaborn:

Task 1: Generate a bar plot that displays the average study hours for each grade, including confidence intervals.

Task 2: Create a bar plot similar to Task 1, but this time, exclude the confidence intervals.

Task 3: Produce a horizontal bar plot showing average study hours for each grade, grouped by age.

Task 4: Construct a box plot to visualize the distribution of study hours for each grade.

Task 5: Create a strip plot to illustrate the distribution of study hours across different grade categories.

Task 6: Develop a count plot to display the frequency or count of each unique value in the grade column.

7.4.6 Distribution Plots in Seaborn

Seaborn provides three types of distribution plots: histograms, Kernel Density Estimate (KDE) plots, and Empirical Cumulative Distribution Function (ECDF) plots. These plots help us understand the distribution of data in a numeric column.

Let's start with histograms. A histogram shows the frequency of occurrences for different values on the x-axis. In Seaborn, you can create a histogram using the displot() function with the kind parameter set to 'hist'. This function requires you to specify the data variable you wish to visualize, such as 'scores', using the x parameter. Once executed, it produces a histogram where the y-axis indicates the number of times each value occurs, typically labeled as 'Count' by default.

When creating a histogram, it's important to choose an appropriate bin size. Too many bins can make the histogram difficult to interpret, while too few bins can result in a loss of precision. You can control the number of bins by adjusting the bins parameter. For example, setting bins=6 will divide the data into six bins.

```
sns.displot(data=score_df_long, kind='hist', x='score', bins=6)
```

Output:

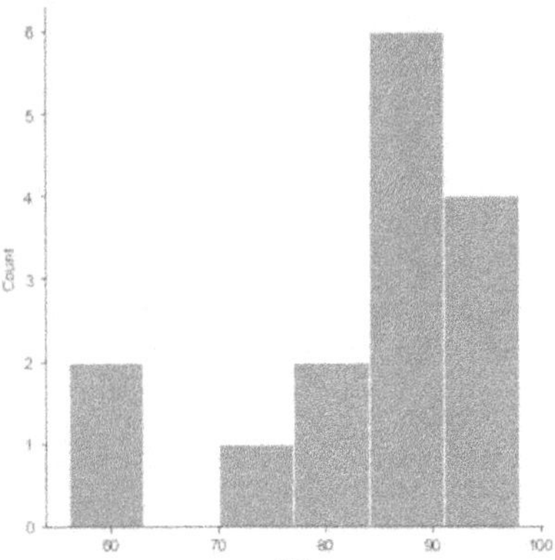

Next, let's explore density plots. A density plot, created with the displot() function and kind='kde', displays the distribution of data using a smoothed curve. It employs a Kernel Density Estimate (KDE) to estimate the probability of a data point occurring at each location along the x-axis. The y-axis represents the probability density. Probability density describes the relative likelihood that a continuous random variable takes on a value in a small interval. The KDE is calculated by considering the distances between data points at each location. Higher concentrations of data points lead to higher KDE values, indicating a higher probability of finding data points in that area. It's important to note that the KDE plot assigns some probability to values beyond the range of the actual data due to the way it is sampled during calculations:

```
sns.displot(data=score_df_long, kind='kde', x='score')
```

Output:

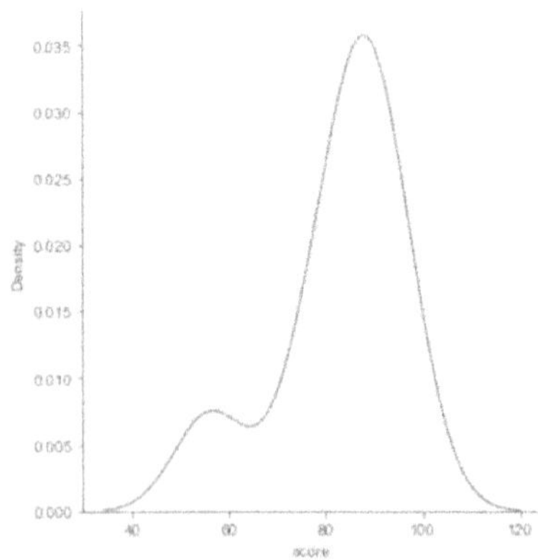

Lastly, let's discuss ECDF plots. An ECDF plot, created using the displot() function with kind='ecdf', shows the percentage of data points that are less than or equal to a particular value on the x-axis. For example, if 80% of the scores are below 90 points, the ECDF plot will show this relationship.

By visualizing the ECDF plot, we can identify percentiles and understand how data is distributed across different values. In the example output, we can observe that 100% of the scores are below 100:

```
sns.displot(data=score_df_long, kind='ecdf', x='score')
```

Output:

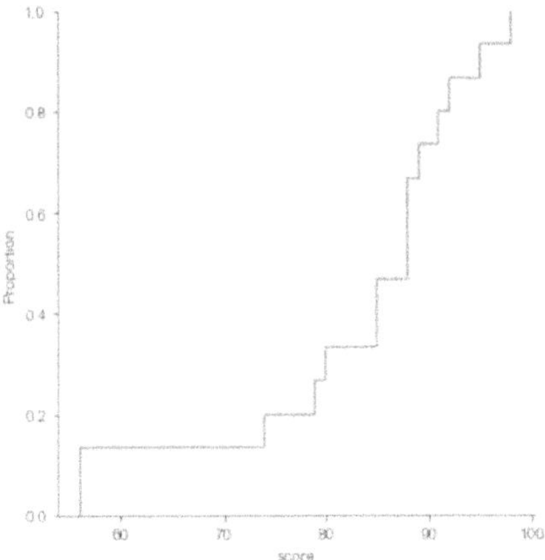

Review Question 7.93
What is the purpose of a histogram in Seaborn?
a. To visualize the probability density function of data
b. To display the percentage of data points below a certain value
c. To show the frequency of occurrences for different values
d. To estimate the kernel density of data points

Review Question 7.94
How can you adjust the precision of a histogram in Seaborn?
a. By controlling the bin size
b. By adjusting the density estimate
c. By changing the orientation
d. By modifying the hue parameter

Review Question 7.95
What does a density plot in Seaborn represent?
a. The percentage of data points below a certain value
b. The probability density of a data point occurring at each location
c. The count of occurrences for different values
d. The cumulative kernel density estimate of the data

Review Question 7.96
How is the KDE (Kernel Density Estimate) calculated in a density plot?
a. By adjusting the bin size
b. By considering the distances between data points
c. By specifying the orientation of the plot
d. By modifying the hue parameter

Review Question 7.97
What does an ECDF plot in Seaborn represent?
a. The percentage of data points above a certain value
b. The frequency of occurrences for different values
c. The kernel density estimate of the data
d. The percentage of data points below or equal to a certain value

Review Question 7.98
What is the purpose of distribution plots in Seaborn?
a. To visualize the correlation between two variables
b. To display the outliers in a dataset
c. To show the relationship between categorical and continuous variables
d. To explore the distribution of data in a numeric column

Exercise 7.5

Using the same dataset as Exercise 7.4, complete the following tasks:
Task 1: Generate a histogram to visualize the distribution of study hours.
Task 2: Produce a density plot for study hours to determine the most probable number of hours a randomly selected student studies.
Task 3: Construct a cumulative distribution plot for study hours to estimate the percentage of students studying more than 10 hours.

7.5 Chapter Summary

In this chapter, you've gained an introductory understanding of Pandas, Matplotlib, and Seaborn for data

visualization. Pandas offers basic tools suitable for exploratory analysis, while Matplotlib provides versatile,

robust plotting. Seaborn complements Matplotlib with a high-level interface optimized for statistical

graphics and visual appeal. Together, these libraries provide a solid foundation for data visualization.

7.6 Solutions to the Review Questions

7.1 B; 7.2 C; 7.3 C; 7.4 C; 7.5 B; 7.6 C; 7.7 C; 7.8 A; 7.9 D; 7.10 C; 7.11 D; 7.12 B; 7.13 C; 7.14 B; 7.15 D;
7.16 D; 7.17 A; 7.18 B; 7.19 D; 7.20 C; 7.21 A; 7.22 C; 7.23 A; 7.24 A; 7.25 C; 7.26 D; 7.27 A; 7.28 B; 7.29
B; 7.30 C; 7.31 B; 7.32 B; 7.33 A; 7.34 D; 7.35 C; 7.36 B; 7.37 B; 7.38 C; 7.39 A; 7.40 D; 7.41 C; 7.42 C; 7.43
C; 7.44 B; 7.45 B; 7.46 B; 7.47 C; 7.48 A; 7.49 C; 7.50 D; 7.51 D; 7.52 D; 7.53 D; 7.54 A; 7.55 B; 7.56 C;
7.57 B; 7.58 B; 7.59 C; 7.60 C; 7.61 B; 7.62 B; 7.63 C; 7.64 C; 7.65 B; 7.66 B; 7.67 A; 7.68 A; 7.69 A; 7.70 C;
7.71 A; 7.72 B; 7.73 C; 7.74 D; 7.75 A; 7.76 B; 7.77 A; 7.78 B; 7.79 C; 7.80 A; 7.81 C; 7.82 C; 7.83 A; 7.84 B;
7.85 C; 7.86 D; 7.87 C; 7.88 C; 7.89 C; 7.90 C; 7.91 D; 7.92 B; 7.93 C; 7.94 A; 7.95 B; 7.96 B; 7.97 D; 7.98 D;

Chapter 8: Time Series and Regression

Chapter Learning Objectives

8.1 Work with time series dataset

8.2 Apply simple linear regression on a real-world dataset

8.1 DatetimeIndex Objects

Time series data is organized by dates and times. While standard analysis methods apply, time series data requires unique operations. For organizing time series data into periods like daily, weekly, or monthly, start by generating the time periods using the start and end dates. Next, reindex the data to these periods, then summarize or visualize it accordingly.

Use Pandas' date_range() function to create time periods, specifying start and end dates, and the freq parameter to set the date frequency. This yields a DatetimeIndex with the generated dates. For example, the following code generates the last day of each month from January 2022 to June 2022:

```python
import pandas as pd
pd.date_range('01/01/2022', '6/30/2022', freq='M')
```

Output:

```
DatetimeIndex(['2022-01-31', '2022-02-28', '2022-03-31', '2022-04-30',
               '2022-05-31', '2022-06-30'],
              dtype='datetime64[ns]', freq='M')
```

Similarly, you can use the date_range() function to obtain other specific date ranges. For example, if you want to get all the business days (Monday through Friday) within a date range, you can use the 'B' frequency:

```python
pd.date_range('01/01/2022', '6/30/2022', freq='B')
```

Output:

```
DatetimeIndex(['2022-01-03', '2022-01-04', '2022-01-05', '2022-01-06',
               '2022-01-07', '2022-01-10', '2022-01-11', '2022-01-12',
               '2022-01-13', '2022-01-14',
               ...
               '2022-06-17', '2022-06-20', '2022-06-21', '2022-06-22',
               '2022-06-23', '2022-06-24', '2022-06-27', '2022-06-28',
               '2022-06-29', '2022-06-30'],
              dtype='datetime64[ns]', length=129, freq='B')
```

To generate specific weekdays within a date range, you can use a similar approach. For instance, the following code generates all the Wednesdays within the date range from January 2022 to April 2022:

```
wed=pd.date_range('01/01/2022', '4/30/2022', freq='W-WED')
wed
```
Output:

```
DatetimeIndex(['2022-01-05', '2022-01-12', '2022-01-19', '2022-01-26',
               '2022-02-02', '2022-02-09', '2022-02-16', '2022-02-23',
               '2022-03-02', '2022-03-09', '2022-03-16', '2022-03-23',
               '2022-03-30', '2022-04-06', '2022-04-13', '2022-04-20',
               '2022-04-27'],
              dtype='datetime64[ns]', freq='W-WED')
```

When using the date_range() function, it's important to know the *offset aliases* for the freq parameter. These aliases specify the frequency of the dates you want to generate. Here are some commonly used aliases:

Frequency	Alias
Daily (default)	D
Business day	B
Weekly	W
Monthly (last day of a month)	M
Monthly (first day of a month)	MS
Quarterly (last day of a quarter)	Q
Quarterly (first day of a quarter)	QS
Annually (last day of a year)	Y
Annually (first day of a year)	YS
Hourly	H
Minutely	T
Secondly	S

To reindex a DataFrame based on a specific date range, you can use a previously created DatetimeIndex object. Let's walk through an example to illustrate this process. First, assume you have a DataFrame containing stock price data, which you read from an Excel file. The DataFrame has a column labeled 'Date' serving as the index, along with 'Open' and 'Close' columns for the stock prices:

```
stock = pd.read_excel('Stock.xlsx', index_col='Date')
stock.head()
```

Output:

Date	Open	Close
2022-01-03	177.830002	182.009995
2022-01-04	182.630005	179.699997
2022-01-05	179.610001	174.919998
2022-01-06	172.699997	172.000000
2022-01-07	172.889999	172.169998

Now, let's say you want to focus only on Wednesdays in your analysis. You have previously generated a

DatetimeIndex object called wed, which contains all the Wednesdays within the date range. To reindex the DataFrame using this wed index, you can use the reindex() method:

```
stock.reindex(wed).head()
```

Output:

	Open	Close
2022-01-05	179.610001	174.919998
2022-01-12	176.119995	175.529999
2022-01-19	170.000000	166.229996
2022-01-26	163.500000	159.690002
2022-02-02	174.750000	175.839996

As you can see, the DataFrame has been reindexed based on the wed index, resulting in only the rows corresponding to Wednesdays remaining in the DataFrame. Reindexing allows you to align your data with a specific date range, making it easier to analyze and compare observations within those time periods.

Review Question 8.1
What is time series data in Pandas?
a. Data organized based on alphabetical order.
b. Data indexed by dates and times.
c. Data sorted by frequency.
d. Data contain dates and times.

Review Question 8.2
Which of the following is NOT a step for organizing time series data into specific time periods?
a. Use the groupby() function.
b. Generate the desired time periods by specifying the start and end dates
c. Summarize or plot the data based on these time periods.
d. Reindex the data based on the specific time periods.

Review Question 8.3
What method can you use to generate time periods in pandas?
a. date_range()
b. generate_periods()
c. create_time_periods()
d. time_index()

Review Question 8.4
What does the following code generate?
```
pd.date_range('01/01/2022', '6/30/2022', freq='M')
```
a. The last day of each month from January 2022 to June 2022.
b. The first day of each month from January 2022 to June 2022.
c. The last minute of each day from January 2022 to June 2022.
d. The first minute of each day from January 2022 to June 2022.

Review Question 8.5
How can you obtain all the business days (Monday through Friday) within a date range?
a. Use the 'B' frequency in the date_range() method.
b. Use the 'WD' frequency in the date_range() method.
c. Use the 'M-F' frequency in the date_range() method.
d. Use the 'BUS' frequency in the date_range() method.

Review Question 8.6
What does the following code generate?
```
wed = pd.date_range('01/01/2022', '4/30/2022', freq='W-WED')
```
a. All the wedding days within the date range from January 2022 to April 2022.
b. All the Wednesdays within the date range from January 2022 to April 2022.
c. All the weekdays within the date range from January 2022 to April 2022.
d. All the weekends within the date range from January 2022 to April 2022.

Review Question 8.7
What are offset aliases used for in the date_range() method?
a. To specify the number of periods to generate.
b. To determine the start and end dates for the time period.
c. To define the frequency of the dates to be generated.
d. To label the time series data.

Review Question 8.8
Which offset alias is used for generating the last day of a quarter?
a. Q
b. QS
c. Y
d. YS

Review Question 8.9
What does the 'MS' offset alias stand for in the date_range() method?
a. Monthly (second day of a month).
b. Monthly (start of the month).
c. Monthly (specific day of the month).
d. Monthly (end of the month).

Review Question 8.10
What is the purpose of reindexing a DataFrame based on a specific date range?
a. To change the order of the rows in the DataFrame.
b. To filter out specific columns in the DataFrame.
c. To align the DataFrame with a specific date range for analysis.
d. To merge multiple DataFrames together.

Review Question 8.11
How can you reindex the stock DataFrame using the 'wed' index in the book example?
a. stock.reindex(wed)
b. stock.reindex('wed')
c. stock.reindex(index='wed')
d. stock.reindex(columns='wed')

Review Question 8.12
What happens to the rows in the DataFrame after reindexing with the 'wed' index in the book example?
a. Only the rows corresponding to Wednesdays remain.
b. All rows corresponding to Wednesdays are removed.
c. New rows are added for Wednesdays.
d. The order of the rows is rearranged randomly.

Review Question 8.13
What is the benefit of reindexing a DataFrame?
a. It changes the underlying data in the DataFrame.
b. It allows for the creation of new columns.
c. It aligns the DataFrame with a specific date range for analysis.
d. It combines multiple DataFrames into a single DataFrame.

8.2 Resample Time-Series Data

When working with datetime indexes, resampling adjusts the frequency of time-series data. There are two types of resampling: downsampling and upsampling.

Downsampling reduces the data frequency, such as converting daily data to monthly data. To do this, use the DataFrame's resample() method, followed by an aggregation function (e.g., `mean()`, `sum()`) that appropriately summarizes the data for the new frequency.

Upsampling increases the data frequency, such as converting daily data to hourly data. This process creates gaps in the data, as there is no actual data for the new, higher frequency intervals. For example, when converting daily data to 12-hour intervals, the new rows will contain missing values (`NaN`). You can fill these missing values with the fillna() method, though upsampling is typically less useful for most analyses, except in specific applications like digital signal processing.

Let's look at examples. To downsample the data to a monthly frequency, use the `resample()` method with the rule `'M'`, which represents months. The following example calculates the monthly mean of stock prices:

```
stock.resample(rule='M').mean().head()
```

Output:

Date	Open	Close
2022-01-31	170.201500	169.861500
2022-02-28	169.635262	169.830001
2022-03-31	164.806956	165.310435
2022-04-30	167.479001	166.820999

To upsample the data to a 12-hour frequency, use the `resample()` method with the rule `"12H"`. Notice that the upsampled data will contain missing values:

```
stock.resample(rule='12H').mean().head()
```

Output:

Date	Open	Close
2022-01-03 00:00:00	177.830002	182.009995
2022-01-03 12:00:00	NaN	NaN
2022-01-04 00:00:00	182.630005	179.699997
2022-01-04 12:00:00	NaN	NaN
2022-01-05 00:00:00	179.610001	174.919998

When downsampling, you can use the `label` and `closed` parameters to control how the data is labeled and which values are included in the aggregation. The `label` parameter determines which edge of the resampling window is used as the index label. By default, it's set to `"right"`, meaning the right edge of the window is used. The `closed` parameter specifies which side of the window includes the boundary value in the aggregation. By default, this is also set to `"right"`, meaning values on the right edge are included.

For example, to downsample the data to quarterly frequency using right labels and closed right edges:

```
stock.resample(rule='Q', label='right', closed='right').mean().head()
```

Output:

Date	Open	Close
2022-03-31	168.026774	168.163549
2022-06-30	167.479001	166.820999

If you prefer left labels and closed left edges, adjust the parameters accordingly:

```
stock.resample(rule='Q', label='left', closed='left').mean().head()
```

Output:

Date	Open	Close
2021-12-31	167.865901	168.057869
2022-03-31	167.972382	167.191904

It's generally advisable to keep both parameters consistent (either both set to `"left"` or both set to `"right"`) to ensure that the data for the label date is included in the aggregation. One of the main advantages of downsampling is that it simplifies data visualization by reducing noise. Aggregating values into lower frequencies helps highlight overall trends and patterns, making plots easier to interpret.

Review Question 8.14
What is downsampling in the context of datetime indexes?
a. Moving data from a lower frequency to a higher frequency.
b. Moving data from a higher frequency to a lower frequency.
c. Filling missing values in the data.
d. Rearranging the order of the rows in the data.

Review Question 8.15
What is upsampling in the context of datetime indexes?
a. Moving data from a lower frequency to a higher frequency.
b. Moving data from a higher frequency to a lower frequency.
c. Filling missing values in the data.
d. Rearranging the order of the rows in the data.

Review Question 8.16
What does downsampling using the 'M' rule do?
```
df.resample(rule='M').mean().head()
```
a. Calculates the head (first) of the values for each month.
b. Calculates the mean of the values for each month.
c. Fills missing values in the data.
d. Calculates the mean of first five rows of the values for each month.

Review Question 8.17
What does upsampling using the '12H' rule do?
```
df.resample(rule='12H').mean().head()
```
a. Calculates the head (first) of the values for every 12 hours.
b. Fills the mean of the head values for every 12 hours.
c. Fills the NaN for every 12 hours.
d. Fills the NaN for every 24 hours.

Review Question 8.18
In which application is upsampling commonly used?
a. Financial forecasting.
b. Digital signal processing.
c. Weather prediction.
d. Stock market analysis.

Review Question 8.19
What is the main limitation of upsampling?
a. It introduces missing values in the data.
b. It rearranges the order of the rows in the data.
c. It requires applying an aggregate method.
d. It is only suitable for monthly frequency.

Review Question 8.20
What is the purpose of the label and closed parameters when downsampling data?
a. They determine the frequency of the downsampling.
b. They control the aggregation method used in downsampling.
c. They define the range of values to be included in the downsampling.
d. They customize the labeling of the index and the inclusion of values in the aggregate calculation.

Review Question 8.21
How do you use the right bin edge as the index in downsampling?
a. Set the label parameter to 'right'
b. Set the bin parameter to 'right'
c. Set the closed parameter to 'right'
d. Set the bin_edge parameter to 'right'

Review Question 8.22
How do you include the values on the right bin edge in the aggregation in downsampling?
a. Set the label parameter to 'right'
b. Set the bin parameter to 'right'
c. Set the closed parameter to 'right'
d. Set the bin_edge parameter to 'right'

Review Question 8.23
When downsampling data to quarterly frequency, which combination of label and closed parameters should be used for consistency?
a. 'middle' for label and 'middle' for closed.
b. 'left' for label and 'right' for closed.
c. 'right' for label and 'left' for closed.
d. 'right' for label and 'right' for closed.

Review Question 8.24
What is one benefit of downsampling data?
a. It increases the frequency of the data.
b. It reduces the noise in the data.
c. It fills missing values in the data.
d. It rearranges the order of the data.

Review Question 8.25
How can downsampling enhance the interpretability of plots?
a. By increasing the frequency of the data.
b. By reducing missing values in the data.
c. By reducing noise in the data.
d. By rearranging the order of the data.

Exercise 8.1

Given the following sales data:
```
np.random.seed(42)
data = np.random.randint(10, 101, size=100)
df = pd.DataFrame(data, columns=['Quantity'])
```
Complete the following tasks:
Task 1: Generate a DatetimeIndex object for the first 100 days of 2024
Task 2: Reindex the sales data with the object created in Task 1
Task 3: Generate a DatetimeIndex object for all weekdays of the first 100 days of 2024
Task 4: Reindex the sales dataframe to include the week days only
Task 5: Calculate weekly sales average of the original data

8.3 Work with Rolling Windows

Rolling windows, also known as moving windows, provide a method to smooth trendlines in noisy data by aggregating values over a specified number of consecutive rows. To create rolling windows in Pandas, you can use the rolling() method. Let's consider an example where we want to calculate the average of the 'Open' and 'Close' values over a window of 3 rows. We can achieve this with the following code:

```
df = stock[['Open','Close']].query('Date <= "01/31/2022"').rolling(window=3).mean()
df.head()
```

Output:

Date	Open	Close
2022-01-03	NaN	NaN
2022-01-04	NaN	NaN
2022-01-05	180.023336	178.876663
2022-01-06	178.313334	175.539998
2022-01-07	175.066666	173.029999

In the resulting DataFrame, you may notice that the first two rows have missing values. This occurs because the window size is set to 3 and the min_periods parameter is not set, which requires 3 consecutive non-missing values for the aggregation to take place.

To avoid missing values at the beginning of the rolling window, you can set the min_periods parameter to 1. This means that the mean will be computed for each window as long as there is at least one valid value present. However, if you have a sequence of missing values longer than the specified min_periods, the resulting window will contain missing values:

```
df = stock[['Open','Close']].query('Date <= 
"01/31/2022"').rolling(window=3, min_periods=1).mean()
df.head()
```

Output:

Date	Open	Close
2022-01-03	177.830002	182.009995
2022-01-04	180.230003	180.854996
2022-01-05	180.023336	178.876663
2022-01-06	178.313334	175.539998
2022-01-07	175.066666	173.029999

Rolling windows provide a useful technique to smooth out data trends by aggregating values over a specified window size. By adjusting the window size and handling missing values using the min_periods parameter, you can tailor the rolling window operation to suit your data analysis needs.

Running totals, also known as cumulative sums, provide another method to smooth trendlines in noisy data. A running total represents the sum of a sequence of numbers and gets updated each time a new number is added to the sequence.

To calculate a running total, you can utilize the expanding() method in Pandas. This method creates a running aggregation of the data in a DataFrame. Unlike a rolling window that moves both the front and back edges of the window, an expanding window only moves the back edge. As a result, the size of the aggregation window expands until it includes the entire DataFrame. Similar to the rolling() method, the expanding() method also supports the use of the min_periods parameter.

In the example below, the sum() method is applied, but it's important to note that other aggregate methods can be used with the expanding() method as well. For instance, you can chain the mean() method after the expanding() method to obtain a running average of the data in the rows. First, the sale DataFrame:

```
# Sample data for the sale DataFrame
data = {
    'date': ['2023-01-01', '2023-01-03', '2023-01-05',
             '2023-01-08', '2023-01-10', '2023-01-12',
             '2023-01-15', '2023-01-17', '2023-01-20',
             '2023-01-22'],
    'sale amount': [100, 150, 200, 120, 180, 220, 170, 190, 210, 160]
}
sale = pd.DataFrame(data)
sale.head(2)
```
Output:

	date	sale amount
0	2023-01-01	100
1	2023-01-03	150

To calculate the running total of the sale amount, you can use the expanding() method as shown below:

```
sale['running_total'] = sale['sale amount'].expanding().sum()
sale.head()
```
Output:

	date	sale amount	running_total
0	2023-01-01	100	100.0
1	2023-01-03	150	250.0
2	2023-01-05	200	450.0
3	2023-01-08	120	570.0
4	2023-01-10	180	750.0

The sale DataFrame now has an additional column running_total, which represents the running total of the sale amount column. Each row in the running_total column represents the cumulative sum of the sale amount column up to that point. The running total gets updated as each new row is processed.

Review Question 8.26
What is the purpose of using rolling windows in data analysis?
a. To calculate the sum of values over a specified window
b. To smooth trendlines in noisy data by aggregating values
c. To remove missing values from the dataset
d. To rearrange the order of rows in the data

Review Question 8.27
Which method in Pandas is used to create rolling windows?
a. windows()
b. resample()
c. expanding()
d. rolling()

Review Question 8.28
Why do the first six rows in the resulting DataFrame have missing values?

```
df = stock[['High','Low']].query('Date <=
"01/31/2020"').rolling(window=7).mean() df.head(6)
```

a. The rolling window is set to 6 instead of 7.
b. The min_periods parameter is set to 6.
c. The data is not available for the first seven rows.
d. The min_periods parameter is not set, resulting in missing values.

Review Question 8.29
What does setting the min_periods parameter to 1 achieve?

```
df = stock[['High','Low']].query('Date <=
"01/31/2020"').rolling(window=7, min_periods=1).mean() df.head(7)
```

a. It calculates the sum of values for each window.
b. It eliminates missing values from the rolling window.
c. It calculates the mean for each window, even with fewer valid values.
d. It adjusts the window size to include all rows in the DataFrame.

Review Question 8.30
How can rolling windows be customized to handle missing values within rolling windows?
a. By adjusting the window size parameter
b. By excluding missing rows from the calculation
c. By setting the min_periods parameter appropriately
d. By using the fillna() method after the rolling calculation

Review Question 8.31
Which method in Pandas is used to calculate a running total or average?
a. rolling()

b. running()
c. expanding()
d. sum()

Review Question 8.32
What is the difference between a rolling window and an expanding window?
a. Rolling windows move both the front and back edges, while expanding windows only move the back edge.
b. Rolling windows include the entire DataFrame, while expanding windows include a subset of rows.
c. Rolling windows sum the values, while expanding windows take the mean.
d. Rolling windows are used for categorical data, while expanding windows are used for numerical data.

Review Question 8.33
What does the additional column x in the expanding() method output represent?

```
sale['x'] = sale.expanding().sum()
```

a. The average of the sale amount column.
b. The maximum value in the sale amount column.
c. The cumulative sum of the sale amount column.
d. The total count of rows in the sale amount column.

8.4 A Time Series Analysis Example

Here's an example of fictitious sales data for a retail store chain that includes timestamps for each transaction. We can use this data to demonstrate grouping by time periods:

```python
import numpy as np
np.random.seed(42)
data = {
    'Timestamp': pd.date_range(start='2023-01-01', periods=100, freq='H'),
    'Store Location': np.random.choice(['New York', 'Los Angeles', 'Chicago'], size=100),
    'Product Category': np.random.choice(['Electronics', 'Clothing', 'Furniture'], size=100),
    'Sales': np.random.randint(100, 1000, size=100),
    'Products Sold': np.random.randint(10, 50, size=100),
    'Customers Served': np.random.randint(5, 30, size=100)
}
sales_df = pd.DataFrame(data)
sales_df.head()
```

The output will be a DataFrame containing the sales data with timestamps:

	Timestamp	Store Location	Product Category	Sales	Products Sold	Customers Served
0	2023-01-01 00:00:00	Chicago	Furniture	791	25	18
1	2023-01-01 01:00:00	New York	Furniture	212	12	16
2	2023-01-01 02:00:00	Chicago	Furniture	929	29	23
3	2023-01-01 03:00:00	Chicago	Electronics	596	33	27
4	2023-01-01 04:00:00	New York	Furniture	541	42	19

Now, we can group the data by different time periods using Pandas' resample function. Here's an example:

```python
daily_sales = sales_df.resample('D', on='Timestamp').sum()
daily_sales.drop(['Store Location', 'Product Category'], axis=1).head()
```

Output:

	Sales	Products Sold	Customers Served
Timestamp			
2023-01-01	13362	796	452
2023-01-02	13500	746	429
2023-01-03	13868	801	409
2023-01-04	13307	781	386
2023-01-05	1396	81	66

By grouping the data into different time periods, such as hourly, daily, or weekly, you can analyze sales trends and patterns over time. Feel free to modify the code and explore other time periods or add more statistics to gain further insights into the retail store's performance.

Exercise 8.2

You are working as a data analyst for a bakery store, and you have been given a dataset that contains daily sales data from January 1, 2022 to June 30, 2023. Your task is to perform time series analysis on the data using pandas to gain insights and make informed business decisions.

Dataset:
The dataset "bakery.csv" contains sales data for a bakery with the following columns:
Timestamp: The date and time when each sale occurred. Stored as a datetime data type.
Item: The name of the bakery item that was sold in each transaction. Stored as text strings.
Quantity: An integer indicating how many units of the given item were sold in each transaction.
Unit Price: A numeric value indicating the per-unit price of the bakery item.
Amount: A calculated numeric column storing the total amount of each transaction. This is obtained by multiplying the Quantity and Unit Price columns.

Task 1: Load the dataset into a pandas DataFrame and set the "Timestamp" column as the index.
Task 2: Generate a DatetimeIndex object for the entire period of sales data. Use 'daily' for frequency.
Task 3: Reindex the DataFrame using the generated DatetimeIndex.
Task 4: Resample the sales data to a monthly frequency and calculate the sum of sales for each month.
Task 5: Calculate the 7-day rolling average of the sales data.
Task 6: Calculate the running total of the sales data.

8.5 ARIMA

Time series analysis is a powerful tool in business data analytics, allowing analysts to make forecasts and understand trends over time. One of the most widely used models in this domain is the Autoregressive Integrated Moving Average (ARIMA) model. This section will explain ARIMA, including its components, how to build an ARIMA model, and an example to illustrate the process.

The ARIMA model consists of three key components:

1. *Autoregressive (AR) Component*: This part of the model specifies that the evolving variable of interest is regressed on its own lagged (prior) values. The number of lagged observations included in the model is denoted by `p`. Think of it like predicting today's ice cream sales based on the sales from the last few days. For example, if you look at the past 3 days to predict today's sales, then the number of past days you use is `p`, and in this case, `p = 3`.

2. *Integrated (I) Component*: This component involves differencing the data to make it stationary, i.e., to remove trends and seasonality. Sometimes, our data has trends or patterns that can make forecasting difficult. The integrated component helps by removing these trends to make the data more stable and easier to predict. For instance, you might notice that ice cream sales are higher on weekends. To make the data more consistent (stationary), you adjust for these weekly patterns. If you need to make this adjustment once, then the number of times you need to adjust the data is called `d`, and in this case, `d = 1`. The 'd' refers to the degree of differencing in the ARIMA model. Differencing is a statistical technique that transforms a time series dataset. By "differencing" the data, we can remove these trends or seasonal components and make the data more stable, or "stationary".

In the context of ice creams example, if ice cream sales are higher on weekends, this is a weekly pattern or seasonality. To make the data stationary, you might subtract the sales of each Sunday from the previous Sunday, the sales of each Monday from the previous Monday, and so on. This is called first-order differencing, and in this case, d = 1.

Continue with the ice cream example. The data shows two clear patterns: 1) Weekly cycle: Sales peak on weekends and dip on weekdays. 2) Yearly cycle: Sales are much higher in summer months than in winter. To make this data stationary for ARIMA modeling, we might need two rounds of differencing (d=2):

1) First differencing (d=1): Subtract each day's sales from the same day last week. This removes the weekly pattern but leaves the yearly trend.

2) Second differencing (d=2): Take the result from step 1 and subtract the value from 52 weeks ago (same day last year). This addresses the yearly seasonality.

After these two rounds of differencing, the remaining data should be relatively stationary, with no clear repeating patterns. The variations left are likely due to random fluctuations or other factors not tied to weekly or yearly cycles.

In this case, d=2 in the ARIMA model because we needed two levels of differencing to achieve stationarity. The goal is to use the smallest value of d that makes the data stationary, as over-differencing can introduce unnecessary complexity to the model.

3. *Moving Average (MA) Component*: This part of the model specifies that the regression error is a linear combination of error terms whose values occurred contemporaneously and at various times in the past. The number of lagged forecast errors in the prediction equation is denoted by `q`. This part uses past forecast

errors to improve future predictions. Imagine if you knew that your past ice cream sales predictions were off by 5 ice creams on average; you could use that information to make better predictions. If you consider errors from the past 2 days, then the number of past errors you use is the `q`, and in this case, `q = 2`. An ARIMA model is typically expressed as ARIMA(p, d, q). So, the ice creams model would be ARIMA(3, 1, 2), or ARIMA(3, 2, 2) depending on the d value you choose in the above example.

Building an ARIMA model involves the following four steps:

1. *Make the Time Series Stationary*: Stationarity means that the statistical properties of the time series do not change over time. This is usually achieved through differencing. A series is differenced by subtracting the previous observation from the current observation. This can be repeated `d` times until the series is stationary.

2. *Identify Parameters (p, d, q)*: The parameters of the ARIMA model need to be specified. This can be done using techniques such as Autocorrelation Function (ACF) and Partial Autocorrelation Function (PACF) plots. ACF is a measure of the correlation between the time series with a lagged version of itself. For instance, at lag 5, ACF would compare series at time instant 't1'…'t2' with series at instant 't1-5'…'t2-5'. PACF measures the correlation between the time series with a lagged version of itself but after eliminating the variations already explained by the intervening comparisons. Eg. at lag 5, it will check the correlation but remove the effects already explained by lags 1 to 4.

The ACF and PACF plots for the time series are then used to identify the parameters for ARIMA:

p: The lag value where the PACF chart crosses the upper confidence interval for the first time. If you notice closely, in PACF, after a certain number of lags, the correlation will drop towards zero and remain so. This point is the indicative Q-value.

q: The lag value where the ACF chart crosses the upper confidence interval for the first time.

d: In an ARIMA model we transform a time series into stationary one(series without trend or seasonality) using differencing. 'd' refers to the number of differencing transformations required by the time series to get stationary.

3. *Fit the ARIMA Model*: Once the parameters are identified, the ARIMA model can be fit to the time series data.

4. *Make Predictions*: The fitted model can then be used to make forecasts.

Let's walk through an example of building an ARIMA model using Python.

```python
import matplotlib.pyplot as plt
from statsmodels.tsa.arima.model import ARIMA
from statsmodels.graphics.tsaplots import plot_acf, plot_pacf
```

```python
# Load example time series data
stock = pd.read_excel('Stock.xlsx')
stock['Date'] = pd.to_datetime(stock['Date'])

# EDA by ploting the time series
plt.figure(figsize=(10, 4))
plt.plot(stock['Date'], stock['Open'])
plt.title('Example Time Series')
plt.show()

# Differencing the data to make it stationary
data_diff = stock.diff(2).dropna()

# Plot ACF and PACF
fig, ax = plt.subplots(1, 2, figsize=(16, 4))
plot_acf(data_diff['Open'], ax=ax[0])
plot_pacf(data_diff['Open'], ax=ax[1])
plt.show()
```

Output:

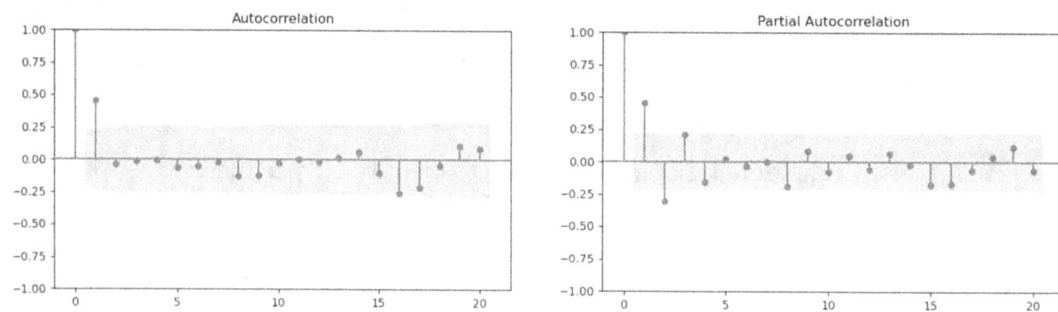

Based on the provided ACF and PACF plots, we can infer the following:

The 'p' value is where the PACF chart crosses the upper confidence interval for the last time before trailing off. In this case, it appears to be at lag 1.

The 'q' value is where the ACF chart crosses the upper confidence interval for the last time before trailing off. In this case, it also appears to be at lag 1.

So, a good starting point for 'p' and 'q' in the ARIMA model would both be 1. Please note that these are just starting points. The actual parameters that give the best fit for your model might be different and you may need to try different combinations.

```python
# Fit the ARIMA model
model = ARIMA(stock['Open'], order=(1, 2, 1))
model_fit = model.fit()
# Print the model summary
```

```
print(model_fit.summary())
```

Output:

```
                               SARIMAX Results
==============================================================================
Dep. Variable:                   Open   No. Observations:                   82
Model:                 ARIMA(1, 2, 1)   Log Likelihood                -219.750
Date:                Thu, 27 Jun 2024   AIC                            445.499
Time:                        11:54:42   BIC                            452.645
Sample:                             0   HQIC                           448.364
                                 - 82
Covariance Type:                  opg
==============================================================================
                 coef    std err          z      P>|z|      [0.025      0.975]
------------------------------------------------------------------------------
ar.L1         -0.1274      0.108     -1.176      0.239      -0.340       0.085
ma.L1         -0.9998      9.190     -0.109      0.913     -19.013      17.013
sigma2        13.4354    123.059      0.109      0.913    -227.757     254.627
===================================================================================
Ljung-Box (L1) (Q):                   0.04   Jarque-Bera (JB):                 3.79
Prob(Q):                              0.84   Prob(JB):                         0.15
Heteroskedasticity (H):               0.93   Skew:                            -0.37
Prob(H) (two-sided):                  0.85   Kurtosis:                         3.77
===================================================================================
```

Here's a breakdown of the output of the ARIMA model (Optional):

Model and Parameters: The model used is an ARIMA(1, 2, 1). This means it's an Autoregressive Integrated Moving Average model with two autoregressive term (AR), one differencing term (I), and two moving average term (MA).

Log Likelihood, AIC, BIC, and HQIC: These are measures of the goodness of fit of the model. The lower these values, the better the model fits the data (except the Log Likelihood).

Coefficients: ar.L1 is the coefficient of the first order autoregressive terms. An autoregressive term in a time series model is a value that is a linear function of the previous value(s) in the series. In this case, ar.L1 is the coefficient for the first lagged value of the series.

ma.L1 is the coefficient of the first order moving average terms, respectively. A moving average term in a time series model is a value that is a linear function of the current and various past noise (or error) terms. In this case, ma.L1 is the coefficient for the first lagged noise term.

sigma2: This is the variance of the residuals (errors).

P>|z|: This is the p-value associated with the respective coefficient. If it's less than 0.05, it suggests that the respective coefficient is statistically significant.

Ljung-Box (L1) (Q): This is a test statistic for checking if the residuals are independently distributed (i.e., no autocorrelation). A p-value (Prob(Q)) close to 1 suggests the residuals are independently distributed.

Jarque-Bera (JB): This is a test statistic for checking if the residuals are normally distributed. A p-value (Prob(JB)) close to 1 suggests the residuals are normally distributed.

Heteroskedasticity (H): This is a test statistic for checking if the residuals have constant variance (i.e., homoscedastic). A p-value (Prob(H)) close to 1 suggests the residuals have constant variance.

Skew: This measures the asymmetry of the residuals distribution. A value close to 0 suggests the residuals are symmetrically distributed.

Kurtosis: This measures the "tailedness" of the residuals distribution. A value close to 3 suggests the residuals have a similar kurtosis to a normal distribution.

Note: while these statistics provide a lot of information about your model, it's also important to plot your residuals and visually check for any patterns or anomalies.

```python
# Forecast future demand
forecasted_demand = model_fit.forecast(steps=7)
X = stock['Open'].values
size = int(len(X) * 0.8)
train, test = X[0:size], X[size:len(X)]
history = [x for x in train]
predictions = list()

for t in range(len(test)):
  model = ARIMA(history, order=(1,2,1))
  model_fit = model.fit()
  output = model_fit.forecast()
  yhat = output[0]
  predictions.append(yhat)
  obs = test[t]
  history.append(obs)
  print('predicted=%f, expected=%f' % (yhat, obs))
```

Output:

```
predicted=177.317718, expected=172.360001
predicted=172.839090, expected=171.160004
predicted=171.165533, expected=171.779999
predicted=171.607914, expected=168.710007
predicted=168.883370, expected=168.020004
predicted=167.927850, expected=167.389999
predicted=167.283964, expected=170.619995
predicted=170.157764, expected=163.919998
predicted=164.556579, expected=165.020004
predicted=164.666733, expected=168.759995
predicted=168.139978, expected=168.910004
predicted=168.749852, expected=166.460007
predicted=166.588852, expected=161.119995
predicted=161.468225, expected=162.250000
predicted=161.888935, expected=155.910004
```

```
predicted=156.375444, expected=159.250000
predicted=158.507230, expected=161.839996
```

```
# Visualization of the forecast
plt.plot(test)
plt.plot(predictions, color='red')
plt.show()
```

Output:

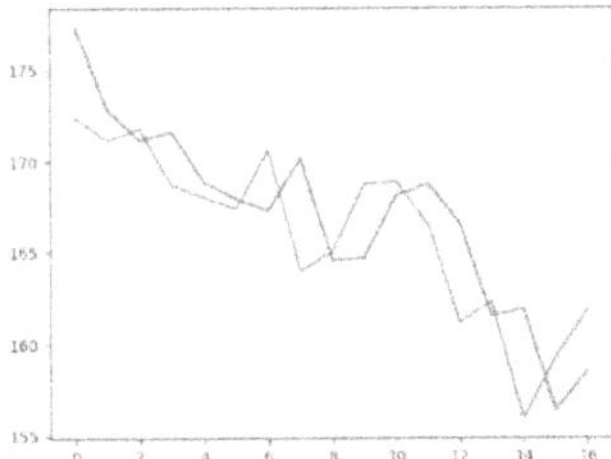

Review Question 8.34
What does ARIMA stand for in time series analysis?
a. Automatic Regression In Moving Averages
b. Autoregressive Integrated Moving Average
c. Advanced Regression Integrated Model Analysis
d. Automated Responsive Iterative Moving Average

Review Question 8.35
Which component of ARIMA deals with making the time series stationary?
a. Autoregressive (AR)
b. Integrated (I)
c. Moving Average (MA)
d. None of the above

Review Question 8.36
In an ARIMA(p,d,q) model, what does 'p' represent?
a. The number of times differencing is applied
b. The number of lagged forecast errors in the prediction equation
c. The number of lagged observations included in the model
d. The degree of polynomial trend in the forecast

Review Question 8.37
Which of the following is NOT a step in building an ARIMA model?
a. Make the Time Series Stationary
b. Identify Parameters (p, d, q)
c. Fit the ARIMA Model
d. Perform cluster analysis

Review Question 8.38
What technique is used to identify the 'q' parameter in an ARIMA model?

a. Partial Autocorrelation Function (PACF) plot
b. Autocorrelation Function (ACF) plot
c. Differencing
d. Moving average calculation

Review Question 8.39
In the context of ARIMA modeling, what does making a time series "stationary" mean?
a. Ensuring the data points are equally spaced in time
b. Removing all outliers from the data
c. Making sure the statistical properties of the series do not change over time
d. Arranging the data in ascending order

Exercise 8.3

Building Your Own ARIMA Model
Task 1: Load the Data. Choose a real-world time series dataset. You can use a dataset such as airline passenger data, stock prices, temperature, sales, or any other dataset with a time component.
Task 2: Visualize the Data. Plot the time series data to get a sense of its characteristics.
Task 3: Make the Series Stationary. Apply differencing to make the series stationary.
Task 4: Identify Parameters (p, d, q). Use ACF and PACF plots to identify the values of `p` and `q`.
Task 5: Fit the Model. Fit an ARIMA model to the data using the identified parameters.
Task 6: Make Predictions. Use the model to make future predictions and plot these predictions. Compare to the real data.

8.6 Correlations

While descriptive analysis examines historical data, predictive analysis forecasts future values using independent variables (IVs) to predict a dependent variable (DV). Regression is a key tool in predictive analysis, with linear regression assuming a linear relationship between variables.

Before applying linear regression, it's crucial to check for correlation between variables. Correlation indicates a relationship between two or more variables, which can be visualized using scatter plots.

To illustrate linear regression, we'll use the Housing dataset from the 1990 California census. Although dated, it serves as an accessible example for learning regression analysis basics.

The Housing dataset contains ten columns:

1. longitude: Distance west
2. latitude: Distance north
3. housingMedianAge: Median age of houses in a block
4. totalRooms: Total rooms in a block
5. totalBedrooms: Total bedrooms in a block

6. population: Total people in a block
7. households: Total households in a block
8. medianIncome: Median household income (in tens of thousands of USD)
9. medianHouseValue: Median house value (in USD)
10. oceanProximity: Location relative to the ocean

Exploring this dataset helps us understand relationships between variables and apply linear regression techniques. Scatter plots are a simple way to visualize correlations between two variables. In linear relationships, the data points form a straight line, showing how the dependent variable (y) changes with the independent variable (x).

To begin, let's load the data excluding the "longitude" and "latitude" columns for simplicity. Here's an example code using pandas:

```
columns_excluded = ['longitude', 'latitude']
df=pd.read_csv('housing.csv', usecols=lambda c: c not in
columns_excluded)
df.head(2)
```
Output:

	housing_media n_age	total_roo ms	total_bedro oms	populati on	househo lds	median_inc ome	median_house_ value	ocean_proxi mity
0	41.0	880.0	129.0	322.0	126.0	8.3252	452600.0	NEAR BAY
1	21.0	7099.0	1106.0	2401.0	1138.0	8.3014	358500.0	NEAR BAY

In the code above, we create a list called columns_excluded containing the column names we want to exclude from the dataset. Then, we use the usecols parameter in pd.read_csv() to read the CSV file while excluding the specified columns. The resulting DataFrame, df, is displayed using df.head(2).

Now, let's explore the relationship between the "median_house_value" and "total_rooms" variables using a scatter plot. We can utilize the Seaborn library to create the plot:

```
import seaborn as sns
sns.relplot(data=df, x='total_rooms', y='median_house_value')
```
Output:

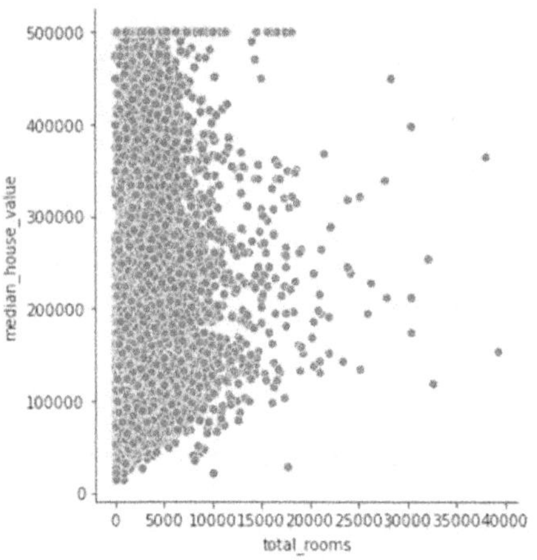

The resulting scatter plot visualizes the correlation between the "total_rooms" and "median_house_value" variables. From the plot, we can observe a weak positive linear relationship between the two variables. This indicates that as the number of total rooms increases, the median house value also tends to increase.

Next, let's consider the relationship between the "median_house_value" and "population" variables:

```
sns.relplot(data=df, x='population', y='median_house_value')
```

Output:

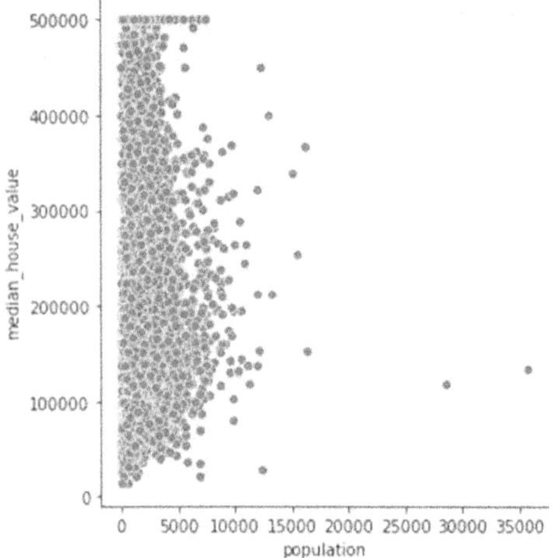

The resulting scatter plot shows that there isn't a distinct linear relationship between the "population" and "median_house_value" variables. However, it's important to note that in densely clustered data, like the one shown in this plot, correlations and data clusters might be concealed or not immediately evident.

To efficiently generate scatter plots for multiple pairs of data points, you can leverage the pairplot() method from the Seaborn library. This method constructs a grid of plots, where each cell corresponds to a specific combination of x and y variables. By default, scatter plots are used for most cells in the grid. However, when a variable is paired with itself, it wouldn't make sense to display a scatter plot, so a histogram or KDE plot is used instead. Additionally, to avoid each relationship is plotted twice, use the corner parameter:

```
sns.pairplot(data=df, diag_kind='kde', corner=True)
```

Output:

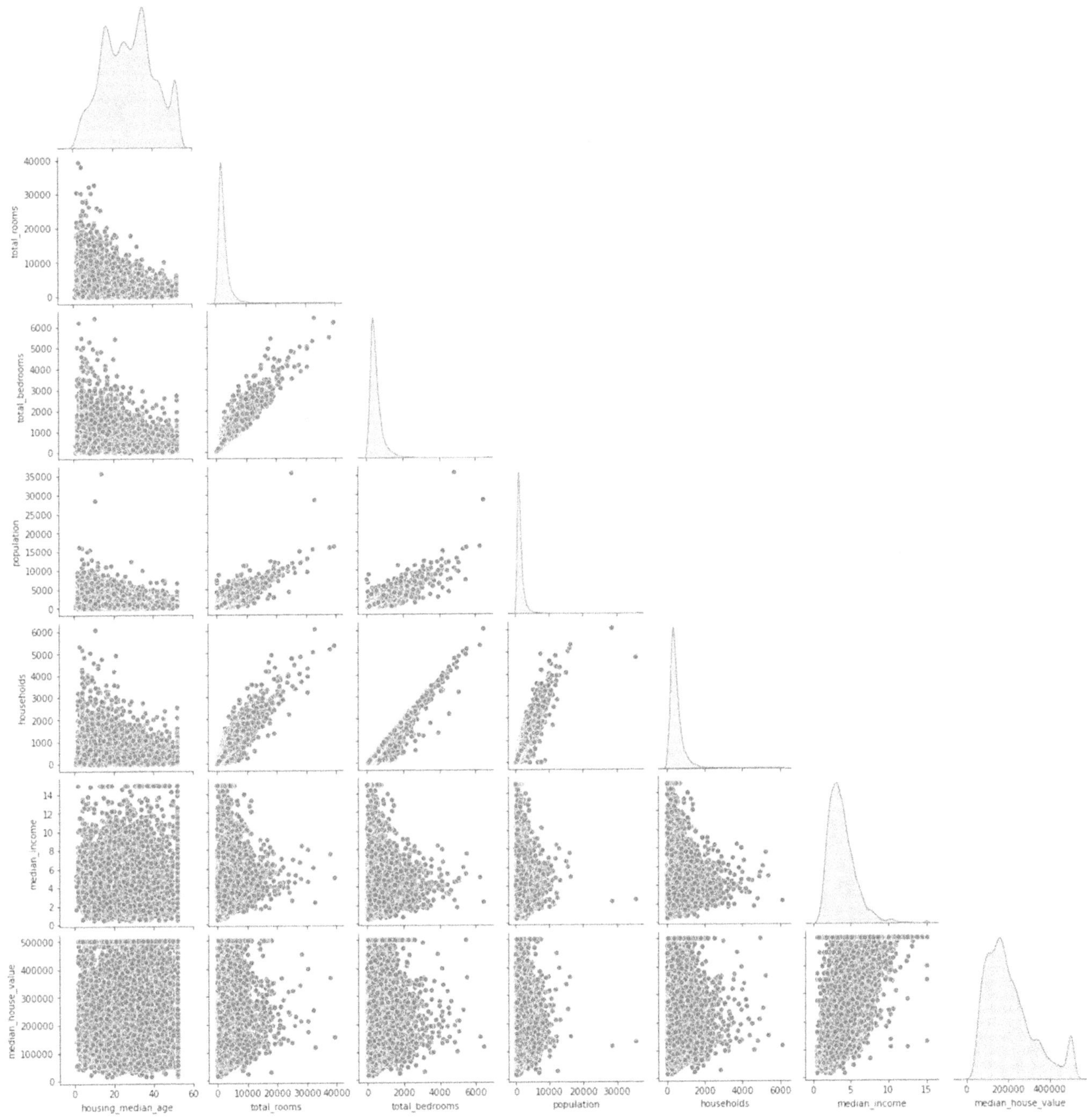

Another approach to identify correlations between variables is by calculating the Pearson correlation coefficient, also known as the r-value. The r-value is a numeric value ranging between 1.0 and -1.0 that quantifies the strength and type of linear correlation between two variables. A high positive r-value close to 1.0 indicates a strong positive correlation, while a high negative r-value close to -1.0 signifies a strong negative correlation.

It's important to note that the r-value only detects linear relationships and may overlook other types of correlations. Therefore, it is recommended to utilize both scatter plots and r-values in combination to identify correlations accurately.

To obtain the r-values for the relationships between each pair of numeric variables in a DataFrame, you can use the corr() method in Pandas. Additionally, when the method is applied, the r-value for a variable paired with itself will be 1.0. To enhance readability, you can filter the data by the "median_house_value" column after calling the corr() method. Furthermore, sorting the values in the "median_house_value" column in descending order facilitates the identification of variables with the strongest correlations.

Use caution when interpreting correlations from corr() for categorical variables encoded as integers. The corr() method will calculate correlations for all numeric columns, even when invalid for categorical data. Here's an example code that uses the corr() method, filters the results by the "median_house_value" column, and sorts the values in descending order:.

```python
df.drop(columns=['ocean_proximity']).corr()[['median_house_value']]\
.sort_values(by='median_house_value', ascending=False)
```
Output:

	median_house_value
median_house_value	1.000000
median_income	0.688075
total_rooms	0.134153
housing_median_age	0.105623
households	0.065843
total_bedrooms	0.049686
population	-0.024650

The above table shows the correlation coefficients (r-values) between each numeric variable and the "median_house_value" variable. The output will help identify the variables with the strongest correlations, allowing for a deeper understanding of the relationships within the dataset.

A heatmap, also known as a heat map, is a visual representation of data where values are represented using different shades of color. In order to create a heatmap using the correlation data calculated by the Pandas corr() method, you can utilize the heatmap() method from the Seaborn library. This method constructs a grid and assigns colors to the cells of the grid based on their respective values. Here is an example code:

```python
df1 = df.drop(columns=['ocean_proximity'])
sns.heatmap(data=df1.corr(), cmap='Blues', vmin=-1.0, vmax=1.0)
plt.xticks(rotation=45)
```

```
plt.show()
```
Output:

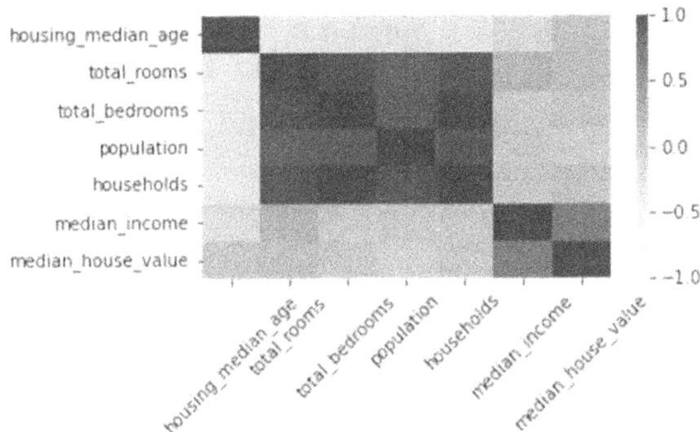

In the above figure, the colors of the cells indicate the strength and direction of the correlation, with lighter shades representing stronger negative correlations, darker shades indicating stronger positive correlations, and shades with a medium shade of blue representing weaker or no correlation.

If you want to create a condensed version of the heatmap, you can modify the code as follows:

```
sns.heatmap(data=df1.corr()[['median_house_value']].sort_values(by='med
ian_house_value', ascending=False), annot=True, cmap='Blues',
cbar=False, fmt=f'.2f')
```
Output:

	median_house_value
median_house_value	1.00
median_income	0.69
total_rooms	0.13
housing_median_age	0.11
households	0.07
total_bedrooms	0.05
population	-0.02

In this code, we first sort the correlation matrix based on the "median_house_value" column. Then, we use sns.heatmap(). Setting annot=True adds numerical annotations to the cells, displaying the correlation values. We use cbar=False to remove the colorbar and fmt='.2f' to format the annotations as floating-point numbers with two decimal places.

Review Question 8.40
What is the main difference between descriptive analysis and predictive analysis?
a. Descriptive analysis involves historical data, while predictive analysis focuses on future values.
b. Descriptive analysis utilizes regression models, while predictive analysis uses descriptive statistics.

c. Descriptive analysis predicts unknown values, while predictive analysis examines past data.

d. Descriptive analysis uses multiple independent variables, while predictive analysis uses a single dependent variable.

Review Question 8.41

What is the main assumption to be checked before applying linear regression?

a. The existence of a linear relationship between independent and dependent variables.

b. The presence of multiple independent variables.

c. The availability of historical data for analysis.

d. The use of descriptive statistics for decision-making.

Review Question 8.42

What type of variables are used in predictive analysis to forecast the value of a dependent variable?

a. Dependent variables.

b. Independent variables.

c. Categorical variables.

d. Continuous variables.

Review Question 8.43

What does correlation refer to in the context of linear regression?

a. The relationship between independent variables.

b. The relationship between dependent variables.

c. The relationship between variables in a linear manner.

d. The relationship between variables in a non-linear manner.

Review Question 8.44

What is one of the simplest approaches to identify the correlation between two variables?

a. Utilizing linear regression models.

b. Using box plots to visualize the data.

c. Examining the distribution pattern through a scatter plot.

d. Applying descriptive statistics.

Review Question 8.45

What is the purpose of using pairplot() from Seaborn?

a. To create KDE plots for diagonal cells.

b. To generate scatter plots for all pairwise combinations of variables.

c. To eliminate redundant plots in the grid.

d. To visualize the distributions of each variable.

Review Question 8.46

What type of plots are used in the diagonal cells of the pair plot generated by pairplot() in seaborn?

a. Scatter plots.

b. Box plots.

c. Histograms or KDE plots.

d. Bar plots.

Review Question 8.47

What parameter can be set to remove redundant plots in the pair plot grid in seaborn?

a. scatter_kind

b. diag_kind

c. corner

d. redundant_plots

Review Question 8.48

What does the pair plot generated by pairplot() allow us to visualize?

a. The correlations between variables.

b. The distributions of each variable.

c. The outliers in the dataset.

d. The summary statistics of each variable.

Review Question 8.49

What is the Pearson correlation coefficient?

a. A measure of the strength and type of linear correlation between two variables.

b. A measure of the spread of data points around the mean.

c. A measure of the central tendency of a dataset.

d. A measure of the association between categorical variables.

Review Question 8.50

What is recommended to accurately identify correlations between variables?

a. Utilizing only scatter plots.

b. Utilizing only r-values.

c. Utilizing both scatter plots and r-values in combination.

d. Utilizing the mean value of each variable.

Review Question 8.51

How can you obtain the r-values for the relationships between each pair of variables in a DataFrame?

a. By using the scatter() method in Pandas.

b. By using the corr() method in Pandas.

c. By using the plot() method in Pandas.

d. By using the describe() method in Pandas.

Review Question 8.52

What should be considered when using the corr() method in Pandas?

a. The presence of categorical variables of numeric format in the dataset.

b. The need to convert all variables to integers.

c. The exclusion of variables with a weak correlation.

d. The calculation of p-values in addition to r-values.

Review Question 8.53

What is a heatmap?

a. A visual representation of data using different shades of color.

b. A scatter plot with a gradient color scheme.

c. A bar chart displaying categorical data.

d. A line plot showing the trend of a variable over time.

Review Question 8.54

What do the colors in a heatmap of correlation data represent?

a. The type of relationship between variables.

b. The spread of data points.

c. The strength and direction of correlation.

d. The frequency of data values.

Review Question 8.55
What does the annot=True parameter in the sns.heatmap() function do?
a. Adds numerical annotations to the cells, displaying the correlation values.
b. Removes the colorbar from the heatmap.
c. Sets the colormap for the heatmap.
d. Formats the annotations as floating-point numbers.

8.7 Simple Linear Regression

As explained in the last section, a regression model is a tool used to predict the value of a dependent variable based on the values of one or more independent variables. To create and utilize a regression model in Python, we can make use of the Scikit-learn library, also known as sklearn. However, keep in mind that sklearn is not the only library available for building regression models in Python.

The procedure for creating and utilizing a regression model using Scikit-learn involves four steps:

Step 1: Splitting the dataset into training and test datasets. This allows us to train the model on the training dataset and evaluate its performance on the test dataset. The train_test_split() function is used to split the dataset into these two subsets. You can specify the criteria for splitting, or randomly assign values to each subset. The random_state parameter allows you to have the same split every time you execute the code.

Step 2: Creating the regression model using the training dataset. We need to import the LinearRegression class from Scikit-learn and create an instance of it. By calling the fit() method on this instance and passing the training dataset, we can train the regression model and fit a regression line to the data. The regression line represents the relationship between the independent and dependent variables.

Step 3: Evaluating the model using the test dataset. The test dataset is used to assess the accuracy and performance of the regression model. By calling the score() method on the regression model instance and passing the test dataset, we can obtain the R^2 regression score. This score indicates the proportion of the variance in the dependent variable that can be attributed to the independent variable. A higher R^2 score signifies a better fit.

Step 4: Using the trained model to make predictions. Once the model has been validated, we can utilize it to predict the values of the dependent variable based on the independent variables. The predict() method accepts the x values (independent variables) from the test dataset and returns the predicted y values (dependent variable). These predicted values can be compared to the actual values to assess the accuracy of the model.

To practice these steps, you can use the following code:

```python
from sklearn.model_selection import train_test_split
from sklearn.linear_model import LinearRegression
from sklearn.metrics import mean_squared_error
# Step 1: Split the data into training and test datasets
x_train, x_test, y_train, y_test =
```

```
train_test_split(df[['median_income']], df[['median_house_value']],
test_size=0.33, random_state=42)
# Step 2: Create the model using the training dataset
linearModel = LinearRegression()
linearModel.fit(x_train, y_train)
# Step 3: Validate the model with the test dataset
score = linearModel.score(x_test, y_test)
print("R-square: ", score)
# Step 4: Make predictions and measure the performance with MSE
y_predicted = linearModel.predict(x_test)
print(y_predicted)
mse = mean_squared_error(y_test, y_predicted)
print("Mean Squared Error: ", mse)
```

Output:

```
R-square:  0.4725720683367075
[[115039.43337818]
 [150515.68435298]
 [190110.86953694]
 ...
 [204942.37123844]
 [228324.73027994]
 [159354.49150091]]
Mean Squared Error:  7028461448.5409775
```

In this code, we import the necessary functions and classes from Scikit-learn: train_test_split for splitting the dataset and LinearRegression for creating the linear regression model.

In Step 1, we split the data into training and test datasets using the train_test_split() function. We pass the independent variable (df[['median_income']]) and dependent variable (df[['median_house_value']]) to be split, along with the desired test size and a random state for reproducibility.

In Step 2, we create an instance of the LinearRegression class and fit the model to the training dataset using the fit() method.

In Step 3, we validate the model by calling the score() method on the trained model and passing the test dataset (x_test and y_test). The returned score represents the R^2 regression score.

In Step 4, we utilize the trained model to make predictions by calling the predict() method and passing the independent variable values (x_test). The predicted values are stored in the y_predicted variable. The Mean Squared Error (MSE) is a measure of how close a fitted line is to data points. A lower MSE means a better fit to the data.

The output shows the R^2 score, predicted values of the dependent variable (y_predicted) based on the independent variable (x_test) and the MSE value of the model.

After obtaining the predicted values from the regression model, you can visualize the regression by plotting the predicted data. This plot allows you to observe the relationship between the independent variable and the predicted values of the dependent variable.

To plot the predicted data, enter the following code in a new cell:

```
predicted = pd.DataFrame(y_predicted, columns=['value_predicted'])
combined = predicted.join([x_test.reset_index(drop=True),
y_test.reset_index(drop=True)])
melted = pd.melt(combined, id_vars=['median_income'],
value_vars=['median_house_value','value_predicted'],
var_name='price_type', value_name='price_value')
sns.relplot(data=melted, x='median_income', y='price_value', hue='price_type')
```

Output:

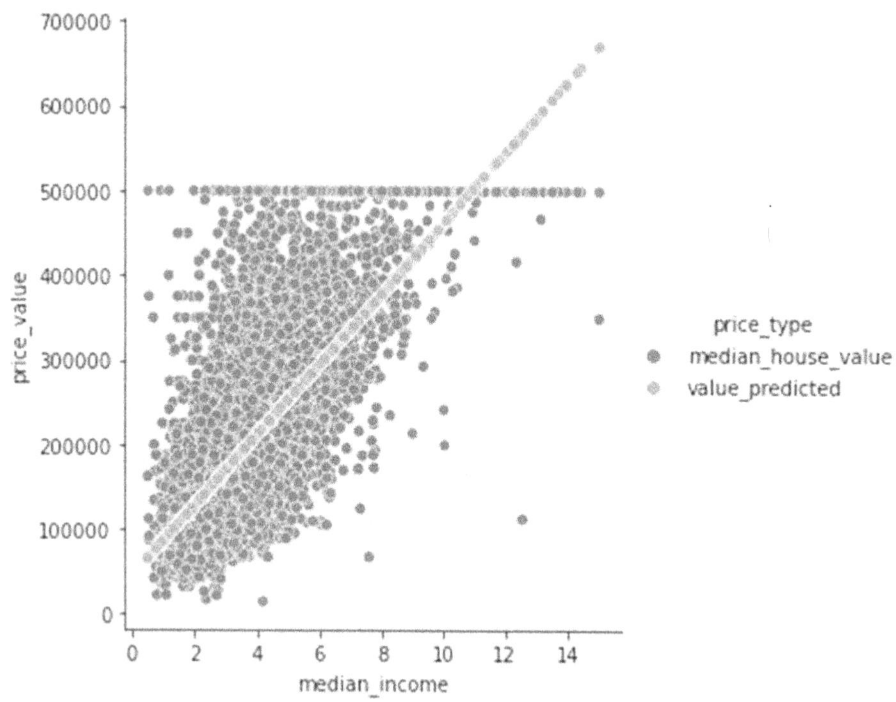

The above figure shows a scatter plot where the x-axis represents the median_income and the y-axis represents the price_value. The hue parameter is used to distinguish between the actual house values ('median_house_value') and the predicted values ('value_predicted') by color. The resulting plot visualizes the regression line by showing how the predicted values form a straight line through the scatter plot data.

To evaluate a regression model further, you can analyze the *residuals*, which are the differences between the actual values of the dependent variable and the predicted values. The residuals provide insights into the accuracy of the predictions and can help identify any patterns or biases in the model. To calculate and visualize the residuals, follow these steps:

```
# Calculate the residuals by subtracting the predicted values from
# the actual values
combined['residual'] = combined.median_house_value -
combined.value_predicted
# Plot the residuals
g = sns.relplot(data=combined, x='median_income', y='residual')
# draw a horizontal line where the y axis is 0
# use dashed line style
for ax in g.axes.flat:
    ax.axhline(0, ls='--')
```

Output:

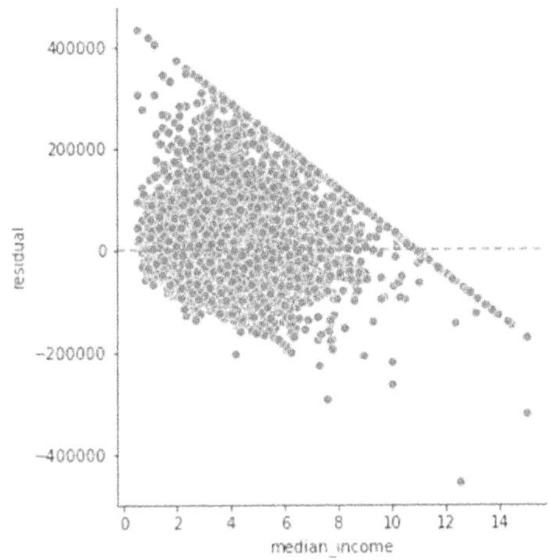

The above figure shows a scatter plot where the x-axis represents the median_income and the y-axis represents the residuals. Each point on the plot represents the difference between the actual median_house_value and the corresponding predicted value.

By analyzing the residuals, you can gain insights into the model's performance. A residual value of 0 indicates an accurate prediction. Positive residuals indicate that the prediction was too low, while negative residuals indicate that the prediction was too high. By examining the distribution and patterns of the residuals, you can identify any systematic errors or areas where the model consistently overestimates or underestimates the values.

Additionally, the code includes a dashed horizontal line at y=0 to indicate the ideal scenario where the predictions perfectly match the actual values. This line helps visually assess the deviation of the residuals from zero.

Review Question 8.56
What is the purpose of a regression model?
a. To predict the value of an independent variable based on the values of one or more dependent variables.
b. To predict the value of a dependent variable based on the values of one or more independent variables.
c. To evaluate the accuracy of a dataset split into training and test subsets.
d. To assess the performance of a classification algorithm.

Review Question 8.57
What is the purpose of splitting the dataset into training and test subsets in regression modeling?
a. To evaluate the accuracy of the model.
b. To visualize the relationship between the variables.
c. To fit a regression line to the data.
d. To assess the performance of the independent variable.

Review Question 8.58
Which function is used to split the dataset into training and test subsets in Scikit-learn?
a. train_test_split()
b. fit()
c. score()
d. split()

Review Question 8.59
What does the fit() method do in Scikit-learn's LinearRegression class?
a. Splits the dataset into training and test subsets.
b. Evaluates the model using the test dataset.
c. Trains the regression model and applies a regression line to the data.
d. Computes the R^2 regression score.

Review Question 8.60
What does the score() method in Scikit-learn's LinearRegression class return?
a. The R^2 regression score.
b. The predicted values of the dependent variable.
c. The coefficients of the regression line.
d. The variance in the independent variable.

Review Question 8.61
What does the predict() method in Scikit-learn's LinearRegression class do?
a. Splits the dataset into training and test subsets.
b. Fits a regression line to the data.
c. Computes the R^2 regression score.
d. Predicts the values of the dependent variable based on the independent variables.

Review Question 8.62
In this book, which library is commonly used for creating and utilizing regression models in Python?

a. NumPy
b. Pandas
c. Matplotlib
d. Scikit-learn

Review Question 8.63
What does the R^2 score represent?
a. The proportion of the variance in the independent variable.
b. The accuracy of the model.
c. The proportion of the variance in the dependent variable that can be attributed to the independent variable.
d. The difference between the predicted and actual values of the dependent variable.

Review Question 8.64
Which step of the regression modeling process involves fitting a regression line to the data?
a. Step 1: Splitting the dataset into training and test datasets.
b. Step 2: Creating the regression model using the training dataset.
c. Step 3: Evaluating the model using the test dataset.
d. Step 4: Using the trained model to make predictions.

Review Question 8.65
What is the purpose of plotting the predicted data in regression analysis?
a. To visualize the relationship between the independent variable and the predicted values of the dependent variable.
b. To visualize the relationship between the independent variable and the actual values of the dependent variable.
c. To visualize the relationship between the residuals and the dependent variable.
d. To observe the regression line formed by the predicted values.

Review Question 8.66
What does the "hue" parameter in the seaborn relplot() function represent?
a. The x-axis variable.
b. The y-axis variable.
c. The color distinction between different groups of data.
d. The type of regression analysis performed.

Review Question 8.67
What does the pd.melt() function do in the provided code?

```
melted = pd.melt(combined, id_vars=['median_income'],
value_vars=['median_house_value','value_predicted'],
var_name='price_type', value_name='price_value')
```

a. Combines the test data and the predicted data.
b. Reshapes the DataFrame by melting columns into a single column.
c. Resets the index of the DataFrame.
d. Creates a scatter plot of the data.

Review Question 8.68
What can be inferred from the scatter plot in terms of the linear regression model?
a. The accuracy of the model.
b. The performance of the model.

c. The strength of the relationship between the independent and dependent variables.
d. The difference between the actual and predicted values.

Review Question 8.69
What are residuals in the context of regression analysis?
a. The differences between the actual values of the independent variable and the predicted values.
b. The differences between the actual values of the dependent variable and the predicted values.
c. The differences between the training and test datasets.
d. The differences between the independent and dependent variables.

Review Question 8.70
What insights can be gained from analyzing the residuals in a regression model?
a. The accuracy of the model's predictions.
b. The performance of the model's independent variables.
c. Any systematic errors or biases in the model.
d. The relationship between the independent and dependent variables.

Review Question 8.71
What does the dashed horizontal line at y=0 represent in the residuals scatter plot of a regression?
a. The median_income value.
b. The residuals.
c. The ideal scenario where the predictions perfectly match the actual values.
d. The deviation of the residuals from zero.

Review Question 8.72
What does a positive residual value indicate in the regression analysis of the book?
a. The prediction was too low.
b. The prediction was too high.
c. The prediction was accurate.
d. There is no relationship between the independent and dependent variables.

Review Question 8.73
How can analyzing the residuals help in evaluating a regression model?
a. By assessing the accuracy of the predictions.
b. By identifying systematic errors or biases in the model.
c. By understanding the relationship between the independent and dependent variables.
d. By determining the optimal values of the independent variables.

8.8 Case study: Higher Education Debt and Income

Data Description:

The dataset used in this analysis is sourced from the U.S. Department of Education's website

(https://collegescorecard.ed.gov/data/). It consists of field of study-level data files covering the pooled

award years 2014-15, 2015-16 through 2017-18, 2018-19. The dataset provides information on cumulative

debt at graduation and earnings one, two, three, and four years after graduation. Its primary objective is to assist prospective postsecondary students in making informed decisions about enrollment.

The dataset contains institution identifiers, academic program information, credential levels, distance education availability, and financial metrics for postsecondary institutions. Unique IDs like UNITID from IPEDS identify each institution. CIP codes classify academic disciplines and credential levels categorize degree types. The distance education field indicates if programs can be completed remotely. Median debt fields show typical federal loan debt for graduating borrowers in each program. Median earnings fields display alumni pay 1-4 years after completing credentials.

Tasks for loading data:

1. Place the education.csv file in the default folder. Read only selected columns into a DataFrame named df:

```
import pandas as pd
selected_columns = ['INSTNM', 'CONTROL', 'CIPCODE', 'CREDLEV',
                    'DEBT_ALL_STGP_ANY_MDN', 'EARN_MDN_1YR',
                    'EARN_MDN_4YR', 'DISTANCE']
df = pd.read_csv('education.csv', usecols=selected_columns)
df.head()
```

Tasks for Data Cleaning:

2. Rename columns for easy of handling in code:

```
column_names = {'INSTNM': 'name',
                'CONTROL': 'type',
                'CIPCODE': 'major',
                'CREDLEV': 'degree',
                'DEBT_ALL_STGP_ANY_MDN': 'debt',
                'EARN_MDN_1YR': 'income1',
                'EARN_MDN_4YR': 'income4',
                'DISTANCE': 'delivery'}
df = df.rename(columns=column_names)
df
```

3. Identify missing values in each field and determine the reasons for their absence. In the df, the 'PrivacySupressed' indicates that the data is missing. You need to decide on an appropriate strategy for handling missing values, such as imputation or deletion, based on the specific field and the impact on the analysis. We will just delete those rows with any missing data:

```
df = df[~df[['debt', 'income1', 'income4']].apply(lambda x:
x.str.contains('PrivacySuppressed')).any(axis=1)]
df
```

4. Check the data types of each variable and ensure they are correctly assigned.

```
df.info()
```

Output:

```
<class 'pandas.core.frame.DataFrame'>
Int64Index: 29545 entries, 16 to 233918
Data columns (total 8 columns):
 #   Column    Non-Null Count  Dtype
---  ------    --------------  -----
 0   name      29545 non-null  object
 1   type      29545 non-null  object
 2   major     29545 non-null  int64
 3   degree    29545 non-null  int64
 4   debt      29545 non-null  object
 5   income1   29545 non-null  object
 6   income4   29545 non-null  object
 7   delivery  29545 non-null  int64
dtypes: int64(3), object(5)
memory usage: 2.0+ MB
```

5. Convert variables to their appropriate data types (e.g., numeric, categorical, datetime) to facilitate analysis and modeling. First, we want to convert the 'type' column from 'object' to 'categorical'. By converting the data type to 'category', you can take advantage of the memory efficiency and potential performance improvements when working with categorical data in pandas.

```
# Convert the column to the 'category' data type
df['type'] = df['type'].astype('category')
df.info()
```

Output:

```
<class 'pandas.core.frame.DataFrame'>
Int64Index: 29545 entries, 16 to 233918
Data columns (total 8 columns):
 #   Column    Non-Null Count  Dtype
---  ------    --------------  -----
 0   name      29545 non-null  object
 1   type      29545 non-null  category
 2   major     29545 non-null  int64
 3   degree    29545 non-null  int64
 4   debt      29545 non-null  object
 5   income1   29545 non-null  object
 6   income4   29545 non-null  object
 7   delivery  29545 non-null  int64
dtypes: category(1), int64(3), object(4)
memory usage: 1.8+ MB
```

Next, the 'debt', 'income1', and 'income4' columns should be converted to int64 data type:

```
df['debt'] = pd.to_numeric(df['debt'], errors='coerce')
df['income1'] = pd.to_numeric(df['income1'], errors='coerce')
df['income4'] = pd.to_numeric(df['income4'], errors='coerce')
df.info()
```

Output:

```
<class 'pandas.core.frame.DataFrame'>
Int64Index: 29545 entries, 16 to 233918
Data columns (total 8 columns):
 #   Column    Non-Null Count  Dtype
---  ------    --------------  -----
 0   name      29545 non-null  object
 1   type      29545 non-null  category
 2   major     29545 non-null  int64
 3   degree    29545 non-null  int64
 4   debt      29545 non-null  int64
 5   income1   29545 non-null  int64
 6   income4   29545 non-null  int64
 7   delivery  29545 non-null  int64
dtypes: category(1), int64(6), object(1)
memory usage: 1.8+ MB
```

6. Identify any duplicate records in the dataset.

```
duplicate_rows = df.duplicated()
num_duplicates = duplicate_rows.sum()
num_duplicates
```

Output:

65

Remove any duplicate records in the dataset, ensuring that each observation is unique.

```
df_no_duplicates = df.drop_duplicates()
df_no_duplicates.duplicated().sum()
```

Output:

0

7. Pay attention to key fields like institution ID or program code to avoid duplication issues. In our case, we don't want to see two different debts for the same institution, major, and degree.

```
duplicate_rows = df_no_duplicates.duplicated(subset=['name', 'type',
'major', 'degree'])
num_duplicates = duplicate_rows.sum()
num_duplicates
```

Output:

119

In a new cell, enter the following:

```
df_no_duplicates2 = df_no_duplicates.drop_duplicates(subset=['name',
'type', 'major', 'degree'])
duplicate_rows = df_no_duplicates2.duplicated(subset=['name', 'type',
'major', 'degree'])
duplicate_rows.sum()
```

Output:

0

8. Detect and assess outliers in numerical variables that may significantly impact the analysis. We will use boxplot to visualize it. In a boxplot, outliers are identified as individual data points that fall outside the whiskers (two horizontal lines outside the box) of the plot. The whiskers represent the range within which most of the data points lie, while the outliers are considered to be extreme values.

```
df_no_duplicates2.boxplot(column=['debt', 'income1', 'income4'])
```

Output:

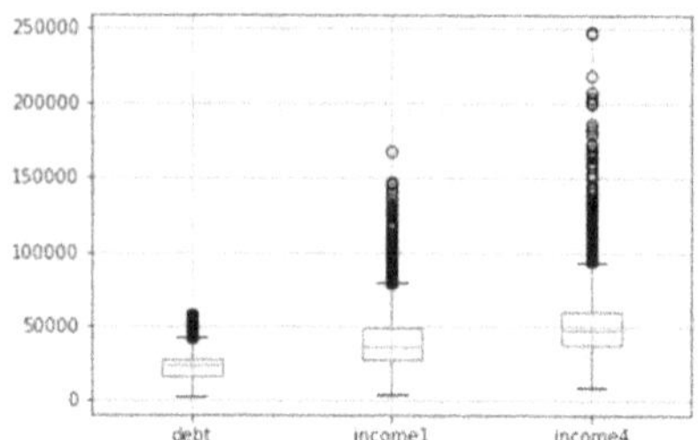

As you can see, there are quite a few outliers in each of the three columns. There are more than one way to identify outliers. We will use 1.5*IQR for upper and lower boundaries and remove any data points that are outside of the boundaries. Enter the following code in a new cell:

```
df2 = df_no_duplicates2.copy()
for col in ['debt', 'income1', 'income4']:
    mean = df2[col].mean()
    median = df2[col].median()
    q1 = df2[col].quantile(0.25)
    q3 = df2[col].quantile(0.75)
    # Use statistical techniques for each column
    # Interquartile range (IQR)
    iqr = q3 - q1
    lower_bound = q1 - 1.5 * iqr
    upper_bound = q3 + 1.5 * iqr
    outliers_iqr = df2[(df2[col] < lower_bound) | (df2[col] > upper_bound)]
    df2 = df2[(df2[col] >= lower_bound) & (df2[col] <= upper_bound)]
```

Try boxplot again and you can see all outliers are gone:

```
df2.boxplot(column=['debt', 'income1', 'income4'])
```

Tasks for Data Preparation:

9. Feature engineering is about creating new features or variables based on the existing data, such as calculating the difference between median income 4 years after graduation and median income 1 year after graduation.

```python
df2['income_diff'] = df2.loc[:, 'income4'] - df2.loc[:, 'income1']
df2
```

A new column named 'income_diff' is added to the data frame.

Tasks for Data Aggregation in a Business Data Analytics Project:

10. Summarize Data by Institution. Aggregate data at the institution level to obtain key metrics such as

average debt and median earnings.

```python
institution_agg = df.groupby('name').agg({
    'debt': ['mean', 'median'],
    'income1': ['mean', 'median'],
    'income4': ['mean', 'median']
})
institution_agg.columns = ['Mean Debt', 'Median Debt', 'Mean Income
1yr', 'Median Income 1yr', 'Mean Income 4yr', 'Median Income 4yr']
institution_agg = institution_agg.sort_values(by='Mean Income 4yr',
ascending=False)
institution_agg.to_pickle('institution.pickle')
institution_agg.head()
```

11. Group Data by Field of Study. Group data based on the field of study (CIP code) to analyze trends and

patterns within specific academic disciplines.

```python
major_agg = df.groupby('major').agg({
    'debt': ['mean', 'median'],
    'income1': ['mean', 'median'],
    'income4': ['mean', 'median'],
    'name': 'count'
})
major_agg.columns = ['Mean Debt', 'Median Debt', 'Mean Income 1yr',
'Median Income 1yr', 'Mean Income 4yr', 'Median Income 4yr', 'Count']
major_agg = major_agg.sort_values(by='Mean Income 4yr',
ascending=False)
major_agg.to_pickle('major.pickle')
major_agg.head()
```

12. Analyze Data by Credential Level. Aggregate data based on credential levels (e.g., certificates, associate's

degrees, bachelor's degrees) to compare outcomes across different educational achievements.

```python
degree_agg = df.groupby('degree').agg({
    'debt': ['mean', 'median'],
    'income1': ['mean', 'median'],
    'income4': ['mean', 'median'],
    'name': 'count'
})
degree_agg.columns = ['Mean Debt', 'Median Debt', 'Mean Income 1yr',
'Median Income 1yr', 'Mean Income 4yr', 'Median Income 4yr', 'Count']
```

```
degree_agg = degree_agg.sort_values(by='Mean Income 4yr',
ascending=False)
degree_agg.to_pickle('degree.pickle')
degree_agg.head()
```

Tasks for Data Visualization:

13. Visualize Institutional type Comparison. Create bar charts to compare key metrics such as debt and earnings across different institutions.

```
import seaborn as sns
import matplotlib.pyplot as plt
id_vars = ['type']
value_vars = ['debt', 'income1', 'income4']
melted_data = pd.melt(df, id_vars=id_vars, value_vars=value_vars,
var_name='Category', value_name='Value')
sns.barplot(x='type', y='Value', hue='Category', data=melted_data)
plt.title('Debt and Income by Institution Types')
plt.xlabel('Institution Types')
plt.ylabel('Amount')
plt.legend(title='Category', loc='upper center')
plt.show()
```

14. Compare Debt and Earnings by Credential Level. Use grouped bar charts or stacked bar charts to compare debt levels and earnings across different credential levels.

```
import seaborn as sns
import matplotlib.pyplot as plt
id_vars = ['degree']
value_vars = ['debt', 'income1', 'income4']
melted_data = pd.melt(df, id_vars=id_vars, value_vars=value_vars,
var_name='Category', value_name='Value')
ax = sns.barplot(x='degree', y='Value', hue='Category', data=melted_data)
plt.title('Debt and Income by Credential Level')
plt.xlabel('Degree Types')
plt.ylabel('Amount')
plt.legend(title='Category', loc='upper left')
tick_labels = ['UG Certs/Diplomas', 'Associate', 'Bachelor', 'Post-Bac Cert']
# Get the current tick locations
current_ticks = ax.get_xticks()
# Set the tick locations and labels
ax.set_xticks(current_ticks)
ax.set_xticklabels(tick_labels)
plt.show()
```

15. Plot Scatterplots for Relationships. Create scatterplots to explore relationships between variables, such as debt and earnings:

```
selected_columns = ['debt', 'income1', 'income4']
```

```
sns.pairplot(df[selected_columns])
```

From the output, you may notice the debt does not have a high correlation with either incomes. However, the two incomes are highly correlated.

Tasks for Simple Regression Analysis:

16. Variable Selection. Based on the output of Task 15 above, we can identify the dependent variable (response variable) be the fourth year income and independent variable (predictor variable).be the first year income.

17. Model Building. Split the dataset into training and testing sets to evaluate the performance of the regression model.

```
from sklearn.model_selection import train_test_split
from sklearn.linear_model import LinearRegression
x_train, x_test, y_train, y_test = train_test_split(df[['income1']],
df[['income4']], test_size=0.33, random_state=42)
```

18. Apply simple linear regression by fitting the model with the training data.

```
linearModel = LinearRegression()
linearModel.fit(x_train, y_train)
```

19. Assess the model's goodness of fit using evaluation metrics such as R-squared.

```
score = linearModel.score(x_test, y_test)
print(score)
```

20. Model Evaluation. Evaluate the performance of the regression model using the testing dataset.

Calculate residuals and plot them to see how close to zero to evaluate the performance of the model.

```
y_predicted = linearModel.predict(x_test)
predicted = pd.DataFrame(y_predicted, columns=['value_predicted'])
combined = predicted.join([x_test.reset_index(drop=True),
y_test.reset_index(drop=True)])
combined['residual'] = combined.income4 - combined.value_predicted
g = sns.relplot(data=combined, x='income1', y='residual')
for ax in g.axes.flat:
    ax.axhline(0, ls='--')
```

Extra challenges:

In the dataset from the Department of Education, there are several interesting questions that data analytics can help answer:

1. How does the debt at graduation vary across different fields of study?
2. Is there a relationship between the level of education (credential level) and incomes?
3. Do students who complete undergraduate certificates or diplomas have different earning potentials compared to those with associate's or bachelor's degrees?
4. Are there significant differences in debt and earnings between different types of institutions?
5. How do the earnings of graduates change over time, specifically one, two, three, and four years after graduation?
6. Can we identify any patterns or trends in the relationship between debt and earnings across various fields of study?
7. Is there a significant difference in earnings between students who complete their programs through distance education and those who do not?
8. Can we predict post-completion earnings based on the field of study and the cumulative debt at graduation?
9. How does the debt and earnings vary across different institutions, and are there any outliers or notable exceptions?
10. Are there any correlations between the debt, earnings, and other variables such as institution size or geographic location (need additional publicly available data)?

8.9 Chapter Summary

In this chapter, you learned time series analysis for historical patterns and trends in temporal data, enabling informed forecasts. Linear regression models relationships between variables, providing prediction and estimation capabilities. This chapter introduced these techniques through a real-world case study analyzing government data on higher education debt and incomes. We encourage further improving of skills by analyzing additional real-world datasets using the methods covered here.

8.10 Solutions to the Review Questions

8.1 B; 8.2 A; 8.3 A; 8.4 A; 8.5 A; 8.6 B; 8.7 C; 8.8 A; 8.9 B; 8.10 C; 8.11 A; 8.12 A; 8.13 C; 8.14 B; 8.15 A; 8.16 B; 8.17 D; 8.18 B; 8.19 A; 8.20 D; 8.21 A; 8.22 C; 8.23 D; 8.24 B; 8.25 C; 8.26 B; 8.27 D; 8.28 D; 8.29 C; 8.30 C; 8.31 C; 8.32 A; 8.33 C; 8.34 B; 8.35 B; 8.36 C; 8.37 D; 8.38 B; 8.39 C; 8.40 A; 8.41 A; 8.42 B; 8.43 C; 8.44 C; 8.45 B; 8.46 C; 8.47 C; 8.48 A; 8.49 A; 8.50 C; 8.51 B; 8.52 A; 8.53 A; 8.54 C; 8.55 A; 8.56 B; 8.57 A; 8.58 A; 8.59 C; 8.60 A; 8.61 D; 8.62 D; 8.63 C; 8.64 B; 8.65 A; 8.66 C; 8.67 B; 8.68 C; 8.69 B; 8.70 C; 8.71 C; 8.72 A; 8.73 B;

Chapter 9: Levels of Data Analytics

Chapter Learning Objectives

9.1 Assess the effectiveness and limitations of descriptive analytics.
9.2 Use diagnostic analytics techniques to understand the reasons behind certain outcomes.
9.3 Define and explain the key concepts and terminologies related to predictive analytics.
9.4 Define and explain the key concepts and terminologies related to prescriptive analytics.

9.1 Introduction

In business data analytics, understanding the different types of data analysis is key for making informed decisions and driving strategic initiatives (Al-Sai, et al., 2022). The four primary levels of data analytics—descriptive, diagnostic, predictive, and prescriptive—each serve a unique purpose and provide distinct insights that collectively enhance a business's ability to interpret and leverage data (Balali et al., 2020). This section will introduce these four levels, highlighting their definitions, similarities, and differences, and explaining their importance in the broader context of business data analytics.

Descriptive analytics is the most basic level of data analysis. It focuses on summarizing historical data to understand what has happened in the past. This level involves the use of data aggregation and data mining techniques to provide insights into past trends and patterns. Common tools and methods used in descriptive analytics include reports, dashboards, and data visualizations. For example, a retail store might use descriptive analytics to calculate the total sales for the past month, the average purchase value, and the most popular products.

Diagnostic analytics investigates deeper into the data to understand the causes of past outcomes. This level goes beyond merely describing what happened by examining the underlying reasons and factors that influenced these outcomes. Diagnostic analytics employs techniques such as drill-down, data discovery, and correlation analysis. Continuing with the retail store example, diagnostic analytics could be used to investigate why certain products sold more than others by analyzing factors like marketing campaigns, seasonal trends, or customer demographics.

Predictive analytics uses statistical models and machine learning techniques to forecast future events based on historical data. This level aims to predict what is likely to happen in the future by identifying patterns and trends that suggest future outcomes. Predictive analytics often involves regression analysis, time series analysis, and predictive modeling. The retail store might use predictive analytics to forecast next month's sales, anticipate stock levels needed for high-demand products, or predict customer behavior based on past purchasing patterns.

Prescriptive analytics goes one step further by not only predicting future outcomes but also suggesting actions to achieve desired results. This level combines predictive models with optimization algorithms and decision analysis to recommend the best course of action. Prescriptive analytics helps businesses determine the best way to handle future scenarios to maximize opportunities and minimize risks. The retail store can use prescriptive analytics to determine optimal pricing strategies, inventory management practices, and marketing efforts to boost sales and profitability.

While each level of data analytics builds on the previous one, they serve distinct purposes:
Descriptive vs. Diagnostic: Descriptive analytics focuses on "what happened," whereas diagnostic analytics seeks to explain "why it happened."
Predictive vs. Descriptive/Diagnostic: Predictive analytics looks forward to "what is likely to happen," based on past data, while descriptive and diagnostic analytics look backward to understand past events.
Prescriptive vs. Predictive: Prescriptive analytics not only predicts future outcomes but also suggests actions to influence those outcomes, making it the most advanced and action-oriented level.

Differentiating these four levels of analytics is important because each provides unique insights and supports different stages of decision-making. By understanding and leveraging each level appropriately, businesses can gain a comprehensive view of their operations, identify root causes of issues, anticipate future trends, and make data-driven decisions to optimize performance.

Together, these four levels of data analytics create a robust framework for business data analytics. Descriptive and diagnostic analytics help businesses understand and learn from past performance. Predictive analytics prepares them for future scenarios, and prescriptive analytics provides actionable recommendations to achieve desired outcomes. By integrating all four levels, businesses can create a continuous cycle of improvement, leveraging data to drive strategic initiatives, enhance operational efficiency, and achieve long-term success.

Review Question 9.1
What is the primary focus of descriptive analytics?
a. Predicting future outcomes
b. Suggesting actions to achieve desired results
c. Summarizing historical data
d. Understanding the causes of past outcomes

Review Question 9.2
Which level of data analytics involves the use of data aggregation and data mining techniques?
a. Predictive analytics
b. Prescriptive analytics
c. Diagnostic analytics
d. Descriptive analytics

Review Question 9.3
What does diagnostic analytics seek to explain?
a. What is likely to happen in the future
b. What actions to take to achieve desired results
c. What happened in the past
d. Why past outcomes occurred

Review Question 9.4
Which level of data analytics uses statistical models and machine learning techniques?
a. Descriptive analytics
b. Diagnostic analytics
c. Predictive analytics
d. Prescriptive analytics

Review Question 9.5
What is the primary purpose of prescriptive analytics?
a. To summarize historical data
b. To understand the causes of past outcomes
c. To predict future outcomes
d. To suggest actions to achieve desired results

Review Question 9.6
Which level of data analytics is the most advanced and action-oriented?
a. Descriptive analytics
b. Diagnostic analytics
c. Predictive analytics
d. Prescriptive analytics

Review Question 9.7
What is the difference between descriptive and diagnostic analytics?
a. Descriptive analytics focuses on "what happened," whereas diagnostic analytics seeks to explain "why it happened."
b. Descriptive analytics focuses on "why it happened," whereas diagnostic analytics seeks to explain "what happened."
c. Descriptive analytics focuses on "what is likely to happen," whereas diagnostic analytics seeks to explain "what happened."

d. Descriptive analytics focuses on "what happened," whereas diagnostic analytics seeks to explain "what is likely to happen."

Review Question 9.8
How does predictive analytics differ from descriptive and diagnostic analytics?
a. Predictive analytics looks forward to "what is likely to happen," based on past data, while descriptive and diagnostic analytics look backward to understand past events.
b. Predictive analytics looks backward to "what happened," based on past data, while descriptive and diagnostic analytics look forward to understand future events.
c. Predictive analytics looks forward to "why it happened," based on past data, while descriptive and diagnostic analytics look backward to understand past events.
d. Predictive analytics looks backward to "why it happened," based on past data, while descriptive and diagnostic analytics look forward to understand future events.

Review Question 9.9
How does prescriptive analytics differ from predictive analytics?
a. Prescriptive analytics not only predicts future outcomes but also suggests actions to influence those outcomes.
b. Prescriptive analytics only predicts future outcomes, while predictive analytics suggests actions to influence those outcomes.
c. Prescriptive analytics only suggests actions to influence future outcomes, while predictive analytics predicts those outcomes.
d. Prescriptive analytics predicts future outcomes based on past data, while predictive analytics suggests actions to influence those outcomes.

Review Question 9.10
Why is it crucial to differentiate the four levels of analytics?
a. Because each level provides unique insights and supports different stages of decision-making.
b. Because each level uses the same techniques and supports the same stage of decision-making.
c. Because each level provides the same insights and supports different stages of decision-making.
d. Because each level provides unique insights and supports the same stage of decision-making.

Review Question 9.11
What do descriptive and diagnostic analytics help businesses with?
a. Understanding and learning from past performance.
b. Preparing for future scenarios.
c. Providing actionable recommendations to achieve desired outcomes.
d. Leveraging data to drive strategic initiatives.

Review Question 9.12
What does predictive analytics prepare businesses for?
a. Understanding and learning from past performance.
b. Future scenarios.
c. Providing actionable recommendations to achieve desired outcomes.
d. Leveraging data to drive strategic initiatives.

Review Question 9.13
What does prescriptive analytics provide to businesses?
a. Understanding and learning from past performance.
b. Preparation for future scenarios.

c. Actionable recommendations to achieve desired outcomes.
d. Summarization of historical data.

9.2 Descriptive Analytics

Descriptive analytics is the initial phase of data analysis focused on summarizing and interpreting historical data to provide insights into what has happened over a specific period (Adama and Okeke, 2024). It involves the use of statistical techniques to describe the main features of a collection of data quantitatively. This level of analytics is important for understanding past performance and establishing a foundation for further analysis.

Summarizing historical data is important for several reasons (Margherita, 2022). Firstly, it allows businesses to identify patterns and trends that inform strategic decisions. By examining past data, companies can understand the outcomes of past actions and initiatives, which helps in assessing their effectiveness and making necessary adjustments. Secondly, summarized historical data provides a factual basis for predicting future performance. By analyzing past trends, businesses can make informed forecasts about future outcomes, aiding in planning and resource allocation. Lastly, summarizing historical data enables clear communication of insights to stakeholders. Through easily interpretable summaries and visualizations, businesses can convey complex information in a straightforward manner, facilitating better decision-making and alignment among all involved parties.

In the field of statistics, there are several key descriptive measures that are often used to understand and interpret data:

The *mean* is the average value of a dataset, which is calculated by summing all the values and dividing by the number of values. It provides a central point of the data distribution.

The *median* is the middle value in a dataset, effectively separating the higher half from the lower half. This measure is particularly useful in skewed distributions as it is not affected by extreme values.

The *mode* is the most frequently occurring value in a dataset. It can be useful in identifying the most common or popular item in a dataset.

The *range* is the difference between the maximum and minimum values in a dataset. It provides a quick measure of the overall spread of the data.

Quartiles divide the dataset into four equal parts. The first quartile (Q1) represents the 25th percentile, the second quartile (Q2) is the median, and the third quartile (Q3) represents the 75th percentile. These measures provide information about the distribution of data and are useful for identifying potential outliers.

The *interquartile range (IQR)* is the difference between the third and first quartiles (Q3 - Q1). It provides a measure of variability that is less sensitive to extreme values than the range.

Skewness is a measure of the asymmetry of the probability distribution of a dataset. It indicates whether the data is skewed to the left (negative skewness) or right (positive skewness) of the mean.

Kurtosis measures the "tailedness" of the probability distribution of a dataset. It provides information about the shape of the distribution, indicating whether it is more peaked or flat compared to a normal distribution.

The *standard deviation* is a measure of the dispersion or spread of values in a dataset. It indicates how much the values deviate from the mean, providing an understanding of data variability.

Variance is the average of the squared differences from the mean. It's closely related to standard deviation (being its square) and is another measure of variability in a dataset.

These measures collectively provide a comprehensive summary of the dataset, aiding in data analysis and interpretation. Each measure offers unique insights into the characteristics of the data, allowing for a more thorough understanding of its distribution, central tendency, and variability.

Additionally, in the field of data analysis, visualization techniques play a crucial role in understanding and interpreting data (Inastrilla, 2023).

Among these techniques, *charts* are commonly used. Bar charts are used to compare categorical data, with rectangular bars representing the frequency or value of each category. Line charts are ideal for showing trends over time, with data points connected by a line to depict continuous data. Pie charts are used to show the proportions of a whole, with each slice representing a category's percentage of the total.

Another important visualization technique is the use of *histograms*. Histograms display the distribution of a dataset by grouping data points into bins and showing the frequency of data points within each bin. This helps in understanding the underlying distribution of data, such as normal distribution, skewness, and kurtosis. *Box plots*, or box-and-whisker plots, provide a visual summary of data distribution, highlighting the median, quartiles, and potential outliers. They are particularly useful for comparing distributions across different datasets. These visualization techniques collectively provide a comprehensive view of the data, aiding in data analysis and interpretation.

Review Question 9.14
What is the initial phase of data analysis that focuses on summarizing and interpreting historical data?
a. Predictive analytics

b. Descriptive analytics
c. Diagnostic analytics
d. Prescriptive analytics

Review Question 9.15
Which measure is particularly useful in skewed distributions as it is not affected by extreme values?
a. Mean
b. Mode
c. Median
d. Standard deviation

Review Question 9.16
What does a bar chart represent?
a. The distribution of a dataset
b. The proportions of a whole
c. Trends over time
d. Comparison of categorical data

Review Question 9.17
What does a histogram display?
a. The proportions of a whole
b. Trends over time
c. The distribution of a dataset
d. Comparison of categorical data

Review Question 9.18
What is the role of standard deviation in a dataset?
a. It represents the most common value.
b. It represents the middle value.
c. It represents the average value.
d. It measures the dispersion or spread of values.

Review Question 9.19
What does a line chart represent?
a. The distribution of a dataset.
b. The proportions of a whole.
c. Trends over time.
d. Comparison of categorical data.

Review Question 9.20
What does a pie chart represent?
a. The distribution of a dataset.
b. The proportions of a whole.
c. Trends over time.
d. Comparison of categorical data.

Review Question 9.21
What does a box plot provide?
a. A visual summary of data distribution.
b. The most common value in a dataset.

c. The average value of a dataset.
d. The middle value in a dataset.

Review Question 9.22
What does a box plot highlight?
a. The mean and mode of a dataset.
b. The median, quartiles, and potential outliers of a dataset.
c. The most common item in a dataset.
d. The average value of a dataset.

Review Question 9.23
Which quartile represents the median of a dataset?
a. First quartile (Q1)
b. Second quartile (Q2)
c. Third quartile (Q3)
d. Fourth quartile (Q4)

Review Question 9.24
How is the interquartile range (IQR) calculated?
a. Q2 - Q1
b. Q3 - Q2
c. Q3 - Q1
d. Q4 - Q1

Review Question 9.25
What does skewness measure in a dataset?
a. The central tendency
b. The variability
c. The asymmetry of the probability distribution
d. The range of the data

Review Question 9.26
Which of the following best describes what kurtosis measures?
a. The center of the distribution
b. The spread of the distribution
c. The asymmetry of the distribution
d. The "tailedness" or peakedness of the distribution

9.3 Diagnostic Analytics

Diagnostic analytics focuses on understanding the reasons behind historical outcomes (Muneeswaran, et al., 2021). Unlike descriptive analytics, which summarizes past data to show what has happened, diagnostic analytics goes deeper to explain why things happened. It involves a thorough examination of data to identify patterns, correlations, and root causes of specific events or trends. By uncovering these insights, organizations can make more informed decisions and implement strategies to improve future performance.

The primary purpose of diagnostic analytics is to provide a detailed understanding of the factors and conditions that influenced past outcomes(Ibeh et al., 2024). This involves identifying relationships between different variables, understanding the sequence of events, and determining the underlying causes of observed changes. For instance, if a company experiences a sudden drop in sales, diagnostic analytics can help pinpoint the factors responsible, such as changes in market conditions, customer behavior, or internal operational issues.

Diagnostic analytics employs a variety of techniques and tools to explore data and uncover insights. Some of the most commonly used methods include:

1. *Data Discovery and Drill-Down Analysis*: This involves exploring large datasets to identify patterns and anomalies (Balali et al., 2020). Drill-down analysis allows analysts to break down high-level data into more detailed views, enabling them to investigate specific aspects of the data more closely. Imagine you have sales data for an entire year for a retail company. Initially, you might look at the total annual sales to get a general sense of performance. If you notice a dip in sales during a particular month, you can drill down to look at weekly or daily sales data for that month. Further drill-down might reveal that sales dipped due to a specific product category underperforming. This detailed analysis helps you pinpoint where the problem lies and investigate why it happened.

Through this book, you've discovered that Pandas offers features for filtering and grouping features, which helps isolate specific subsets for detailed analysis. For instance, we can filter sales data by region or product category and then group it to observe patterns within each subset.

2. *Correlation Analysis*: This technique examines the relationships between different variables to determine how changes in one variable may be associated with changes in another. Correlation analysis can help identify potential causes of observed outcomes by highlighting significant relationships within the data. Suppose you're analyzing the relationship between advertising spend and sales revenue. By performing correlation analysis, you might discover a strong positive correlation, indicating that increased advertising spend is associated with higher sales revenue. This insight can help the company make informed decisions about future advertising budgets. Pandas provides robust tools for data manipulation and analysis. We can use the `corr()` method to calculate the correlation matrix of a dataset, which reveals the relationships between different variables.

To further validate these findings, we can perform a hypothesis test. Hypothesis testing is a statistical method that is used in making statistical decisions using sample data. It is basically an assumption that we make about the population parameter. For instance, if we want to test whether our observed correlation between advertising spend and sales revenue is statistically significant, we could set up a null hypothesis stating that there is no correlation between the two variables. We then use the data to calculate a test statistic (based on the correlation coefficient and the size of the dataset) and determine the probability (p-value) of obtaining our observed data if the null hypothesis were true. If this probability is below a predetermined threshold (commonly 0.05), we reject the null hypothesis and conclude that there is a statistically significant correlation. This process provides a rigorous, quantifiable basis for decision-making.

3. *Root Cause Analysis*: This method aims to identify the fundamental reasons behind observed events or trends (Abdelrahman and Keikhosrokiani, 2020). By systematically examining the data, root cause analysis helps uncover the underlying factors that contribute to specific outcomes, allowing organizations to address these issues directly. A manufacturing company notices an increase in defective products. Through root cause analysis, they might find that a specific machine on the production line is malfunctioning. By addressing the root cause (the faulty machine), they can reduce the number of defective products, improving overall quality and efficiency.

To dissect cause-effect relationships, we can employ statistical tests or regression analysis using Python packages such as SciPy for statistical tests and Statsmodels or Scikit-learn for regression analysis. For instance, a linear regression can be performed to scrutinize how fluctuations in advertising spend influence sales. These Python packages provide robust tools for conducting root cause analysis, enabling us to understand the relationships between variables and make data-driven decisions.

These techniques and tools are essential for businesses to understand their data deeply, make informed decisions, and implement effective strategies to address underlying issues and improve performance.

Review Question 9.27
What is the focus of diagnostic analytics?
a. Summarizing past data
b. Predicting future outcomes
c. Understanding the reasons behind historical outcomes
d. Visualizing data

Review Question 9.28

What does drill-down analysis allow analysts to do?
a. Identify patterns and anomalies
b. Break down high-level data into more detailed views
c. Perform correlation analysis
d. Conduct root cause analysis

Review Question 9.29
What does correlation analysis examine?
a. The relationships between different variables
b. The sequence of events
c. The underlying causes of observed changes
d. The patterns and anomalies in large datasets

Review Question 9.30
What is the purpose of a hypothesis test in diagnostic analytics?
a. To identify patterns and anomalies
b. To make statistical decisions using experimental data
c. To break down high-level data into more detailed views
d. To visualize data

Review Question 9.31
What does root cause analysis aim to identify?
a. The relationships between different variables
b. The fundamental reasons behind observed events or trends
c. The patterns and anomalies in large datasets
d. The sequence of events

Review Question 9.32
What can a company do if it experiences a sudden drop in sales?
a. Use diagnostic analytics to pinpoint the factors responsible
b. Use descriptive analytics to summarize past data
c. Use predictive analytics to predict future outcomes
d. Use prescriptive analytics to recommend actions

Review Question 9.33
What does data discovery involve?
a. Exploring large datasets to identify patterns and anomalies
b. Breaking down high-level data into more detailed views
c. Performing correlation analysis
d. Conducting root cause analysis

Review Question 9.34
What does the corr() method in Pandas calculate?
a. The correlation matrix of a dataset
b. The sequence of events
c. The underlying causes of observed changes
d. The patterns and anomalies in large datasets

Review Question 9.35
What is the purpose of a null hypothesis in hypothesis testing?

a. To identify patterns and anomalies
b. To make statistical decisions using experimental data
c. To state that there is no correlation between two variables
d. To visualize data

Review Question 9.36
What can a manufacturing company do if it notices an increase in defective products?
a. Use root cause analysis to find the specific machine on the production line that is malfunctioning
b. Use descriptive analytics to summarize past data
c. Use predictive analytics to predict future outcomes
d. Use prescriptive analytics to recommend actions

9.4 Predictive Analytics

Predictive analytics uses historical data, statistical algorithms, and machine learning techniques to forecast future outcomes (Lepenioti, 2020). It aims to predict future events based on patterns and trends observed in past data. By analyzing current and historical data, predictive analytics provides insights that help organizations make proactive, data-driven decisions (Adesina, 2024).

The primary purpose of predictive analytics is to anticipate future trends and behaviors. This capability allows businesses to plan effectively, allocate resources efficiently, and mitigate potential risks. For example, a retail company might use predictive analytics to forecast future sales, helping it to manage inventory levels and optimize staffing.

Several techniques and tools are commonly used in predictive analytics, each serving unique purposes: *Regression analysis* is a statistical method for modeling the relationship between a dependent variable and one or more independent variables. Its primary purpose is to predict the value of the dependent variable based on the values of the independent variables. For instance, regression analysis can be used to predict future sales by analyzing past sales and advertising spend.

Another important technique is *time series analysis* involves analyzing time-ordered data points to identify trends, patterns, and seasonal variations. This method is particularly useful for forecasting future values based on historical data, such as predicting monthly sales performance.

Lastly, *machine learning algorithms* allow computers to learn from data and make predictions or decisions without explicit programming. They enhance prediction accuracy by learning from large datasets and include examples such as decision trees, neural networks, and support vector machines. Together, these techniques provide a robust framework for making informed predictions in various business contexts.

Python is a versatile programming language with a wide range of libraries that make it ideal for predictive analytics. Here, we explore several practical applications:

To implement simple linear regression, certain Python packages are commonly used. The Pandas package is typically used for data manipulation and analysis. It offers data structures and operations for manipulating numerical tables and time series. The Scikit-learn library, on the other hand, provides simple and efficient tools for predictive data analysis and is built on NumPy, SciPy, and matplotlib. Within Scikit-learn, the train_test_split() function is used to split the dataset into random train and test subsets. The LinearRegression function, also from Scikit-learn, is used to perform linear regression. It fits a linear model with coefficients to minimize the residual sum of squares between the observed targets in the dataset, and the targets predicted by the linear approximation. Finally, the mean_squared_error function from Scikit-learn's metrics module is used to compute the mean squared error regression loss. This function provides a risk metric corresponding to the expected value of the squared (quadratic) error or loss. It is a popular choice for evaluating the performance of a regression model.

In Python, the Statsmodels library is often used for time series forecasting. It provides a suite of powerful tools for statistical modeling, including time series analysis. The Pandas package, again, is used for data manipulation and analysis. It provides data structures and operations for manipulating numerical tables and time series, which are essential for time series forecasting. The ARIMA (AutoRegressive Integrated Moving Average) function from the statsmodels.tsa.arima.model module is used to fit an ARIMA model to the data. This model is a generalization of an autoregressive moving average (ARMA) model and is widely used in time series forecasting. The Matplotlib library is used for creating static, animated, and interactive visualizations in Python. It provides a way to visualize the historical data and the forecasted values, which is key for understanding the performance of the forecasting model.

Machine learning models can be used for more complex predictive tasks. There are numerous models that can be utilized for these tasks. One such model is the Decision Tree Regressor, which is a part of the Scikit-learn library in Python. This model is particularly beneficial in real-world business environments due to its simplicity and interpretability. Decision Tree Regressor uses a tree-like model of decisions. It does not require any assumptions about the relationship between the variables, making it suitable for non-linear relationships. It's also more interpretable than linear regression as it provides clear rules for prediction. The Decision Tree Regressor operates by defining independent and dependent variables. In terms of coding, it is very similar to the simple regression, both models are implemented similarly using the Scikit-learn library in Python. The primary difference lies in the instantiation of the model (LinearRegression() vs DecisionTreeRegressor()), but the steps for splitting the data, fitting the model, making predictions, and evaluating the model are essentially the same.

Review Question 9.37
What is the primary purpose of predictive analytics?
a. To analyze past data
b. To anticipate future trends and behaviors
c. To create machine learning models
d. To perform regression analysis

Review Question 9.38
Which technique in predictive analytics is used to model the relationship between a dependent variable and one or more independent variables?
a. Time series analysis
b. Regression analysis
c. Machine learning
d. Data manipulation

Review Question 9.39
What is the purpose of time series analysis in predictive analytics?
a. To identify trends, patterns, and seasonal variations in time-ordered data points
b. To predict the value of the dependent variable based on the values of the independent variables
c. To make predictions or decisions without explicit programming
d. To manipulate numerical tables and time series

Review Question 9.40
What is the role of machine learning algorithms in predictive analytics?
a. To provide a way to visualize the historical data and the forecasted values
b. To fit a linear model with coefficients to minimize the residual sum of squares between the observed targets in the dataset, and the targets predicted by the linear approximation
c. To learn from data and make predictions or decisions without explicit programming
d. To manipulate numerical tables and time series

Review Question 9.41
What is the purpose of the mean_squared_error function in Scikit-learn's metrics module?
a. To split the dataset into random train and test subsets
b. To perform linear regression
c. To measure the model performance
d. To fit an AutoRegressive Integrated Moving Average (ARIMA) model to the data

Review Question 9.42
What is the purpose of the ARIMA function in the statsmodels.tsa.arima.model module?
a. To split the dataset into random train and test subsets
b. To perform linear regression

c. To compute the mean squared error regression loss
d. To fit an AutoRegressive Integrated Moving Average (ARIMA) model to the data

Review Question 9.43
What is the purpose of the Matplotlib library in Python?
a. To provide a way to visualize the historical data and the forecasted values
b. To perform linear regression
c. To compute the mean squared error regression loss
d. To fit an AutoRegressive Integrated Moving Average (ARIMA) model to the data

Review Question 9.44
What is the Decision Tree Regressor in the Scikit-learn library?
a. A type of machine learning model that uses a tree-like model of decisions
b. A function to split the dataset into random train and test subsets
c. A function to perform linear regression
d. A function to compute the mean squared error regression loss

Review Question 9.45
What is the primary difference between the implementation of the simple regression and the decision tree regressor in Python?
a. The steps for splitting the data
b. The steps for fitting the model
c. The instantiation of the model
d. The steps for evaluating the model

Review Question 9.46
What does the train_test_split() function do in Scikit-learn?
a. It fits a linear model with coefficients to minimize the residual sum of squares between the observed targets in the dataset, and the targets predicted by the linear approximation.
b. It splits the dataset into random train and test subsets.
c. It computes the mean squared error regression loss.
d. It fits an AutoRegressive Integrated Moving Average (ARIMA) model to the data.

Review Question 9.47
What is the purpose of the Pandas package in Python?
a. To provide data structures and operations for manipulating numerical tables and time series
b. To perform linear regression
c. To compute the mean squared error regression loss
d. To fit an AutoRegressive Integrated Moving Average (ARIMA) model to the data

Review Question 9.48
What is the primary purpose of regression analysis in predictive analytics?
a. To predict the value of the dependent variable based on the values of the independent variables
b. To identify trends, patterns, and seasonal variations in time-ordered data points
c. To make predictions or decisions without explicit programming
d. To manipulate numerical tables and time series

9.5 Prescriptive Analytics

Prescriptive analytics is the process of using data to determine the best course of action (Lepenioti, et al., 2020). It builds on descriptive and predictive analytics by not only anticipating future outcomes but also suggesting actions to achieve desired results (Bertsimas and Kallus, 2020). Prescriptive analytics is like having a GPS for decision-making. It doesn't just tell you where you are (descriptive analytics) or predict where you might end up (predictive analytics); it guides you on the best path to reach your goals. By analyzing data, prescriptive analytics provides specific recommendations on what actions to take to achieve the best possible outcomes.

Imagine a ride-sharing app. Using prescriptive analytics, it can suggest the most efficient routes for drivers, helping them avoid traffic and maximize passenger pickups. This ensures that drivers earn more, passengers wait less, and the service operates efficiently.

Prescriptive analytics offers numerous benefits to businesses (Sharma et al., 2022). It evaluates various scenarios and recommends optimal strategies, enabling businesses to make informed decisions based on data rather than relying solely on intuition. For example, a company deciding to launch a new product might use prescriptive analytics to assess market trends, customer preferences, and competitive landscape. This data-driven approach can lead to more accurate predictions and better strategic planning.

Another significant benefit of prescriptive analytics is improved efficiency. By analyzing data patterns and trends, businesses can allocate resources more effectively, thereby reducing waste. For instance, a manufacturing company might use prescriptive analytics to optimize its production schedule, ensuring that machinery and labor are utilized efficiently while minimizing downtime. This can lead to significant cost savings and improved operational efficiency.

Lastly, prescriptive analytics can help maximize profits by optimizing operations. By identifying the most profitable strategies and eliminating inefficiencies, companies can increase their profitability. For example, a retailer could use prescriptive analytics to determine the optimal inventory levels, striking a balance between having enough stock to meet customer demand and minimizing storage costs. This could result in increased sales, reduced inventory costs, and ultimately, higher profits. Consider a pharmaceutical company deciding on production levels for a new drug. Prescriptive analytics can analyze demand forecasts, production costs, and market trends to suggest the optimal quantity to produce. This helps avoid overproduction (which ties up capital) or underproduction (which leads to lost sales).

To effectively implement prescriptive analytics, businesses rely on a variety of techniques and tools. These methods help organizations navigate complex decision-making processes by optimizing resources, simulating different scenarios, and analyzing potential outcomes. Let's explore some key approaches that enable businesses to make data-driven decisions and maximize their potential.

Optimization is all about finding the best solution from a range of feasible options, much like choosing the best path to reach a destination. Businesses often face problems that require allocating limited resources—whether it's time, money, or materials—to maximize outcomes.

Linear Programming (LP) is one of the most common optimization techniques. It's used when the relationship between variables is linear, making it ideal for problems like resource allocation. For example, a manufacturing company might use LP to determine the optimal mix of products to produce, maximizing profit while staying within budget and resource constraints.

Integer Programming is similar to linear programming, but the decision variables must be integers. This is useful in situations where items can't be divided, such as determining the number of trucks needed for delivery routes. By using integer programming, a logistics company can efficiently plan its fleet, minimizing costs while ensuring all deliveries are made on time.

Nonlinear Programming (NLP) comes into play when relationships between variables are nonlinear. This is often seen in complex financial models or engineering problems where the effect of one variable on another isn't constant. For instance, a tech company developing new products might use NLP to optimize design features that affect cost and performance, striking the best balance between the two.

Simulation techniques help businesses model complex systems and explore the impact of different strategies without real-world risks.

Monte Carlo Simulations use random sampling to understand uncertainty in forecasts and assess risks. Imagine a finance team wanting to predict future stock prices. They can use Monte Carlo simulations to model thousands of potential price paths, helping them understand the range of possible outcomes and plan for various market conditions. This technique provides insights into the likelihood of different scenarios, allowing for better risk management.

Bootstrap is another powerful simulation technique that involves repeatedly sampling from a dataset with replacement to assess the variability of estimates. For example, a marketing team analyzing customer purchase patterns can use the bootstrap method to estimate the variability in average customer spending across different periods. This allows businesses to understand the stability of their models and predictions, improving decision-making under uncertainty.

Scenario Analysis involves evaluating outcomes under various hypothetical situations. It's like playing "what if" games with business strategies. For example, a retailer might use scenario analysis to explore how changes in consumer behavior, like a shift to online shopping, would impact sales. By analyzing different scenarios, businesses can develop contingency plans and be better prepared for unexpected changes in the market.

Decision analysis provides a structured approach to making complex decisions by evaluating possible outcomes using tools like decision trees and utility theory.

Decision Trees are visual tools that map out decisions and their potential consequences, much like a flowchart. Each branch represents a choice, and the outcomes lead to further decisions. For example, a company deciding whether to launch a new product can use a decision tree to evaluate different strategies, weighing potential profits against risks. This visual representation helps simplify complex decisions by breaking them down into manageable parts.

Utility Theory assesses the value or utility of different decisions, helping businesses choose the most beneficial option. It's particularly useful when outcomes are uncertain. For instance, a financial planner might use utility theory to help clients decide between investment options, considering both potential returns and the client's risk tolerance. By evaluating decisions based on their overall utility, businesses can ensure they align with their strategic goals and stakeholder preferences.

In Python, there are several libraries that can be used for prescriptive analytics. One of them is PuLP, which simplifies solving linear optimization problems. It allows you to define objective functions, constraints, and decision variables easily. This makes it accessible for beginners who want to optimize resources in various scenarios, such as minimizing costs or maximizing profits.

Another useful approach in Python is simulating scenarios with Monte Carlo simulations. Libraries like NumPy and SciPy are great for this purpose. These simulations involve running numerous trials to generate probabilistic forecasts, helping businesses understand potential risks and outcomes in uncertain situations.

Python also offers tools for creating decision trees, which are useful for visualizing decision-making processes. Libraries like Scikit-learn make it straightforward to implement these trees. They help evaluate outcomes based on different scenarios and are useful for breaking down complex decisions into manageable parts.

Most of these topics are beyond the scope of this book, but we'll explore a simple linear programming example using Python below.

Example 9.1: Linear Programming with Python
Problem:
Scott Shop Co. wants to optimize inventory levels for two products, Product A and Product B, over the next six months. The quantities of these products are represented by decision variables x (Product A) and y (Product B).

Objective:
The goal is to maximize the total revenue of these products. The revenue for Product A is $3 and for Product B is $5. Thus, the objective function can be expressed as:

Maximize Z= 3x + 5y

Constraints:
1. Budget Constraint: The cost for Product A is $2 per unit, and for Product B, it is $3 per unit. The total cost should not exceed $100: 2x + 3y <= 100;
2. Minimum Stock Constraint: There should be at least 10 units of each product in stock: x>=10; y>=10;
This problem is a linear programming problem that can be solved using Python libraries such as SciPy or PuLP. Below is a Python solution that sets up and solves this problem (You may need to run !pip install pulp to install the package).

Here's a Python solution using the PuLP library to solve the linear programming problem:

```python
import pulp
# Create a linear programming problem
problem = pulp.LpProblem("Inventory Optimization", pulp.LpMaximize)
# Define decision variables
x = pulp.LpVariable('x', lowBound=10, cat='Integer')  # Product A
y = pulp.LpVariable('y', lowBound=10, cat='Integer')  # Product B
# Objective function
problem += 3 * x + 5 * y, "Total Revenue"
# Constraints
problem += 2 * x + 3 * y <= 100, "Budget Constraint"
# Solve the problem
problem.solve()
# Output the results
print("Optimal quantities:")
```

```
print(f"Product A (x): {pulp.value(x)}")
print(f"Product B (y): {pulp.value(y)}")
print(f"Total Cost: ${pulp.value(x)*2+pulp.value(y)*3}")
print(f"Total Revenue: ${pulp.value(problem.objective)}")
```

Output:
```
Optimal quantities:
Product A (x): 11.0
Product B (y): 26.0
Total Cost: $100.0
Total Revenue: $163.0
```

Review Question 9.49
What is the primary purpose of prescriptive analytics?
a. To analyze past data
b. To anticipate future trends and behaviors
c. To suggest actions to achieve desired results
d. To perform regression analysis

Review Question 9.50
How does a ride-sharing app benefit from prescriptive analytics?
a. It suggests the most efficient routes for drivers
b. It predicts future traffic conditions
c. It analyzes past traffic data
d. It performs regression analysis on traffic data

Review Question 9.51
How does a company benefit from using prescriptive analytics when deciding to launch a new product?
a. It can assess market trends, customer preferences, and competitive landscape
b. It can predict future market trends
c. It can analyze past sales data
d. It can perform regression analysis on sales data

Review Question 9.52
How does a manufacturing company benefit from using prescriptive analytics?
a. It can optimize its production schedule
b. It can predict future production needs
c. It can analyze past production data
d. It can perform regression analysis on production data

Review Question 9.53
How does a retailer benefit from using prescriptive analytics?
a. It can determine the optimal inventory levels
b. It can predict future inventory needs
c. It can analyze past inventory data
d. It can perform regression analysis on inventory data

Review Question 9.54
What is the purpose of optimization in prescriptive analytics?

a. To find the best solution from a range of feasible options
b. To predict the best solution
c. To analyze past solutions
d. To perform regression analysis on solutions

Review Question 9.55
What is the purpose of Linear Programming (LP) in prescriptive analytics in the book example?
a. To determine the optimal mix of products to produce
b. To predict the optimal mix of products
c. To analyze past product mixes
d. To perform regression analysis on product mixes

Review Question 9.56
What is the purpose of Integer Programming in prescriptive analytics in the book example?
a. To efficiently plan a logistics company's fleet
b. To predict the number of trucks needed for delivery routes
c. To analyze past delivery routes
d. To perform regression analysis on delivery routes

Review Question 9.57
What is the purpose of Nonlinear Programming (NLP) in prescriptive analytics in the book example?
a. To optimize design features that affect cost and performance
b. To predict the effect of one variable on another
c. To analyze past relationships between variables
d. To perform regression analysis on relationships between variables

Review Question 9.58
What is the purpose of Monte Carlo Simulations in prescriptive analytics?
a. To understand uncertainty in forecasts and assess risks
b. To predict future stock prices
c. To analyze past stock prices
d. To perform regression analysis on stock prices

Review Question 9.59
What is the primary purpose of using the bootstrap method in data analysis?
a. To increase the size of the dataset
b. To eliminate outliers from the data
c. To assess the variability of estimates
d. To predict future customer behavior

Review Question 9.60
What is the purpose of Scenario Analysis in prescriptive analytics?
a. To evaluate outcomes under various hypothetical situations
b. To predict the impact of changes in consumer behavior
c. To analyze past consumer behavior
d. To perform regression analysis on consumer behavior

Review Question 9.61
What is the purpose of Decision Trees in prescriptive analytics?
a. To analyze past decisions

b. To predict the outcomes of decisions
c. To map out decisions and their potential consequences
d. To perform regression analysis on decisions

Review Question 9.62
What is the purpose of Utility Theory in prescriptive analytics?
a. To analyze past decisions
b. To predict the utility bills of involved businesses
c. To assess the value of different decisions
d. To perform regression analysis on decisions

Review Question 9.63
How does prescriptive analytics help a pharmaceutical company deciding on production levels for a new drug in the book example?
a. It can predict the demand for the new drug
b. It can suggest the optimal quantity to produce
c. It can analyze past production levels
d. It can perform regression analysis on production levels

Review Question 9.64
What is the primary purpose of PuLP in Python?
a. To define objective functions, constraints, and decision variables easily
b. To simulate scenarios with Monte Carlo simulations
c. To create decision trees
d. To visualize decision-making processes

Review Question 9.65
What is the primary purpose of Monte Carlo simulations in Python?
a. To define objective functions, constraints, and decision variables easily
b. To simulate scenarios using random sampling techniques
c. To create decision trees
d. To visualize decision-making processes

9.6 Integrating the Four Levels

In business data analytics, four levels—descriptive, diagnostic, predictive, and prescriptive—work together to transform raw data into actionable insights. Understanding how these levels interact is important for leveraging the full power of data. Here's a quick recap of we have learned:

Descriptive Analytics provides a summary of historical data, answering questions like "What happened?" For example, a retail company may analyze sales data to determine trends and patterns over time. This foundational level helps businesses understand their past performance.

Diagnostic Analytics goes a step further by exploring the reasons behind past events. It answers "Why did it happen?" Using the same retail example, diagnostic analytics might examine sales declines, considering factors like seasonality, promotions, or external events that influenced sales.

Predictive Analytics uses historical data to forecast future trends. It answers "What could happen?" By applying models to past data, businesses can anticipate customer behavior or market trends. For instance, a retailer might use predictive analytics to forecast next quarter's sales based on historical trends and current market conditions.

Prescriptive Analytics provides actionable recommendations by analyzing data and predicting outcomes. It answers "What should we do?" Building on the insights from the previous levels, it helps businesses make optimal decisions. In our retail example, prescriptive analytics could suggest the best inventory levels to meet anticipated demand while minimizing costs.

The flow from descriptive to prescriptive analytics provides a structured approach to decision-making, allowing businesses to leverage data at each stage for better outcomes.

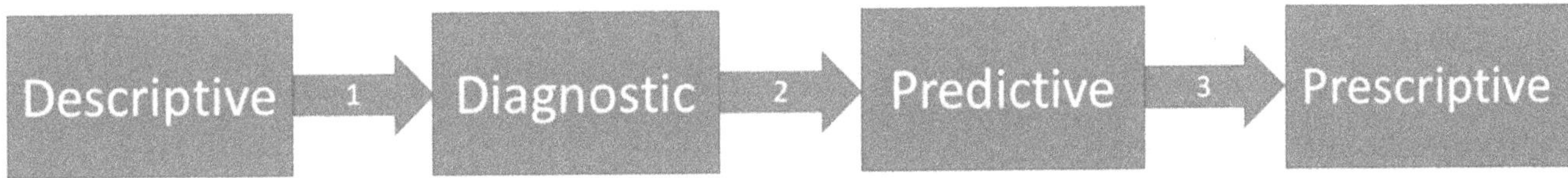

Figure 9.1 The Flow of Data Insights.

1. Descriptive to Diagnostic:
Descriptive Analytics: This first step involves summarizing historical data to answer "What happened?" For example, a retail store might analyze last year's sales data to identify trends, such as which products sold best during certain months.
Diagnostic Analytics: Next, businesses go deeper to understand "Why did it happen?" Using the previous sales data, the store might investigate why certain products spiked in sales—perhaps due to successful promotions or seasonal demand. This step involves looking for patterns and correlations that explain past performance.

2. Diagnostic to Predictive:
Predictive Analytics: Armed with insights from the diagnostic phase, businesses move to predictive analytics to answer "What could happen in the future?" Building on our example, the store could use past data and identified patterns to predict future sales trends. For instance, if a particular product tends to sell well before

holidays, predictive models can forecast increased demand during those periods. Techniques like regression analysis or machine learning algorithms help in making these forecasts.

3. Predictive to Prescriptive:

Prescriptive Analytics: Finally, prescriptive analytics provides actionable recommendations based on predictive insights, answering "What should we do?" In our retail example, if the store predicts high demand for certain products, prescriptive analytics might suggest optimal inventory levels to maximize sales while minimizing excess stock. This step often involves optimization models that take various constraints into account, such as budget limits or storage capacity.

Integrating all four levels of analytics empowers businesses to make informed, data-driven decisions. By using descriptive analytics, companies gain a clear picture of past performance. Diagnostic analytics uncovers the reasons behind successes or failures, providing deeper insights. Predictive analytics anticipates future trends, helping businesses prepare for upcoming challenges. Finally, prescriptive analytics offers actionable recommendations, enabling organizations to achieve their strategic goals.

Here's a simplified example of how these levels might be integrated into a project (Building a comprehensive analytics pipeline):

1. Data Collection and Cleaning:

Gather historical sales data from various sources like CRM systems, e-commerce platforms, and marketing tools. Clean the data by removing duplicates, handling missing values, and standardizing formats to prepare it for analysis. For instance, if dates are in different formats, convert them to a uniform format.

2. Descriptive Analysis:

Use Pandas to generate summary statistics such as mean, median, and standard deviation of sales figures. Visualize sales trends over time using line charts and bar graphs to identify patterns, such as seasonal peaks or declining sales periods. This helps in understanding the data's basic characteristics. For example, plotting monthly sales to observe trends, identifying peak months, and seeing overall growth.

3. Diagnostic Analysis:

Investigate factors affecting sales by performing correlation analysis. Look at the relationship between sales and variables like marketing spend, customer demographics, or external economic indicators. Use scatter plots to visualize these relationships. For example, analyzing the impact of a specific marketing campaign on sales by comparing sales figures before and after the campaign.

4. Predictive Modeling:

Build a regression model to forecast future sales based on historical data and identified factors such as marketing spend and economic trends. This helps in anticipating future demand. For example, using a linear regression model to predict next quarter's sales based on past sales data and current marketing budget.

5. Prescriptive Analysis:

Apply optimization techniques, such as linear programming, to determine the ideal inventory levels that maximize profits while meeting forecasted demand. This ensures efficient resource allocation. For example, optimizing inventory to avoid overstocking or stockouts, ensuring that resources are used efficiently while meeting customer demand.

Review Question 9.66
What does Descriptive Analytics provide?
a. A summary of historical data
b. The reasons behind past events
c. A forecast of future trends
d. Actionable recommendations by analyzing data and predicting outcomes

Review Question 9.67
What does Diagnostic Analytics explore?
a. A summary of historical data
b. The reasons behind past events
c. A forecast of future trends
d. Actionable recommendations by analyzing data and predicting outcomes

Review Question 9.68
What does Predictive Analytics use historical data for?
a. Summarizing historical data
b. Exploring the reasons behind past events
c. Forecasting future trends
d. Providing actionable recommendations by analyzing data and predicting outcomes

Review Question 9.69
What does Prescriptive Analytics provide?
a. A summary of historical data
b. The reasons behind past events
c. A forecast of future trends
d. Actionable recommendations by analyzing data and predicting outcomes

Review Question 9.70

What is the first step in the flow of data insights according to the book?
a. Descriptive to Diagnostic
b. Diagnostic to Predictive
c. Predictive to Prescriptive
d. Prescriptive to Descriptive

Review Question 9.71
What is the final step in the flow of data insights according to the book?
a. Descriptive to Diagnostic
b. Diagnostic to Predictive
c. Predictive to Prescriptive
d. Prescriptive to Descriptive

Review Question 9.72
What does the Descriptive Analysis step involve in building a comprehensive analytics pipeline?
a. Gathering historical sales data
b. Investigating factors affecting sales
c. Building a regression model to forecast future sales
d. Using Pandas to generate summary statistics and visualize sales trends

Review Question 9.73
What does the Diagnostic Analysis step involve in building a comprehensive analytics pipeline?
a. Gathering historical sales data
b. Investigating factors affecting sales
c. Building a regression model to forecast future sales
d. Using Pandas to generate summary statistics and visualize sales trends

Review Question 9.74
What does the Predictive Modeling step involve in building a comprehensive analytics pipeline?
a. Gathering historical sales data
b. Investigating factors affecting sales
c. Building a regression model to forecast future sales
d. Using Pandas to generate summary statistics and visualize sales trends

Review Question 9.75
What does the Prescriptive Analysis step involve in building a comprehensive analytics pipeline?
a. Gathering historical sales data
b. Investigating factors affecting sales
c. Building a regression model to forecast future sales
d. Applying optimization techniques to determine the ideal inventory levels

9.7 Chapter Summary

In this chapter, we introduced the four levels of data analytics: descriptive, diagnostic, predictive, and prescriptive. While these types of analytics have been discussed throughout the book, this chapter provides a comprehensive summary of them.

9.8 References

Abdelrahman, O., & Keikhosrokiani, P. (2020). Assembly line anomaly detection and root cause analysis using machine learning. IEEE Access, 8, 189661-189672.

Adama, H. E., & Okeke, C. D. (2024). Harnessing business analytics for gaining competitive advantage in emerging markets: A systematic review of approaches and outcomes. International Journal of Science and Research Archive, 11(2), 1848-1854.

Adesina, A. A., Iyelolu, T. V., & Paul, P. O. (2024). Leveraging predictive analytics for strategic decision-making: Enhancing business performance through data-driven insights. World Journal of Advanced Research and Reviews, 22(3), 1927-1934.

Al-Sai, Z. A., Husin, M. H., Syed-Mohamad, S. M., Abdin, R. M. D. S., Damer, N., Abualigah, L., & Gandomi, A. H. (2022). Explore big data analytics applications and opportunities: A review. Big Data and Cognitive Computing, 6(4), 157.

Balali, F., Nouri, J., Nasiri, A., Zhao, T., Balali, F., Nouri, J., ... & Zhao, T. (2020). Data analytics. Data Intensive Industrial Asset Management: IoT-based Algorithms and Implementation, 105-113.

Bertsimas, D., & Kallus, N. (2020). From predictive to prescriptive analytics. Management Science, 66(3), 1025-1044.

Ibeh, C. V., Asuzu, O. F., Olorunsogo, T., Elufioye, O. A., Nduubuisi, N. L., & Daraojimba, A. I. (2024). Business analytics and decision science: A review of techniques in strategic business decision making. World Journal of Advanced Research and Reviews, 21(2), 1761-1769.

Inastrilla, C. R. A. (2023, September). Data visualization in the information society. In Seminars in Medical Writing and Education (Vol. 2, pp. 25-25).

Lepenioti, K., Bousdekis, A., Apostolou, D., & Mentzas, G. (2020). Prescriptive analytics: Literature review and research challenges. International Journal of Information Management, 50, 57-70.

Margherita, A. (2022). Human resources analytics: A systematization of research topics and directions for future research. Human Resource Management Review, 32(2), 100795.

Muneeswaran, V., Nagaraj, P., Dhannushree, U., Ishwarya Lakshmi, S., Aishwarya, R., & Sunethra, B. (2021). A framework for data analytics-based healthcare systems. In Innovative Data Communication Technologies and Application: Proceedings of ICIDCA 2020 (pp. 83-96). Springer Singapore.

Sharma, A. K., Sharma, D. M., Purohit, N., Rout, S. K., & Sharma, S. A. (2022). Analytics techniques: descriptive analytics, predictive analytics, and prescriptive analytics. Decision intelligence analytics and the implementation of strategic business management, 1-14.

9.9 Solutions to the Review Questions

9.1 C; 9.2 D; 9.3 D; 9.4 C; 9.5 D; 9.6 D; 9.7 A; 9.8 A; 9.9 A; 9.10 A; 9.11 A; 9.12 B; 9.13 C; 9.14 B; 9.15 C; 9.16 D; 9.17 C; 9.18 D; 9.19 C; 9.20 B; 9.21 A; 9.22 B; 9.23 B; 9.24 C; 9.25 C; 9.26 D; 9.27 C; 9.28 B; 9.29 A; 9.30 B; 9.31 B; 9.32 A; 9.33 A; 9.34 A; 9.35 C; 9.36 A; 9.37 B; 9.38 B; 9.39 A; 9.40 C; 9.41 C; 9.42 D; 9.43 A; 9.44 A; 9.45 C; 9.46 B; 9.47 A; 9.48 A; 9.49 C; 9.50 A; 9.51 A; 9.52 A; 9.53 A; 9.54 A; 9.55 A; 9.56 A; 9.57 A; 9.58 A; 9.59 C; 9.60 A; 9.61 C; 9.62 C; 9.63 B; 9.64 A; 9.65 B; 9.66 A; 9.67 B; 9.68 C; 9.69 D; 9.70 A; 9.71 C; 9.72 D; 9.73 B; 9.74 C; 9.75 D;